PERPETUAL MIRAGE

ORGANIZED BY MAY CASTLEBERRY

WITH ESSAYS BY
MAY CASTLEBERRY AND MARTHA A. SANDWEISS

JOHN CHÁVEZ, ROBERT COLES, EVAN S. CONNELL, SUSAN DANLY,
WILLIAM H. GOETZMANN, WILLIAM N. GOETZMANN, ANNE HAMMOND,
WILLIAM KITTREDGE, PATRICIA NELSON LIMERICK, JULIE MELLBY,
PETER E. PALMQUIST, LISA PHILLIPS, MARC REISNER,
ROBERT A. SOBIESZEK, THOMAS W. SOUTHALL, KEVIN STARR,
RINA SWENTZELL, RON TYLER, ADAM D. WEINBERG,
TERRY TEMPEST WILLIAMS, SHARYN WILEY YEOMAN

PERPETUAL MIRAGE

PHOTOGRAPHIC NARRATIVES OF THE DESERT WEST

WHITNEY MUSEUM OF AMERICAN ART, NEW YORK

DISTRIBUTED BY HARRY N. ABRAMS, INC., NEW YORK

This book was published on the occasion of the exhibition
"Perpetual Mirage: Photographic Narratives of the Desert West"
at the Whitney Museum of American Art, June 27–September 22, 1996.

The exhibition and catalogue are made possible by grants from
Joanne Leonhardt Cassullo and The Dorothea L. Leonhardt Foundation, Inc.,
The Nathan Cummings Foundation, the National Endowment for the Humanities,
and Furthermore, the J.M. Kaplan Fund publication program.

Research for the exhibition and publication
was supported by income from an endowment established by
Henry and Elaine Kaufman, The Lauder Foundation, Mrs. William A. Marsteller,
The Andrew W. Mellon Foundation, Mrs. Donald A. Petrie,
Primerica Foundation, Samuel and May Rudin Foundation, Inc.,
The Simon Foundation, and Nancy Brown Wellin.

Cover image:
John Hillers
Hopi Pueblo of Walpi, First Mesa, Arizona, 1876 (detail)
From Morgan, *Houses and House-Life of American Aborigines*, 1881
Albumen print, 9¾ x 12¹³⁄₁₆ (25 x 32.8)
Centre Canadien d'Architecture/Canadian Centre for Architecture, Montreal

Library of Congress Cataloging-in-Publication Data
Castleberry, May.
Perpetual mirage : photographic narratives of the desert west /
May Castleberry : with contributions by John Chávez . . .
p. cm.
Includes bibliographical references.
ISBN 0-87427-100-2
1. West (U.S.)–Pictorial works–Bibliography.
2. Illustrated books–West (U.S.)–Bibliography.
3. Deserts–West (U.S.)–Pictorial works–Bibliography.
I. Chávez, John. II. Title.
Z1251.W5C37 1996
[F590.7]
016.978'0022'2–dc20
95-25999 CIP

TABLE OF CONTENTS

DIRECTOR'S FOREWORD

In our collective imagination, the most immediate image of the American desert West is drawn from a now historical body of photographs. Beginning in photography's early days, landscape photographs were used to create dramatic, often idealized visions of the vast, remote drylands, canyons, and majestic mountains of the Western territories.

In the hands of the early photographic pioneers, the medium functioned as a tool of scientific exploration, promoted commercial (and political) development of the West, and educated and thrilled people who would never visit the exotic and remote sites captured by the camera. In later years, as the tradition of Western landscape photography flourished and tourist travel became possible, the masterful photographs of artists such as Ansel Adams contributed to the definition of photography as an independent artistic medium. Even more important, these landscape photographers helped to raise public consciousness about the region's fragility and its essential role in a vital, interlocking ecological system.

Since the mid-nineteenth century, many photographs of the American Southwest have been presented to the public primarily in books. At first handmade, and later mechanically printed and bound, these photographic books enabled the images to speak directly to the viewer in a most effective and intimate fashion and allowed for the construction of complex landscape narratives. Increasingly, however, the exhibition of photographs in museums and galleries has given the individual photographic print a different status — that of landscape painting — and this has charged the photographic image with additional power and authority.

All these developments are explored in depth in this detailed and altogether extraordinary exhibition and publication organized by May Castleberry, the Whitney's librarian and associate curator for Special Collections. *Perpetual Mirage* offers an unprecedented opportunity to explore the ways in which photography and its various forms of presentation and reception — most notably the photographic book — contributed to nothing less than the construction of America's self-image. And perhaps as important, it allows us to delight in as well as better understand the extraordinary art that lies at the heart of this enterprise.

The exhibition has been an exciting collaborative process. Though acknowledged elsewhere in this volume, I want to thank the lenders, authors, and scholars who have contributed to *Perpetual Mirage* and, on behalf of the Trustees of the Whitney Museum of American Art, express our special appreciation to the artists whose vision we celebrate with this exhibition.

DAVID A. ROSS
Alice Pratt Brown Director

"The deserts are not all desert. . . . All that is needed is to explore and declare the nature of the national domain!"
— Clarence King, on the need to survey the 40th parallel country, c. 1867[1]

"Desert is a loose term to indicate land that supports no man;
whether the land can be bitten and broken to that purpose is not proven."
— Mary Austin, *The Land of Little Rain*, 1903[2]

"It is the desert that is truly ours, for we have made it so and must live with the consequences."
— Reyner Banham, *Desert Cantos*, 1991[3]

Alexander Gardner
On the Great Plains, Kansas, 294 Miles West of Missouri River, 1867
Albumen print from Gardner,
Across the Continent on the Kansas Pacific Railroad . . . , 1869
Missouri Historical Society, St. Louis

Alexander Gardner
"Westward the Course of Empire Takes Its Way,"
Laying Track, 300 Miles West of Missouri River, 1867
Albumen print from Gardner,
Across the Continent on the Kansas Pacific Railroad . . . , 1869
Missouri Historical Society, St. Louis

Alexander Gardner
*Yucca Tree, "Spanish Bayonet," on the Great Basin, Southern California,
Sierra Nevada in the Distance, 1,670 Miles from the Missouri River,* 1867–68
Albumen print from Gardner,
Across the Continent on the Kansas Pacific Railroad . . . , 1869
Boston Public Library, Print Department

John Hillers
Hopi Pueblo of Walpi, First Mesa, Arizona, 1876
From Morgan, *Houses and House-Life of the American Aborigines,* 1881
Albumen print, 9¾ x 12¹³⁄₁₆ (25 x 32.8)
Centre Canadien d'Architecture/Canadian Centre for Architecture, Montreal

INTRODUCTION

MAY CASTLEBERRY

Perhaps more than any other region, the deserts and drylands of the American West continue to focus the diverse forces of social, cultural, and natural change that have shaped the American landscape. "Perpetual Mirage" looks at the interaction between the desert West and its interpreters as it has unfolded in the photographic book, a medium that has consistently engaged our perceptions of this region over the past 150 years. The exhibition examines the crucial role of photographic books and those who created them in shaping both the history of photography and the American consciousness of the desert West.

Photographers have particularly favored the photographic book to portray the desert West, whether to capture the scale of the region with extended series of panoramic photographs, to analyze its geologica   embellish its lore with illustrated texts. They h   engage aesthetic, scientific,   to communicate to conte   photographic views of th   eared in railroad and gov   hs have recorded enormo   the land, changes brought   nd water reclamation projects.

These books do more, however, than provide a retrospective record of change for the modern observer. They suggest an awareness of history on the part of the photographers themselves. The region is presented with a visible past, inscribed in pueblos, stones, or modern ghost towns, and located in a natural setting that came to be understood as no less varied than the human settlements dotting the landscape. Photographers observe "lost" landscapes and cultures, represent infinitely deep geological history, or witness the imprint of man in a dry atmosphere that seems to preserve all traces of the past.

The dual awareness of the desert as both a fragile natural environment and a vast, irreplaceable artifact has been reflected in decades of debate over conservation. Particularly in the Southwest, limited water first delayed, then magnified, questions of modern development. For these and other reasons explored in the following essays, this landscape has provoked a wide range of published narrative responses. The seemingly "empty" vista of the desert West now reveals the fissures in the American ethos of development as they have widened in the twentieth century. It is a region that has inspired some of America's toughest confrontations with the natural environment — and some of its most visionary art.

SCOPE OF THE EXHIBITION AND CATALOGUE

The exhibition begins with the Western surveys that preceded the Civil War and continues with the diverse initiatives, by individuals and organizations, that evolved over the next hundred years: the illustrated books that first surveyed an unfamiliar land at the dawn of the photographic era; the photographic albums of the government-sponsored surveys of the later nineteenth century that used photographs by William Bell, William Henry Jackson, John Hillers, and Timothy O'Sullivan as evidence of natural resources in the West; turn-of-the-century travelers' guides that defined the desert as a tourist site; photo-textual documents of the Great Depression by Dorothea Lange and others; mid-twentieth-century conservation "battle books," as they were called, by Ansel Adams, Eliot Porter, and others, which attempted to inform Americans of endangered wildlands; and more recent books by photographers such as Robert Adams, JoAnn Verburg, and Mark Klett, who force us to confront issues of history and change in the desert West, sometimes by photographing the same sites visited by photographers a century before.

The photographs presented here have been shaped and enriched by their position in a sequenced book that intermingles images and interpretive texts. Although many of them are familiar to the public and have received iconic status as individual works of art, their origin — and hence their context — as elements of a larger, usually collaborative, project remains generally unknown.

An inherently multidisciplinary medium, the photographic book is a product of the collaborative ambitions of photographers, authors, and their publishers; the nature of these collaborations is discussed in several of the following essays. In this sense, both the catalogue and the exhibition help document the larger narrative of American publishing history. Together, they encourage a more critical consciousness of the photographic medium and a greater awareness of how it has shaped and reflected our ideas about the landscape.

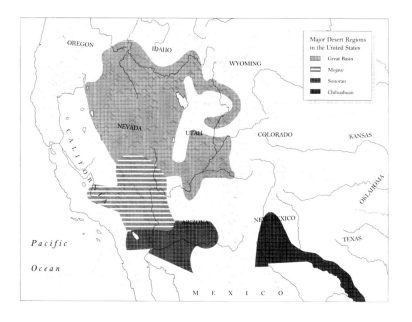

"The overriding influence that shaped the West is the desert. That is the one unifying force. It permeates the plains, climbs to all but the highest mountain peaks, dwells continuously in the valleys, and plunges down the Pacific slope to argue with the sea."

— Walter Prescott Webb, "The American West, Perpetual Mirage," 1957[4]

"Along the eastern side of the Cascades and Sierras, extending into Southern California, are the real deserts. Regions with less than ten inches a year of rainfall, with sparse vegetation, these are not deserts of myth but of actuality."

— Patricia Nelson Limerick, *Desert Passages,* 1985[5]

The region considered in this exhibition encompasses vast stretches of arid land, not all of which may be "true" desert. Because historical and contemporary observers — even the most practiced — have disagreed on the American Desert's nature and extent, the exhibition operates under varied definitions, looking at what the region actually is, as well as what its observers have thought it to be. Geographically, this study considers the drylands of Arizona, New Mexico, Utah, Nevada, and eastern California, and reaches into the more arid areas of Oregon, Wyoming, Texas, Kansas, and Nebraska. This same region may be described, geologically, as taking in much of the Colorado Plateau, the Great Basin, the Rio Grande, and some of the western Great Plains regions.[6]

What is the desert? In modern scientific terms, it is a place where annual rainfall is 10 inches or less, as in the Sonoran and Mojave Deserts. Historical and metaphorical uses, however, broaden the term: an unpeopled wilderness, a "wasteland," or the "Great Desert," which many early nineteenth-century Americans believed covered much of the territory west of the Central Plains. Definitions continue to be disputed, and each generation argues about the extent to which the desert has influenced the perception and development of the American West: derided as a wasteland in the early nineteenth century; charted in the interest of science and economic expansion in the later nineteenth century; embraced for its diversity in the early twentieth century; and, more recently, cited as a product of human mismanagement. Historians and environmentalists have periodically challenged each other no less than prevailing interpretations of the desert. Although one mid-nineteenth-century booster described the American desert as a "Garden of the World,"[7] John Wesley Powell warned in 1878 that most of the West would continually face the political and ecological pressures of a land that cannot be developed or farmed without extensive irrigation. *Report on the Lands of the Arid Regions of the United States* (1878), Powell's sobering account, offered an inclusive definition of the "Arid Regions," which extended from the Central Plains across the Rocky Mountains to the Pacific, excepting only a section of the Northwestern coast. What defined the territory was an annual rainfall averaging less than 20 inches.[8] The true desert areas of the region, with far less rain, were recognized as particularly unsuitable for agriculture and development.

Although the extent of water resources in the West is now fairly well understood, the term "desert" is still debated in reference to the greater West. In 1949, enormous controversy was generated by the article Walter Prescott Webb published in *Harper's* magazine, "The American West: Perpetual Mirage" (from which the title of this exhibition is taken).[9] Webb centered the American desert in the eight states of the Rocky Mountain region — Arizona, Colorado, Idaho, Utah, Nevada, New Mexico, Montana, Wyoming — and defined the eight surrounding states as "the desert rim." (Even California, Webb has argued, is "a semi-desert with a desert heart.")

The exhibition also reflects key stages in the quarrel about the juncture of the desert and human settlement. While it features "natural" landscapes (bearing in mind that almost any landscape observed by the camera has already been shaped by human activity), it also presents numerous outdoor views of settlements seen in relation to the desert. These include archaeological ruins such as Mesa Verde, which may have been abandoned due to drought; long-inhabited Pueblo communities in Arizona and New Mexico, which over centuries adapted to an irregular water supply; and newly created "oasis" cities, which have defied the constraints of the desert climate through modern feats of engineering.

THE DESERT WEST AND THE PHOTOGRAPHIC BOOK

"A rich and beautiful book is always open before us. We have but to learn to read it."
— J. B. Jackson, *Landscape*, 1951[10]

"I suppose I usually work in units of pictures, because I try to reach a diverse audience, and because I know, having lived on the edge of the world, how important books can be. I learned to photograph mostly by studying books, and I try now to keep up through books."
— Robert Adams, *Cottonwoods,* 1994[11]

For the purposes of this exhibition and catalogue, photographic books are defined as bound and printed publications distinguished by original contributions of photographic images, whether they have been printed in runs of a few copies or in larg-er trade editions numbering in the thousands. Such books encompass albums with printed title pages and tipped-in original photographs, as well as the more familiar publications with photographs reproduced by gravure, offset lithography, or other printing techniques.

Emphasized here are photographers who have shown a profound involvement with the landscape of the arid West and the concept of the photographic book as a narrative form. These books present photographic images as part of a coherent theme or sequence, rather than as a collection of individual reproductions. Also included are individual photographs which were created with a larger publishing project in mind.[12]

The intersection of the desert terrain with the medium of the photographic book offers an excellent means of observing how the form of photographic books metamorphosed to accommodate new audiences, attitudes, and printing techniques. The development traced here was partly a response to economic conditions: the Western photographic book began with perhaps the most substantial commercial and government patronage in the history of photographic publishing, an end product of the monumental survey projects of the nineteenth century. As the desert West continued to appeal to the American imagination, so the publishing industry followed. But the photographic book may also have a particular expressive tie to the West and to the vocation of the photographer. It offers a means of presenting numerous photographs of a region whose open space overwhelms — or minimizes — individual photographs and human scale, and whose historic monuments encourage storytelling. The sequential format enables the photographer to convey panoramic vastness through a series of images and explore the natural and cultural diversity of a region that resists uniform approaches.

Emphasis on the book form also reveals a relatively unknown, but seminal, aspect of the work of many important photographers. We can here see Ansel Adams and Edward Weston as organizers of books who worked in fertile collaboration with writers, editors, and publishers. In so doing, we can trace how these activities and connections shaped their better-known careers as masters of the individual print. We can also better understand Laura Gilpin's development as a photographer by observing how she evolved as an author, historian of the Southwest, and photographic book designer. Just as significantly, a focus on the book brings to light many important works by less well-known photographers, such as the comprehensive photographic and archaeological record of Mesa Verde created by scientist Gustaf Nordenskiöld in 1893, or the illustrated desert travel book, *A Modern Prairie Schooner on the Transcontinental Trail: The Story of a Motor Trip* (1919), by independent desert traveler

A.J. Russell
Bitter Creek Valley, Panoramic, 1868
Albumen print, 13 x 16 (33 x 40.6)
Union Pacific Museum, Omaha

A.J. Russell
On the Mountains of the Green River, Smiths Buttes, 1868
Albumen print from Russell, *The Great West Illustrated* . . . , 1869
Union Pacific Museum, Omaha

Caroline Poole. With or without the stature or finances needed to overcome the considerable obstacles to publishing, these photographers had a strong interest in the book form and somehow found the wherewithal to publish. Because of her interest in the photographic book, Laura Gilpin spent her savings to print several of her early books; because of previous difficulties in controlling the quality and content of his productions, Ansel Adams organized a publishing company with editor Nancy Newhall and other friends and family.

PHOTOGRAPHIC BOOKS AND THE CONSUMER

Inordinately expensive to produce, photographic books were especially vulnerable to economic pressures and shifts of public taste. Therefore, as artifacts, they do not supply a balanced view of social history, but they make excellent barometers for gauging the interests — or fantasies — of the historical consumer.

A comparison of the A.J. Russell photographs chosen for publication in *The Great West Illustrated* (1869) with those that were left out may reveal the machinations of the railroad officials intent on using the album as a promotional tool: only the right half of Russell's two-part *Bitter Creek Valley, Panoramic* was published. The unpublished left half depicted a harsh and waterless landscape, perhaps too reminiscent of the image of the Great Desert that boosters were trying to forget, while the published image, under the title *On Mountains of the Green Valley, Smith's Buttes,* presented a watery vista.[13]

By the turn of the century a much expanded publishing industry could and did respond to broader consumer demands. The market for books at this time, aimed at the middle and upper-middle classes, was filled with cowboy books illustrated by artists such as Frederic Remington and books about Indians replete with photographs by figures such as Edward Curtis and Charles Fletcher Lummis. The photographic book had been the medium of choice for documenting exotic cultures.

The American public largely turned away from photographic books about the West after World War I. Interest in the region adequate to sustain photographic publishing finally revived after the Great Depression of the 1930s, but with a new focus. This era saw the growth of photodocumentary articles on the rural poor in magazines like *Life* and *Survey Graphic*, and regional issues came to the fore in a new genre of photodocumentary books by photographers such as Berenice Abbott and Walker Evans. As a consequence of vanguard articles within such publications, and with growing evidence of a national audience for photographic books focused on contemporary social problems, a venturesome photographic book on Dust Bowl migrants, *An American Exodus* (1939) by Dorothea Lange and agricultural economist Paul Taylor, could be financed and published. The book's dust jacket pointed to "an urgent national problem to which attention has already been directed by John Steinbeck's *The Grapes of Wrath*."

In each historical period, printing technologies greatly affected the form of the photographic book as well as the size and cost of the edition—and hence determined the audience the book reached.[14]

PRINTING TECHNOLOGIES

Between 1839, when the invention of photography was announced, and 1880, when technological advances allowed a full-toned photographic image to be printed simultaneously with type, relatively few books were illustrated with original photographs. Beginning in the 1840s, survey leaders were so eager to publish more accurate illustrations with their reports that a number of them took up the considerable challenge of experimenting with the new medium of photography, and daguerreotypists accompanied scientists, military personnel, and illustrators into the field. Though many of these efforts failed because of the cumbersome nature of the photographic equipment, some photographs were produced and used as reference by draftsmen, whose drawings were then reproduced as engravings and lithographs in the published reports. These books anticipated post-Civil War survey reports, in which illustration would increasingly rely on photographic information, and, for many uses, be replaced by the photographic image altogether.

Between the 1860s and the 1890s, one technique of combining the direct photographic image with text in book form flourished: original photographs (usually albumen prints) were often tipped in on the pages of books. This method derived from the first book to be illustrated with photographs, William Henry Fox Talbot's *The Pencil of Nature*, published in London between 1844 and 1846, which featured tipped-in salt-paper photographs. The technique is seen in many books in the first section of this exhibition, including *The Great West Illustrated*, published by the Union Pacific Railroad with original albumen prints by A. J. Russell, and *Photographs Showing Landscapes, Geological and Other Features. . . Geographical and Geological Explorations and Surveys West of the One Hundredth Meridian* (c. 1876) with original albumen prints by William Bell and Timothy O'Sullivan. Because of the hand labor involved in printing photographs and pasting them in, most albums illustrated with original photographs were produced in editions of fewer than two hundred copies. Their distribution was consequently limited to an elite clientele. *The Great West Illustrated*, for example, fetched the exorbitant price of $75 in 1869.

To reach larger audiences, publishers through the 1870s still depended on engravers and lithographers to translate photographs into easily reproduced line drawings. Some artists and craftsmen loosely copied photographs; others worked from a pho-

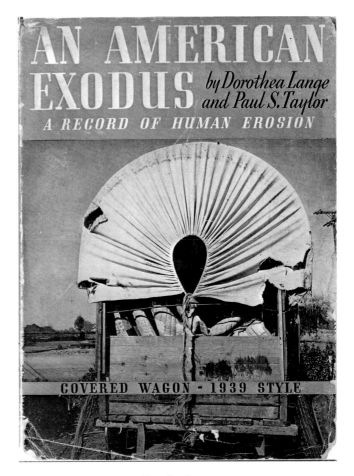

Dorothea Lange
Dust jacket from Lange and Taylor,
An American Exodus: A Record of Human Erosion, 1939
Library Collection, Whitney Museum of American Art, New York

John K. Hillers
Inner Gorge of Toroweap – Looking East
Heliotype from Dutton,
Tertiary History of the Grand Cañon District with Atlas, 1882

*process
time frame*

tographic impression that had been printed on a woodblock. Once this intermediary process of copying or tracing was completed, the image could be produced in editions of many thousands. This intervention persisted through the later nineteenth century, even after substantial advances were made in photographic printing. Even the most objective scientific publications (such as Clarence King's 1878 *Systematic Geology*) included drawings that dramatically altered and tinted the photographs on which they were based — sometimes for practical reasons, for example, to emphasize scientific content by exposing underlying rock structures; sometimes in an attempt to render Western landscapes more picturesque and appealing to Eastern audiences.

Photolithographic and related processes (most of which depended on a photographically prepared gelatin printing surface) came into wide use by the 1870s. Although the best of these processes, including collotype and heliotype, produced a full range of tones (as in the heliotype reproductions of John Hillers' photographs in Clarence Dutton's 1882 *Tertiary History of the Grand Cañon District*), the fragility of the gelatin printing surface limited most editions to under a few thousand copies. Photogravure, a continuous-tone printing method with an etched copper plate as a printing surface, came into use by the 1880s. The velvety, smoky tones seen in Gustaf Nordenskiöld's *The Cliff Dwellers of the Mesa Verde, Southwestern Colorado* (1893) result from this technique, and Edward S. Curtis's twenty-volume *North American Indian* (1907–30) includes some fifteen hundred gravure reproductions.

The halftone process, which came into wide use in the 1890s, so reduced the cost and increased the possible output of the presses that it revolutionized illustrated publishing. The halftone screen converts a photograph to an easily inked and printed dot pattern, which, when printed, reads to the naked eye as gradated tones. Over the next century, the halftone process would be incorporated into a variety of older printing processes that had been adapted for commercial use, most frequently relief printing, photogravure, and offset lithography.

Relief printing and photogravure were considered the "quality" commercial techniques through the 1950s. Since then, the increasingly versatile method of offset lithography has dominated the printing industry. Virtually all the books in the exhibition published after 1960 were printed by offset lithography. In 1950, Ansel Adams insisted on the dense inks and richly articulated tones of photoengraving for *The Land of Little Rain*, but by the early 1960s he reluctantly allowed an edition of *This Is the American Earth* to be printed in the less expensive process of offset lithography so that its message would reach a broader audience. The accuracy of offset lithography has greatly advanced since 1960.

The illustrations in the present volume were reproduced by offset lithography incorporating halftone photography. The tritone and duotone illustrations were printed from separations made in a camera, not electronically. These illustrations translate, but of course do not exactly duplicate, the look of the original photographs or reproductions of photographs from which they were made. Despite this remove, it becomes apparent that visual images in books can function simultaneously as art objects and artifacts. This awareness broadens, rather than circumscribes, our appreciation of photography and the book.

———————————

The essays here are intended to trace the rich history of the photographic book and the great diversity of viewpoints that have been used to interpret the landscape over the past one hundred and fifty years. Following Martha A. Sandweiss' overview of the photographic book in the arid West, twenty short essays focus on key books — individual works of singular importance to the history of the photographic book and the history of the region. By inviting authors from different fields to contribute to this catalogue, we hope to demonstrate the richness and diversity of the cultural attitudes that produced these books. Although written from a broad range of personal and scholarly perspectives, the essays consistently address similar questions: How did audiences come to learn about an unfamiliar landscape through photographic books? How have photographic books communicated ideas that other media have not? How or when have photographers and authors changed public attitudes about the landscape?

In another sense, these essays provide a guide to attitudes of previous generations and reveal the diverse thinking that a new generation of readers has brought to these photographic books. They open up a wider vista, in which we may recognize the shifting, overlapping, and sometimes opposing interpretations that continue to define and redefine the American desert. In these accounts, history remains a vital force; past opinions and images are constantly recalled and transformed to address pressing questions about the landscape — its past, its conservation, and its transformation — that continue to make the arid West a region of perpetual reinterpretation and fascination.

1. Rossiter W. Raymond, "Biographical Notice of Clarence King," *Transactions of the American Institute of Mining Engineers XXXIII* (1903), p. 631, cited in Thurman Wilkins, with Caroline Lawson Hinkley, *Clarence King: A Biography* (Albuquerque: University of New Mexico Press, 1988), p. 101.

2. Mary Austin, *The Land of Little Rain* (Boston and New York: Houghton Mifflin Company; Cambridge, Massachusetts: The Riverside Press, 1903), p. 3.

3. Reyner Banham, "The Man-Mauled Desert," in Richard Misrach, *Desert Cantos* (Albuquerque: University of New Mexico Press, 1987), p. 1.

4. Walter Prescott Webb, "The American West: Perpetual Mirage," *Harper's Magazine*, 214 (May 1957), p. 25.

5. Patricia Nelson Limerick, *Desert Passages: Encounters with the American Deserts* (Albuquerque: University of New Mexico Press, 1985), p. 4.

6. Alpine regions such as Yosemite — seen and publicized as the oases or distinctive "wonder places" of the West as early as the mid-nineteenth century— lie outside the scope of this study. Because of space limitations, and to maintain a focus on the most arid regions of the West, the exhibition excludes some well-known work from the mountain West, such as William Henry Jackson's Tetons and Colorado photographs and Carleton Watkins' Yosemite views.

7. See Earl Pomeroy, *In Search of the Golden West* (New York: Alfred A. Knopf, 1957) p. 31 n, discussing C.W. Dana, *The Garden of the World, or the Great West. . .* (Boston: Wentworth and Company, 1856).

8. John W. Powell, *Report on the Lands of the Arid Regions of the United States, with a More Detailed Account of the Lands of Utah* (Washington, D.C.: Government Printing Office, 1878); Mary C. Rabbitt, *Minerals, Lands, and Geology for the Common Defence and General Welfare, Volume l, Before 1879; United States Geological Survey: A History of Public Lands, Federal Science and Mapping Policy,* *and Development of Mineral Resources in the United States*, (Washington, D.C.: US Government Printing Office, 1979), pp. 252–55.

9. Webb, "The American West," p. 26.

10. *Landscape 1* (Spring 1951), p. 5, cited in D.W. Meinig, "Reading the Landscape: An Appreciation of W. G. Hoskins and J. B. Jackson," *The Interpretation of Ordinary Landscapes: Geographical Essays* (New York: Oxford University Press, 1979), p. 195.

11. *Cottonwoods: Photograp'* [ ] thsonian Institution Press, 1994), [ ]

12. To show a few of the [ ] ial photographs, and other prin [ ] unpublished albums, postcards, [ ] in the exhibition.

13. Thanks to Donald Snod [ ] r this and other information on *T* [ ]

14. For further reading on the techniques and the development of the photographic book, see Robert Taft, *Photography and the American Scene: A Social History, 1839–1889* (New York: The Macmillan Company, 1938); Lucien Goldschmidt and Weston Naef, *The Truthful Lens* (New York: The Grolier Club, 1980); David Margolis, *To Delight the Eye* (Dallas: DeGolyer Library, Southern Methodist University, 1994); William Welling, *Photography in America: The Formative Years, 1839–1900* (New York: Cromwell, 1978); John Szarkowski, *Photography Until Now*, exh. cat. (New York: The Museum of Modern Art, 1990); Alan Trachtenberg, *Reading American Photographs: Images as History, Mathew Brady to Walker Evans* (New York: Hill and Wang, 1989); Alex Sweetman, "Photobookworks: The Critical Realist Tradition," in Joan Lyons, ed., *Artists' Books: A Critical Anthology and Sourcebook* (Rochester, New York: Gibbs M. Smith in association with Visual Studies Workshop Press, 1985).

Timothy O'Sullivan
Kearsarge Mining Co., Kearsarge, Colorado, 1871
Albumen print from Wheeler, *Photographs Showing . . . the Western*
Territory . . . 1871, 1871
The Metropolitan Museum of Art, New York; Purchase, Joseph Pulitzer
Bequest and The Horace W. Goldsmith Foundation Gift, 1986

DRY LIGHT:
PHOTOGRAPHIC BOOKS
AND THE ARID WEST

MARTHA A. SANDWEISS

If one takes a broad view of geography and — for the moment — a dim view of geopolitical boundaries, it can be argued that the rich tradition of photographically illustrated books about the arid West actually begins in Canada. In the spring of 1858, a young Irishman named Humphrey Lloyd Hime hired on as official photographer for the Assiniboine and Saskatchewan Exploring Expedition, charged with documenting for the Canadian government the geology, natural history, and topography of the country. Working with the laborious wet-plate negative process, Hime struggled through extremes of hot and cold, violent weather, and sky-darkening swarms of grasshoppers "beyond all calculation" to produce photographs that could be redrawn as engravings for the official expedition report.[1]

Not all of Hime's photographs, which include Indian portraits, pictures of the settlement at Red River, and images of the Hudsons Bay Company's forts, deal directly with the arid landscape. But among the photographs is a startling image of the western Canadian prairies, brutal in its depiction of the harsh land. A razor-straight horizon slashes across a bleak landscape. The sky is a void, the foreground a lifeless plain decimated by a recent grasshopper plague. And there, lying on the ground, is a bleached white bone — perhaps human, perhaps animal — and the unmistakable form of a human skull. The picture is frightening for its intimation of human frailty in the face of nature, for its suggestion of personal failure and national defeat. When redrawn as a printed illustration in the expedition report in 1860, the image became considerably more cheery, with geese added to the sky and the prairie tinted a promising green. The immense Red River prairies, the accompanying text asserted, "seem to promise a bountiful recompense to millions of our fellow-men."[2] If such willful optimism anticipates the tone of the photographically illustrated books that would be published in the United States during the late 1860s and 1870s, the photograph itself remains utterly unlike any photograph made in the arid American West during the mid- to late nineteenth century. Rather than open possibili-

ties, it seems to close them.

The Hime photograph resonates with the ideas made popular in the United States some thirty-five years earlier with the publication of the official report of Major Stephen Long's government-sponsored exploring expedition to the Rocky Mountains in 1819–20. Expedition chronicler Edwin James was outspokenly blunt about the seemingly endless stretches of arid prairie thatseparated the Mississippi Valley settlements from the Rockies. "In regard to this extensive section of country," he wrote, "we do not hesitate in giving the opinion, that it is almost wholly unfit for cultivation and of course uninhabitable by a people depending upon agriculture for their subsistence."[3] Underscoring this assessment were the words blazoned across the engraved map that accompanied the official expedition report —"Great American Desert" — signifying the seeming emptiness of the place and its apparent inutility to Americans steeped in Jeffersonian rhetoric about the agrarian base of national democracy. For several decades, these words could be found inscribed across the vast middle section of American maps, not only describing an area of sparse European-American settlement, but actually shaping the perceptions of travelers and would-be settlers. Empty and barren, the "Great American Desert" seemed an impediment to national expansion, a geographic barrier precluding the peopling of the continent.

Yet by the 1860s and 1870s, when American photographers began to travel in greater numbers into the interior West, and photographically illustrated books emerged as a new kind of bookmaking, the seeming emptiness of the arid land was just what made it so alluring. It provided a blank slate upon which Americans could project and inscribe grand narratives of national life, narratives which, in the beginning, inevitably stressed success and growth, never failure or defeat. The photographic books produced by the great railroad surveys and the government-sponsored exploring expeditions reimagined James' "Great American Desert" as a land of possibilities and promise; not simply as a

Humphrey Lloyd Hime
The Prairie Looking West, 1858
Albumen print, 5½ x 7 (13.2 x 17.8)
National Archives of Canada, Ottawa

A.J. Russell
Dale Creek Bridge, General View, 1868
Albumen print from Russell, *The Great West Illustrated . . .* , 1869
Union Pacific Museum, Omaha

landscape of small, self-sufficient farms, but also as the locus of interesting scenery, natural resources, and promising town sites that could link the urban centers of East and West. Given the physical features of the plains and deserts — so devoid of such comfortingly familiar and picturesque sites as wooded glens or babbling brooks — this more optimistic view presented a conceptual challenge. The illusive emptiness and strange topography of the arid West resisted easy incorporation into the national myth of manifest destiny that emphasized economic growth and political expansion. Photographs of treeless prairies and waterless deserts, as Humphrey Lloyd Hime had shown, had the unsettling potential to suggest that the arid West *lacked* the necessities of settled life. But photography has always been a subjective medium, despite its documentary roots. In simply deciding what to include and what to exclude from the frame, a photographer can convey a point of view and shape the way we understand an image. Carefully composed, carefully edited pictures are like the short scenes from which longer narrative stories can be crafted. The photographers, writers, and publishers who collaborated on the photographic books produced in the 1860s and 1870s found ways to shape dense tales of pictures and words that served to normalize the arid West even as they documented its unusual topography. Their photographic books both reflected and contributed to the creation of broader cultural and political dialogues about the place of the West in national life and about the shape of American life itself.

The photographic books about the arid American West produced between 1869 and the present fall into three rough conceptual categories. The earliest books and albums — including work produced for the Union Pacific and Kansas Pacific railroads by A. J. Russell and Alexander Gardner and the government survey reports with photographic (or photographically based) illustrations by Timothy O'Sullivan, William Bell, William Henry Jackson, and John K. Hillers — are implicitly forward-looking, reflecting the economic interests of the photographers' institutional patrons. It might seem ironic that photography, a medium inherently well-suited to recording a present or the traces of a past, should be adapted as a predictive medium. But the West encountered in the photographic books illustrated by Russell or Gardner, Jackson or O'Sullivan, is invariably a West of the future, a place where economic investment will be rewarded and immigrants will meet with a prosperous future.

If such a reading of the landscape relies upon a kind of willing erasure of its human past and of the increasingly complex realities of Native American life, later nineteenth- and early twentieth-century photographers reimagined this human past as central to their story. Photographic narratives fashioned by such photographers as Charles Fletcher Lummis, Adam Clark Vroman, Edward S. Curtis, and Laura Gilpin looked to the past — not the future — to find the real and metaphoric importance of the arid West. Still ignoring the contemporary Indian peoples, they found in the region's historic and prehistoric past a "history old as Egypt" that conferred cultural legitimacy on one of the Western world's newest nations.[4]

Since the 1930s, the desert West has become a site for the inscription of new stories — stories about the human despoliation of the natural landscape, the limited ability of an arid land to support urban growth, the tensions that arise when different peoples share a common space, the possibilities of learning from the cyclical patterns of nature. If the earliest photographic books about the arid West looked to an Edenic future and later ones imagined an Edenic past, the focus of the widely diverse books published in the past sixty years is — broadly speaking — on the immensely complicated present and the potential consequences of our human behavior.

Despite these changing stories and the changing reproduction technologies that make a lavish 1870s book with tipped-in albumen photographs quite different from a contemporary book with laser-scanned color reproductions, all of the photographically illustrated books included in this catalogue were produced with certain common assumptions in mind: that photography is an effective narrative medium; that printed words can expand and amplify the meanings suggested by photographic images; that photographic books are an engaging and persuasive form of communication; and that in the arid West are scenes of extraordinary visual interest and stories of broad national appeal.

The use of photography as a narrative medium extends back to the earliest days of photography in the American West. San Francisco photographer Robert Vance took his collection of three hundred California daguerreotypes east to New York in the fall of 1851 and presented them in sequential order in an exhibition hall, along with a printed narrative that he himself distributed in the gallery. That same year, John Wesley Jones made an extraordinary overland trip from California to St. Louis, documenting the route with a reported 1,500 daguerreotypes that he intended to convert into a moving panorama with sequential painted scenes of the trail to the goldfields. These projects drew from the marketing strategies developed by such painter-entrepreneurs as George Catlin and John Mix Stanley, who had presented their "Indian gallery" paintings in the 1830s and 1840s with narratives that explicated their carefully arranged pictures. They were inspired, too, by the popularity during the 1840s of

moving panoramas — long, crudely painted canvases that scrolled across a stage from one reel to another and brought Western subjects to audiences across America. Like the "Indian galleries," these "moving pictures" relied upon a combination of spoken words and sequenced images to convey a story. In mimicking these popular presentations, Vance and Jones suggested that photography, too, could tell complex narrative stories that unfolded across time and space.[5]

While daguerreotypes could be redrawn and engraved for inclusion in printed books, the true era of the photographic book did not really begin until the late 1850s, when changing photographic technologies permitted American photographers to produce positive photographic prints on paper. As before, these photographs could be redrawn for engraved reproductions, but they could also now be tipped in to bound book sheets. The earliest Western book to be illustrated with tipped-in photographs was George Fardon's *San Francisco Album* (1856), which used thirty-one carefully sequenced landscapes and architectural views to lay out a grand civic agenda for the city's glorious future. No book illustrated with original photographs would deal with the less settled parts of the arid West for another thirteen years, a gap that speaks to the complicated economics of this sort of bookmaking.

From the 1850s into the 1880s, the production of books with tipped-in photographic illustrations was both expensive and labor-intensive. Leave aside for a moment the work involved in making a wet-plate negative outside of a studio — a process that could easily take thirty to sixty minutes for a single exposure. Making the prints was time-intensive too. To make a single photographic print, a photographer had to place a sheet of sensitized paper in contact with the negative and expose it to direct sunlight for a half-hour or so. The print then had to be finished and hand-mounted on paper or board mounts. Finally, these mounted photographs had to be bound together with printed sheets of text, a process that could be complicated by the bulk of the mounted pictures. Books illustrated with original photographs relied on two distinctive instruments of mass production — the printing press and the camera. But in the end, they could be joined only through hand labor.

By contrast, books illustrated with engravings or woodcut illustrations made *after* photographs were much cheaper to mass-produce. Artists would redraw by hand the image depicted in the photographic view and their printing plates could be inked and printed along with the blocks of type for the text, forming a single, seamless page of words and image. But it is a stretch to call such projects photographically illustrated books. Visually, they are similar to earlier books illustrated with engravings made after drawings or paintings. Sometimes the illustrations have a detail that betrays their photographic origins, but often this is not the case. The specificity, the persuasive authenticity of the eyewitness view, is inevitably lost.

Given the cost of producing books with actual bound-in photographic prints, it is not surprising that relatively few such illustrated books on the arid West were published between the 1860s and 1880s. And those that were varied widely, from modest commemorative books representing small private investment schemes, to the grand railroad and survey albums that signal a more ambitious agenda for political change and economic expansion.

The strictly commemorative projects — such as *Journey Through the Yellowstone National Park and Northwestern Wyoming* (1883) — used photographs more as illustrative, anecdotal material than as images central to the argument of the book, and were printed in small quantities as keepsakes for travelers. Travel accounts promoting private development schemes — such as *Our Indian Summer in the Far West* (1880) or George Street's *Che! Wah! Wah!* (1883) — aimed at a broader audience, but kept photography in a supporting role, with the few tipped-in photographs simply amplifying the lengthy upbeat narrative. Likewise, the English railroad investor William Blackmore used tipped-in photographs in his promotional book *Colorado: Its Resources, Parks, and Prospects as a New Field for Emigration. . .*(1869), but the number and content of the images vary from copy to copy, suggesting that he viewed pictures more as generic illustrations than as independent sources of information.[6]

The great monuments of photographic bookmaking during the albumen print era — the only projects in which photographs themselves assume pride of place — were the products of corporate ambition and governmental largesse. Alexander Gardner's *Across the Continent on the Kansas Pacific Railroad (Route of the 35th Parallel)* (c. 1869); A.J. Russell's *The Great West Illustrated* (1869), published for the Union Pacific Railroad Company; and the various books of pictures done by Timothy O'Sullivan and William Bell for Lieutenant George M. Wheeler's survey of the lands west of the 100th meridian (published in the 1870s) were produced by well-financed sponsors who had much to gain by promoting a particular and easily communicated vision of the West's future. Carefully sequenced photographs combined with minimal text make these large-scale books both entertaining picture albums and more complicated narratives of political expansion and industrial growth.

The linear organization of the Russell and Gardner albums echoes the photographers' routes of travel. The Gardner album follows the east to west search for a suitable southern railroad line; and the Russell album follows actual railroad construction west from Omaha to Salt Lake City, a city whose very existence and prosperity testify to what awaits the Western immigrant. Each album conveys a progressive, forward-looking vision of Western historical development, confirming that man will inevitably prevail over nature and that American civilization will spread across the land.

Such a story is conveyed, in its essentials, by the photographs alone. But the brief printed captions flesh out the story and inadvertently reveal the sometimes uneasy connections between image and text: the printed words simultaneously reinforce and undercut the messages conveyed by the photographs. The descriptive literalism of the photographs was both an asset and a liability. The preface of *The Great West Illustrated*, for example, notes the photographer's conviction that photographs offer "the most comprehensive manner in which a positive and substantial knowledge" of the region can be conveyed. Yet the pictures of visual interest are not always coincident with the narrative purpose of the project. Photographs of the Dale Creek Bridge, for example, may provide visual evidence of the engineers' mastery of the difficult Western terrain. But only the printed caption can provide the information that there are trout in the stream, representing the natural bounty that awaits the traveler or would-be settler. Likewise, the captions for Russell's photographs of *Valley of the Great Laramie from the Mountains* and *Source of the Laramie River* transform these landscapes into sites of abundant game; and the text accompanying *Among the Timber at Head of Little Laramie River* speaks of the gold mines and quartz beds that are hidden from the photographer. Russell was adept at depicting scenery and documenting engineering feats; but explicating the land's natural wealth was more easily accomplished through words.[7]

There is a tension created by the simultaneous belief in the photograph as an unimpeachable witness and the lack of faith in its ability to convey the full story. Consider, for example, the album of twenty-five albumen prints made by Timothy O'Sullivan and William Bell between 1871 and 1874, as members of Lieutenant Wheeler's Survey: *Photographs Showing Landscapes, Geological, and Other Features, of Portions of the Western Territory of the United States* (c. 1876). Earlier albums of Wheeler survey prints from the 1871–73 seasons had appeared as bound volumes of albumen prints mounted on boards with simple printed titles and credits. Depicting sites of scenic, historic, and geologic interest, the photographs were meant to be read as self-evident records of the West's varied terrain. But in this later volume, nothing remains self-evident. The mounted pictures are interleaved with paragraph-long "descriptive legends" that shape a reader's understanding of the photographs and place the pictures in service to a higher goal — an elaborate narrative tale of Western economic development that relies on the simultaneous inflation of natural resource potential and devaluation of contemporary Native American cultures. And if the pictures often stress what is *different* about the geography and geology of the arid West, the captions remind the reader of what is familiar about this strangely unfamiliar landscape.

The argument about the West's economic potential begins with the first photograph and caption. *Snow Peaks, Bull Run Mining District, Nevada* (1871) shows the rugged winter terrain of the Sierras, but is of interest because it depicts a route to newly discovered silver mines. A sequence of four photographs of the remote Conejos Canyon of southwestern Colorado is presented not just for its beauty, but because "in all of our unoccupied territory there is no spot which offers greater advantages to the settler than this."[8] Such boosteristic language runs through to the concluding photograph of the Snake River Canyon in Idaho, presented as a prospective site for gold mining and set in the midst of a region with good pasturage and an abundance of game. The possibilities for this site are boundless, now that is has been "freed from the terror of hostile Indians."[9]

This marginalization of the land's native inhabitants is the central subtheme of the text that accompanies the photographs. The Apaches are "true savages," now being converted on reservations into productive farmers.[10] The Navajos, likewise, are making "good progress towards civilization" since their military subjugation, and the Zunis exhibit a "form of government and obedience to authority that would not compare unfavorably with some modern centres of civilization."[11]

Just as the text attempts to deny complex cultural differences and the possibilities of cultural conflict, so it also works to deny the off-putting features of the very geography the photographs so vividly depict. The saguaro cactus — surely the most dramatic example of the radically different flora to be found in the arid West — is normalized through its caption as an important source of food. And following several photographs of the Grand Canyon of the Colorado — pictures that underscore the harsh inaccessibility of much of the Southwest — is a picture of Apache Lake, Arizona, whose "conditions of beauty and fertility effectually prove that Arizona, in its entirety, is not the worthless desert that by many it has been supposed to be."[12]

The Wheeler album, like Russell's *Great West Illustrated* or Gardner's *Across the Continent*, can be read as a kind of seamless corporate statement that nullifies the voice or vision of the individual photographer. This is not to say that O'Sullivan and Bell, Gardner and Russell, didn't each have a personal grace and style that distinguish their pictures from those of their contemporaries. But in these books, their vision is made subservient to the

Timothy O'Sullivan
*View on Apache Lake, Sierra Blanca Range, Arizona.
Two Apache Scouts in the Foreground*, 1873
Albumen print from Wheeler,
*Photographs Showing . . . the Western Territory . . .
1871, 1872, 1873, and 1874*, 1874–75
The Denver Art Museum

grander vision articulated through the careful sequencing and captioning of their pictures — a captioning that in each case is done by an unidentified hand, orchestrating the drama like an omniscient narrator.

The refinement of reproductive printing technologies in the early 1890s opened new possibilities for the use of photography in printed books and soon ended the era of tipped-in photographic illustrations. The halftone process allowed technicians to transfer a screened photographic image to a specially prepared metal plate that produced an image of countless tiny dots. The space between these dots could be etched away and the plate then printed with regular printer's ink. Images with near-photographic detail could thus be reproduced directly onto the sheet that held the printed word, and the laborious handwork required for producing and tipping in photographs could be eliminated. The more difficult and expensive gravure process allowed technicians to produce even finer continuous-tone images, also from metal plates that could be inked and printed on a press.

These changes in reproduction technologies evolved at the same time as changes in photographic technologies that made photography a simpler and less arduous craft. The dry-plate negatives that came into wide use in the 1880s freed photographers from the burden of having to sensitize a sheet of glass for every exposure, and greatly reduced the bulk of equipment and chemicals that had to be carried into the field. Photography thus became a more attractive leisure-time pursuit for countless Americans. The widespread marketing of the simple Kodak camera in the 1890s ("You push the button, we'll do the rest") brought still more amateurs into the field and made the photography of remote sites simpler than ever.

These technological changes coincided with broad shifts in cultural thinking about the arid West. The massacre at Wounded Knee in late December 1890 brought to an end decades of US military action against the West's native peoples. Confined to reservations and no longer a threat to settlement or economic development, Western Indians could more easily be consigned to a safely remote and exotic past — where they were transformed into benign symbols of America's unique cultural heritage.

A similar shift in thinking occurred with regard to the more remote areas of the desert West. Photographs by Gardner, Russell, O'Sullivan, and Bell had been used to demystify the desert landscape by showing it as a place that could be developed for industrial purposes. But photographers of the late nineteenth and early twentieth centuries showed less interest in the possible *future* of the arid land than in its storied *past*. Suddenly the ruins at Mesa Verde, what Laura Gilpin called "a living monument to a forgotten race," seemed more interesting than the prospective site for a railroad bed or a mountain laced with silver ore.[13] And the Southwest in general seemed alluring not for what *could* happen there, but for what already *had*. Photographer Frederick Monsen described Navajo and Hopi country in *With a Kodak in the Land of the Navajo* (1909) as "a land of extinct volcanoes and shadowy canyons, a land of a dead and forgotten people."[14] In the work of photographers such as Monsen or Charles Lummis or Edward Curtis, the people and the land could be remythologized together and transported to a dim and shadowy past.

The work of these romanticists is more personal in tone than the earlier photographic books produced by the railroad and survey photographers. Improvements in the ease and safety of Western travel, coupled with the technological advances that made cameras simpler to operate, meant that photographers could more easily travel on their own without either financial or logistical support. They could thus pursue personal interests and operate more independently than had their predecessors, many of whom were contract workers. And as photomechanical reproduction techniques became widespread throughout the printing industry, photographers gained an increasing number of options for the reproduction of their photographs. It is ironic that a mechanical reproduction process should afford photographers a broader role in book production than the older method, which relied on the hand-processing of individual photographs. But because books with large numbers of tipped-in photographs were generally produced by institutional sponsors, photographers rarely had a chance to control the presentation of their work. When photographically illustrated books became cheaper and easier to make, photographers could remain a part of the production process: they could even become writers.

George Wharton James, Charles Fletcher Lummis, Edward Curtis, Frederick Monsen, Gustaf Nordenskiöld, Laura Gilpin — in the first third of the twentieth century all became photographer-authors, using the medium of the photographically illustrated book to shape viewers' understanding of their pictures of the arid West. Their elegiac voices amplify the sense of loss we feel in their photographs; the words and images work together to create a seamless message. At the risk of minimizing the many differences among these photographers, it can be said that they all viewed their travels through the Southwest as enlightening journeys of self-discovery; shared a romantic fascination with the historic cultures of the region; and valued anthropology, but were otherwise relatively uninterested in the scientific issues that had engaged many of their nineteenth-century predecessors. If the arid West that emerges in the photographic books of the nineteenth century is a place awaiting the shaping hand of the entrepreneurial engineer, the West of these early twentieth-century books awaits the more gentle tread of the tourist.

Historical tourism remains a central theme in the photographically illustrated state guides published for the Southwestern states under the aegis of the Works Progress Administration in the late 1930s and 1940s. But during this period, the arid West also emerges as a newly vital and complicated *social* landscape in the books of photographers (all Westerners themselves) such as Ansel Adams, Dorothea Lange, or Laura Gilpin. In their publications, the present finally becomes as engaging a subject as either an imagined future or a storied past. Gilpin's portraits of contemporary Pueblo and Southwestern Hispanic life, published in *The Pueblos: A Camera Chronicle* (1941) and *The Rio Grande, River of Destiny* (1949), reveal few hints of social tensions. But in acknowledging the very presence of these people as contemporary participants in regional life, she had moved well beyond the backwards-looking romanticism of her earlier work on Mesa Verde (1927), introducing instead the theme of social and cultural accommodation to the arid landscape that would become central to her most important work, *The Enduring Navaho* (1968). Ansel Adams' work underwent a similar shift in focus. His pictures in *Taos Pueblo* (1930) had emphasized the timeless aspects of Pueblo life and given visual amplification to Mary Austin's romantic text. In *Born Free and Equal* (1944), however, he directly addressed the politics of the federal government's decision to intern Japanese-Americans during World War II. Dorothea Lange likewise viewed the West as a social and political landscape. In *An American Exodus: A Record of Human Erosion* (1939), she used her photographs to turn nearly a century of American iconography of the West on its head. In this searing book on displaced workers, the road West leads not to hope but to continued despair. And the heartbreak is all the worse because the immigrants trudging westward carry with them impossibly high expectations fueled by the enduring visual icons and literary myths of the West as a land of possibilities.

The West thus emerges as a contested social space in photographic books published in the 1930s, but not until the 1960s does it become a contested natural landscape as well. Ansel Adams' *This Is the American Earth* (1960) and Eliot Porter's *The Place No One Knew: Glen Canyon on the Colorado* (1963) invert the tradition of nineteenth-century Western photographic books by calling into question the beneficence of industrial development. Since words can shape our understanding of pictures in powerful and unexpected ways, one can almost imagine selected works by either Adams or Porter serving the developers who financed some of the earliest photographically illustrated books. But Adams and Porter worked instead with the Sierra Club, a conservation group

that had its own agenda to promote. The texts of their books make certain that we understand the natural beauty documented in the photographs as something to be cherished and protected, not exploited and developed. Pictures and words work together as examples of moral suasion. Shown the inherent value and beauty of the natural world, we're asked to honor it.

Adams and Porter only implicitly acknowledge the threat of development. Their contemporary successors are more direct. The new suburban houses found in the pictures of Robert Adams or Lewis Baltz, the cheap tract homes sprouting up on the Southwestern Indian reservations photographed by Skeet McAuley, signal a more complicated way of looking at the arid West as both a natural and social landscape. The lines drawn in Adams' and Porter's work seem cut-and-dry: preservation is good; development a destructive evil. But the moral lines are less clearly drawn in the newer work, where development is not so much an evil as a kind of aesthetically interesting, moral complication. The transformative power of industrial culture, so fervently hoped for by the publishers of early photographically illustrated books, is viewed here more warily. Its promise and its potential to betray seem perilously alike.

If the future — represented by sprawling new Western communities — seems considerably complicated in recent photographic books, so is the Western past, which stubbornly refuses to go away. Old cultural patterns, enduring social problems, and long historical memories inform the community life along the Mexico-United States border documented by photographer Jay Dusard in *La Frontera* (1986). The legacy of America's internal nuclear testing haunts the landscapes of Richard Misrach's *Bravo 20: The Bombing of the American West* (1990). Once imagined as a land of infinite possibilities, the West is here reimagined as a place bounded and tethered by its past.

The nineteenth-century photographers whose pictures were tipped into books had little to say about the ways in which their images were enveloped by texts. Since the 1890s, however, the texts of virtually all the photographically illustrated books about the arid West have been written either by the photographer or a close collaborator. Photographer Dorothea Lange and her husband, the sociologist-writer Paul Taylor, worked together to compile the pictures and words for *An American Exodus*; Edward Weston and his wife, Charis Wilson Weston, likewise worked as a photographer-writer team to produce *California and the West* (1940). Ansel Adams actively collaborated with writer Mary Austin in *Taos Pueblo* (1930); after Austin's death, however, he selectively borrowed and edited her writings to serve as captions for his photographs in *The Land of Little Rain* (1950). Words in all these books explicate a particular picture or create a parallel image with

Skeet McAuley
Biker at Navajo tribal government grounds, Window Rock, Arizona, 1984
From McAuley, *Sign Language: Contemporary Southwest Native America,* 1989
Collection of the artist; courtesy Terry Etherton Gallery, Tucson, Arizona

Laura Gilpin
The Rio Grande Yields Its Surplus to the Sea, 1947
From Gilpin, *The Rio Grande, River of Destiny . . . ,* 1949
Gelatin silver print, 15¹³⁄₁₆ x 9¹³⁄₁₆ (40.2 x 24.9)
Amon Carter Museum, Fort Worth, Texas; Gift of the artist

language. In either case, the model is of partnership, with word and image reinforcing each other.

Precisely because it disrupts this expectation about the cozy agreement between image and text, between the intent of the photographer and the intent of the writer, Skeet McAuley's book *Sign Language* (1989) forces us to rethink the way photographically illustrated books work. McAuley photographs the ways in which the Navajo and White Mountain Apache people alter their physical landscape — recording the green grass on a Monument Valley football field, the painted murals at a Navajo college, the anonymous tract housing being constructed near White River, Arizona. If turn-of-the-century photographers of Southwestern Indian life crafted an illusory image of unchanging traditional life and passive native subjects, McAuley's photographs seem very much about the complexities of contemporary change and the active agency of his Indian subjects. It comes as a shock, then, to read the commentaries on the photographs, adapted from the oral comments of Navajo medicine man Mike Mitchell. The picture of a huge concrete culvert carrying water through a desert landscape near Shiprock, New Mexico, seems to me a statement — one that could have been conveyed through any number of pictures of Western dams and water projects — about the hubris of those who would deny that aridity imposes limitations on human activity. Mitchell, however, responds to the picture with a meditation about the holiness of water. A picture of a boy on a motorcycle in front of some prefabricated buildings in Window Rock, Arizona, seems a commentary on how contemporary consumer culture has become a part of everyday Navajo life. But for Mitchell the most interesting part of the picture is the rock formation in the background, which inspires a story about the sacred qualities of rocks.[15]

I bristle when I think of some government functionary in 1875 writing a caption for Timothy O'Sullivan's pictures of Southwestern Indians that renders the subjects benign and unthreatening. O'Sullivan's photographs seem to suggest something much more interesting about the possibilities for cultural exchange. But Mike Mitchell's commentaries likewise deny the cultural complexities preserved in McAuley's photographs. If I don't bristle at his comments, I suppose it is because I grant him the moral authority to comment on a world that is his and not mine.

O'Sullivan's and McAuley's two vastly different photographic book projects nevertheless make a similar point. Photographic meaning is not only culture-specific, it is malleable. When photographs appear in books, they invite consideration in the context of words, and words shape the way we understand pictures. Look at any one of the photographs featured in this catalogue, cover up the accompanying words, and just look at the image. Chances are a story will emerge as the picture stirs memories and associations – perhaps of a childhood trip or a recent vacation, a favorite film, a misadventure in the backyard, or a dimly recalled history book. Pictures can sustain any number of readings. But words rein them in, reinforcing one reading at the expense of others. It's words that make a book of Eliot Porter's Glen Canyon photographs less a lyric account of desert light than a meditation about loss and the destruction of the natural world. It's words that transform Timothy O'Sullivan's Southwestern landscapes into pictures of exploitable land. It's words that make Skeet McAuley's pictures of the vernacular landscape into symbolic representations of a Navajo worldview.

Do photographs gain or lose in imaginative power when they appear in books, harnessed by words? One might argue that the pictures grow in authority as publications bring them to a broad audience; but that they lose imaginative resonance because words limit the possibilities for divergent personal interpretations. One might also argue, however, that this very directedness is what makes photographs and photographic books so compelling as cultural objects. By enforcing a particular reading of pictures, the text of a photographically illustrated book asks all readers to understand the photographs in the same way; to understand that

Lange's *An American Exodus* pictures show sharecroppers stuck in a system they are helpless to change, or that A. J. Russell's Union Pacific photographs prove the triumph of American engineering know-how. Photographically illustrated books, and the photographs they include, thus become more potent instruments of communication and persuasion. And photographic books about the arid West become indices of the nation's changing cultural anxieties.

For nearly 130 years, these regional books have proved an important medium for the dissemination of cultural and political ideas about national life. "The West is America, only more so," a historian remarked recently.[16] And, indeed, in these books we can trace changing national concerns, as an emphasis on the necessity for political expansion is replaced by anxieties about the hazards of human settlement in a fragile landscape; a disinterest in the Indian and Spanish inhabitants of the nineteenth-century West is supplanted by an interest in the region as a gathering place of peoples; a faith in growth is displaced by a concern for limits. The Great American Desert, it turns out, is not an empty space. It is more like a grand national stage where the central tensions of American life are revealed in sharp relief under the clear, harsh light of the dry desert skies.

1. Henry Youle Hind, *Narrative of the Canadian Red River Exploring Expeditions* (London: Longman, Green, Longman and Roberts, 1860), I, pp. 296–97.

2. Ibid., p. 135.

3. Edwin James, *Account of an Expedition from Pittsburgh to the Rocky Mountains Under the Command of Major Stephen H. Long* (Philadelphia: Carey and Lea, 1822–23), II, p. 361.

4. Laura Gilpin, *The Pueblos: A Camera Chronicle* (New York: Hastings House, 1941), p. 7.

5. For more on Vance, Jones, and the narrative tradition in Western American photography, see Martha A. Sandweiss, "Undecisive Moments: The Narrative Tradition in Western Photography," in Martha A. Sandweiss, ed., *Photography in Nineteenth-Century America*, exh. cat. (Fort Worth, Texas: Amon Carter Museum, 1991), pp. 99–129.

6. For more on these books, see the catalogue by David Margolis, with introduction by Martha A. Sandweiss, *To Delight the Eye: Original Photographic Book Illustrations of the American West*, exh. cat. (Dallas: DeGolyer Library, Southern Methodist University, 1994). Also deserving of mention in any review of early photographically illustrated books is Charles Granville Johnson's interesting *The Territory of Arizona, Embracing a History of the Territory. . .*(San Francisco: Vincent Ryan & Co., 1869). Johnson was promoter, writer, and photographer for this publication, which was intended to illustrate the navigability of the lower Colorado River, and thus was perhaps the first to write and illustrate a photographic book. He proposed to sell by subscription twenty-five parts of his series, each of which would feature one or more tipped-in albumen photographs supported by a brief text. But only three parts appeared. The failure of the project speaks to the financial difficulties of producing and marketing this sort of book without broad institutional support.

7. A.J. Russell, *The Great West Illustrated in a Series of Photographic Views Across the Continent; Taken Along the Line of the Union Pacific Railroad West from Omaha, Nebraska . . .* (New York: Union Pacific Railroad Company, 1869). The photographic captions all appear at the front of the book in an annotated table of contents.

8. See the descriptive legend for view no. 18 in *Photographs Showing Landscapes, Geological and Other Features, of Portions of the Western Territory of the United States, Obtained in Connection with Geographical and Geological Explorations and Surveys West of the 100th Meridian, Seasons of 1871, 1872, 1873, and 1874* (Washing-ton, D. C.: War Department, Corps of Engineers, c. 1876).

9. Ibid., descriptive legend for view no. 25.

10. Ibid., descriptive legends for view nos. 8 and 9.

11. Ibid., descriptive legends for view nos. 10 and 15.

12. Ibid., descriptive legend for view no. 7.

13. Laura Gilpin, *The Mesa Verde National Park* (Colorado Springs: Gilpin Publishing Co., 1927), n.p.

14. Frederick Monsen, *With a Kodak in the Land of the Navajo* (Rochester: Eastman Kodak Company, 1909), p. 5.

15. See Mitchell's commentaries in Skeet McAuley, *Sign Language: Contemporary Southwest Native America* (New York: Aperture, 1989), pp. 58 and 48.

16. Clyde Milner, introduction to Clyde A. Milner, Carol A. O'Connor, and Martha A. Sandweiss, *The Oxford History of the American West* (New York: Oxford University Press, 1994), p. 3, where the author expands on a remark about California attributed to the writer Wallace Stegner.

SURVEYING
AN UNFAMILIAR LAND
1840–1880

Timothy O'Sullivan
Black Cañon, from Camp 8, Looking Above, 1871
Albumen print from Wheeler,
Photographs Showing . . . the Western Territory . . . 1871, 1871
The Metropolitan Museum of Art, New York; Purchase, Joseph Pulitzer
Bequest and The Horace W. Goldsmith Foundation Gift, 1986

pp. 30–31: Timothy O'Sullivan
Wall inthe Grand Cañon, 1871 (detail)
Albumen print from Wheeler,
Photographs Showing . . . the Western Territory . . . 1871, 1872, and 1873, 1871
Private Collection

Timothy O'Sullivan
Black Cañon, Colorado River, Looking Above from Mirror Bar, 1871
Albumen print from Wheeler,
Photographs Showing . . . the Western Territory . . . 1871, 1871
The Metropolitan Museum of Art, New York; Purchase, Joseph Pulitzer
Bequest and The Horace W. Goldsmith Foundation Gift, 1986

Timothy O'Sullivan
Eroded Strata, Near Cottonwood Springs, Nevada, 1871
Albumen print from Wheeler,
Photographs Showing . . . the Western Territory . . . 1871, 1871
The Metropolitan Museum of Art, New York; Purchase, Joseph Pulitzer Bequest
and The Horace W. Goldsmith Foundation Gift, 1986

opposite: Timothy O'Sullivan
Cereus Giganteus, Arizona, 1871
Albumen print from Wheeler, *Photographs Showing . . .*
the Western Territory . . . 1871, 1871
The Metropolitan Museum of Art, New York; Purchase, Joseph Pulitzer Bequest
and The Horace W. Goldsmith Foundation Gift, 1986

We begin with the idea of the "emptiness" of the inland West that dominated most Anglo-American conceptions of portions of the region in the early nineteenth century: a vast wilderness, a "trackless desert" extending beyond the Missouri River to the Pacific Slope.

After the war with Mexico (1846–48) and the discovery of gold in California in 1848, military and commercial interests joined forces in surveying the newly acquired territories, as they had done after the Louisiana Purchase. The US government ordered the army to undertake extensive surveys to mark the new boundary with Mexico and examine the adjacent terrain in such illustrated publications as the *Report on the United States and Mexican Boundary Survey* by William Emory, published between 1857 and 1859. Draftsmen who could create detailed maps and record sites to guide future military campaigns were important members of these survey teams. In the mid-1850s, the government also authorized a series of exploratory trips to find the best railroad route from the Mississippi River to the Pacific" — the transcontinental connection being essential for the development of the West. The thirteen-volume "Pacific Railroad Surveys" (*Reports of Explorations and Surveys, to Ascertain the Most Practicable and Economical Route for a Railroad from the Mississippi River to the Pacific Ocean*), published between 1855 and 1860, not only traced potential links between the termini, but also provided a wealth of documentation about the diverse country that had been charted. Overall, however, the lithographs and engravings that illustrated these early volumes provide less than precise records. They frequently blend documentation with aesthetic conventions derived from European pictorial traditions, so much so that the topography of the New World sometimes takes on attributes of the Old World.

During an expedition through Navajo country in 1849, Richard Kern made the first known sketches of Canyon de Chelly (p. 45), the same site that Timothy O'Sullivan would photograph some twenty years later (p. 65). A comparison of their works suggests why photographers began to supplant all but the most exceptional draftsmen on topographic surveys.[1] Kern's fine watercolor sketches of Canyon de Chelly blur the geological stratification so precisely recorded in O'Sullivan's photographs. Without days to study a site, or the use of photographs as reference, very few draftsmen could capture either the particularity required by geologists or the speed of execution demanded by generals. As Kern regularly noted in his diary, encounters with hostile Indians frequently prevented his party from remaining long at any site (Kern was killed while on an expedition in Utah during 1853). Yet until after the Civil War, when photographic equipment was adapted for travel through this rugged terrain, expeditions depended primarily on draftsmen for visual records of the territory they crossed.

With the end of the war, commercial and governmental organizations made the exploration of the West a paramount goal. Two railroads, the Kansas Pacific and the Union Pacific, raced to commission prominent photographers to document their proprietary routes across the West and convince prominent citizens that theirs was the superior path for a planned transcontinental railroad. A. J. Russell photographed the Union Pacific's northern route across Nebraska, Wyoming, and Utah (the winning track),

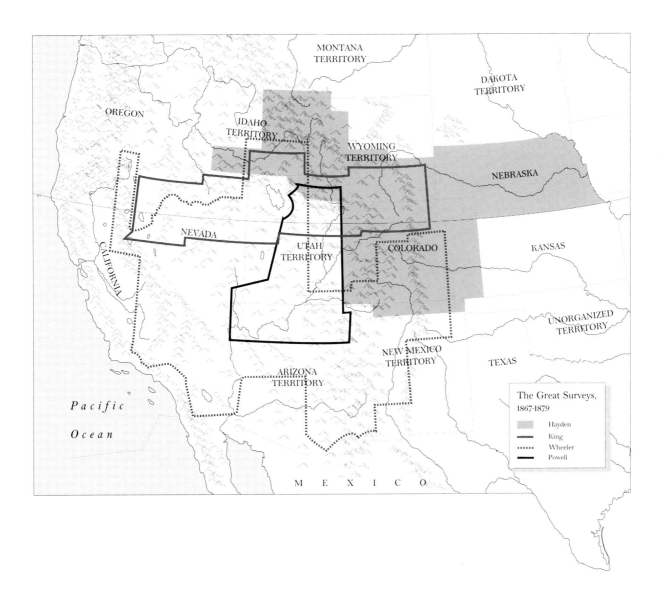

The Great Surveys,
1867-1879

	Hayden
	King
	Wheeler
	Powell

which was already under construction. The Union Pacific then published a lavish album of Russell's photographs for distribution to investors and congressmen. Meanwhile, Alexander Gardner, the famed Civil War photographer, was invited to shoot the Kansas Pacific's more southern route from St. Louis, across the Southwest, and on to California.

These vast projects required more capital than private industry could assemble, and the US government eagerly increased its participation in the westward enterprise. In his inaugural address of 1868, President Ulysses S. Grant acknowledged that the federal government was expecting to exploit mineral deposits in the West to pay off the huge national debt that had accrued during the war. In a speech referring to the transcontinental railroad, Grant said, "It looks as though Providence has bestowed upon us a strong box in the precious metals locked up in the sterile mountains of the far west and which we are now forging the key to unlock, to meet the very contingency that is upon us." Stating that "it may be necessary to insure the facilities to these riches, and it may be necessary also that the general government should give its aid to secure access," Grant continued the policy that would generate intensive exploration of the West by the US government through the next decade.[2]

Beginning with geologist Clarence King's exploration of the 40th parallel in 1867, the government sponsored the four projects that have come to be known as the "Great Surveys." These meticulously described, mapped, illustrated, and photographed the inland Western territory and its resources over the next twelve years. They were led by Clarence King (1867–79), F.V. Hayden (1867–79), John Wesley Powell (1872–79), and Lieutenant George M. Wheeler (1871–79).[3] Competing with each other to locate mineral resources, optimal transportation routes, areas for settlement, and indigenous peoples who might aid or interfere with their plans, they crisscrossed the West. King moved east from California across northern Nevada, Utah, Colorado, and southern Wyoming — across the 40th parallel country. After surveying Nebraska and parts of Idaho and Wyoming (most notably Yellowstone), Hayden concentrated during 1873–76 on the mountainous regions of Colorado. Powell worked principally in Utah, including territory he had first traversed as a private citizen in 1869, by descending the Green and Colorado Rivers from northern Utah through the Grand Canyon of Arizona to the California border. Meanwhile, Wheeler out-distanced them all by covering most of the land from central California east to Texas, and from the Mexican border north to Idaho and Wyoming (72,250 square miles in 1873 alone).

As the only career army man among the survey directors, Lieutenant Wheeler concentrated on preparing topographical maps that could be used for military purposes. Clarence King's reconnaissance, although reputed for its innovative and controversial geological theories, insisted on practical results, especially in economic geology, and provided a model of organizational and scientific standards for the three other surveys.[4] Powell also made scientific studies of indigenous peoples, an interest he would later pursue as the first director of the Bureau of Ethnology.

In each of these expeditions, photography, particularly in its published forms, played a crucial part. It was the medium of choice to document geology and topography and to convey the land's richness and natural beauty. Some of the most respected photographers of the Civil War, such as Timothy O'Sullivan, were enlisted. Others who later rose to acclaim were introduced to the craft while working on a survey (John Hillers, for example, had joined Powell's group as an oarsman, but soon mastered photographic technique and became Powell's primary photographer). The survey leaders had no question about the importance of photography: Lieutenant Wheeler regularly halted his breakneck pace so that O'Sullivan could wait hours for a favorable light, or would shorten a day's march in order to camp where the photographer wished to make an exposure the next morning.

These survey photographs and their public presentation were the expeditions' lifeline to the East. During the winter hiatus, Hayden, Powell, and Wheeler would generally return to Washington, where they would lobby Congress for appropriations to finance the next year's work. Individual prints and gifts of photographic albums proved to be effective tools with which to unlock federal coffers. Many of these images and texts were further disseminated through collections of stereographs and individual photographic prints, marketed to the broad audiences curious about the American West.

Whether for science or scenery, the vast majority of the photographic records assembled within the scientific reports of the 1870s and into the early 1880s are devoted to representations of eroded canyons, mesas, and strata of the Grand Canyon and other monumental geological phenomena. These records presented the West as a "geological clock," one that measured time and space on a scale that reduced humanity to an unexpectedly small role, as in Clarence Dutton's description of the Grand Canyon in *Tertiary History of the Grand Cañon District* (1882). These accounts not only recorded potential riches but vividly instructed readers that the West was an amazingly different geographical region.

MAY CASTLEBERRY

1. Two such exceptional draftsmen, the artist Thomas Moran and the geologist and topographer William Henry Holmes, worked alongside photographers during the surveys of the 1870s. Often informed by photographic records of the same sites, their drawings for publications such as *Tertiary History of the Grand Cañon District* (1882) present graphic information that photographs did not and could not.

2. Mary C. Rabbitt, *Minerals, Lands, and Geology for the Common Defence and General Welfare, Volume 1, Before 1879; US Geological Survey: A History of Public Lands, Federal Science and Mapping Policy, and Development of Mineral Resources in the United States* (Washington, D.C.: United States Government Printing Office, 1979), pp. 179–80.

3. Elisabeth Hodermarsky, assistant curator of Prints at the Yale University Art Gallery, kindly provided her notes for a Yale University Art Gallery exhibition on the "Great Surveys."

4. Clifford M. Nelson and Mary C. Rabbitt, "The Role of Clarence King in the Advancement of Geology in the Public Service, 1867–1881," in Alan E. Leviton, Peter U. Rodda, Ellis L. Yochelson, and Michele L. Aldrich, eds., *Frontiers of Geological Exploration of Western North America* (San Francisco: Pacific Division American Association for the Advancement of Science, 1982), p. 19.

Curtis Burr Graham after John Mix Stanley
Group of Plants Exhibiting the Vegetation on the Gila
Lithograph from Emory, *Notes of a Military Reconnoissance* [sic] . . . , 1848
DeGolyer Library, Southern Methodist University, Dallas

PRINTS VS. PHOTOGRAPHS, 1840–1860

RON TYLER

As Lieutenant John Charles Frémont arose from his camp in the Wind River Mountains on the morning of August 10, 1842, he paused to admire the "lofty snow peak. . .glittering in the first rays of the sun" opposite his campsite. "The scenery becomes hourly more interesting and grand, and the view here is truly magnificent," he wrote in his journal. "The sun has just shot above the wall, and makes a magical change. The whole valley is glowing and bright, and all the mountain peaks are gleaming like silver. Though these snow mountains are not the Alps, they have their own character of grandeur and magnificence, and will doubtless find pens and pencils to do them justice."[1] Frémont, the first Western explorer to take a daguerreotype camera with him, tried on that morning to do some measure of justice to the peaks, setting up his apparatus to photograph this stunning view.

The artist and inventor Samuel F.B. Morse had introduced the daguerreotype process to America in April 1839, at precisely the right moment to influence the exploration of the American West.[2] The United States incorporated into its borders a vast domain during the 1840s — Texas in 1845, the Oregon Territory in 1846, and California and the desert Southwest in 1848, a result of the war against Mexico. This expansion threatened the "integrity of the Union" according to Colonel John J. Abert, commander of the Topographical Engineers, who felt the solution was a transcontinental railroad from the Mississippi to the Pacific.[3] The necessity of such a road became even more apparent in 1849, when the discovery of gold in California brought more than 100,000 immigrants to the sparsely settled mission and rancho country.

The government responded with extraordinary reconnaissances to explore the West and integrate it into the Union, disseminating the findings through the proven methods of the illustrated book and the factual travel account that had gained widespread acceptance during the eighteenth century.[4] These books constituted one of the most popular genres in bookmaking during what one historian has called the Second Great Age of Discovery, and explorers from Russia, Great Britain, France, and Germany produced colorful tomes documenting their circumnavigations and other explorations, including pictures of the flora and fauna, geology, and people and their habitations.[5] The American expeditions began with Lewis and Clark's trip to the

Pacific Northwest in 1803–06, Zebulon M. Pike's tour of the Southwest in 1807, and Major Stephen H. Long's expeditions to the Great Plains in 1820–21. Government exploration peaked during the two decades before the Civil War, with at least eighteen expeditions sending engineers, scientists, and artists into virtually every corner of the West,[6] but, of the earliest expeditions, only Long had artists with him — Samuel Seymour and Titian Ramsay Peale — as an integral part of the scientific team. His report, *Account of an Expedition from Pittsburgh to the Rocky Mountains. . .*, edited by Edwin James and published in both Philadelphia and London in 1823, was the first American contribution to the genre.[7]

The paintings and drawings of the expeditionary artists had served a need, but the British polymath William Henry Fox Talbot was widely perceived to have answered the demand of the newly emerging scientific community for precise, accurate, and objective images of nature when he published his "photogenic drawings" in *The Pencil of Nature*. Images could now be photographed through a microscope, telescope, or directly from nature. Seth Eastman used a daguerreotype camera in his Indian research, and Frederick Catherwood took one to the jungles of the Yucatán to aid in his study of the Mayan ruins.

In attempting to photograph the Rockies, then, Frémont was hoping to add the daguerreotype to the grand tradition of illustrated exploration books. He might well have been influenced by the success that photographer Edward Anthony had enjoyed on Professor James Renwick's Northeast Boundary survey in 1840–42. Had Frémont been equally as successful on that cold August day in 1842, Seymour and Peale might well have been among the last of the expeditionary artists.[8] But he failed — so completely that he did not even mention his attempts in the official record. His efforts are known only through the expedition's financial records (which document payments for the equipment) and the secret journal of his assistant, Charles Preuss, a troubled, German-born and -trained cartographer.[9] Frémont had first tried to photograph Independence Rock on August 2. "He spoiled five plates that way," Preuss complained. "Not a thing was to be seen on them. That's the way it often is with these Americans. They know everything, they can do everything, and when they are put to a test, they fail miserably. . . ." Frémont tried again on August 5 with similar results, and again, apparently his last effort, on

Charles Koppel
Water Line and Shores of the Ancient Lake (Colorado Desert)
Toned lithograph from *Reports of Explorations and Surveys . . . 1857*, 1857
Amon Carter Museum, Fort Worth, Texas

Curtis Burr Graham after John Mix Stanley
San Diego
Lithograph from Emory, *Notes of a Military Reconnoissance* [sic] . . . , 1848
DeGolyer Library, Southern Methodist University, Dallas

August 10. By then even Preuss was sympathetic: "The same as before, nothing was produced," he wrote. "This time it was really too bad, because the view was magnificent."[10]

Lithographer Edward Weber of Baltimore copied Preuss' small sketches for Frémont's *Report on an Exploration of the Country Lying Between the Missouri River and the Rocky Mountains, on the Line of the Kansas and Great Platte Rivers* (Washington, D.C., 1843), the second US contribution to the "literature and art of fact."[11] Even in these modest prints, the artist's advantage over the camera is apparent: in *Central Chain of the Wind River Mountains*, for example, Preuss included a panorama that suggests the majesty and range of the peaks, something that the daguerreotype could not do. Even if Frémont had been able to conquer the technical difficulties inherent in the process, the narrowness of the aperture would have forced him to put several plates together to form a panorama as comprehensive as the one that Preuss sketched.[12]

Failure dampened Frémont's enthusiasm for photography, and he did not take the apparatus with him on his next three expeditions. Like the other explorers, he continued to rely on the topographic artist and the cartographer to provide the visual dimensions for his reports. Preuss remained with him on his second expedition, and the young Philadelphia artist Edward Kern enlisted on the third. Richard Kern joined his brother for Frémont's fourth expedition in 1848, which ended in disaster when they were lost in the mountains during the winter.[13] Henceforth, most of the expeditions into the newly acquired Southwest included artists as a part of the scientific corps: artist and daguerreotypist John Mix Stanley provided paintings for Lieutenant William H. Emory's *Notes of a Military Reconnoissance* [sic], *from Fort Leavenworth, in Missouri, to San Diego, in California, Including Part of the Arkansas, Del Norte, and Gila Rivers* (Washington, D.C., 1848), which chronicled Colonel Stephen W. Kearny's march across the Southwest from Santa Fe to San Diego, bringing the first images of the ancient civilizations of the region to the American public.[14] The Kern brothers provided illustrations for Lieutenant James H. Simpson and Lieutenant Lorenzo Sitgreaves' expeditions in 1849 and 1851, and Franklin R. Grist and John Hudson accompanied Captain Howard Stansbury on his expedition to the Great Salt Lake in 1849.[15]

Topographic artists rather than photographers illustrated the two most important publications of the 1850s: the multivolume reports accompanying the United States-Mexican Boundary Survey and the Pacific Railroad Surveys. Stanley and ten other artists — Heinrich Bauldin Möllhausen, Friedrich W. von Egloffstein, Gustavus Sohon, Richard H. Kern, John C. Tidball, Albert H. Campbell, James G. Cooper, John Young, William P. Blake, and

Charles Koppel — produced the approximately 725 illustrations accompanying the dozen quarto volumes of the *Reports of Explorations and Surveys, to Ascertain the Most Practicable and Economical Route for a Railroad from the Mississippi River to the Pacific Ocean*; only one of these illustrations is acknowledged to have been copied from a daguerreotype.[16] Stanley is known to have made daguerreotypes on Isaac I. Stevens' 1853–54 survey between the 47th and 49th parallels, but it is unclear whether he used them for any of the approximately sixty lithographs he supplied to accompany Stevens' report.[17]

John Russell Bartlett, the third commissioner of the United States-Mexican Boundary Survey, declined to take a daguerreotype camera with him, despite the fact that he had been impressed with the photographs that Catherwood had made of the Mayan ruins in 1842. Lieutenant William H. Emory, Bartlett's successor, also worked without a camera, leaving artists Arthur C.V. Schott, John E. Weyss, and Augustus de Vaudricourt to produce the approximately 379 illustrations of the border and its people for his two-volume *Report on the United States and Mexican Boundary Survey* (Washington, D.C., 1857–59). Bartlett himself provided most of the illustrations for his privately published, two-volume *Personal Narrative of Explorations and Incidents in Texas, New Mexico, California, and Chihuahua. . .* (New York, 1854).[18]

Many of these images are similar to what a photographer might have produced. Möllhausen's portraits and genre scenes of the Southwest Indians, made on Lieutenant Amiel W. Whipple's 35th parallel expedition, for example, are straight-on views that could have come from a photograph, and Charles Koppel's *Colorado Desert and Signal Mountain*, from Lieutenant R.S. Williamson's survey across Southern California, seems to exhibit characteristics of a photograph: the field of vision is fairly narrow and the objects in the foreground are larger and diminish in proportion as they vanish toward the horizon. *The Plaza and Church of El Paso* even suggests a photographic perspective, with the cropped structure at the left, the group of people and building that disappear into the right margin, and the foreground rising up to meet the viewer.[19]

But most of the landscape views in illustrated books of this period contain a much wider panorama than the camera lens could then encompass. Seth Eastman, an artist who taught topographic art at West Point, explained in his textbook that the artist should provide his commander with accurate information on "what obstacles will be presented to his ascent, and to what extent the ground will admit of manoeuvres."[20] Lieutenant Edward G. Beckwith, who conducted the exploration of the central route for the Pacific Railroad Surveys, qualified Eastman's principles a bit:

Friedrich W. von Egloffstein after a sketch by Joseph Christmas Ives
Black Cañon
Engraving from Ives, *Report Upon the Colorado River of the West*, 1861
DeGolyer Library, Southern Methodist University, Dallas

Curtis Burr Graham after John Mix Stanley
The Ruins of the Casa Grande (The Founders of Which Are Unknown)
Lithograph from Emory, *Notes of a Military Reconnoissance* [*sic*] . . . , 1848
DeGolyer Library, Southern Methodist University, Dallas

The landscape views are presented with no purpose of presenting the beauties of the scenery of the country, but to illustrate its general character, and to exhibit on a small scale the character of its mountains and cañones, and of its plains and valleys, in their respective positions and extents, as seen in nature. . . .They are taken, as will be seen at once, from elevated positions, and consequently partake somewhat of a panoramic character, and being of great extent, the ordinary inequalities of the surfaces of plains and slopes are not perceptible.[21]

Needless to say, this was difficult to accomplish with a daguerreotype and might well explain why photography was not used more frequently in expeditionary publications before the Civil War. In addition, most of the artists, overcome with the exoticism and vastness of the new country and its people, fell back on the vocabulary of Romanticism, mixing elements of the picturesque with the images they knew their East Coast audiences would appreciate.[22]

Meanwhile, daguerreotypists experienced their first real success in the Trans-Mississippi West, but the results of their work were not published until decades later. As a sub-assistant in the scientific corps for the Creek Boundary Expedition of 1850, William C. Mayhew made a number of daguerreotypes. At least two handsome examples survive. They may well be the earliest extant photographs of the Trans-Mississippi American West, but none of them found their way into contemporaneous publications or were even known to exist until the 1970s.[23]

Three years later, in 1853, Frémont succeeded in his efforts to document the American West through photography. Inspired by the great German naturalist Alexander von Humboldt, who had urged in his recently published *Cosmos* that photography be employed in scientific exploration, Frémont resolved to try again on his final expedition. There had been several technical improvements in photographic processes since his first attempt. He held a competition between thirty-eight-year-old Solomon N. Carvalho, an established painter and daguerreotypist, and a "photographist" named Bomar, who used the waxed-paper negative process. Frémont chose Carvalho for the expedition because he succeeded in making a plate before Bomar could develop his negative. Despite the enormous hardships of another winter passage through the mountains, including having to leave his daguerreotype equipment buried in the snow, Carvalho came away with a number of plates, among them the *Cheyennes on Big Timber River* and a panorama from the summit of one of the mountains near the Grand River, made while he stood in waist-deep snow.[24]

Upon his return to New York, Frémont employed photographer Mathew Brady to copy the images by the collodion (wetplate) process so he could give prints to the artists hired to produce the engravings for his book. But he got involved in presidential politics instead and never published the report of this trip. He probably still had some of the prints thirty years later: they appear to have been used by the engravers of the illustrations in his *Memoirs of My Life* (Chicago, 1887). But both the original daguerreotypes and the Brady negatives seem to have been destroyed in a warehouse fire in 1881.[25] If Frémont had been as successful in 1842 as Carvalho was in 1853, photography might have caught on more quickly, and the visual history of the West might well have been different.

Despite this lackluster record, the documentary promise of the photograph continued to attract expedition commanders. In 1857–58, Lieutenant Joseph Christmas Ives carried "a little photographic apparatus" along on his exploration of the Colorado River as far as the Grand Canyon. But he was not upset when his darkroom tent and equipment blew away in a gale, noting "that [it] was of comparatively little importance." Only one of the seventy-six illustrations in his *Report upon the Colorado River of the West* — *Robinson's Landing, Mouth of Colorado River* — was copied after a photograph he had made. Möllhausen and Friedrich W. von Egloffstein provided the remaining images, including impressive painted and drawn views of *Black Cañon* and *Mojave Canyon*.[26]

Photographers accompanying Lieutenant James H. Simpson into the Great Basin of Utah and Captain William F. Raynolds up the Missouri and Yellowstone Rivers in 1859–60 had similar unsuccessful experiences with photography. Using the wet-plate process, J.D. Hutton, a topographer and assistant artist under Raynolds, set out on July 13, 1860 to make a photograph of the Great Falls of the Missouri River, but returned to camp that evening only "having indifferently accomplished" his purpose.[27] C.C. Mills, the photographer on Simpson's 1859 expedition, apparently had even less success, and Simpson considered the effort a complete failure:

I am informed that in several of the Government expeditions a photographic apparatus has been an accompaniment, and that in every instance, and even with operators of undoubted skill the enterprise has been attended with failure. The cause lies in some degree in the difficulty in the field, at short notice, of having preparations perfect enough to secure good pictures, but chiefly in the fact that the camera is not adapted to distant scenery. For objects very close at hand, which of course, correspondingly contracts the field of vision, and for single portraits of persons and small groups, it does very well; but as, on exploring expeditions, the chief desideratum is to daguerreotype extensive mountain chains and other notable objects having considerable extent, the camera has to be correspondingly distant to take in the whole field, and the consequence is a want of sharpness of outline and in many instances, on

Richard Kern
Ruins of an Old Pueblo in the Cañon of Chelly, 1849
From Simpson, *Journal of a Military Reconnaissance . . .* , 1852
Wash on paper, 9¼ x 5 (23.5 x 12.7)
The Ewell Sale Stewart Library, Academy of Natural Sciences of
Philadelphia

account of the focal distance not being the same for every object within the field of view, a blurred effect, as well as distortion of parts. In my judgment, the camera is not adapted to explorations in the field, and a good artist, who can sketch readily and accurately, is much to be preferred.[28]

Simpson's and Ives' criticisms sum up the expeditionary commander's concern about photography. The apparatus was a lot of trouble, requiring training and expertise — Carvalho estimated that it took him approximately two hours to make a plate, with most of the time being spent in setting up and stowing the equipment — and the results usually were not that good.

Consequently, expeditionary artists compiled, and lithographers and engravers reproduced, the extraordinary visual record of America's expansion into the arid West. Between 1843 and 1863, the government printing office alone authorized at least twenty-six separate, illustrated volumes, all, with the exception of Charles Wilkes' *Narrative of the United States Exploring Expedition. . . .*(1838–44), relating solely to the American West and containing more than 1,750 separate images. The books were issued in editions ranging from 100 copies to 53,000 copies, meaning that the government produced almost 24,500,000 prints of the West in a twenty-year period, an unprecedented financial and artistic investment in exploration and publication.[29]

1. John C. Frémont, *The Exploring Expedition to the Rocky Mountains*, intro. by Herman J. Viola and Ralph E. Ehrenberg (Washington, D.C.: Smithsonian Institution Press, 1988), p. 61.

2. Beaumont Newhall, *The Daguerreotype in America*, 3rd rev. ed. (New York: Dover Publications, 1976), p. 15; Richard Rudisill, *Mirror Image: The Influence of the Daguerreotype on American Society* (Albuquerque: University of New Mexico Press, 1971), p. 45.

3. Abert is quoted in William H. Goetzmann, *Army Exploration in the American West, 1803–1863* (Austin: Texas State Historical Association, 1991), pp. 209–10; see also pp. 355–89.

4. The circumnavigational exploits of Captain Cook, La Pérouse, and others had been chronicled in handsome publications and widely circulated. See William H. Goetzmann, *New Lands, New Men: America and the Second Great Age of Discovery* (New York: Viking Penguin, 1986), pp. 5–12; Barbara Maria Stafford, *Voyage into Substance: Art, Science, Nature, and the Illustrated Travel Account, 1760–1840* (Cambridge, Massachusetts: The MIT Press, 1984), pp. 1–29, 440; Bernard Smith, *European Vision and the South Pacific* (New Haven, Connecticut: Yale University Press, 1988); idem, *Imagining the Pacific: In the Wake of the Cook Voyages* (New Haven, Connecticut: Yale University Press, 1992). See also *Travel in Aquatint and Lithography, 1770–1860, from the Library of J.R. Abbey* (Folkestone and London: Dawsons of Pall Mall, 1972).

5. Spain also sent a number of exploring expeditions around the world, but, unlike the other nations, did not publish the findings. For example, see Warren L. Cook, *Flood Tide of Empire: Spain and the Pacific Northwest, 1543–1819* (New Haven, Connecticut: Yale University Press, 1973), pp. 4–5; and Iris H.W. Engstrand, *Spanish Scientists in the New World: The Eighteenth-Century Expeditions* (Seattle: University of Washington Press, 1981), p. 3.

6. Goetzmann, *New Lands, New Men*, pp. 5–12.

7. Goetzmann, *Exploration and Empire: The Explorer and the Scientist in the Winning of the American West* (Austin: Texas State Historical Association, 1993), pp. 1–64.

8. Rudisill, *Mirror Image*, pp. 77–101.

9. "Subvoucher, New York, 6 May 1842, U.S. to James R. Chilton," and "Abstract of Disbursements on Account of Military and Geographical Surveys West of the Mississippi. . .," in Donald Jackson and Mary Lee Spence, eds.,

The Expeditions of John Charles Frémont, Vol. 1: Travels from 1838 to 1844 (Urbana: University of Illinois Press, 1970), pp. 145, 379, 384; Andrew Rolle, *John Charles Frémont: Character as Destiny* (Norman: University of Oklahoma Press, 1991), p. 37, concludes that Frémont, recalling the several accounts of the Lewis and Clark expedition that were published before the official version, ordered his men not to keep journals so that his would be the only record of the trip, but points out that army policy also forbade the keeping of journals while in "enemy territory."

10. Frémont seems to indicate that the day was August 10, Preuss August 11; Jackson and Spence, *The Expeditions of John Charles Frémont*, p. 255; Charles Preuss, *Exploring with Frémont: The Private Diaries of Charles Preuss, Cartographer for John C. Frémont on His First, Second, and Fourth Expeditions to the Far West*, trans. and ed. by Erwin G. and Elisabeth K. Gudde (Norman: University of Oklahoma Press, 1958), pp. 32, 35, 38.

11. Frémont, *The Exploring Expedition*, p. 5; Ron Tyler, *Prints of the West* (Golden, Colorado: Fulcrum Publishers, 1994), pp. 73–74; Stafford, *Voyage into Substance*, p. xx.

12. Early daguerreotypists made panoramas by framing multiplate daguerreotypes side by side. See Newhall, *The Daguerreotype in America*, p. 50, for the story of the Langenheims' five-plate panorama of Niagara Falls.

13. The young Edward Kern had hoped to acquire daguerreotype experience on the trip; Robert V. Hine, *In the Shadow of Frémont: Edward Kern and the Art of Exploration, 1845–1860*, 2nd ed. (Norman: University of Oklahoma Press, 1982), p. 16. Jackson and Spence, *The Explorations of John Charles Frémont*, p. xxxiii, say that Frémont took a daguerreotype camera with him on his second expedition, but the only suggestion of this, a document related to the purchase of a daguerreotype camera, is later explained (pp. 379, 384) as being for the first expedition.

14. Although he used no photographic equipment on the Emory expedition, Stanley apparently learned the daguerreotype process soon after it was available in this country. He is recorded in the Maine *Democrat* in October 1841 as having gone to Fort Gibson, Arkansas, to photograph Indians; see Peter E. Palmquist, "Robert H. Vance: The Maine and Boston Years (1825–c. 1850)," *The Daguerreian Annual 1991* (Lake Charles, Louisiana: The Daguerreian Society, 1991), p. 210. See also Robert Taft, *Photography and the American Scene* (New York: Dover Publications, 1964), p. 289; idem, *Artists and Illustrators of the Old West, 1850–1900* (New York: Charles Scribner's Sons, 1953), pp. 269–73.

15. Taft, *Photography and the American Scene*, pp. 223–24, 484–85; Julia Ann Schimmel, "John Mix Stanley and Imagery of the West in Nineteenth-Century American Art," Ph.D. diss. (New York: New York University, 1983), pp. 60–70; David J. Weber, *Richard H. Kern, Expeditionary Artist in the Far Southwest, 1848–1853* (Albuquerque: University of New Mexico Press, 1985); Hine, *In the Shadow of Frémont*; Brigham D. Madsen, ed., *Exploring the Great Salt Lake: The Stansbury Expedition of 1849–1850* (Salt Lake City: University of Utah Press, 1989).

16. The engraving, *Placer Mining by the Hydraulic Method, Michigan City* [California], is in W.P. Blake's report on the geology of the Great Basin in the twelve-volume *Reports of Explorations and Surveys, to Ascertain the Most Practicable and Economical Route for a Railroad from the Mississippi River to the Pacific Ocean* (Washington, D.C., 1855–61), V. Many of the 725 illustrations are natural history drawings of flora, fauna, and geological formations.

17. Stanley wrote to his fiancée, Alice Caroline English, from St. Louis on May 16, 1853, that he planned to "make many captives — on paper and plate"; quoted in Schimmel, "John Mix Stanley," p. 104. See also Stevens, *Reports of Explorations and Surveys*, XII: pp. 87, 103–04. There is some question as to how many pictures Stanley supplied, because the credits in different editions of Stevens' *Report* vary; see Taft, *Artists and Illustrators*, p. 275, n. 56.

18. Robert V. Hine, *Bartlett's West: Drawing the Mexican Boundary* (New Haven, Connecticut: Yale University Press, 1968), pp. 14–15, 90; Victor Wolfgang von Hagen, *Maya Explorer: John Lloyd Stephens and the Lost Cities of Central America and Yucatán* (Norman: University of Oklahoma Press, 1948), pp. 205–06, 208–09.

19. This picture is credited to Augustus de Vaudricourt in Emory's *Report*, but it may well be by John Russell Bartlett, since there is a sepia wash in the Bartlett Papers at John Carter Brown Library, Providence, Rhode Island, that is quite similar to this chromolithograph; see Hine, *Bartlett's West*, pl. 5. For a discussion of the relationship between paintings and early photographs, see Peter Galassi, *Before Photography: Painting and the Invention of Photography*, exh. cat. (New York: The Museum of Modern Art, 1981), pp. 13–29.

20. Seth Eastman, *Treatise on Topographical Drawing* (New York: Wiley & Putnam, 1837), p. 22.

21. John W. Gunnison and Edward G. Beckwith, "Report," in *Reports of Explorations and Surveys*, II, p. 126. See Albert Boime, *The Magisterial Gaze: Manifest Destiny and American Landscape Painting c. 1830–1865* (Washington, D. C.: Smithsonian Institution Press, 1991), for an interpretation of this characteristic in landscape painting. At the same time Beckwith was contending that the views did not intend to present the "beauties of the scenery," Attorney George Gibbs was advising Henry Rowe Schoolcraft that Congress would appropriate "any amount of public money" for an expensive "picture book";

quoted in Brian W. Dippie, *Catlin and His Contemporaries: The Politics of Patronage* (Lincoln: University of Nebraska Press, 1990), p. 176.

22. Tyler, *Prints of the West*, pp. 6–9.

23. One is a portrait of the expedition naturalist, Dr. Samuel W. Woodhouse of Philadelphia, and the other shows the survey party in camp in central Oklahoma, about three miles west of the present-day town of Quay. The unpublished manuscript for the Creek Boundary Expedition is in the Philadelphia Academy of Natural Science. See John S. Tomer and Michael J. Brodhead, eds., *A Naturalist in Indian Territory: The Journals of S.W. Woodhouse, 1849–50* (Norman: University of Oklahoma Press, 1992), pp. 206–08; Weston J. Naef and James N. Wood first published the Mayhew daguerreotypes in *Era of Exploration: The Rise of Landscape Photography in the American West, 1860–1885*, exh. cat. (Buffalo: Albright-Knox Art Gallery; New York: The Metropolitan Museum of Art, 1975), p. 30.

24. Rolle, *John Charles Frémont*, pp. 150–160; Solomon Nunes Carvalho, *Incidents of Travel and Adventure in the Far West*, ed. by Bertram Wallace Korn (Philadelphia: The Jewish Publication Society of America, 1954), pp. 83–84, 128, 145, 188.

25. A badly damaged daguerreotype of what might be the Cheyenne village on the Big Timber in the Brady collection at the Library of Congress may be the only surviving image of the 1853 expedition; Rudisill, *Mirror Image*, pp. 105–06.

26. Joseph Christmas Ives, *Report upon the Colorado River of the West* (Washington, D.C., 1861), p. 34. See also Taft, *Photography and the American Scene*, p. 266. The photograph from which *Robinson's Landing. . .* was made has not been traced.

27. Taft, *Photography and the American Scene*, pp. 266–67; Naef and Wood, *Era of Exploration*, pp. 29, 77. A small photograph of Great Falls, attributed to Hutton, is in the Western Americana Collection at the Beinecke Rare Book and Manuscript Library, Yale University.

28. J.H. Simpson, *Report of Explorations in Great Basin of Territory of Utah in 1859* (Washington, D.C., 1876), p. 8, quoted in Taft, *Photography and the American Scene*, pp. 266–67. The Civil War delayed the publication of Simpson's report. As a result, his critical comments about photography were not published until 1876 — by which time the stunning landscape photographs of Andrew J. Russell, William Henry Jackson, Timothy O'Sullivan, William Bell, and others, published in official government surveys, had rendered his remarks obsolete.

29. Tyler, *Prints of the West*, p. 105. Goetzmann, *New Lands, New Men*, p. 178, estimates that the federal government published sixty volumes relating to the West; the cost of publication would have represented one-quarter to one-third of the entire federal budget during any given year in this period.

A.J. Russell
Embankment, East of Granite Canyon
(Granite Canyon, from the Water Tank), 1868
Albumen print from Russell, *The Great West Illustrated . . .* , 1869
Union Pacific Museum, Omaha

PHOTOGRAPHY, RAILROADS, AND NATURAL RESOURCES IN THE ARID WEST: PHOTOGRAPHS BY ALEXANDER GARDNER AND A.J. RUSSELL

SUSAN DANLY

Just after the Civil War, two competing railroad companies commissioned veteran photographers Alexander Gardner and A.J. Russell to record the landscape along two proposed rail routes west of the Mississippi River.[1] The Kansas Pacific and the Union Pacific knew that as the United States Congress and potential private investors contemplated the photographs of these two routes, the topographical advantages and disadvantages of each would be revealed. Gardner's album, *Across the Continent on the Kansas Pacific Railroad (Route of the 35th Parallel)*, promoted a route that would begin on the prairies in Kansas, head due west to Colorado, and then dip southward to skirt the Rocky Mountains.[2] As the route then turned westward again, it would pass through the extremely arid territories of northern New Mexico, Arizona, and Southern California. Then, moving northward through the central valley of California, the railroad would eventually meet the Pacific coast at San Francisco. Russell's album, *The Great West Illustrated in a Series of Photographic Views Across the Continent; Taken Along the Line of the Union Pacific Railroad*, documented a more northerly route. The Union Pacific had already established an eastern railhead in Omaha and had begun construction on a route that ran across the high plains of Wyoming and cut through the western mountain ranges of Utah. This would become the route of the first transcontinental railroad, when in May 1869, just outside Salt Lake City, the Union Pacific joined the Central Pacific Railroad, which had built its way eastward from San Francisco.

An analysis of the photographs in the albums produced by Gardner and Russell provides a means of better understanding the railroads' political agenda and the public's romantic perception of the Western landscape. The layouts of the individual albums convey very different narrative meanings through the visual sequence of images and texts — both written and implied. The means by which Gardner's and Russell's photographs were distributed to the public also suggests how they can be "read" —

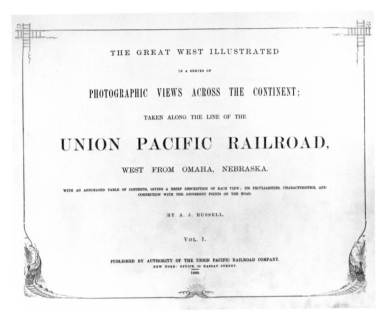

Title page from Russell, *The Great West Illustrated . . .* , 1869
Union Pacific Museum, Omaha

A.J. Russell
Sphynx of the Valley, 1869
Albumen print from Russell, *The Great West Illustrated* . . . , 1869
Union Pacific Museum, Omaha

both in terms of the specific pictorial modes chosen by each photographer and the type of topography they were commissioned to record. Although we have no record that the two men knew of one another's work, their photographs were produced for a similarly diverse audience of Washington politicians, railroad investors, and the general public. In addition to large-format photographic prints issued in expensive albums, their photographs appeared in government-sponsored scientific reports and as cheap stereoscopic cards. These photographs thus served several functions: to encourage federal and private investment, to document the Western topography, to promote economic development in the Western territories, and to entertain and educate the public.

One of the most critical and dramatically illustrated issues raised by the albums had to do with water. Without a reliable source of water, the steam-powered railroad engines could not run and the land could not be cultivated. Thus, white settlement in the West hinged on the availability of water. This essay, therefore, will concentrate on the photographs as they relate to the presence and absence of water in the Western landscape. While Gardner's images purposely play down the presence of water, Russell's photographs and his accompanying text emphasize its abundance.

Made in 1867, long before railroad construction on the southerly route began, Gardner's album draws attention to the flatness of the Western landscape and thus implies the relative ease of laying track.[3] The presence of water and its geologic action on the terrain presented potential problems for railroad builders. It is the absence of such obstacles that Gardner sought to capture in his album. There are no uncrossable rivers among his photographs, no insurmountable peaks, no wild Indians. He emphasizes instead the panoramic view, the emptiness and openness of the prairie and the desert. Gardner seems to have eschewed the comfortable vantage point, instead opting for one that captured the limitless horizontal expansiveness of space in the American West. His desert images, especially, are "anti-picturesque" in their avoidance of familiar pictorial devices, such as laterally positioned trees to suggest perspectival recession, or human figures to suggest relative scale. He uses the arid and barren landscape of the Southwestern territories as a metaphor for endless economic expansiveness.

On the other hand, Russell's scenes, photographed in 1868 and 1869, while the northern route of the Union Pacific was under construction, served a very different purpose.[4] They concentrated on newly built trestles, the transport of materials, and, most important, on the wealth of natural resources made available by the railroad. They draw attention both to the heroic engineering efforts of man and the picturesque nature of the landscape. By deliberately using the picturesque mode in making his photographs, Russell relied on a traditional form of landscape imagery to put his viewers at ease in the unfamiliar landscape of the West. His photographs suggest a land that is easily settled and soon filled with fences, fields, and even towns.

Gardner's album of 127 photographic plates begins in St. Louis and ends in San Francisco. The first third of the album consists of scenes taken on the prairies of Kansas; the second third includes views of the foothills of the Colorado Rockies and the mountain passes into northern New Mexico; and the last third depicts panoramas of the desert landscape of Arizona and the gentle, rolling hills of Southern California. Taken as a whole, the album builds its visual narrative from reassuring views of the new towns popping up on the plains of Kansas, to the more remote and barren desert mesas, and culminates with images of green California hills filled with groves of live oak. The dramatic contrast between the fertile and the arid West is strongest in the landscape photographs in the latter part of the album. Viewing the photographs in the narrative sequence that follows Gardner's travels in both space and time, the viewer experiences a sense of relief crossing from the dry, almost featureless desert into the promised land of California, with its hillsides covered in flowers even in February. William J. Palmer's official report on the railroad survey, published in 1869, provided a narrative text that further underscored Gardner's visual narrative:

Here, also we leave behind all our old friends of the desert and the plains, the artemisia, the Spanish bayonet, and the cactus, and are ushered through groves of live oak into fertile fields of wheat and barley, well watered meadows, vineyards, and orange orchards.[5]

Unlike the pictures in Gardner's album, which follow sequentially from east to west, William Palmer's 1869 *Report of the Surveys*, with Gardner's photographs, is organized according to the natural resources and topography as they relate directly to the economic needs of the railroad. For example, the Gardner photograph of a characteristic desert plant is accompanied by an assessment of its potential commercial value:

Dr. Parry supposes that the Yucca, or Spanish bayonet, with which this desert is abundantly covered, and which is also found abundantly in New Mexico and Arizona, will come into value for the manufacture of ropes, mattresses, etc., for which I believe it is already considerably used in California.[6]

Gardner's photographs of the native population are presented amidst a discussion of the strong military presence in the West and serve to allay the railroad investor's fears about the pos-

A.J. Russell
The Windmill at Laramie, 1868
Albumen print from Russell, *The Great West Illustrated . . . ,* 1869
Union Pacific Museum, Omaha

Alexander Gardner
Ancient Pueblo Town of Zuni, Western New Mexico, 1868
Albumen print from
Across the Continent on the Kansas Pacific Railroad . . ., 1869
Boston Public Library, Print Department

Alexander Gardner
Partridge Creek, Western Base of Mogoyon Range, Arizona; Mescal Plant in
Foreground, 1,280 Miles from Missouri River, 1867
Albumen print from
Across the Continent on the Kansas Pacific Railroad . . ., 1869
Missouri Historical Society, St. Louis

sible dangers of the region. The Zuni appear flanked by soldiers, and their ancient pueblos are given historical reference in the caption, which quotes a description of the site written by the sixteenth-century Spanish explorer Coronado:

In this town there may be some 200 houses, all compassed with walls, and I think that, with the rest of the houses, which are not so walled, there may be 500. They are very excellent, good houses, of three or four or five lofts high, wherein are good lodgings and fair chambers with ladders instead of stairs. The people of this town seem to me of reasonable stature and witty. In this place is found some quantity of gold and silver, very good; also turquoise. That which these Indians worship is the water, for they say it causeth their corn to grow.[7]

Because this is the only caption of any length in Gardner's album that refers to the presence of water, it deserves special scrutiny. Coronado, who was searching for gold in the Southwest in 1540, concludes that it is water, not gold, that the Zuni nation treasures most. By further emphasizing the high degree of civilization in terms of urban architecture, reliance on agriculture, and personable demeanor, Coronado's text also underscores the reasonableness of the Zuni religious beliefs.

In sharp contrast to Gardner, Russell provides many more detailed captions that point directly to the natural resources of the West. The fifty photographic images in *The Great West Illustrated* are introduced by a preface that explicitly states the economic intentions of his patron, the Union Pacific Railroad:

It is therefore believed that the information contained in this Volume. . . is calculated to interest all classes of people, and to excite the admiration of all reflecting minds as to the colossal grandeur of the Agricultural, Mineral, and Commercial resources of the West are brought into view.

The annotated table of contents that follows is filled with factual information about each plate — the height of the railroad trestles, the number of miles from the railhead, the closest source of water. But even one of the most desolate of views in the album, *Embankment, East of Granite Canyon*, is accompanied by a narrative that suggests the promise of a picturesque valley just out of sight: "The road-bed in this view is filled in fifty feet, and is one thousand feet in length. The station is situated five hundred forty miles west of Omaha, at the head of a beautiful valley fifteen miles in width, which extends north and east fifty miles." The description of the windmill at Laramie reads: "These mills used for raising water, are self regulating, ingenious in construction, and durable, having never failed to supply the demands of the railroad." Taken together, these seemingly bare-boned facts suggest a landscape rich in the resources needed for railroad construction, such as coal and timber, and a continuous supply of water.

Both Gardner and Russell also introduce another significant feature to the cultural geography in their photographic depictions of the arid West. They make visual comparisons between the man-made and natural monuments of the West and those of ancient Egypt. The mysterious sphinx has its equal in a natural rock formation in Utah, and the inscriptions on El Moro made by native tribes and the Conquistadors are seen as rivals to the hieroglyphs found on the pyramids. Such comparisons were readily exploited by travel writers of the period, who similarly fixed on such well-known historic sites to lure their readers westward. As one such author proclaimed:

What a wild land we live in! A few puffs of a locomotive had transformed us from civilization to solitude itself. This was the "great American desert". . . . A mysterious land with its wonderful record of savages and scouts, battles and hunts. We had a vague idea then that a sphinx and a score of pyramids were located somewhere on it.[8]

Such images were aimed at a popular audience as well as a scientific one. Ferdinand V. Hayden published thirty Russell photographs in his book *Sun Pictures of Rocky Mountain Scenery* (1870). Hayden, a prominent professor of mineralogy and geology at the University of Pennsylvania who was responsible for several of the important geological surveys of the 1870s, selected Russell's images because they afforded a great opportunity for the armchair tourist to study the natural history of the West:

I shall ask the reader to travel with me along the line of the Union Pacific Railroad, wandering aside here and there, to cull a flower or examine an Indian village or read some wonderful legend which attaches to most every portion of this country. We shall also delay now and then to study rock and unearth their fossil contents; and in many we may also take a look at some of nature's grand old ruins, which are infinitely more remarkable than those which have been hidden for centuries in the tangled and almost impenetrable forest of Central America.[9]

Among the "grand old ruins" most frequently depicted by photographers, artists, and writers of the nineteenth century were the castellated cliffs along the Green River in Wyoming. Although Russell's photograph of this site shows a barren landscape eroded by wind and water, his caption in *The Great West Illustrated* makes pointed reference to the railroad and growing town that lay just over the hill:

The standpoint for this view is nearly two thousand feet above the Railroad, which can be seen, winding through the bottom lands three miles away; farther off can be seen the dim outline of Green River City. The town is built of unburnt brick, and when this view was taken contained two thousand inhabitants.

Alexander Gardner
The Mojave Desert, in the Great Basin, California, Sierra Nevada in the Distance, 1,650 Miles from the Missouri River, 1867–68
Albumen print from
Across the Continent on the Kansas Pacific Railroad . . . , 1869
Boston Public Library, Print Department

Alexander Gardner
Two Races at Fort Mojave, Arizona, 1867–68
Albumen print from
Across the Continent on the Kansas Pacific Railroad . . . , 1869
Boston Public Library, Print Department

Alexander Gardner
Crossing of the Sierra Nevadas, California, Techapa Pass, California,
1,720 Miles West of the Missouri River, 1868
Albumen print from
Across the Continent on the Kansas Pacific Railroad . . . , 1869
Boston Public Library, Print Department

This site along Green River also evoked references to the historical past. In the pages of *Picturesque America,* one of the most widely read travel books of the period, the cliffs of the Green River are literally defined by the convergence of nature and the railroad: "All about one, lie long troughs, as of departed rivers; long level embankments, as of railroad tracks or endless fortifications."[10]

Another adaptation of Russell's photographs for a popular audience occurred when his stereoscopic views, taken for the Union Pacific, were converted to lantern slides. Stephen J. Sedgwick, a prominent lecturer in New York, used them to illustrate his series of popular lectures on the railroad, which he gave throughout New England, New York, and Pennsylvania between 1870 and 1879.[11] Sedgwick also sold Russell's photographs: the albums cost $75, the stereoscopic views cost $2 per dozen, and individual "parlor views" (14 x 17-inch mounted prints) cost $1.50 each. Commending the educational value of such images, the Brooklyn *Daily Times* noted:

The accuracy, boldness and delicacy of detail which characterize the pictures have elicited the enthusiastic approbation of twenty thousand people. We congratulate the audience which has had the pleasure of attending these lectures thus far. Certain we are that these magnificent pictures will long remain in their minds and will often be recalled with delight. The lessons inculcated with them must have an elevating and refining tendency.[12]

Gardner's photographs also reached a broad audience as stereoscopic cards, and as wood engravings used to illustrate William Bell's 1869 book, *New Tracks in North America: A Journal of Travel and Adventure.*[13] As the subtitle for Bell's book suggests, this publication was largely aimed at a popular audience. Such books fueled the imagination of armchair travelers on the East Coast and provided information whose truthfulness, the authors boasted, was attested to by the photographs. Ironically, the pictorial narrative in these same books also helped to establish a romantic ideal about the Western landscape. This was a landscape that, however arid, barren, and forbidding to Eastern eyes, could ultimately be settled and developed. The dwindling native populations would soon be under the control of the United States military. The land's natural resources were there for the white population to exploit and the natural wonders of its landscape were there for the tourist to admire.

Although Gardner's and Russell's photographs were initially aimed at a narrow audience of politicians and railroad investors, their eventual impact was widespread. Through lantern slide lectures, travel books, and the ubiquitous stereoviewer, their images of the Western landscape had the potential to reach a broad segment of the American middle class. The photographs laid out visual stories confirming the railroads' claims that they would one day traverse the vast expanses of the West, capitalize on its natural resources (ranging from abundant supplies of water and timber to desert plants), and establish a network of cities and farms that would provide economic opportunity for countless Americans. In the early days of Western expansion, the arid West was just one of many obstacles that could be overcome easily with ingenuity and railroad technology. Photography made the task seem simple and, even more important, inevitable.

1. Both Gardner and Russell had worked as photographers during the Civil War. For a more complete history of their work, see Susan Danly, "The Railroad Photographs of A.J. Russell and Alexander Gardner," Ph.D. diss. (Providence, Rhode Island: Brown University, 1983).

2. Gardner's photographic career as a whole and the Kansas Pacific railroad survey in particular are discussed in more detail in Brooks Johnson, *An Enduring Interest: The Photographs of Alexander Gardner*, exh. cat. (Norfolk, Virginia: The Chrysler Museum, 1991).

3. This southern route was not completed until construction of the Atchison, Topeka and Santa Fe Railroad in 1887.

4. For further discussion of Russell's work in connection with the construction of the transcontinental railroad, see Susan Danly, "Andrew Joseph Russell: 'The Great West Illustrated,'" in Susan Danly and Leo Marx, eds., *The Railroad in American Art: Representations of Technological Change* (Cambridge, Massachusetts: The MIT Press, 1988), pp. 93–112.

5. William J. Palmer, *Report of the Surveys Across the Continent in 1867–'68 on the 35th and 32nd Parallels, for a Route Extending the Kansas Pacific Railway to the Pacific Ocean at San Francisco and San Diego* (Philadelphia: W.B. Selheimer Printer, 1869), p. 132.

6. Ibid.

7. This text appears as the caption for plate 83 in the Gardner album; see the copy in the Boston Public Library.

8. W. E. Webb, *Buffalo Land* (Philadelphia: Hubbard Bros., 1872), p. 118.

9. Ferdinand V. Hayden, *Sun Pictures of Rocky Mountain Scenery* (New York: J. Bien, 1870), p. 18.

10. E. L. Burlingame, "The Plains and the Sierras," in William Cullen Bryant, ed., *Picturesque America* (New York: D. Appleton and Co., 1874), II, p. 174.

11. The most complete holdings of Sedgwick material and related Russell imagery are located at the Beinecke Rare Book and Manuscript Library at Yale University. See for example, Stephen J. Sedgwick, *Catalogue of Stereoscopic Views of Scenery in All Parts of the Rocky Mountains, Between Omaha and Sacramento* (New York: 1874). This publication reproduces some of Russell's photographs as wood-engravings and provides lists of those that were available for sale, although Sedgwick does not name Russell as the maker.

12. Ibid., n.p.

13. William A. Bell, *New Tracks in North America: A Journal of Travel and Adventure Whilst Engaged in the Survey for a Southern Railroad to the Pacific Ocean During 1867–8*, 2 vols. (London: Chapman and Hall, 1869). A participant in the Palmer survey, Bell chose six of Gardner's photographs to reproduce as wood-engravings in his book, noting that "with few exceptions, all are exact copies of photographs taken on the spot" (I, p. ix).

Timothy O'Sullivan
Pyramid and Tufa Domes, Pyramid Lake, Nevada, 1868
Reproduced in King, *Systematic Geology*, 1878
Albumen print, 7¹³⁄₁₆ x 10¹¹⁄₁₆ (19.8 x 27.1)
Yale Collection of Western Americana, Beinecke Rare Book and Manuscript Library,
Yale University, New Haven, Connecticut

DESOLATION, THY NAME IS THE GREAT BASIN: CLARENCE KING'S 40TH PARALLEL GEOLOGICAL EXPLORATIONS

WILLIAM H. GOETZMANN

Timothy O'Sullivan (1840–1882) was the earliest photographer of the real "Great American Desert." On two major post-Civil War surveys of the arid West, O'Sullivan, with his mule-powered ambulance and large wet-plate camera, photographed the vast empty wastes of the Great Basin, Death Valley, the lower Grand Canyon, the Wasatch Range, and the Uintas. He breathed the dust, drank the alkali water of desert pools, hobnobbed with miners in the underground landscapes of the Comstock Lode, and nearly died of starvation and exposure in America's grandest canyon. His photographs, much admired today for their surrealistic, abstract qualities, reflected his own direct experience of these desolate lands, not the vicarious propaganda of some promoter of the photographic picturesque.

O'Sullivan began his Western labors with Clarence King's United States Geological Explorations of the 40th Parallel in 1867.[1] King, a veteran of the earlier California Geological Survey, had scaled the Sierras and mapped and geologized what he called "the top of California." He became well known in both literary and scientific circles as a bon vivant, a splendid writer, a connoisseur of the arts, and a flamboyant adventurer. He also had a distinct talent for science, honed at the Sheffield Scientific School at Yale. So bright and so well connected was he that at the termination of the California Surveys, Secretary of War Edwin Stanton made him director of the 40th Parallel Surveys — a much coveted assignment.

Timothy O'Sullivan was King's photographer for the years 1867, 1868, and 1869 as the 40th Parallel parties struggled across the Basin and Range country, mapping and geologizing along a two-hundred-mile swath of territory that encompassed the designated transcontinental railroad route from Nevada's Sierras to the Front Range of the Rockies. Between 1871 and 1873, O'Sullivan served as the photographer on Lieutenant George M. Wheeler's United States Geographical Survey West of the 100th Meridian.[2] On both surveys, O'Sullivan had assistants back in Washington developing his striking wet-plate negatives. Clarence King and George Wheeler thus successfully introduced the camera as

Timothy O'Sullivan
Pyramid and Tufa Domes – Pyramid Lake – Nevada
Photolithograph from King, *Systematic Geology*, 1878
DeGolyer Library, Southern Methodist University, Dallas

Gilbert Munger
Eocene Bluffs, Green River, Wyoming
Chromolithograph from King, *Systematic Geology*, 1878
DeGolyer Library, Southern Methodist University, Dallas

Timothy O'Sullivan
Rhyolite Columns, Karnak, Montezuma Range, Nevada
Photolithograph from King, *Systematic Geology*, 1878
DeGolyer Library, Southern Methodist University, Dallas

a tool to record geological formations more accurately — and photographs became an important aspect of visual discourse in science. King's volumes featured photolithographs; Wheeler's volumes were illustrated by heliotypes.[3]

King's survey produced the most exciting scientific results. Between 1870 and 1878, King published *Final Reports or Monographs*, seven large volumes that represented a landmark in sophisticated scientific work, including one volume, *Mining Industry* (1870), written with James D. Hague, that described and illustrated the latest in mining techniques and machinery. He also authorized publication of Yale paleontologist Othniel Charles Marsh's *Odontornithes: A Monograph on the Extinct Toothed Birds of North America* (1880), which described and pictured the avians that coexisted with and evolved from dinosaurs of the Cretaceous period. O'Sullivan's work appeared in three of King's *Final Reports: Mining Industry* by James D. Hague and King (1870); *Descriptive Geology* (1877) by Arnold Hague and Samuel F. Emmons; and King's masterpiece, *Systematic Geology* (1878).[4]

Rather than provide a dispassionate description of the terrain, *Systematic Geology* was nothing less than a history of Western geology told in incredibly dramatic terms. King departed from British geologist Charles Lyell's uniformitarian gospel, according to which changes in the earth and its creatures were invariably gradual. In the vast American West, King had found innumerable evidences of sudden changes or huge catastrophes — not unlike the recent discovery of the collapse of a Pleistocene ice dam near Grand Coulee in the inland Northwest, a collapse that shaped entire geological contours of the inland Northwest.[5] Today this mixture of uniformitarianism and catastrophism described by King is designated by geologists as "punctuated equilibrium."[6]

King orchestrated an immense drama, in which mountains rose to "Himalayan" heights of 30,000 feet and then, due to relatively rapid erosion during the entire Paleozoic period, sank — mountain and lowland reversing in what King referred to as "a distinctly catastrophic process analogous to that of modern faults."[7] Huge inland seas resulted — the lofty Wasatch Mountains became an atoll in a billowing ocean that rose and fell, leaving shallow seas and marshy shores where the Rockies now stand, an environment that fostered dinosaurs during the long Carboniferous period and Mesozoic era. Late in the Mesozoic era came the Cretaceous period, in which the seas turned shallow and then the Great Plains abruptly domed, obliterating what King called a "mediterranean ocean" on the present Great Plains, as all the water drained off into the present Gulf of Mexico or toward the Pacific. At the end of the Cretaceous period, "a tremendous orographical disturbance" occurred.[8] The volcanic activity and fractures and huge lava beds of the Miocene and Pliocene epochs represented to King, in the jargon of his day, tremendous exhibitions of "telluric energy." After each major event, according to King, "not a species remained."[9]

King pondered the causes of these abrupt changes for the rest of his life. For a brief time he believed in a theory that energy was generated from the earth's core. Lord Kelvin's Laws of Thermodynamics, which posited that the cooling of the earth meant that loss of energy (entropy) is a constant, seemed to confirm his theories. Then, as Kelvin's theory about the rate of the cooling of the earth was gradually discredited, King's theory likewise faded. There is no doubt, however, that King's volumes were influential — even C.S. Peirce, America's foremost philosopher of science — was impressed by his theories. He considered them superior to those of Lyell.[10]

While he probed deeply into nature, King also presented his work in novel, even contrasting ways. He hired Timothy O'Sullivan to photograph and hence scientifically "objectify" many of the important geological landscapes along the 40th parallel. Modeled somewhat after Josiah Dwight Whitney's *Yosemite Book* (1868), which contained fifty of Carleton E. Watkins' original photographs, King's *Final Reports* were among the first American exploration books to feature the "realism" of photolithographs.

O'Sullivan made about 177 photographs for King's survey from 1867 to 1869. Of these, seventeen appeared in *Systematic Geology*, together with nine brilliantly colored chromolithographs from paintings by Gilbert Munger, apparently included to add the dramatic picturesque to King's grand story. All this work was done by the famous lithography firm of Julius Bien & Co. of New York.

Descriptive Geology, published the year before *Systematic Geology* under King's supervision, featured twenty-eight O'Sullivan photolithographs by Bien & Co., many of them more geologically meaningful than those in King's *Systematic Geology*. *The Horse Shoe Curve – Green River – Wyoming* (pl. I, opp. p. 192), for example, not only shows the great power of the Green River's erosion (a uniformitarian concept), but the massive uplifts and tiltings of the Mesozoic formations. Plate II, *Summit Valley – Uintas Mountains*, not only shows the river cutting down through many layers of sedimentary rock, but also clear evidence of faulting and fracturing and the immense "telluric energy" of the Miocene and Pliocene volcanic period.

By contrast, only a few of O'Sullivan's pictures in King's *Systematic Geology* stand out geologically, and then only subtly in relation to King's story. Plate XIII (opp. p. 338), *Eocene Bluffs – Green River – Wyoming*, is a good example of how O'Sullivan's

Timothy O'Sullivan
Eocene Bluffs, Green River, Wyoming
Photolithograph from King, *Systematic Geology*, 1878
DeGolyer Library, Southern Methodist University, Dallas

Gilbert Munger
Uinta Range, Colorado, Cañon of Lodore
Chromolithograph from King, *Systematic Geology*, 1878
DeGolyer Library, Southern Methodist University, Dallas

treatment of a monumental site is changed in the chromolitho-graph. The same site appears romanticized in Gilbert Munger's chromolithograph, plate XIV (opp. p. 390). Munger, like Thomas Moran, William Henry Jackson, and A.J. Russell, captures the whole monumental sweep of this formation. O'Sullivan, by con-trast, seems to say "a bluff is just a bluff."[11] Close inspection, how-ever, does reveal geological layering, uplifting, whole periods of aqueous sediment representing thousands of years, then, to the left, evidence of synclinal folding, and on top, a thick layer of brown sandstone. King felt that both O'Sullivan's laconic close-up and Munger's panoramic chromolithograph demonstrated geo-logic detail sufficiently.[12]

Another interesting photolithograph is plate XXI (opp. p. 644), *Rhyolite Columns – Karnak – Montezuma Range – Nevada*. Here is an amazing, organ-pipe stack of crystallized volcanic rhyo-lite perhaps 100 feet high (measured by the scale of the mammoth wet-plate camera in the middle of the photograph). Clearly this site speaks of fracture, fire, and telluric energy on a startling scale. A third photolithograph, *Pyramid and Tufa Domes – Pyramid Lake – Nevada*, plate XXIII (opp. p. 514), suggests the earlier exis-tence of the great inland sea and the intrusive volcanic eruptions.

Why King left out so many other O'Sullivan photographs from his lavishly illustrated volumes remains a mystery. Many of the omitted images are striking: the wonderfully stark view of O'Sullivan's photo wagon in the sand dunes of the Great Basin's Carson Desert; the nonchalant view of a man resting near some alkali springs in the desolate Ruby Valley of Nevada; the almost sinister view of a smoking volcanic fissure in that same Ruby Valley; the important, even majestic panorama of the twisted, uplifted folds of the Green River; the revealing *Cañon of the Colorado Near the Mouth of the San Juan River*, and the pioneering views of the underground landscape of the Savage and Gould and Curry mines of the Comstock Lode in Nevada.

Weston J. Naef and James Wood, in *Era of Exploration*, as-sert that "O'Sullivan was directed by both King and the geologist S.F. Emmons to make photographs that provided evidence for King's theory of 'catastrophism' and Emmons's more sober prin-ciple of 'mechanical geology' – an outgrowth of King's think-ing."[13] There is no evidence for this in the relevant archival collections and, as noted, King's theory was a combination of uni-formitarianism and catastrophism. The O'Sullivan photographs utilized by King, together with their laconic captions, do little to especially highlight "catastrophism"; what they reveal, rather, are ongoing processes of sedimentary layering and erosion, but only periodical volcanism and sudden crustal faulting.

King's selection of illustrations is occasionally flawed. Surely in the interests of accuracy he would not have approved of plate

V (opp. p. 148), a grossly inaccurate Munger chromo of Lodore Canyon with tepees and natives at home on an inaccessible ledge, partway up the canyon wall, embellished from one of O'Sullivan's more striking, unpublished photographs. King must have known that whatever Indians lived thereabouts did not live in Plains Indians' tepees. Yet he opted for the chromolithograph rather than for the more accurate O'Sullivan photographic original, in which no tepees appear.

O'Sullivan is justly acclaimed for his matter-of-fact realistic photography, which seems to come across as a nonchalance toward the arid dimensions of the 40th parallel. There was not much beauty in such a desolate and arid region. Certainly, in his photographs, O'Sullivan was not inviting friends to visit his lonely camps, nor do his photographs indicate much future for "development." On the contrary, they portray the extreme aridity, heat,

boring terrain, and day-by-day difficulties in a thoroughly non-mythical landscape.

But this contradiction between exploration's lonely difficulties and King's dandified, heroic ways (he climbed mountains in a derby hat and lemon yellow gloves) was reflected in *Systematic Geology*. It was a work of well-informed, careful, and sophisticated science, yet it was a grand romantic narrative punctuated by O'Sullivan's unembellished photographs and Munger's sometimes garish and inaccurate chromolithographs. King himself could never make up his mind whether he wanted to be a scientist or a connoisseur of the arts à la John Ruskin. The contradictions therefore between O'Sullivan's "factual" photographs and Munger's colorful chromolithographs seem to reflect a "chromo civilization" fast giving way to the depressing realities of an industrial age, which King in his *Mining Industry* and later extensive mining ventures helped to bring West.[14]

1. Clarence King produced numerous publications from his exploration and survey of the 40th parallel, which mapped along the 40th parallel from the California Sierras to the Front Range of the Rockies for one hundred miles north and south of the parallel. Each year, from 1871 to 1878, he published an *Annual Report*. He also published *Final Reports or Monographs* and an *Atlas* (see note 4 below).

See also William H. Goetzmann, *Exploration and Empire* (New York: Alfred A. Knopf, 1967), esp. chap. XII, "The West of Clarence King," pp. 430–66, and portfolio III, *Images of Progress: The Camera Becomes Part of Western Exploration*, pp. 603–48.

2. For Wheeler, see *United States Geographical Surveys West of the One Hundredth Meridian*, "Annual Reports 1869–1884." The reference in the present text is to George M. Wheeler, *Final Reports or Monographs*, 7 vols. (Washington, D.C.: US Government Printing Office, 1875–89): I, *Geographical Report* (1889); II, *Astronomy and Barometric Hypsometry* (1877); III, *Geology* (1875); IV *Paleontology* (1877); V, *Zoology* (1875); VI, *Botany* (1878); VII, *Archaeology* (1879).

Wheeler also published sixteen "Unclassified Publications" and approximately ninety-six maps. See also for Wheeler, Goetzmann, *Exploration and Empire*, chap. XI, "The Army Way," pp. 390–430, and Doris Ostrander Dawdy, *George Montague Wheeler: The Man and the Myth* (Athens, Ohio: Swallow Press/Ohio University Press, 1993), passim.

3. A heliotype transferred the negative onto a metal plate rather than onto a lithographic stone and hence was much sharper and clearer.

4. Following are the seven volumes of *Final Reports or Monographs* as well as an *Atlas* (Professional Papers of the Engineer Dept., U.S. Army, no. 18, Washington, D.C.) between 1870 and 1878: I, *Systematic Geology*, (1878); II, *Descriptive Geology* (1877); III, *Mining Industry* (1870); IV, parts 1 and 2, *Paleontology*, part 3,

Ornithology (1877); V, *Botany* (1871); VI, *Microscopical Petrography* (1876); VII, *Odontornithes: A Monograph on the Extinct Toothed Birds of North America*; *Atlas* (1876).

5. Michael Parfit, "The Floods That Carved the West," *The Smithsonian*, 26 (April 1995), pp. 48–58.

6. Thurman Wilkins, *Clarence King*, rev. ed. (Albuquerque: University of New Mexico Press, 1988), p. 221n.

7. Clarence King, *Systematic Geology* (Washington, D.C.: Government Printing Office, 1878), p. 732.

8. Ibid., p. 356.

9. See Goetzmann, *Exploration and Empire*, pp. 462–64, as well as pp. 430–66 in general, for a briefer chronicle of King's Survey.

10. Wilkins, *Clarence King*, p. 223.

11. Weston J. Naef and James Wood, *Era of Exploration: The Rise of Landscape Photography in the American West 1860–1885* (Boston: New York Graphic Society, 1975), p. 135, declare that O'Sullivan's views were "among the least picturesque of all western landscape photographs."

12. King, *Systematic Geology*, pp. 388–90.

13. Naef and Wood, *Era of Exploration*, p. 57.

14. While on the 40th Parallel Survey, both King and James D. Hague served as mining consultants. Josiah Dwight Whitney wrote: "The King of Diamonds has all the work he can do now examining mines and. . .never charges less than $5,000 for looking. . ."; quoted in Wilkins, *Clarence King*, pp. 188–89.

WE ARE WHAT WE SEE: PHOTOGRAPHY AND THE WHEELER SURVEY PARTY

WILLIAM KITTREDGE

New Haven, the home of Yale University, surely one of the sites of privilege in our culture, was supposed to be a frightening town. William Finnigan, a friend from years ago in Montana, wrote about underclass life in New Haven for *The New Yorker* in ways that made the city sound vividly dangerous. But what I saw on my taxicab trip from the railroad station to the removes of the Beinecke Library was dreary and looked more defeated than threatening — empty commonplace storefronts, asphalt thick with potholes — another urban wasteland, where our most disenfranchised citizens survive as best they can.

Thoughts of where I was, inside almost entirely sealed envelopes of contrasting realities, were part of what moved me so deeply during the next hours, as I sat in a Beinecke reading room, enjoying the silences and leafing gingerly through the elegant pages of a book of photographs printed by Lieutenant George M. Wheeler as part of his report on the US Army survey he led into the American Southwest in the 1870s.

Those photographs of that once-upon-a-time West were art, as was the book itself, huge but perfectly proportioned and elegant, and powerfully moving to a Westerner like me. What did this art, I could not stop wondering, an art done with the notion of furthering settlement in the West, have to do with what we, our society, have become, and with the run of injustices that we the privileged, people like me, have learned to look away from?

In late September of 1870, when he was hired by Lieutenant Wheeler to act as photographer on a military exploration into the Great Basin the following spring, Timothy O'Sullivan was around thirty years old and a proven field photographer.

As a very young man, O'Sullivan spent the years just before the Civil War learning his trade under the direction of Alexander Gardner, a first-rate technician, in the studio of the renowned Mathew Brady in Washington, D.C. When war began,

Timothy O'Sullivan
Wall in the Grand Cañon, 1871
Albumen print from Wheeler,
Photographs Showing . . . the Western Territory . . . 1871, 1871
The Metropolitan Museum of Art, New York; Purchase, Joseph Pulitzer
Bequest and The Horace W. Goldsmith Foundation Gift, 1986

O'Sullivan worked first as a field assistant to Brady, then, under obviously demanding conditions, as a battlefield photographer for the Army, again under the supervision of Gardner. O'Sullivan's photographs of the dead in the strewn aftermath of battle, and of the ruined cities of the South, are impressive and vividly memorable, if not yet much distinguished by what can be identified as a personal style.

After the war, O'Sullivan returned to studio work in Washington. In April 1867, he was hired by Clarence King to serve as photographer for a scientific and mapping survey of the unexplored lands of the Great Basin along the 40th Parallel, a strip one hundred miles wide, reaching from the Sierra Nevada Mountains to the Rockies. Congress had authorized $100,000 for King's expedition, and expected specific information in return — most urgently, accurate maps to use while trying to make informed decisions about settlement, and specific information about the location of mineral deposits — coal for the railroads, and silver and gold which would lure miners, enrich the nation, and result in settlement.

King was a privileged young man, a recent graduate of Yale's Sheffield Scientific School, who believed that periods of slow geologic change such as the present were shattered by life-threatening catastrophes which drive evolutionary change, that geology could be thought of as the history of God's occasionally violent recreation of the earth. King found nature to be often threatening, as in this description of the Great Basin plains: ". . .a procession of whirl-wind columns slowly moving across the desert in spectral dimness. A white light beat down, dispelling the last trace of shadow, and hung above the burnished shield of hard, pitiless sky."[1]

It's a vision which reminds us of Revelation, or the early novels of Paul Bowles, set in North Africa. King may have hired O'Sullivan because, after his battlefield experience, he seemed to be the perfect photographer to record such a vision. It's impossible to know if O'Sullivan shared such quasi-religious ideas with King, but the arc of his career makes it clear that he was always working in pursuit of his own artistic objectives.

It is also clear that O'Sullivan proved himself to be tough and

William Bell
Perched Rock, Rocker Creek, Arizona, 1872
From Wheeler, *Photographs Showing . . . the Western Territory. . .
1871, 1872, and 1873*
Albumen print, 10⅞ x 8 (27.6 x 20.3)
The Denver Art Museum

determined, capable of first-quality photography while deep in the rigors of traveling for months in hard country; that he was an expert technician and a developing artist, capable of showing us what he had been seeing in a quite particular way.

Lieutenant George Wheeler, when he hired O'Sullivan in 1870, had just been made chief of a United States Army expedition to explore and map "territory lying south of the Central Pacific Railroad, embracing parts of eastern Nevada and Arizona."[2] Army leaders were unhappy with the usurpation of the military's role as the nation's explorers by civilians like King, F.V. Hayden, and John Wesley Powell, and Wheeler was an Army man, less interested in geological or natural history (although scientists accompanied all his expeditions) than in promoting Army objectives.

The Army understood settlement to be the future of the West, and protection of settlers from raids by native peoples to be its role in that future. Accurate topographical maps of the West were essential. Lieutenant Wheeler was clearly determined to assert Army leadership in the exploration of the West by providing those maps; Wheeler was firm in his sense that the Army's mission in the West was to assist in the bringing of civilization and order (law) to what was understood as wilderness.

Wheeler's expedition assembled on May 3, 1871, at a remote railroad stop called Halleck Station (or Fort Halleck), near Elko, Nevada, and headed out, pack trains of mules carrying their provisions and scientific instruments, across the extremely arid Basin and Range country of Nevada. Temperatures reached 118 degrees. They crossed Death Valley one long night in July, on their way to the Inyo Mountains. As Wheeler described it, "The route lay for more than 39 miles in light, white, drifting sand, which was traversed between 5 a.m. and 6 p.m., the center of the desert being reached about the meridian." He adds that other marches "have extended from fifty to sixty or even eighty hours, with scarcely a single halt."[3]

This sounds, to anyone experienced in that country, not so much like an expression of iron will in the pursuit of duty as an inadvertent admission of incompetence. News clippings from the time, in a scrapbook which may have belonged to Wheeler, show him capable of inexcusable cruelties (as in the case of the boy outside Belmont, in central Nevada, who was hung from a raised wagon tongue by his thumbs, civilian guides who may have perished in the Death Valley country, and the native men mistreated and on at least one occasion shot and killed). A clipping from the scrapbook reports that "The Wheeler Exploring Party. . .seems to have been composed of brutes, if not worse."[4] But the clippings are unattributed, and we cannot know if the stories have any basis in actuality.

The self-serving pointlessness of Wheeler's next move seems unmistakable. With flat-bottomed boats brought from San Francisco, Wheeler set out to ascend two hundred miles of the Colorado River, from Camp Mohave to Diamond Creek in the Grand Canyon. It was a daunting notion, likely an attempt by Wheeler to connect his name to a glamour topic in Western exploration and help establish himself as a visible presence before his Army superiors and Congress.

The trip was unnecessary. In 1857 Lieutenant Joseph Ives, with Dr. John Stong Newberry, a geologist, had gone upriver to the Black Canyon (just down from present-day Hoover Dam), then overland, the first significant scientific exploration of the Grand Canyon. John Wesley Powell had come down the canyon in 1869, and was repeating the trip as Wheeler went upstream. The territory, in other words, had already been explored. On September 16, Wheeler's party of thirty-five scientists, boatmen, soldiers, and fourteen Indians set out, pulling their boats with tow lines. By September 23, they were in the Black Canyon, walls of stone rising 1,700 feet above them. Wheeler wrote of confronting "points at which a stillness like death creates impressions of awe."

O'Sullivan and his photographic crew set their own pace in their own boat, called the *Picture*. On September 27, just upstream from the foot of Boulder Canyon, they caught up with the major party, who were off the river, caulking their boats. By September 29 the expedition was above the mouth of the Virgin River. The labor was extraordinarily difficult but their surroundings were astonishingly grand.

Then, on October 11, disaster. In Wheeler's words, "The boat ran back against the rocks almost a perfect wreck, and its contents were washed down below the overhanging rocks. A stout case containing my most valuable public and private papers and data for a great share of the season's report, which for the first time had not been taken out of the boat at a portage, was lost, as well as valuable instruments, the astronomical and meteorological observations, and worse than all the entire rations of the boat."[5]

It seemed the ultimate defeat, but they pushed on, and on October 19 reached their destination, Diamond Creek, having taken thirty-three days to fight their way two hundred miles upstream. The downriver trip, back to Camp Mohave, where the expedition disbanded, took five days.

O'Sullivan set out for Washington, D.C. with a large collection of negatives, most of which were lost during the trip. Wheeler produced a ninety-four-page report on the expedition and a preliminary topographical map. But the principal consequence of the expedition was the remarkable photography which survived the trip to the East. Timothy O'Sullivan's photographs of the Black Canyon are capable of moving us profoundly through

Timothy O'Sullivan
Ancient Ruins in the Cañon de Chelle, N.M., 1873
Albumen print from Wheeler,
Photographs Showing . . . the Western Territory . . . 1871, 1872, and 1873, c. 1874
Hallmark Photographic Collection, Hallmark Cards, Inc.,
Kansas City, Missouri

Timothy O'Sullivan
Old Mission Church, Zuni Pueblo, New Mexico, 1873
Albumen print from Wheeler,
Photographs Showing . . . the Western Territory . . . 1871, 1872, and 1873, 1874
Centre Canadien d'Architecture/Canadian Centre for Architecture,
Montreal

Timothy O'Sullivan
Shoshone Falls, Snake River, 1874
Albumen print from Wheeler,
Photographs Showing . . . the Western Territory . . .
1871, 1872, 1873, and 1874, c. 1875
Hallmark Photographic Collection, Hallmark Cards, Inc.,
Kansas City, Missouri

their contemplations of darkness and light, in the canyon and on the occasionally gleaming water beneath a white sky.

On first looking at reproductions of O'Sullivan's photographs, as a Westerner whose sense of actuality was largely formed in the outback rangeland and rimrock country of the West, I was moved to think that this at last was real and not false to what I knew. O'Sullivan's work brought me back to what was most omnipresent in the West I knew as a child, which I am tempted to name as stillness, although we know its motions are incessant; it is the indifferent paradise. I saw intimations of what I take to be my true situation in the mirror of O'Sullivan's photography.

Wheeler was delighted with O'Sullivan's work, but by the time Congressional appropriations for his 1872 survey were approved, O'Sullivan was working for Clarence King's 40th Parallel Exploration, in California and the Green River region of western Wyoming and Colorado.

O'Sullivan was replaced by the photographer William Bell, whose work was capable, vivid, quite precise in its evocation of the physical West, and much respected by photographic historians. Yet it is often abstract in ways that lead me to think of the forms Cézanne saw in Provence. But ultimately Bell seems to me to be a journeyman. His work, I think, is not distinguished by the insights generated from what I see as O'Sullivan's personal and perhaps intuitive agenda. Looking at O'Sullivan's work, I begin to sense something that seems true about what it is like to be human — isolated, with companions, on this planet, with no given knowledge of why — I begin to see my own existence in the mirror of his photographs.

In 1873, O'Sullivan was back with Wheeler, this time in Arizona and New Mexico, the Sierra Blanca Mountains and Canyon de Chelly, photographing both land forms and native people in defeated but not dying cultures. In November, ending what he may have sensed was his final year in the West, O'Sullivan went alone to photograph Shoshone Falls on the Snake River, at the point where it cut its canyon through the plains of southern Idaho.

This was actually a rephotography project. O'Sullivan had first visited Shoshone Falls in 1868, with Clarence King, who was both attracted and repelled by the ceaselessness and power of the rushing water, which he ultimately took to be threatening and fearful. O'Sullivan photographed the falls from below, focusing upstream into the torrent, the metaphor. In 1873, O'Sullivan spent at least three more days photographing Shoshone Falls, his last work in the West. In attempting to understand what drew him back there, it is perhaps useful to think of another explorer in the West, Meriwether Lewis at the Great Falls of the Missouri on

June 13, 1805, and the trouble he had naming what he saw: "...from the reflection of the sun on the spray or mist which arises from these falls there is a beautiful rainbow produced which adds not a little to the beauty of this majestically grand scenery. After writing this imperfect description I again viewed the falls and was so much disgusted with the imperfect idea which it conveyed of the scene I was determined to draw my pen across it and begin again, but then reflected that I could not perhaps succeed...."[6]

The Lewis and Clark Expedition and the Wheeler Survey, like the other federally sponsored research expeditions into the West, were primarily designed as scientific searches for evidence of what would be useful to settlement and commerce. In his reports on their field work, long after it was finished, Wheeler consistently describes O'Sullivan's photographs in prose designed to encourage and reassure potential settlers for the West, using O'Sullivan's vision as an instrument to promote what was taken, by most Americans and certainly by Army men in his time, as one of our most serious national purposes.

But O'Sullivan was attempting to photograph, I cannot help but think, ineffable significances in the flow of light and energies which is real but not nameable, the place we ultimately inhabit. Making sense of where we are, and why we live — such work is the challenge before the mind of any major artist.

O'Sullivan's final photographs in the West, particularly my favorite, looking downriver over Shoshone Falls, mist glowing above the canyon of our descent, can be thought of as attempts at locating and naming himself within the overwhelming complexity of that which is actual. Timothy O'Sullivan died in January 1882 of tuberculosis, a young man with the good fortune to have done some striking work that has proved vastly useful to Westerners in their attempts to make sense of themselves as partly formed by their homeland, if such origins offered any solace.

It is our misfortune, as a society, that this kind of work is so often locked away from us. We see ourselves in our art, and we are moved to understand, again, that we are all of us nothing if not fragile and in this together. In consequence, we may be sometimes moved to empathy, and compassion, and even the pursuit of public enfranchisement. The Whitney Museum and the Beinecke Library perform a great service in bringing these photographs out to display before a wide public.

1. Clarence King, "The Range," *Atlantic Monthly*, 28 (May 1871), pp. 611–12.

2. Richard Bartlett, *Great American Surveys* (Norman: University of Oklahoma Press, 1980), p. 338.

3. Lieutenant George M. Wheeler, *Geographical Report*, Vol. I. In *Report Upon United States Geographical Surveys West of the 100th Meridian*, 45.

4. Bancroft Library, University of California, Berkeley, Wheeler Scrapbook, P-W 32, vol. I.

5. Wheeler, *Geographical Report*, pp. 164–65.

6. Gary E. Moulton, ed., *The Journals of the Lewis & Clark Expedition*, Vol. 4. April 7–July 27, 1805 (Lincoln: University of Nebraska Press, 1987).

DISCOVERING
A HUMAN PAST,
INVENTING
A SCENIC WEST,
1880–1930

John K. Hillers
Pueblo de Santo Domingo, New Mexico, 1880
From Morgan, *Houses and House-Life of the American Aborigines*, 1881
Albumen print, 9⅝ x 12¹³/₁₆ (24.7 x 32.9)
Centre Canadien d'Architecture/Canadian Centre for Architecture, Montreal

pp. 68–69: Gustaf Nordenskiöld
The Cliff Palace, 1891 (detail)
Photogravure from Nordenskiöld, *The Cliff Dwellers of the Mesa Verde. . .* , 1893
Private collection

John K. Hillers
Pueblo de Taos, North, New Mexico, 1880
From Morgan, *Houses and House-Life of the American Aborigines*, 1881
Albumen print, 9⅝ x 12¹³⁄₁₆ (25 x 32.5)
Centre Canadien d'Architecture/Canadian Centre for Architecture, Montreal

Toward the end of the century, ethnography succeeded topography as the prime focus of photographically illustrated government reports and rapidly grew to dominate private publications. While government-sponsored survey reports began to disclose the rich cultural heritage of the Southwest prior to the Civil War and in the decade following, the founding of the Bureau of Ethnology in 1879 established Native American cultures as a subject of continuous government-sponsored research. Apart from these projects, the new discipline of archaeology, with its important base of evidence among the pueblos and ruins of the Southwest, led to a number of important photographic publications by private individuals.

Houses and House: Life of American Aborigines (1881), an anthropological study written by Lewis Henry Morgan with photographs by John Hillers, was published under the imprint of the Bureau of Ethnology. Through views of settlements, this work depicted the ways in which the Pueblo Indians in particular sited their dwellings in relation to the landscape of the Southwest. Somewhat later, an independent archaeological study by Gustaf Nordenskiöld, documented in *The Cliff Dwellers of the Mesa Verde, Southwestern Colorado, Their Pottery and Implements* (1893), gave Europeans and Americans the first comprehensive study of the ancient Indian ruins in southern Colorado.

The 1890 census report declared the frontier closed, but this official statement merely confirmed what most Americans already knew — just a few pockets of true wilderness remained in the territory of the United States. What was very nearly lost became increasingly treasured, and the era was marked by the formation of new national preserves: Grand Canyon was declared a National Park in 1906, some twenty-five years after Yellowstone was named America's (and the world's) first National Park. Popular interest in native cultures also reached a zenith around the turn of the century, as a belief in the imminent eclipse of these cultures became commonplace. Significant photographic books documenting the Southwest proliferated, fueled by the missions of professional and amateur archaeologists and ethnologists determined to avert a loss of cultural heritage.

With the backing of publishers both commercial and private, many photographic book projects on American Indians were undertaken, none more important than Edward Curtis' twenty-volume *The North American Indian; Being a Series of Volumes Picturing and Describing the Indians of the United States, and Alaska* (1907–30). Written, illustrated, and published by Curtis, with a foreword by Theodore Roosevelt, and field research conducted under the patronage of J. Pierpont Morgan, this project involved nearly three decades of photographic work among native cultures. (Several of the Southwest volumes, including landscape views, are featured in this exhibition, as well as several of the large, exhibition-scale photogravure plates that were issued in portfolios accompanying the volumes.)

Curtis' work became increasingly stylized as the years passed and as he sought to depict traditional costumes and ceremonies that were less and less common in contemporary life. His often romantic manipulations of his subjects, which have inspired much criticism in recent years, were admired by most

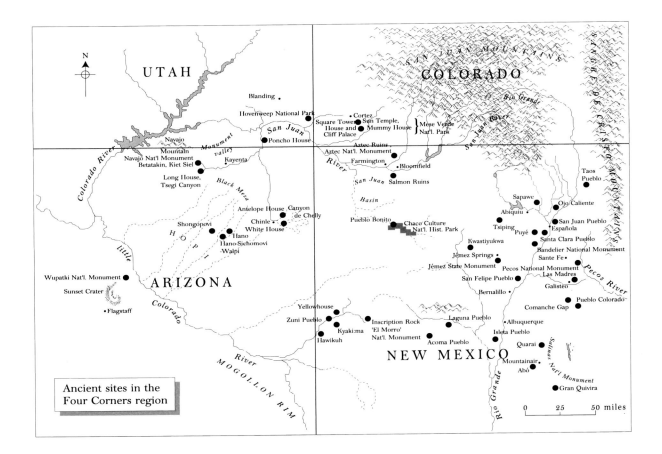

Ancient sites in the Four Corners region

of his contemporaries, including prominent ethnologists, and many Native Americans valued his prodigious field work and the historical information it provided, if only as reference to earlier tribal practices.

Yet by the time Curtis completed the project in 1930, he was bankrupt, in large part because the lavish publishing standards upon which his patron J. Pierpont Morgan had insisted had outpriced some of the most likely collectors.[1] The volumes failed to sell in sufficient quantity even before the Great Depression put an end to the so-called golden age of book collecting, and even at a time when the Indian Wars were still remembered as a burning national issue.

Although interest in the Southwest and the desert West was slower to develop than that in the "wonderlands" of Yosemite, Yellowstone, and coastal California, by the 1890s a conjunction of technological innovation and renewed patronage made the Southwest a site of relentless promotion. The development of smaller cameras and roll film enabled non-professionals to take up photography. Likewise, the technology of halftone printing transformed the publishing business by greatly reducing the cost of printing illustrated books and expanding the number of copies that could be produced. Commercial houses and corporate sponsors quickly took advantage of these innovations to preach the virtues of the Southwest to a growing popular audience. The Santa Fe Railroad (which had completed a southern route across the West in the 1880s) and its partner, the Harvey House hotels and tours, became lavish patrons and publish-

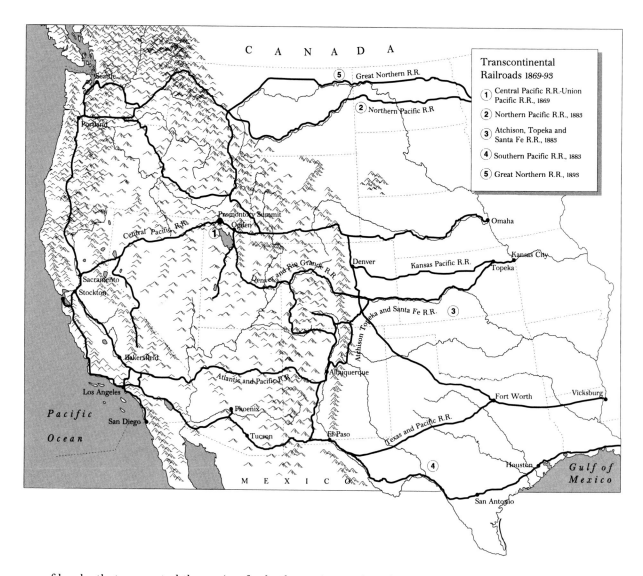

ers of books that promoted the region for both tourism and settlement. A late example of this phenomenon, Frederick Monsen's *With a Kodak in the Land of the Navajo* (1909), demonstrates how easy it had
become to visit the territory Richard Kern had struggled across nearly eighty years before.

A growing public interest in the archaeology of the Southwest was reflected in many popular
accounts. Photographs by Adam Clark Vroman (a Pasadena bookseller who traveled extensively in the
region), showing an expedition up the Enchanted Mesa to examine the ruins on top, were widely published. The archaeologist Adolph F.A. Bandelier wrote a fanciful historical novel of the Anasazi culture,
The Delight Makers (1890), which was later illustrated with photographs by his friend Charles Fletcher
Lummis, an amateur in archaeology (and in almost every field related to the Southwest of that time).
Lummis was typical of a new type of adventurer who was drawn to the Southwest at the turn of the century: for Lummis, photography was only one facet of his involvement in the region, and his scholarly turn
of mind was balanced by an ardor to share his enthusiasm for the region's deserts, mesas, and pueblos

with the rest of the country. It was Lummis who coined the slogan "See America First," and he meant the Southwest above all.

With the relative ease of travel by railroad (and later by automobile), the once forbidding deserts and arid lands became magnets for artists and tourists who found there a sense of isolation and a theater of the sublime. Books by photographers such as J. Smeaton Chase also promoted the healthful climate and the remarkable flora of the Southern California deserts. Perhaps ironically, such works helped to turn a provincial outpost like Palm Springs into a popular resort within a few decades. The American Southwest also became the landscape in which travelers came to see a storied American embedded in archaeological ruins said by Lummis and others to rival those of Europe and t

Even as the technological horizon widened, the turn of the century brought a return and a respect for the communitarian life — which led photographers such as Lummis, Vro Moon to pay particular attention to the Pueblo Indians. The Arts and Crafts Movement, par ential in California, spawned an extraordinary number of fine presses devoted to hand-prin ing. (It is out of this tradition that the Grabhorn Press in 1930 published *Taos Pueblo* by Ansel Adams and Mary Austin.) Supported by small groups of West Coast book lovers, these private presses also gave rise to personal accounts of the increasingly familiar desert landscapes of Arizona, Nevada, and California, such as Caroline Poole's desert travel narrative, *A Modern Prairie Schooner on the Transconti-nental Trail: The Story of a Motor Trip* (1919).

As more Americans became familiar with the arid West, their desire to protect the region extended to the least hospitable desert areas. Multiple editions of John Van Dyke's *The Desert: Further Studies in Natural Appearances* (of which one edition of 1916 is illustrated with J. Smeaton Chase's photographs) helped create a generation of "desert lovers" with a new aesthetic appreciation for the landscape. Van Dyke had spent a year in the desert to restore his health; in *The Desert*, he applied his skills as an art historian to analyze the terrain's multihued vistas. Many of these publications extol the Grand Canyon and other sites at the moment when these areas were being named, primarily during the tenure of President Theodore Roosevelt, as National Parks or Monuments.

MAY CASTLEBERRY

1. D. W. Wright, archivist at The J. Pierpont Morgan Library, graciously provided this and other information on Edward S. Curtis.

Gustaf Nordenskiöld
The Cliff Palace, 1891
Photogravure from Nordenskiöld,
The Cliff Dwellers of the Mesa Verde . . ., 1893
Private collection

MESA VERDE

EVAN S. CONNELL

"'Boom-boom-boom-boom-boom,' came the rhythmic sound of the war drums of Cliff Palace,
and 'boom-boom-boom-boom' bounced back the echoes,
from the cliffs that lined the beautiful Mesa Verde Canyon,
wherein this great cliff city is located."
Silent Water and Long Bow, who were tramping through the
junipers that carpet most of the great green tableland. . . .

So begins Arthur W. Monroe's 1950 novel, *Silent Water: The Romance and Tragedy of the American Cliff Dwellers.* It is beyond doubt a romance, all but submerged in syrup, which ends some two hundred pages later as the hero and his true love, Laughing Flower, wend their way homeward: "For them life had drawn itself into perfect shape — and perhaps it was the shape of a heart."

The author, who for several years worked as a ranger at Mesa Verde National Park in southwestern Colorado, knew how difficult life must have been in those cliff houses; nevertheless, he succumbed to the allure of the ruins and concocted a prehistoric idyll. It should be remarked, however, that Mr. Monroe had plenty of company.

W.H. Holmes, a geologist-topographer assigned to the 1874–76 Hayden Survey, departed from approved bureaucratic style to observe that as one views certain crags in this region, "he is unconsciously led to wonder if they are not ruins of some ancient castle, behind whose mouldering walls are hidden the dread secrets of a long-forgotten people. . . ."[1]

Dr. Jesse Fewkes arrived in 1908, dispatched by the Bureau of American Ethnology. Dr. Fewkes had been excavating prehistoric sites for two decades, so it would be reasonable to expect a steady hand on the spade; but late one afternoon near the so-called Sun Temple there appeared "an influence" which assumed the form of a huge bird much like an eagle and Dr. Fewkes realized that the sun had returned to its abode to deliver a message. This apparition identified itself as the archaic god of fire and said it was followed by the Kachinas, its children, who would communicate their thoughts. From a nearby grove of cedars came a rustling noise. Various shadowy personages emerged. First was an old man wearing the kilt of a priest who declared that he inhabited Aztec Pueblo, forty miles away. This spectral figure said Aztec was being excavated, which Dr. Fewkes knew quite well because archaeologist Earl Morris was working there. The apparition

went on to say that Morris was doing a good job. Then the Kachinas spoke up. They, too, applauded all this scientific investigation, specifically praising the National Geographic Society for sponsoring a project in Chaco Canyon some distance south of Mesa Verde. Finally: "The last visitor disappeared as noiselessly as the others and as the darkness increased I followed the trail on foot back to my camp, pondering on the visitation. . . ."

In 1917 the heights of fancy were scaled by a Denver woman, Virginia McClurg, whose Colorado Cliff Dwellings Association presented a drama titled *The Marriage of the Dawn and the Moon.* At the conclusion of this spectacle — written, costumed, and directed by Mrs. McClurg — the audience settled down to a feast of roast calf, baked ears of maize, and peaches, thus participating more fully in a prehistoric experience. Although the banquet sounds delicious, it is not what Mesa Verde people ate. In winter they ate cornbread, beans, and dried meat — fox, deer, coyote, rabbit — whatever could be hit with an arrow or a club. Spring brought cornbread and beans, juniper berries, wild onions, edible roots, tansy mustard, and a funguslike growth called puffball. Then came squash, more beans, more cornbread, maybe piñon nuts.

Photographer Laura Gilpin, who visited Mesa Verde twice during the 1920s, worked early in the morning before tourists arrived. According to her biographer, Martha Sandweiss, Gilpin wanted to convey an impression of how things used to be, or ought to be. Years later these dramatic soft-focus prints would embarrass Gilpin, but at that time she remarked: "The atmosphere of antiquity which emanates from these age-old ruins takes possession of all who behold them."[2]

Just about everybody who visits Mesa Verde is affected. This gigantic sandstone bluff dominates the Montezuma Valley so thoroughly that it demands recognition. One struggles for an appropriate metaphor because Green Table seems inadequate.

Gustaf Nordenskiöld
The Balcony House, 1891
Photogravure from Nordenskiöld,
The Cliff Dwellers of the Mesa Verde . . . , 1893
Private collection

Mesa Verde becomes a reef, perhaps a Crusader's castle. Gilpin likened the successive promontories to "giant piers awaiting the arrival of some leviathan ship." And as the road curls upward through the shadow of the north rim it is easy to imagine that one is gliding toward a reef or pier, or the ramparts of Acre which fell to the Moslems in 1291 A.D. — just as the last Mesa Verde people were abandoning their homes.

Navajos and Utes who drifted into southwestern Colorado a couple of centuries later refused to enter this city of the dead; and the first Spaniards to see Mesa Verde did not climb to the top, as we know from the journal of Father Silvestre Vélez de Escalante.[3] So it was not until the late nineteenth century, when gringo prospectors, ranchers, and US Government topographers explored the territory that human voices disturbed the lizards and rats occupying these apartments.

Tom Outland — a character in Willa Cather's novel *The Professor's House* — reported his first view of the ruins with poetic disbelief: "Far up above me, a thousand feet or so, set in a great cavern in the face of the cliff, I saw a little city of stone, asleep. . . . The falling snow-flakes, sprinkling the piñons, gave it a special kind of solemnity. . . . I knew at once that I had come upon the city of some extinct civilization."[4]

Who found this dead city? Although the argument has persisted for a hundred years, Richard Wetherill and his brother-in-law Charles Mason usually receive credit. Wetherill's father, a Quaker from Pennsylvania, brought the family to Colorado in 1880 and settled near the town of Mancos just east of the Mesa. Utes in the vicinity did not like an unending cavalcade of Bearded Mouths who regarded land as property to be annexed, but the old Quaker never carried a gun and partly for this reason they allowed his cattle to forage in the Mesa Verde branch canyons.

One December afternoon, Richard Wetherill and Charlie Mason were looking for strays when they noticed an apartment house on the face of a distant cliff. They made their way up to it and wandered through room after room, leaving boot tracks in dust that had been accumulating for centuries. Wherever they looked they saw painted clay mugs, bowls, water jars, and other household objects, as though the people who lived here might come home at any moment. After picking up a few souvenirs, Wetherill and Mason returned to the ranch, but whenever possible they and Richard's younger brothers would explore the canyons. As more apartments were discovered their collection of artifacts increased. They thought the people of Durango might be interested, so in the spring of 1889 the Wetherill collection went on display. Several hundred citizens visited the exhibit and there was talk of buying the relics. Nothing happened.

The Wetherills took their antique cooking pots, black-and-

Gustaf Nordenskiöld
Ruin 18, Mountain Sheep Cañon, 1891
Photogravure from Nordenskiöld,
The Cliff Dwellers of the Mesa Verde . . . , 1893
Private collection

white ladles, stone axes, arrowheads, and broken mugs across the San Juan range to Pueblo. The citizens of Pueblo, being more sophisticated, ought to be interested, they thought. Not at all. The exhibition was ridiculed.

On to Denver. Surely the cosmopolitan people of Denver would understand. Again they were rejected. Despite this, the Wetherill brothers — Richard, Clayt, Win, Al, John — and Charlie Mason continued to search the canyons and by the following spring they had located almost two hundred cliff houses.

News of their discoveries brought quite a few visitors to the Wetherill ranch, among them a prosperous Connecticut druggist with a taste for mountaineering, Frederick Chapin. Unlike most sightseers, Chapin did not go pot-hunting; he seemed content to sketch and photograph, and upon returning to Connecticut he wrote a paper for the Appalachian Mountain Club. After a second visit in 1890 he wrote *The Land of the Cliff-Dwellers*, which included photos and data from both excursions.

In style and outlook Chapin was very much the nineteenth-century romantic. "How long," he asks, "since human foot had trod those sandstone floors?" A secluded cavern moves him to speculate: "A stronghold surely it was, impregnable to a foe armed only with arrows. . . . Perchance these remote fortresses were subjected to a long siege by crafty Ute or fiery Apache, wherein the heroic defenders stood out to the last. . . ."

Chapin's theory has been dismissed by anthropologists, but other nineteenth-century ideas were no less fanciful. A journalist writing for the Mancos *Times* thought the Mesa Verde natives may have been serfs condemned to mine gold for their Spanish masters, while the apartments were castles erected for grandees "much after the feudal customs obtaining at that period in Spain." And it was commonly held that Montezuma's Aztecs once governed this region.

A young Swedish tourist, Gustaf Nordenskiöld, learned of the cliff dwellings while visiting Denver and decided to spend a week at Alamo Ranch. Late one evening, exhausted by a thirty-mile buggy ride from the Durango railroad station, he drove into the yard, told the Wetherills who he was, and asked if they would show him around Mesa Verde.

Nordenskiöld came from a family of scientists, all the way back to his great-great-grandfather, who had been director general of saltpeter boileries in Finland. Gustaf's father, Nils, chief of the mineralogical department at the Swedish Royal Academy, had been the first man to navigate a Northeast Passage — which earned him the title of baron. The Wetherills knew about Baron Nordenskiöld's famous voyage, so they were more than simply pleased to welcome young Gustaf.

Nordenskiöld wrote to his parents that on his first trip with Richard and Al they rode twenty-four miles down the Mancos Valley and entered a cliff house by descending steps cut into the rock by people who had lived there centuries ago.[5] Next day he studied and copied some ancient petroglyphs.

When he returned to Alamo Ranch a week later he was obsessed. He notified his parents that he meant to stay at least a month, possibly two months. He wanted to find out who these people were, where they went, and why.

A letter to his father, dated July 2, 1891, mentions that the Wetherills had acquired a great many items which they would sell for $8,000. Could this material be purchased for display in Sweden? And he comments that no photographs exist of these astonishing ruins. He wonders if his camera might be shipped to Colorado, along with a barometer. Nils Nordenskiöld shipped the barometer and camera, but replied that funds to purchase this collection were unavailable.

Gustaf went home in the spring of 1892, and like Frederick Chapin he at once began to write about his experience. *The Cliff Dwellers of the Mesa Verde, Southwestern Colorado: Their Pottery and Implements* was published in Swedish by the Royal Printing Office in 1893, just two years before Nordenskiöld's death from tuberculosis. His monograph concluded: "It is reserved for future research to carry out a careful investigation of the numerous archaeological remains. . . ."[6] Photographs of Mesa Verde hung on the walls of his gloomy medieval apartment in Stockholm, and the dining room tablecloth bore a design copied from a bowl he had unearthed.

The artifacts he wanted to buy eventually were displayed at a Minneapolis industrial exposition. Later they became part of the Wetherill exhibition at the 1893 Chicago World's Fair — less than aesthetically housed in a fake cliff dwelling at the end of an artificial canyon — where they competed with a Ferris wheel, cotton candy booths, Egyptian belly dancers, and other midway attractions.

Alfred Vincent Kidder, who would become the leading American archaeologist of his time, reached Mesa Verde in 1907. While exploring the canyons with his friend and associate Jesse Nusbaum — who would be appointed superintendent of the National Park — he noticed a cliff house so high on the wall that it seemed inaccessible. After a difficult, dangerous climb, across a narrow ledge with a long drop below, Kidder and Nusbaum got there. Elated, excited, positive that nobody had visited this apartment for at least six hundred years, they peered through a crevice and saw an upended slab of rock. On it Richard Wetherill had scratched a message: "What fools these mortals be."

1. F. V. Hayden, "Report of William H. Holmes," in *Geological and Geographical Survey of the Territories (U.S.): Tenth Annual Report of the United States Geological and Geographical Survey of the Territories.* (Washington, D.C.: US Government Printing Office, 1878), p. 390.

2. Laura Gilpin, *The Mesa Verde National Park: Reproductions from a Series of Photographs by Laura Gilpin* (Colorado Springs: The Gilpin Publishing Company, 1927), n.p.

3. Joseph Cerquone, *The Domínguez-Escalante Expedition* (Denver: The Domínguez-Escalante Expedition Bicentennial, 1976).

4. Willa Cather, *Willa Cather: Later Novels* (New York: Library of America, 1990), p. 220.

5. Olof W. Arrhenius, *Stones Speak and Waters Sing: The Life and Works of Gustaf Nordenskiöld* (Mesa Verde, Colorado: Mesa Verde National Park and Mesa Verde Museum Association, 1984), p. 6.

6. Ibid., p. 12.

Edward S. Curtis
Cañon de Chelly – Navaho, 1904
Photogravure from
The North American Indian: Large Plates Supplementing Volume I, 1907
Yale Collection of Western Americana, Beinecke Rare Book and
Manuscript Library, Yale University, New Haven, Connecticut

THE ARCADIAN LANDSCAPES OF EDWARD S. CURTIS

WILLIAM N. GOETZMANN

Perhaps the largest and most beautifully printed book of photographs of the American West is Edward Sheriff Curtis' *The North American Indian*, published between 1907 and 1930, in an edition of approximately 270. The lavish twenty-volume set — actually twenty volumes of text and twenty portfolios of plates — was one of this century's first "multimedia" presentations. Text, photographs, and Edison wax cylinder sound recordings together document the culture of more than eighty Indian tribes throughout western North America. The text volumes are copiously illustrated with tinted drawings and plates made from Curtis' photographs; the large-scale portfolio of sepia-toned photogravures is now widely collected as a separate volume, and its plates are reproduced as icons of Native American culture. These grand images, taken by Edward Curtis and, for the most part, printed by his Seattle studio manager Adolph Muhr, represent a self-Consciously aesthetic narrative of American Indian life. They are an artistic attempt to reach through the scientific information collected on American Indian cultures, in order to capture its "essence." Whether Curtis, through his photographs, discovered some fundamental truths about Native American life, or merely projected turn-of-the-century European-American stereotypes onto native peoples has long been the subject of debate.

In fact, Curtis' photographs of American Indians in relation to the natural landscape fit squarely into the American aesthetic tradition of their time. In particular, Curtis' landscape settings reveal a profound nostalgia for a pre-industrial, Arcadian existence that the artist "embodied" in his views of American Indian life. The five volumes of *The North American Indian* that concern Southwestern tribes (vols. I, II, XII, XVI, and XVII) are set in the stark, arid landscape of Arizona and New Mexico. The magic of Curtis' photography turns these lands into a lush Eden, enjoyed by nonmaterialistic people who bathed themselves in the cool desert springs, built their houses from the earth and trees, and picked their nourishment from the bounty of the desert.

In order to understand the iconography of Edward Curtis it is important to understand how *The North American Indian* evolved. Curtis created his images for a distinct audience, and experimented with different modes of photography before per-

fecting the style that made him famous. In fact, the story of this tremendous project is not only a testimony to one artist's single-minded perseverance over three decades, but a fascinating episode in American cultural history. The tale begins not in the West, but among one particular "tribe" in New York.

VIEWS OF A VANISHING RACE

The evening at the Waldorf-Astoria in March 1905 couldn't have gone better for Seattle photographer Edward Curtis. Although his bill for the use of the grand ballroom totaled an astronomical $1,300, most of New York's social luminaries made an appearance. They came to see Curtis' spectacular lantern show and multimedia presentation of the "Vanishing American" — motion pictures, Edison cylinder recordings, stereopticon views, photographs and engravings of Southwestern Indian tribes. At the conclusion of the soirée, several of the most powerful women in America, including Mrs. Stuyvesant Fish, Mrs. Jay Gould, Mrs. Herbert Satterlee (daughter of Pierpont Morgan), Mrs. Douglas Robinson, and Mrs. Frederick Vanderbilt purchased copies of Curtis' photographs.[1] That evening, to the assembled guests and journalists in attendance, the photographer described his grandiose dream: to create a monumental documentary record of American Indian life, to preserve the last vestiges of native existence before acculturation destroyed it altogether — to capture the vanishing frontier.

Few of the assembled blue bloods realized that Curtis was proposing the impossible. By 1905, the vanishing frontier, at least in the Western United States, had already vanished. No one understood this more than Edward Curtis himself. He had spent the last eight years photographing Native American people in the Northwest and Southwest and had been hard pressed to document any visual evidence of Indians in a "pre-contact" state. For instance, his views of the Hopi, taken in 1900, show dancers with baggy cloth trousers beneath their antelope costumes and women with calico dresses rather than woolen robes.[2] These early shots, while true to turn-of-the-century Southwestern Indian life, were not the pictures that made him famous. Only after he learned to

Edward S. Curtis
Acoma and Enchanted Mesa, 1904
Gelatin silver print, 5¾ x 7¾ (14.7 x 19.7)
Centre Canadien d'Architecture/Canadian Centre for Architecture,
Montreal

eliminate modern details did Curtis' more familiar romantic image of Indians take shape. In describing his giant project, Curtis was proposing something that could only be delivered through the magic of photography — a visual re-creation of cultures as they once were, or at least as the artist and his models would like to remember them.

The audience that night who applauded Curtis' nostalgic portraits of Indian chiefs and views of a bygone era could hardly be called disinterested observers of the vanished frontier. New York railroad tycoons were the financiers who had opened up the West to transcontinental traffic and directly hastened the end of traditional Native American life. Jay Gould, Cornelius Vanderbilt, Pierpont Morgan, Jr., E.H. Harriman, Curtis' earliest patron, and James J. Hill, Curtis' personal friend, fought titanic financial battles for control of the American rails during the late nineteenth century. Among them, by 1906, they owned more than half the railroads in America. Of the 228,000 miles of track that crisscrossed the continent, Vanderbilt controlled 22,500 miles from New York to Chicago, Morgan interests controlled 18,000 miles in the Southeast, Gould owned 17,000 miles in the Mississippi Valley, E.H. Harriman owned 21,000 miles of central and trans-Mississippi track, and Hill controlled 21,000 miles of northern routes to the Pacific.[3]

American capitalism and politics worked hand in hand at the end of the nineteenth century to enforce the "civilizing" of the American Indian tribes. In particular, there is evidence that as early as 1868 United States policy was to use the Western railroad system as a means to confront the Indian nations and "clean out Indians as we encounter them."[4] Indiscriminate slaughter of the vast buffalo herds, particularly on railroad lands, hastened the decimation of the Plains Indians. By 1890, hostile Indians and roving herds no longer threatened the vast commercial network controlled by the railroad tycoons; however, memories of the violent Indian wars were still fresh. Nonetheless, given their success in civilizing the frontier, the assembled captains of industry could afford a bit of romantic nostalgia for bygone days. In fact, the successful development of the Western territories depended in part upon replacing the threatening image of American Indians with a pacific one.[5]

The following year, 1906, a letter from President Theodore Roosevelt, and in all likelihood a good word from Mrs. Herbert Satterlee, won Curtis an audience with the mighty Pierpont Morgan. Curtis sought Morgan's patronage of his *North American Indian* project, asking for $15,000 per year for five years.[6] His plan was to use the Morgan money to produce one hundred sets of the book, priced at $5,000 each. The way Curtis may have seen it, success required sales to only twenty-five percent of New

York's famous 400. According to Curtis' biographer Barbara A. Davis, Morgan agreed to give $75,000 to Curtis in exchange for twenty-five sets of *The North American Indian*, three hundred large photographic prints, and two hundred small ones. In addition, he persuaded Curtis to make his profit on volume rather than margin by lowering the price to $3,000 per set. Thus, for his commitment to purchase twenty-five sets of the book at $3,000 each, Morgan got an additional five hundred of Curtis' fine photographic prints, so admired by the financier's daughter, and he earned the immediate reputation as a patron of American Indian culture! Although Morgan preferred to remain anonymous about his support of the project, Curtis insisted on spreading the word. On the heels of the deal, one newspaper headline read "Morgan Money to Save Indians from Oblivion."[7]

It took twenty-three years and an estimated $1.2 million dollars, but Curtis delivered on the deal. Unfortunately, he woefully underestimated the cost of the project and overestimated the social set's commitment to preserving Native American culture. Shortly after the beginning of the project, the Wall Street panic of 1907 made subscriptions from wealthy New York patrons difficult to obtain. By 1911, Morgan was forced to increase his patronage of the project by investing an additional $60,000. The photographer also sought bank loans and private investment from Seattle businessmen to finance the remainder of his annual expenses. His patron died in 1913, leaving Curtis to scramble for additional funding on his own. Ultimately, the Morgan family assumed much of the publication cost of *The North American Indian*. In total, the Morgan contribution to the production of the book amounted to $400,000.[8]

The vast sums of money were primarily used to finance a series of field seasons from 1907 to 1927, in which Curtis and his assistants traveled through the West, camping with tribes, taking photographs, recording songs, making motion pictures, and gathering ethnographic information. Due to the enormous scope of the project, Curtis delegated substantial portions of work to his collaborators and assistants. William Myers, for instance, was responsible for a considerable portion of the ethnography, which in turn was edited by the Bureau of American Ethnology's Frederick Webb Hodge, who was also the editor of the *Handbook of North American Indians*. The printing and preparation of the glass plate negatives developed in the field fell to the master printer Adolph Muhr, who managed Curtis' Seattle darkroom, and who undoubtedly made a significant contribution to the distinctive Curtis photographic style, through negative retouching and decisions regarding exposure of the prints.

In his thirty years of travel among Indian tribes in the West, Curtis proved as adept at wooing powerful and influential Native

Edward S. Curtis
A Feast Day at Acoma, 1904
Photogravure from
The North American Indian: Large Plates Supplementing Volume XVI, 1904
Yale Collection of Western Americana, Beinecke Rare Book and
Manuscript Library, Yale University, New Haven

Edward S. Curtis
Water Carriers, c. 1904
Gelatin silver print, 5⁷⁄₁₆ x 7⁵⁄₈ (14 x 19.5)
Yale Collection of Western Americana, Beinecke Rare Book and
Manuscript Library, Yale University, New Haven

Americans as he was at wooing upper-crust European-Americans. Among the famous Native Americans whom he persuaded to pose for him were Princess Angeline, whose father was the Squamish chief for whom Seattle is named, Nez Percé Chief Joseph, and the Apache chief Geronimo. Curtis apparently had a knack for getting Native Americans to re-create tableaux from their vanished past. For instance, he directed *In the Land of the Head Hunters*, a full-length motion picture made in collaboration with the Kwakiutl people of British Columbia. In the film, villagers build houses, masks, and a whaling canoe in the traditional manner, in order to simulate their pre-contact culture.

THE EVOLUTION OF THE CURTIS STYLE

The idea of historically re-creating past cultures, which became the hallmark of Curtis' style, actually evolved slowly. Its progress may be charted through a series of images of Hopi women at the Walpi Pueblo water hole which the photographer took over a period of twenty-two years, from 1900 to 1921. His first photograph of the scene, taken on a trip through the Southwest in 1900, is a picture of six women visiting the spring with their watering jugs. The photograph, preserved in Yale's Beinecke Library, is *not* included in volume XII, devoted to the Hopi. It shows the women in ordinary modern dress, with print skirts, and various unelaborated hairstyles.[9] The bright light of the scene allowed Curtis to use a narrow aperture for the exposure, which brought the foreground and background into focus. It is an unremarkable, and apparently unposed picture, suggesting that the artist took a "snapshot" view of contemporary Indian life at the time.

Curtis decided to include a different water hole scene in the published illustrations to the text of volume XII. Taken in 1906 and entitled *Gossip at the Water Hole*, it also pictures six Hopi women. This time, however, they are clothed in traditional Atöö robes, and their hair is arranged in a distinctive bilobular style. Although he does not say as much in the text, Curtis asked the women to dress themselves in traditional costume and hairstyles for his photograph. The composition, while stronger than its predecessor due to the darker costumes of the women and the concentration on the foreground, is not particularly powerful, nor does it express any particular relationship between the women and the landscape. Between 1900 and 1906, however, Curtis had developed one of his favorite "tricks" for adding depth to his scenes: he opened the aperture of the camera, rendering the distant pueblo as an unfocused blur on the horizon. Christopher Lyman points out that this "focal recession" was also used to blur modern figures and details, such as tourists viewing the famous Hopi dances.[10]

Curtis made a third view of the water hole, entitled *Loitering at the Spring*, in 1921, and he evidently liked it the best, for he included it as a large plate in the portfolio of photogravures accompanying volume XII. The decision to include it among the thirty-six large-format plates indicates that it qualified as "art" suitable for framing. Like the 1906 version, the picture shows six women in traditional "holiday" clothing and hairstyle, with the background out of focus. In this final version of the subject, Curtis made full use of the expressive possibilities of the photogravure process. Copper-plate engraving, in which the photographic image is transferred to a copper plate and light zones are etched away with acid, lends itself well to creating soft-edge "impressions" and rich tonal modulation. The 1921 picture differs from the 1906 version in that the composition is much stronger, and it makes a distinctive aesthetic statement about the relationship between the Indian women and the natural world. The figures are massed monumentally on the right bank of the water hole, their relationship to the water defined by the pottery water vessels perched at the edge of the pool. One woman reaches down to touch the still surface. Unlike the previous view, Curtis elevated and tilted his camera to make the most of the reflective properties of the water, to allow it to "embrace" the stone outcrop where the women stand and to enlarge its significance in the composition. Water collecting, the moment when mankind directly draws sustenance and relief from the wellspring of nature, had now become a sacred act worthy of monumental composition, rather than the pedestrian, everyday occurrence Curtis pictured in 1900.

The perfected "Curtis style" sought to capture not only the historical dress and appearance of his native subjects, but the relationship of the American Indian to the natural world itself. Neither one of these goals was without precedent in turn-of-the-century American culture. Both a scientific and an aesthetic tradition provided the context for Curtis' vision of the American Indian as prehistoric natural man in the pristine landscape.

THE STONE AGE PRESENT

Curtis' historical re-creation of pre-contact Native American culture was criticized from the outset for its inauthenticity. For instance, in 1907, upon the publication of the first volume, Columbia University anthropologist Franz Boas complained of Curtis' lack of objectivity to President Roosevelt, who had contributed an introduction to the volume.[11] Curtis' style of ethnography and photography differed dramatically from that of Boas, who also worked among the Northwest Coast Indian tribes. Unlike Curtis, Boas' ethnographic photographs and motion pictures were often

Edward S. Curtis
Gossip at the Water-Hole
Photogravure from *The North American Indian*, volume I, 1907
Yale Collection of Western Americana, Beinecke Rare Book and
Manuscript Library, Yale University, New Haven, Connecticut

Edward S. Curtis
Loitering at the Spring, 1921
Photogravure from *The North American Indian:
Large Plates Supplementing Volume XII*, 1922
Yale Collection of Western Americana, Beinecke Rare Book and
Manuscript Library, Yale University, New Haven, Connecticut

made against a backdrop that screened out the physical context of his subjects. By breaking the relationship between the individual and the landscape, Boas' photographic documents of the Northwest Coast Indians gave the appearance of ethnographic "objectivity," something which Curtis' pictures lacked. Placing the individual in the landscape, as Curtis did, required aesthetic decisions about whether to allow modern detail and dress. Covering up the background relieved the photographer from "filling in" missing cultural detail.

The differences between Boas the scientist and Curtis the artist ultimately stemmed from Curtis' interest in picturing the past rather than the present. To that end, Curtis eliminated modern details, such as those he took care to record in his earlier pictures; ethnographic facts got in the way of a good picture of native prehistory. While Curtis felt that *The North American Indian* would be important as an extensive and detailed documentary record, the large-plate images he selected for his portfolios stripped away these details in an attempt to synthesize a "typical" image.

Perhaps one reason for turn-of-the-century European-American culture's fascination with American Indians was emerging archaeological evidence that the subsistence technology and perhaps even the ceremonial culture of the European Paleolithic and Neolithic eras resembled that of pre-contact American Indians. In his introduction, Theodore Roosevelt described Curtis' Indian: "His life has been lived under conditions thru which our race past so many ages ago that not a vestige of their memory remains."[12] Evidently, the European-American fascination with Native Americans was, in part, a curiosity about its own distant past. Read in this way, Curtis' sepia-toned images peered into *all* prehistory. They were not only a recreation of Native American past, they were intended as comments upon collective human origins.

Curtis was not alone in using native subjects to recreate the vanished "stone-age" past. Taos artists Joseph Henry Sharp and Eanger Irving Couse, contemporaries of Curtis, posed Taos Pueblo Indians in traditional clothing, and painted them working at traditional tasks such as making pottery and arrowheads, and grinding corn meal. Like Curtis, these two Taos artists eliminated modern detail to create images of Indian people as they once were, before the influence of the white man. Another Western painter who used Indian subjects to consciously re-create prehistory was Maynard Dixon. Like Curtis, Dixon began picturing the West in documentary style, but his work developed a stylized, elemental character. Also like Curtis, he reduced his Indian figures to simple, massive forms as a way of emphasizing the connection to the earth. In *Paleolithic Afternoon* and *Earth-Knower*, Dixon emphasized the formal similarities of Southwestern Indians to the surrounding landscape — just as Curtis juxtaposed native figures with natural features, the formal connection implying a philosophical one.

Perhaps Curtis' most striking juxtapositions of man and landscape are found in photographs taken in Canyon de Chelly and Canyon del Muerto, on the Navajo reservation. In *Cañon de Chelly – Navaho* riders slowly pass weathered stone sentinels, following trails worn by their ancestors. Unlike the famous image taken of the scene by Wheeler expedition photographer Timothy O'Sullivan in 1873, Curtis pictures the canyon from ground level, and exposes the walls for dramatic effect rather than to capture geological detail. The figures are anonymous — a small band of Navajos walking their horses across the sandflats of the canyon stream. In this and other Southwestern views, Curtis rendered his subjects as forms rather than as individuals. Their anonymity accentuates their formal relationship with the landscape — his subjects are often literally "of the land." In other pictures, such as *Offering to the Sun – San Ildefonso, 1925*, a Pueblo worshiper draws his power from the rugged cliffs that both protect the villages and lift them to the sky. In *At the Old Well at Acoma*, 1904, a Keres woman is presented as an indistinct, dark form in a tone similar to the dark well walls. In these landscape views, Curtis' subjects echo the natural world and are thus in harmony with it.

INDIANS AND ARCADIA

Curtis' portrayal of the natural harmony of the American Indian with the landscape reflects broader Arcadian themes in late nineteenth century Romanticism. These themes in turn provide the key to understanding many of Curtis' aesthetic choices. Curtis used setting, pose, and costume to create a primeval vision of European-Americans' own antiquity. Viewers of Curtis' Indians were transported back to an imagined, idyllic moment in their own cultural past. Evidently, part of the appeal of *The North American Indian* to New York society was that the photographer explicitly contrasted the "natural" world of the American Indian with the "commercial" world of his patrons. In his general introduction to volume I, Curtis wrote:

It is thus nearer to Nature that much of Indian life still is; hence its story, rather than being replete with the statistics of commercial conquests, is a record of the Indian's relations with and his dependence on the phenomena of the universe – the trees and shrubs, the sun and stars, the lightning and the rain – for these are to him animate objects.

Volume I of *The North American Indian* focuses heavily on the theme of Indians in the natural landscape. In many ways, the volume represents Curtis' most striking work. It contains images

taken on his trip to Arizona and New Mexico Territory in 1906 —
the first Curtis field season financed by a check from Pierpont
Morgan. Rather than depict Apache and neighboring Mohave
Indians of the Southwest as fierce warriors, Curtis produced
archetypal pictures of mankind in the state of nature. As such,
these images must have been jarring to his audience, raised on
scenes of bloodthirsty Apache marauders. For the caption to the
large-plate photogravure *The Apache*, Curtis wrote:

*This picture might be entitled, 'Life Primeval.' It is the Apache as we
would mentally picture him in the Stone Age. It was made at a point on
the Blood River, Arizona, where the dark, still pool breaks into the
laugh of rapids.*

The picture's caption helps us understand Curtis' landscape
iconography. Curtis shows an Apache man, clothed only in a loin-
cloth and hat, poised between past and present. He stands at the
brink of a "dark, still pool," signifying the Indian past. That era
has come to an end, as the water pours out of the pond into a
rapid — which presumably signifies cultural change. The figure is
turned toward the past, away from the viewer, the reflective surface of the deep pool signifying the subject's state of mind.[13]

In his quest to create Arcadian idylls, Curtis deliberately
chose landscape settings in volumes I and II that contradicted
stereotypes of the arid Southwestern desert. A substantial proportion of the photographs (excluding portraits) uses bodies of water
as major compositional elements. Plates such as *The Pool —
Apache*, *The Mohave*, *The Bathing Pool*, and *Nature's Mirror* create a
sense of the desert lands as a country with leafy bowers, quiet
pools, and tranquil springs, each a sharp contrast to the popular
images of the Arizona desert as a setting for fights between the
US Cavalry and the Indians, painted by Western artists such as
Frederic Remington, Charles Schreyvogel, or Henry Farney.

By the time Curtis began posing his views of scantily clad
Indians in the virgin landscape, there was already a strong tradition of Arcadian photography and painting in American art. In
the 1880s, Thomas Eakins, for instance, made nude photographs
of his students in the Pennsylvania countryside with Arcadian
props such as pan-pipes.[14] Some of these became the basis for his
famous painting *The Swimming Hole* (1884–85), in which an
unspoiled natural pond sets the stage for Eakins and his male
friends, who strip off their clothes — the accoutrements of civilization — and celebrate the beauty of nature. Curtis' Apache subjects
embodied the Whitmanesque ideal — they enjoyed the "Sweet,
sane still nakedness in Nature."[15]

While Eakins was somewhat of an outcast in American art,
re-creations of Arcadia eventually became central to American
artistic culture in the first decade of this century. Perhaps the

Edward S. Curtis
The Apache, 1906
Photogravure from
The North American Indian: Large Plates Supplementing Volume I, 1907
Yale Collection of Western Americana, Beinecke Rare Book and
Manuscript Library, Yale University, New Haven, Connecticut

most elaborate re-creation of the Arcadian past took place at an artist's colony in Cornish, New Hampshire, in 1905, when the group enacted "Masque of 'Ours,' the Gods and the Golden Bowl," a Neoclassical dress-up featuring many of the leading artists of day, including painters George de Forest Brush, Thomas Dewing, Henry Fuller, and Maxfield Parrish.[16] The Cornish colonists photographed themselves dressed as Greek gods and goddesses posing in the beautiful New Hampshire countryside to celebrate sculptor Augustus Saint-Gauden's twentieth anniversary at the colony. The masque celebrated more than their well-known founder, however. It celebrated the Arcadian theme that American artists had long projected onto American Indians. In these and similar Neoclassical *tableaux vivants* enacted by the Cornish colonists, the artists shed the trappings of modern society and donned garb evocative of an ancient, primeval past — perhaps as enthusiastically as Curtis' Indian subjects had stripped off their modern clothing and put on traditional costumes, evoking a simpler period in their own cultural history. The Arcadian views posed by Edward Curtis, using Native American subjects, were strikingly similar in theme to the Neoclassical masque and *tableaux vivants* created by turn-of-the-century artists using themselves as subjects. Like other artists of his time, Curtis was probing the relationship between man and nature — only he was able to use models who knew something about the subject.

THE FATE OF THE NORTH AMERICAN INDIAN

The twentieth and final volume of *The North American Indian* was published in 1930. Curtis had enjoyed wide acclaim at the outset of this mammoth undertaking, but by the time it was completed, he was virtually unknown. The stock market crash of 1929 frightened away many potential customers, as the prices for virtually all art, even masterpieces, dropped precipitously at the end of the 1920s.[17] In 1935, the bound and unbound copies of the book, along with the copper plates used for production were sold to Charles E. Lauriat, a rare book dealer in Boston. Curtis' picture of American Indian life, developed so passionately and thoroughly, appears to have fallen out of fashion, at least until the revival of interest in Curtis' work in the 1970s. After 1930, Curtis suffered from nervous exhaustion, a condition that ended his career as an Indian photographer. He tried his hand at gold mining, with little success, and continued to work intermittently as a cinematographer, shooting some motion picture scenes in 1936 for Gary Cooper's *The Plainsman*. Upon his death in 1952, *The New York Times* noted simply that he was known as a photographer.[18]

The North American Indian was first lauded as the final document of a vanishing race, and then harshly criticized for its romanticization of American Indians. Since its rediscovery twenty-five years ago, it has continued to elicit strongly contrasting opinions.[19] Despite controversy over their value as cultural documents, Curtis' romantic images of American Indians are widely collected and admired. A single set of *The North American Indian* is now worth roughly twice the entire investment in it made by the Morgan family. Curtis has been decried by Native Americans for "lying" about early twentieth-century American Indian culture and also admired for preserving elements of Indian culture and images of ancestors that would otherwise have gone unrecorded.[20] Perhaps these very disagreements attest to his enduring power as an artist. Regardless of their authenticity, Curtis' images of the American Indian are indelibly imprinted on the American imagination.

(I would like to thank Alfred Bush, William H. Goetzmann, George Miles, and William Reese for helpful conversations on this topic.)

1. For an account of the evening, see Barbara A. Davis, *Edward S. Curtis: The Life and Times of a Shadow Catcher* (San Francisco: Chronicle Books, 1985), p. 40.

2. See Curtis' Hopi photographs in the Beinecke Rare Book and Manuscript Library, Yale University, New Haven, Connecticut.

3. Alex Groner, *The American Heritage History of American Business and Industry* (New York: The American Heritage Publishing Company, 1972), p. 200.

4. See Rachel Sherman Thorndike, ed., *The Sherman Letters: Correspondence Between General and Senator Sherman* (New York: 1894), p. 320, quoted in William H. and William N. Goetzmann, *The West of the Imagination* (New York: W.W. Norton and Company, 1986), p. 204.

5. See Alfred L. Bush and Lee Clark Mitchell, *The Photograph and the American Indian* (Princeton, New Jersey: Princeton University Press, 1994), p. xviii.

6. See Davis, *Edward S. Curtis*, p. 44.

7. Ibid., p. 45.

8. Ibid., p. 75.

9. Edward S. Curtis, "Photographs of Hopi Indians," Beinecke Rare Book and Manuscript Library, Yale University, New Haven, Connecticut, exposure no. 750.

10. See Christopher Lyman, *The Vanishing Race and Other Illusions* (New York: Pantheon Books, 1982), p. 76.

11. See William H. Goetzmann, *The First Americans: Photographs from the Library of Congress* (Washington, D.C.: Starwood Publishing, 1991), p. 22.

12. Theodore Roosevelt, "Introduction," in *Edward S. Curtis, The North American Indian*, vol. I (Cambridge, Massachusetts: The University Press, 1907).

13. There is little doubt that Curtis used pictorial depth in his landscape views to signify the dimension of time. He tells us as much in the caption to the first large plate of volume I in which Indians are riding into the sunset. As Curtis put it, the figures are "passing into the darkness of an unknown future...."

14. See Gordon Hendricks, *The Photographs of Thomas Eakins* (New York: 1972), pl. 45.

15. Quoted in Lloyd Goodrich, *Thomas Eakins*, vol. I (Cambridge, Massachusetts: Harvard University Press, 1982), p. 230.

16. See John H. Dryphout, "The Cornish Colony," in *A Circle of Friends: Art Colonies of Cornish and Dublin*, exh. cat. (Durham, New Hampshire: The University Art Galleries, 1985), p. 52.

17. See William N. Goetzmann, "Accounting for Taste: Art and the Financial Markets over Three Centuries," *The American Economic Review*, 5, no. 83 (1993), pp. 1370–76.

18. Davis, *Edward S. Curtis*, p. 79.

19. For two perspectives on Curtis' photographs as ethnographic documents, see Lyman, *The Vanishing Race*, and the review of Lyman's book by William Holm in *American Indian Art Magazine*, 8 (Summer 1983), pp. 68–73.

20. For two Native American scholars' perspectives on Curtis, see George P. Horse Capture, "Foreword," in Christopher Cardozo, ed., *Native Nations: First Americans as Seen by Edward S. Curtis*, (Boston: Bulfinch Press, 1993), and Vine Deloria, Jr., "Introduction," in Lyman, *The Vanishing Race*.

—1601—
TOP OF KATZIMO

MESA, CAÑON AND PUEBLO
BY CHARLES FLETCHER LUMMIS

KEVIN STARR

"The tourist guide"

In 1925 the Century Company of New York published *Mesa, Cañon and Pueblo*, with text and nearly one hundred photographs by Charles Fletcher Lummis, with additional photography by Carl Oscar Borg, Adam Clark Vroman, Ben Wittick, and others. A long book, 517 pages, it selectively incorporated the literary and photographic gatherings of Lummis' forty-year involvement in the Spanish Southwest. Some of the essays had initially appeared in Lummis' first important work, *Some Strange Corners of Our Country: The Wonderland of the Southwest* (1892), an earlier treatment of the subject also published by Century, or in Lummis' *The Land of Poco Tiempo* (1893), published by Charles Scribner's Sons. Other essays incorporated material first presented in Lummis' turn-of-the-century Los Angeles magazine, *Land of Sunshine* (*Out West* after 1902), which Lummis energetically edited and sometimes almost totally composed as a vehicle for the development of Los Angeles as capital city of the Spanish Southwest: "the lands of the sun," as the motto of the magazine phrased it, "[which] expand the soul."

Mesa, Cañon and Pueblo appeared in the midst of a decade when the imaginative presence of the Spanish Southwest — as hinterland, as appropriated heritage, as a metaphor for design and for lifestyle — was transforming, as Lummis had long hoped it would, greater Los Angeles, indeed much of Southern California, into a Spanish S___ theme park. Throughout Sou___ ___ Santa Barbara, Pasadena, and ___ ___ ___lemente, and San Diego — a ___ ___ ___giving Lummis' Spanish Sou___ ___ n and a name. By the time ___ ___thern California architectu___ ___ past anchored in the Spani___ ___d metaphor — which

precursor of L.6's books

possessed the cumulative force of a shaping myth that has survived to this day. In a steady stream of books, articles, and published photographs; in his personal lifestyle at his stone hacienda El Alisal on the Pasadena Arroyo, which he built himself and where he presided as Don Carlos, dressed in a *charro* suit of emerald green wide-wale corduroy and the red sash of the Old Spanish Southwest; in his efforts to preserve the California missions and to establish the Museum of the Southwest on the Arroyo — Charles Fletcher Lummis, Don Carlos to his friends, had fulfilled a mission he first received as a student at Harvard in the late 1870s, when professor of art history Charles Eliot Norton taught his classes to make the past real, make it come alive, put it into context, and, above all else, preserve the American heritage.

Born in Massachusetts in 1859, Charles Fletcher Lummis belonged to a generation of college-trained Easterners (prominent among them was another Harvard man, Lummis' lifelong friend Theodore Roosevelt) who sought renewal through the strenuous life and an imaginative relationship to the vanishing frontier. At Harvard, Norton approached art as the most important recoverable aspect of history. Artistic expression, he taught — poetry, music, painting, architecture, sculpture, metalwork, textile design — idealized and preserved the best energies of a given period. Europe-oriented in his scholarship and Bostonian in his culture, Norton nevertheless looked out to the great American continent, place, and people, as a source of landscape, myth, and legends, which, properly perceived, need make no apologies to Europe. He knew his Dante as well as his Ralph Waldo Emerson and James Russell Lowell. He mastered the architecture of the Middle Ages, but he also appreciated the American forest and the archaeological record of Native American civilization. He helped preserve Niagara Falls from commercial exploitation and served as one of the founders of the Archaeological Institute of America, an organization pioneering the concept that American antiquities were deserving of recovery and preservation. All these lessons Charles Fletcher Lummis pondered in his heart. Very soon, the Spanish Southwest would release them into significant action.

Graduating from Harvard, Lummis turned to journalism. All his life, Lummis would write with the crisp accuracy and terse

Charles Lummis
Top of Katzimo, 1898
Variation of *David Starr Jordan and Party, with the Author, on Summit of the Enchanted Mesa*, 1898
From Lummis, *Mesa, Cañon and Pueblo . . .* , 1925
The Southwest Museum, Los Angeles

Charles Lummis
A Castle on the Rhine? No – an American Ruin:
The Franciscan Church at Abó, N.M., Deserted 1670
Photoengraving from Lummis, *Mesa, Cañon and Pueblo . . . ,* 1925
Library Collection, Whitney Museum of American Art, New York

descriptive power of a skilled journalist. He moved to Chillicothe, Ohio, with his wife Dorothea Roads, a practicing physician, where he edited the *Scioto Gazette* for a few years. He then began to show signs of deteriorating health brought on by the fact that he was, simultaneously, a workaholic and a bounder, given to booze, cigarettes, and a degree of amorous intrigue that, combined with overwork, frequently left him distraught and exhausted. In September 1884, having accepted an offer from publisher Harrison Gray Otis to serve as city editor on the *Los Angeles Times*, Lummis decided to regain his health and to see America first (a slogan he would practically invent) by walking from Ohio to Southern California. It took him 112 days to walk the 3,507 miles, and the resulting travelogue, *A Tramp Across the Continent* (1892), gave proof positive that Charles Fletcher Lummis had found his lifelong theme and métier in the Spanish Southwest.

Here, Lummis discovered, was a region touched by a great drama of landscape and by an equally heroic heritage of history extending back to the Spanish explorers of the sixteenth and seventeenth centuries and, even more ancient, to the Pueblo Indian cultures whose origins, in European terms, were at the least medieval, if not patristic. Sunlight and land forms; mesa, canyon, and desert; pueblo cities of uncertain antiquity; ranch life in the haciendas of New Mexicans whose ancestors had arrived with the conquistadores; Native American communities which, in their simplicity and dignity, their rituals and social structures, seem to have stepped from the pages of a North American *Iliad* or *Odyssey.* Here was a world gloriously proving Norton's assertion that the American continent, American antiquities, and American art were comparable in meaning and aesthetic effect to the best Europe had to offer.

As city editor of the *Los Angeles Times*, Lummis slipped back into his Ohio habits of dissipation and overwork. In 1885 he returned to the Southwest to cover the Apache revolt led by Geronimo in the Arizona Badlands. Resting briefly at the Santa Fe hacienda of Don Manuel Antonio Chaves, Lummis found himself enchanted by the personal civility and dignified lifestyle of this borderland patriarch. Much of the tone and feeling of Old Spain, Lummis believed, survived in the Chaves household, modified by a three-century sojourn in the Southwestern borderlands, where Spain had encountered, and to a certain extent intermingled with, the highly developed Hopi, Navajo, and Zuni cultures. Once again, the lessons of Charles Eliot Norton took hold of Lummis' mind and imagination. In the homes of Santa Fe, especially in the Chaves hacienda, Lummis felt himself in the palpable presence of a past art surviving in altar paintings, *santos,* silver candlesticks mule-packed from Mexico City two centuries earlier, as well as in a thousand daily objects — plates, bowls,

combs, saddlery — all demonstrating an inner coherence of culture, an internal sense of identity that graced life with ritual and
touched all that was said or done with the transforming presence
of tradition.

In 1887 Lummis returned to the Southwest for a third
sojourn: not this time, however, as a dashing reporter for the
Times eager to cover the clash of cavalry bluecoats and Apaches,
but as a near-blind paralytic, felled by the stroke he had long been
courting through dissipation. Returning to the Rancho San
Mateo of his good friend Don Manuel Antonio Chaves, Lummis
was in a terrible state. He had to be pushed around the ranch in a
wheelbarrow. After three long years of patient effort, supported
by Don Manuel and befriended by the Don's son Amado
(returned to New Mexico after taking a law degree in Washington, D.C.), Lummis recovered his eyesight and mobility. It took
him nearly a year to be able to sit atop a horse, he claimed in
My Friend Will (1911), a later account of his stroke and self-rehabil-
itation.

In August 1888, toward the end of his recovery period,
Lummis made fast friends with the great archaeologist and ethnologist Adolph F.A. Bandelier, to whom he attached himself for
the next four years as secretary, research assistant, general facto-
tum, and devoted disciple. In Bandelier's company, Lummis fully
regained his health (5 feet, 7 inches, he boasted, as sinewy and
agile as a panther) as well as absorbing a crash course in archaeology and ethnology. Together, they explored Pueblo cultures in
the vastness of the Pajarito Plateau west of Santa Fe. Lummis kept
his 5 x 8 view camera and glass plates tucked into a knapsack on
his back, schlepped the heavy tripod under his one good arm up
and down pathless cliffs and tangled canyons, and forded icy
streams and ankle-deep sands. Most important, Lummis produced in this period a substantial portion of the ten thousand
glass-plate negatives he would expose in his career as a photographer. In 1892, he accompanied Bandelier to Bolivia and Peru,
where he confirmed his complete physical recovery with a record
ascent of El Misti, a 19,000-foot volcano above Arequipa.

Lummis' *Some Strange Corners of Our Country: The Wonderland of the Southwest* is essentially the first version of *Mesa, Cañon
and Pueblo* (1925). *Some Strange Corners of Our Country*, however,
was not illustrated with photographs by Lummis but with forty
of the elegant wood engravings, based on Lummis' photographs,
for which *Century* magazine was famous. Each book opens with a
plea embodied in the slogan "See America First," a theme significantly expanded in *Mesa, Cañon and Pueblo*. (In the earlier volume,
Lummis provided train routes. In *Mesa, Cañon and Pueblo* he
included a map of the newly constructed highway system.) The
first photograph in *Mesa, Cañon and Pueblo*, that of the ruins of

Charles Lummis
A Detail of the Grand Cañon, 6,000 feet – from River to Rim
Photoengraving from Lummis, *Mesa, Cañon and Pueblo . . .* , 1925
Library Collection, Whitney Museum of American Art, New York

Charles Lummis
The Penitente Crucifixion, San Mateo, 1888. The Black-Hooded Figure at the
Foot of the Cross Is Lying on a Bed of Buckhorn Cactus, 1888
Photoengraving from Lummis, *Mesa, Cañon and Pueblo . . . ,* 1925
Library Collection, Whitney Museum of American Art, New York

A.C. Vroman
A Moqui Coiffure — Doing Up the Virgin Squash-Blossom
Photoengraving from Lummis, *Mesa, Cañon and Pueblo . . . ,* 1925
Library Collection, Whitney Museum of American Art, New York

the Franciscan church at Abo, New Mexico, abandoned in 1670, visually reinforces Lummis' central theme: the Southwest is soaked through with history. "In New Mexico alone," Lummis wrote, "to this day the ruins of the old Franciscan churches and monasteries at Tabira, Abo, Cuarai, Pecos, Giusewa, San Felipe, Santa Clara, Taos, and Acoma (still used, though the monastery is partly in ruins) — these nine temples, if they were in Europe, would be each a household word and a pilgrimage."[1] Lummis next plunged into a description of the Grand Canyon of Arizona so as to establish the second polarity of the Southwest: nature in all its glory, the matrix for the archaeological and human environment. Emphasizing as they do the geological forces that shaped the gigantic gorge, Lummis' photographs of the Grand Canyon are among the best of their era. Indeed, the landscape photography throughout *Mesa, Cañon and Pueblo* is superb, and Lummis deserves more recognition than he has received for his skills as a landscape photographer.

Yet it was rarely nature alone that captured Lummis' eye. He preferred, rather, nature in the human context: the rise of a pueblo city against a canyon wall, as if the settlement itself were a natural creation; El Morro, Inscription Rock, etched with three centuries of Spanish inscriptions (beginning with one made in 1605 by the great colonizer himself, Juan de Oñate), which Lummis presents in a series of skillful close-ups and annotations. One photograph — of Lummis, Stanford University president David Starr Jordan, and their party on the summit of the Enchanted Mesa — is especially revealing in its juxtaposition of the great Southwestern desert spreading below and the urban-attired visitors. (There is at least one derby hat.) The photograph juxtaposes the grandeur of the Spanish Southwest with the presence of urban intellectuals for whom the region offers the last great American territory awaiting interpretation. The lithic archive at El Morro gave Lummis an opportunity to discuss the epic of Spanish exploration and travel in the Southwest in the seventeenth and eighteenth centuries, thus strengthening even further the historical dimension of his argument. Long before American independence, Lummis argued, and visually documented through photography, ancient pueblo civilizations had arisen in this region, possessed of millennial antiquity; and during the Renaissance and Enlightenment, Spanish soldiers and at least one bishop, Don Martin de Elizacochea, had ventured north from Mexico to leave a record of their presence on a strategically sited rock in the midst of a barely explored wilderness.

As a matter of both argument and visual imagery, Lummis' description and photography of the *Penitente* crucifixion rites in San Mateo, New Mexico, on Holy Thursday and Good Friday 1888 bear the most explicit burden of the Europe-Spanish Southwest comparison that was always at work in Lummis' reportage. The comparison, most obviously, is to the Passion Play of Ober- ammergau, enacted every decade since 1633. The *Penitentes,* or Penitent Brothers, were a cult which took root in New Mexico in the seventeenth century. One ritual pushed the reenactment of the Crucifixion to bizarre levels since a *Penitente* was actually cru- cified. Using a great Dalmeyer lens and Prosch shutter and glass negatives, Lummis photographed the ritual, despite the warnings of the Chaves family that the *Penitentes* would kill anyone who wit- nessed it. Lummis photographed the first phase of these illicit rites, explicitly condemned by the Church, with two .44 pistols loaded and at the ready. That was Holy Thursday. Thanks to the intervention of Don Manuel, the Hermano Mayor (Chief Brother) of the *Penitentes* allowed Lummis to photograph the actual crucifixion the next day, March 30, 1888, without fear for his personal safety. "I was the first to bring the astonishing practices of the *Penitentes* to the notice of the world," Lummis justifiably boasted, "and to this day no one else has ever succeeded in pho- tographing their supreme rites."[2]

In a similar way, Lummis visualized and presented the Native Americans of this region in the context of European analogues. In a photograph by A.C. Vroman, a nursing mother becomes a Moqui Madonna. The Moqui snake dance, which Lummis wit- nessed in 1891 and illustrated with photographs by Carl Oscar Borg and Ben Wittick, was an even more ancient ritual than the crucifixion of the *Penitentes.* Moqui hair fashions, especially the coiffure affected by unmarried women, compare with the elabo- rate styles of the European past. "How remote they seem," eulo- gized Lummis of the Moqui people, "farther in centuries than their cliff-perched home in miles from our Civilization! Back to the time of Abraham and the Patriarchal simplicities and sinceri- ties — back even farther to primitive Sanity!"[3]

Lummis' photographs of the Moqui, Navajo, and Hopi, espe- cially the individual portraits, are triumphs of technical skill and humanistic sympathy. Lummis would later publish many of these photographs in *Land of Sunshine/Out West,* using them to prove that the Native American of the Southwest was a dignified and thoroughly coping citizen of the American Republic — and not, as some claimed, a dependent ward of government. He was especial- ly offended by the philosophy behind the Carlisle Indian School in Pennsylvania: namely, that Native Americans, of whatever tribal background, should be extracted from their communities and generically refashioned into mainstream citizens.

For *Mesa, Cañon and Pueblo,* Lummis selected some of the best of his many portraits. Martin Valle, seven times governor of Acoma, poses grandly in a colored blanket that has all the dignity of a Roman toga. Faustin, war captain of Acoma, poses in a gar- den patch, hoe in hand, a centurion turned to peaceful purposes. At the Isleta Pueblo, a woman combs out the long hair of her hus- band, the two of them sitting in the sun, a chubby and healthy child nearby. In another photograph, Lummis captured the sim- ple dignity of an Isleta Pueblo interior: the beds covered by pat- terned blankets, the massy adobe walls, the household utensils arrayed neatly in the corner.

Mesa, Cañon and Pueblo represents the culmination of Lummis' life and work. Forty years earlier, he had found in the Southwest the métier and theme for a lifetime: the Spanish Southwest as the psychological and moral equivalent of Europe. Charles Eliot Norton had first alerted him to such possibilities. Adolph F.A. Bandelier had helped Lummis anchor this awareness in archaeology and historical scholarship. A lifetime of writing had further wedded Lummis to the region. But it was primarily through the camera that Charles Fletcher Lummis saw and re- covered the Southwest most vividly and with the most artistic success. Whatever else he was — journalist, scholar, librarian, preservationist, promoter — Lummis was first and foremost a pio- neer photographer. Camera at the ready, he saw the Spanish Southwest in the last lingering days of wilderness and ancient human glory.

1. Charles F. Lummis, *Mesa, Cañon and Pueblo* (New York and London: The Century Company, 1925), pp. 12–13.

2. Ibid., p. 127.

3. Ibid., p. 158.

J. Smeaton Chase
Sunset and the Sentinel, n.d.
From Van Dyke, *The Desert: Further Studies in Natural Appearances*, c. 1918
Gelatin silver print, 3⅛ x 5½ (7.9 x 14)
Palm Springs Desert Museum, California

A PLEASANT FELLOW IN A NOT SO PLEASANT PLACE: J. SMEATON CHASE AND HIS TRAIL OF GOOD NATURE

PATRICIA NELSON LIMERICK AND SHARYN WILEY YEOMAN

Individuals who have found little to like in the human race have often found a lot to like in the desert. The terms "misanthrope" and "desert-lover" tend to be used as synonyms, with the appeal of the desert lying in the comparative sparseness of the presence of the planet's most active and insistent large mammal. But the example of the California writer J. Smeaton Chase proves that human-hating and desert-loving do not necessarily overlap. Attracted and inspired by the desert, Chase also found a great deal to like in his fellow human beings, and they found a great deal to like in him. While he "felt the magic, the magnetism of the old, wonderful desert," he was not, by that count, a misanthrope. Moreover, Chase's declared "love" for his "fellow men" did not come with racial or ethnic clauses of exclusion. Indian and Mexican people found room within the reach of his fellow feeling.[1]

Born in England in 1864, Chase in his late twenties traveled to the California coast. He took up settlement-house work, affiliating himself with the Bethlehem Institutional Church, which ministered to workers in Los Angeles. His first book, *Yosemite Trails*, was published in 1911 when he was forty-seven, and he moved to Palm Springs the next year. Marrying into a prominent local family, Chase spent the remainder of his life in the desert.

Misanthropes, as a rule, make poor guests and unpleasant visitors. By contrast, the roles of guest and visitor were ones in which Chase excelled. If his book *California Desert Trails* offered evidence of the harsh and difficult nature of arid lands, it also offered a record of Chase's own good nature. His four-month circuit of the Colorado Desert, undertaken in the summer of 1918, followed a loop south from Palm Springs, through California's Colorado Desert to the Colorado River at Yuma, and back to the west and north through the Coachella Valley. At various spots along that trail, Chase visited and chatted his way through terrain that others would think of as essentially uninhabited.

The hardship of desert travel, in fact, made Chase a connoisseur of hospitality, and he responded gratefully to gifts of food, shelter, and conversation. Conversation was a reciprocal gift between host and visitor. With hospitable people along his way,

Chase shared "their supper and breakfast, as well as [their] hopes, trials, and prospects. . . ." Stopping to see a friend's date plantation, Chase found his friend "absent, but the jolly young Canadian foreman and a delightful Mexican family who worked on the place made my stay pleasant and profitable."[2] Although comfortable with solitude and his own company, Chase recorded a variety of pleasant and instructive meetings with prospectors, miners, farmers, irrigation-developers, traders, ranchers, freighters, land-boomers, Indian village-dwellers, Mexican workers, and townspeople. He thus drew a portrait of arid lands that came fully supplied with human beings, their ambitions, their stories, their material artifacts, and their acts of hospitality and hope.

Chase's desert was not, in other words, deserted. He regularly encountered both humans and the evidence of their activity. All along the route, he bought hay and feed for his pony, Kaweah, to supplement the sparse forage. Chase and Kaweah drank at wells and tanks maintained from antiquity to the present by human hands. He walked along the railroad near the Colorado River. He passed near the highway between San Diego and El Centro, and his remarks anticipated later irritation with traffic. "Automobiles were common," he said, "and soon became a nuisance with their obscene noises and the clouds of dust they gave in return for the right of way." Chase made several prolonged stays in desert towns. With its lively and varied population of Indians, Mexicans, and Anglos, the town of Yuma might have been "scorned by people devoted to progress," but Chase reached another judgment. "Altogether," he said, "Yuma comes near my idea of a model town."[3]

Chase's tolerance and good nature earned him the license to be an intelligent critic of the habits of his own species. He was forthright in his condemnation of white American behavior toward Indians and Mexicans. Refused permission to camp near an Indian home, he described this as "the only time I have been denied at an Indian's, but I could not complain, for the Indian had good reason to be suspicious of white strangers." Referring to certain sites where Indians had recently lived, he concluded:

J. Smeaton Chase
In Thousand-Palm Cañon, n.d.
From *California Desert Trails*, 1919
Gelatin silver print, 3⅜₆ x 5½ (8.1 x 14)
Palm Springs Desert Museum, California

"when I come on these abandoned settlements of the Indians, at places where they would no doubt have wished to remain, I take them for links in an old but lengthening chain of wrong." Welcomed by "a kindly Mexican family" living near the Colorado River, he "experienced again the courtesy of these often underrated people." A few days later, he came upon a clearing where a family of Mexicans had once grown corn. But a white settler had not only "ousted" the Mexicans, he proved distinctly their inferiority in the practice of hospitality: "I could not help wishing that the 'damned greasers,' as [the white settler] termed the late occupiers, had been my hosts. Anglo-Saxon superiority has sometimes to be taken for granted."[4]

Chase was troubled, as well, by the qualities of the farming society that whites had created on the land they had taken from Indians and developed, often with Mexican labor. While remarkable in its successes, Imperial Valley farming carried "special drawbacks," manifested in "the slipshod appearance of the farm buildings" and in the odd imbalances of population, as white women followed the habit of spending the summers "inside," in the cooler areas west of the coastal range. Thus, the desert held "a larger percentage than usual of farmers who are unmarried, or whose womenkind do not live, at least continuously, on the farm: and without women the home can hardly be." In this appraisal and others, Chase purposefully distanced himself from the declarations preferred by boosters and boomers. Chase told various desert boosters: "I did not, could not, and would not boom; was, in fact, even averse to booms and boomers; and was more enthralled by desert sunsets than by desert dairies, astounding as these might be." The "mind of the land-boomer," Chase remarked in a judgment shared by many observers of the American West, "is one of the last puzzles that philosophy will solve."[5]

The relics of human history that Chase found in the desert served as powerful reminders of the impermanence of human enterprise. At watering places, he encountered the trash of generations of campers; pottery shards mixed with broken bottles and tin cans. Pieces of pottery seemed, in truth, to be everywhere; "I have often been surprised," Chase said, "at meeting these evidences of bygone populations in the most unlikely places." Petroglyphs testified to the long duration of human occupation. White settlement had left an equally rich collection of ruins: abandoned houses, abandoned stage stations, abandoned railroad tracks, abandoned roads, and, perhaps most notably, abandoned mines, which far outnumbered operating and producing mines. "Mining camps are in their nature evanescent," Chase observed. "The historian of a mining camp must be early on the scene if he is to find anything more than the ground on which it stood."[6]

Even places that looked perfectly vacant turned out to hold

the imprint of human action and memory. Desert emptiness, Chase proved repeatedly, was often in the mind of the beholder. He self-consciously walked and rode in the footsteps of Juan Bautista de Anza, who had led a Spanish party in overland travel to California, and of Francisco Garces, the Spanish friar whose killing by Yuma Indians in 1781 shut down the overland route between northern Mexico and coastal California. Chase followed the path taken by General Stephen W. Kearney and his troops as they traveled, during the Mexican-American War, to their defeat at the battlefield of San Pascual. He noted the routes of the Mormon Battalion, the Gold Rush overland travelers on the southern trail, and the Butterfield Overland Stage line. He came upon remote desert graves, and he heard many stories of men who died of thirst in the desert, men who had, as one desert veteran phrased it, "gone in and stayed."[7]

Chase also traveled through terrain in which humans were invisible and irrelevant. Sometimes this was a matter of exhilaration for him, and sometimes it was a matter of terror. When both foreground and background offered only bare rock, sand, and sparse foliage, the fact that one had spent the night before at a settler's cabin or in an Indian village did not necessarily reduce one's sense of isolation. When the horizon offered only the skeletal outline of a desert mountain or the unbordered spread of a sand basin, yesterday's indications that humans were a vital presence in the desert yielded to today's evidence that humans were nowhere and nothing. In those settings, "the life of towns, of farms, all that signifies humanity, seems totally unreal."[8] Since no writer has ever been more attentive to the human presence in deserts than J. Smeaton Chase, there is particular power in his descriptions of landscapes where the human presence on the planet was entirely invisible.

In contrast to his often evocative words, Chase's photographs were far less subtle. He intended them to appeal to people like himself and thus used no props, no lighting techniques other than the sun, no staging, and no composition except nature's arrangements. "This," the viewer thinks, "is what *I* would have seen if I had been there myself." Chase's purpose in putting images on film was to dispel ignorance, not to create it. His landscapes registered in the photographic record as his eyes took them in; plants and animals appeared in their native surroundings, not isolated like the specimen collections of a scientific expert. Attempting to persuade Americans to reconsider their negative impressions of the desert, Chase presented them with appealing palm-studded canyons hidden in the arid regions, with the incredible beauty and life-sustaining value of water, and the fantastic and variable adaptability of plants and animals. This clear look at reality was an assertion of the worth of arid land, in

J. Smeaton Chase
A Sidewinder Ready for Business, n.d.
From *California Desert Trails*, 1919
Gelatin silver print, 3¼ x 5½ (8.3 x 14)
Palm Springs Desert Museum, California

and of itself. Chase carried bulky, fragile, and awkward photographic equipment at considerable risk to himself, for it took up space that would otherwise have been used for food, water, or forage for his horse. The imperative of showing his beloved desert overrode his concern for his own safety and comfort.

The photograph *In Thousand-Palm Cañon* evokes Egypt and Arabia. The oasis, source of water and life, looks lush in comparison to the monumental and even monstrous scale of the desert. The scene contains both the familiar threats of arid landscape and the Edenic enchantment of a concealed garden. Interpretation of the imagery, in this case or any other, was not left to chance — Chase wrote exuberantly about the pleasure of oases. The thirty-five images accompany 378 pages of text, with the photographs forming a part of the new terms of expression Chase used to grasp this unusual place. The frontispiece, *At Two-Bunch Palms: San Gorgonio Mountain in the Distance*, stands as an allegory for the journey. Through the beautiful snow-capped peak interrupting the horizon, the arid vastness of the middle ground, the familiar palms, and the loyal horse-companion, the photograph draws the viewer into the encounter. In both photos and words, Chase combined celebration with warning. Captioning cholla cactus "the vilest of the vile," he gave danger, pain, and mishap a physical form. Similarly, the sidewinder he photographed emanated from the page at its most threatening, coiled and striking with fangs visible. These figures suggest the incompatibility of comfort with the desert. Pilgrims in this landscape necessarily faced ordeals in the search for a relationship between people and the earth.

Chase's own ordeals tested the limits of his spirit, love of the land, and good will. If he knew where he was going or, more precisely, if he knew where and when he would find water, then he could contemplate the landscape with interest and appreciation. In desert canyons and washes, for instance, Chase could trace the origins of the land forms, noting the clearly marked sculpting powers of water and wind. Thus, in many passages, Chase was enjoying the adventurous life of the geological detective, tracking clues to the mysteries of the origins of the desert's rocky landscape. The pleasures of curiosity were matched by an appreciation of the shapes and colors of forms.

In just as many passages, however, both the detective's inquiry and the aesthete's appreciation collapsed, curiosity went dead, and Chase's odyssey became a nervous trek from oasis to oasis. In Carrizo Creek Canyon, he traveled through "pale, ashy hills" that "looked the very stronghold of drought," with "a scattering of drab brush only serving to mark their ugliness and hopeless aridity." The misery was not limited to afflictions imposed on the eye: "The loose sand made the hardest kind of going, and the sun dealt its fiercest stroke."[9] As one reads Chase's vivid descriptions of slogging through a repellent landscape at the peak of summer heat, it is startling to remember that he was immersing himself in misery out of desire, not necessity. At any moment, he could have interrupted and ended the journey with the simple admission, "This is too hot, too exhausting, too miserable, and, much of the time, too ugly." Instead, he traveled on, and every step reaffirmed an important paradox about the history of attitudes toward arid lands: people who have *loved* deserts have also, unless they were the battiest of masochists, spent a significant part of their time *hating* deserts.

J. Smeaton Chase wanted an immediate and intense experience of the desert; and more often than he wanted it, he got it. He got it sometimes in the form of a segment of cholla cactus immediately and intensely attached to his skin, or to the hide or hoof of his horse. A confirmed and admitted nature-lover, Chase still *hated* that "general enemy," cholla cactus. "I could willingly devote a chapter," he said, "to abusing the cholla."[10] But having hundreds of little cholla needles inserted into one's skin does have a cheerful philosophical effect: it offers an undeniable reminder that the recipient is alive and fully sentient.

The example of cholla supplies us with one answer to the riddle of how and why the desert has been at once so fearful and so attractive. Of all landscapes, the desert provided and provides the world's best reminder that the observer is truly, gratefully alive. Proof of the vitality of the visitor arises instantly from the contrast with a landscape so full of suggestions of death and so sparsely supplied with life's necessity, water. With its "uncompromising reality," as Chase put it, "the desert yields no point of sympathy, and meets every need of man with a cold, repelling No." And yet the repetition of this "No" gave clarity and poignancy to the "Yes" of persistent human life. The desert, Chase told us, "takes away what hides us from ourselves."[11]

In the twentieth century, more and more people have followed in Chase's footsteps and turned to the desert in search of this moment of self-discovery and this feeling of being fully alive. Posterity may find this behavior cryptic and puzzling. Why did so many human beings, already visibly and palpably alive, feel so much in need of proof of that vitality? Why couldn't they just live, without demanding that the universe offer repeated evidence of and testimony to their being? In an age of great self-consciousness and self-inspection, why did they have to travel so far in search of themselves?

Indeed, the greatest value of the answers Chase offered lies precisely in his congeniality. Historical inquiry often focuses on exercises of power and stories of great drama — people involved in conflict, friction, violence, and tension. And yet the price of that focus has been a nearly complete neglect of "nice guy studies." In Western American history, we know a great deal about the doings of unpleasant people, or at least of people rendered operationally unpleasant by the mandates of invasion and conquest. But the thoughts and activities of consistently nice people have received little attention. They are not, in truth, easy subjects to write about. Neither the word "pleasant" nor the word "nice" carries much power when it appears in cold type.

J. Smeaton Chase's example reawakens us to the value of studying the pleasant, the good-natured, the generous, the flexible, the tolerant, the curious, and the hospitable. Without much knowledge of the actions and workings of the good-tempered people in our past, we travel into the future without bearings. And traveling without one's bearings, Chase knew, is not merely nerve-racking, it is also life-threatening.

Repeatedly, Chase remarked on the anxiety generated by the need to choose a route without the benefit of clear directions. Following a "phantom trail," Chase would find himself reduced to "mere guesswork." Geography, under these circumstances, acquired an urgent meaning. A landscape of arroyos meant not only disorientation, but also dangerous and time-consuming ascents and descents, requiring the expenditure of energy and water often not planned for in that day's narrow allotment of resources. "It is this sort of thing," Chase remarked, "that takes the pleasure out of desert travel." A "mistake of direction" was "a thing to be dreaded" — and "dreaded all the more as one gains in desert experience." Under these circumstances, the provision of proper signs and markers was a matter of great urgency and strong emotion.[12]

"This business of guessing, when a mistake may spell disaster," Chase declared, "gradually gets on one's nerves, knocks out the fun, and finally puts one out of humor with desert travel."[13] Whether one experiences it in difficult physical landscapes or in difficult social and political landscapes, this "business of guessing" without the help of proper trails and markers, can, indeed, "knock out the fun." Especially as we wrestle with issues of social justice and environmental preservation, a "mistake of direction" in the paths of humanitarian thinking and responsible social policy can be just as perilous as a "mistake of direction" in the choice of desert trails. In those terms, J. Smeaton Chase is a signpost and a pathmarker in himself. Among those drawn to deserts in the past, he reminds us, have been men and women of decency and tolerance, travelers who have approached both physical nature and human nature in a spirit of hearty and even-tempered curiosity and understanding. The good humor and good nature of people like Chase give us our bearings, helping us steer away from those mistakes of direction which otherwise so wear on our nerves. For the persistence of human life on this varied planet, a campaign in which the value of good nature will match the value of water and other physical resources, J. Smeaton Chase and his counterparts define a necessary trail.

1. J. Smeaton Chase, *California Desert Trails* (Boston and New York: Houghton, Mifflin, 1919), p. 234.

2. Ibid., pp. 114–15, 172.

3. Ibid., pp. 287, 305.

4. Ibid., pp. 231, 150, 320, 326–27.

5. Ibid., pp. 286–87, ix, 329.

6. Ibid., pp. 98, 152, 154.

7. Ibid., p. 252.

8. Ibid., p. 10.

9. Ibid., pp. 250–51.

10. Ibid., p. 56.

11. Ibid., pp. 180, 4, 14.

12. Ibid., pp. 146–47, 194.

13. Ibid., p. 349.

MODERNIST VISIONS
AND
TRADITIONAL VOICES,
1930–1960

Edward Weston
Old Bunk House, Twenty Mule Team Canyon, Death Valley, 1938
From Weston, *California and the West*, 1940
Gelatin silver print, 7½ x 9½ (19.1 x 24.1)
Center for Creative Photography, The University of Arizona, Tucson

pp. 104–05: Laura Gilpin
Storm from La Bajada Hill, New Mexico, 1946 (detail)
From Gilpin, *The Rio Grande, River of Destiny . . .* , 1949
Gelatin silver print, 20 x 24 (50.8 x 61)
Amon Carter Museum, Fort Worth, Texas; Bequest of Laura Gilpin

Edward Weston
Leadfield Club, Death Valley, 1939
From Weston, *California and the West*, 1940
Gelatin silver print, 7¹¹⁄₁₆ x 9⁹⁄₁₆ (19.1 x 24.1)
Center for Creative Photography, The University of Arizona, Tucson

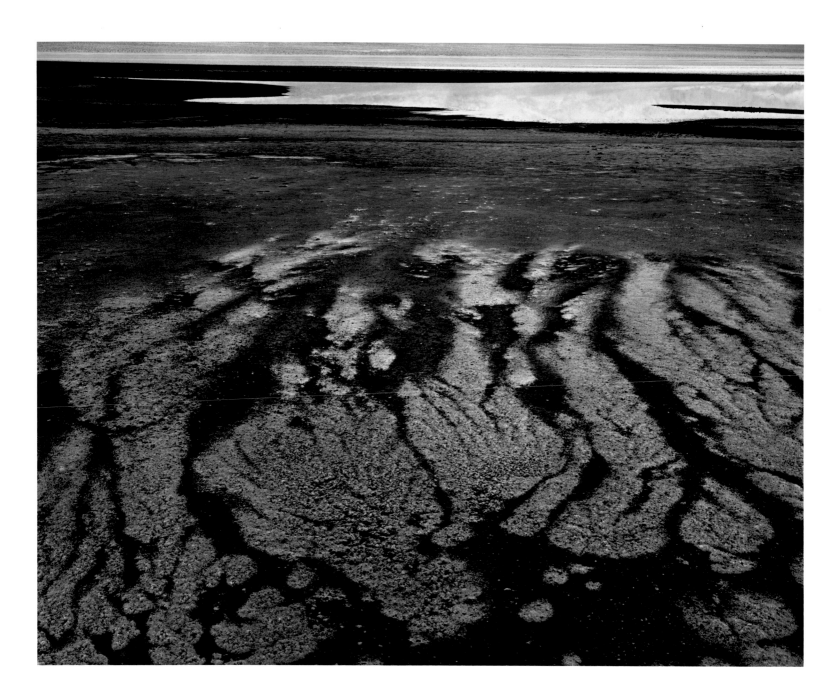

Ansel Adams
Saline Deposits and Pool Near Ballarat, 1941
From Adams, *The Land of Little Rain*, 1950
Ansel Adams Publishing Rights Trust, Carmel, California

Accompanied by the following text:
". . . the pool is never quite dry, but dark and bitter, rimmed about
with the efflorescence of alkaline deposits."

Ansel Adams
Winter Storm, Mount Tom, Sierra Nevada, 1948
From Adams, *The Land of Little Rain*, 1950
Ansel Adams Publishing Rights Trust, Carmel, California

Accompanied by the following text:
"When those glossy domes swim into the alpenglow . . .
you conceive how long and imperturbable are the purposes of God."

The collaboration of Mary Austin and Ansel Adams on *Taos Pueblo* (1930) opens a new chapter in the history of the Western photographic book and the personal engagement of professional photographers in the publishing process. As a fledgling writer, Austin had been encouraged by Charles Fletcher Lummis, but she went beyond his regional advocacy to create some of the finest naturalist writing of this century. Adams also brought a new attitude to the subject. Since the mid-nineteenth century, few photographers immersed in an artistic tradition (whether formally or informally) had chosen to work in the Southwest; with the arrival of Ansel Adams, close on the heels of Paul Strand, the tide turned. Adams played a crucial role in introducing contemporary aesthetics to portrayals of the arid West. Writing to his father from Santa Fe in April 1929, he boasted: "Everyone agrees that I am the only photographer that has come here really equipped to handle the country (pardon my vanity)."[1] Adams wasn't referring to cameras or lenses; he meant modernism. His book with Austin marked the beginning of the Southwest as a primary subject for modernist photographers.

Adams worked under the protection of Mabel Dodge (a doyenne of the avant-garde) and her husband, Antonio Luhan (a Taos Indian). They secured the approval of the tribe for Adams to work in the pueblo, where he photographed both scenes within the buildings and views that situated the pueblo in relation to the Sangre de Cristo Mountains. Though photographed in soft focus (which he would sharpen within a few years), his pictures move toward the crisp geometric structures and stark contrasts of light and shadow pioneered by Alfred Stieglitz and Paul Strand to create monumental images far removed from the more anecdotal, informal photographs of his recent predecessors. Limited to only one hundred copies (plus proofs) by Adams and Austin, *Taos Pueblo* was one of the most lavish volumes of the period. In order to produce the finest images, Adams used book paper coated with photographic emulsion to print the photographs directly on the pages; thus they suggest the tipped-in plates of many nineteenth-century albums but preserve the integration of text and image possible only in a book. The small size of the edition was partially dictated by the unlikelihood of selling many copies in the first year of the Depression; although all were sold in two years, *Taos Pueblo* signaled the end of an era known for its grand editions and avid book collectors.

Six years later, in 1936, Edward Weston applied for a Guggenheim Fellowship to continue "the making of a series of photographic documents of the west." With the stipend, Weston and his companion, Charis Wilson, spent much of 1937–39 traveling across California and Arizona making photographs for their book, *California and the West* (1940). Weston's pictures apply his own version of the abstracting modernist vision to the region, but they also mark a significant shift in his work. In 1930, Weston had written that subject matter meant very little to him; his aesthetic decontextualized and transformed whatever he addressed. Yet, his photographs for the Guggenheim project record a new openness to the world and a desire to accommodate his aesthetic to the function of recording a particular place. Combined in the book with Weston's photographs, Wilson's text reveals a strong concern with everyday life, whether describing a vista in Death Valley or the dead man found in the desert.

Weston chose not to restrict these images to the fine photography world, or even to a fine book, and was willing to have his photographs published in a popular magazine. In exchange for a series of prints, the editor of *Westways* supplied him with maps of the most inhospitable areas and enabled him to purchase a touring car for the trip. The resulting photographic layouts were gathered in book form, in *Seeing California with Edward Weston*, published by the Automobile Association of America in 1939, and aimed at promoting tourism. Here Death Valley, with its eroded landforms and exotic botany, is displayed as just another one of California's easy-to-visit, scenic wonders, a century after it acquired its forbidding name.

Unlike most photographers discussed here, Frederick Sommer shunned the popular photographic book and broader audiences in order to dig more deeply into his own psyche. Having moved to Tucson in 1931 as part of a treatment for tuberculosis, he took up photography in emulation of Stieglitz, Strand, and Weston, especially the latter's images of the Southwest. (In December 1938, toward the end of his Guggenheim tenure, Weston and Wilson visited Sommer in Arizona.) Combining Weston's strategy of photographing a distant landscape so that it appears limitless — without horizon or lateral edges — with Max Ernst's Surrealist dream images, Sommer created disorienting photographs that are barely recognizable as depictions of austere Arizona hills strewn with boulders and spotted with giant saguaro cacti. Sommer recounted that "I found that I was mapping an interior landscape."[2] The Surrealist magazine *VVV* published a pair of these photographs in 1943. Though they have not been published in a book focusing on the desert, these talismanic images have appeared in a number of influential retrospective catalogues edited by Sommer.

Dorothea Lange, more than most of her peers in the West, defined the new commitment by photographers to engage contemporary life. Her collaboration with Paul Taylor, *An American Exodus* (1939), confronts the realities of the Dust Bowl, focusing on the tragic mismanagement of the arid lands of the Southern Plains that led to the impoverishment and the flight of thousands of farmers to a new promised land — California. Lange's work not only created great sympathy for the disenfranchised, but earned the sometimes grudging respect of colleagues who were committed to formalist aesthetics, such as her friends Ansel Adams and Edward Weston. There is no doubt that Lange's ability to merge social advocacy with powerful graphic compositions strongly influenced Adams' decision to use his photography to promote social and ecological causes.[3] These photographers found different methods of approaching the realities of the Great Depression, conceiving their own, increasingly personal and revisionist views and incorporating the documentary style of the picture-stories emerging in new magazines such as *Life* and *Survey Graphic*. This style was extended to a new genre of documentary photobook, among them Lange and Taylor's *An American Exodus*.

Recording the words and capturing pictures of regional Americans where they work and live, *An American Exodus* was one of several such books that promoted a sense of American communities and their

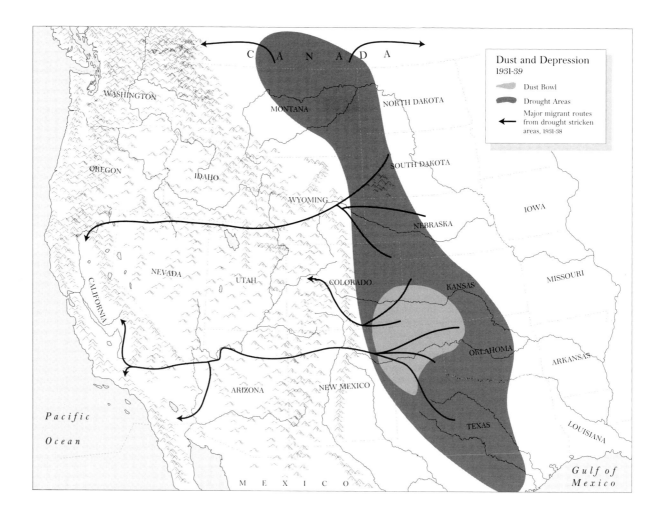

Dust and Depression
1931-39
  Dust Bowl
  Drought Areas
← Major migrant routes
  from drought stricken
  areas, 1931-38

tie to the land. Strongly identifying with their subjects, Laura Gilpin and Laura Adams Armer both spent years exploring traditional and changing Native American communities; their writings and photographs are intertwined in such books as Laura Gilpin's *Pueblos* (1941) and Laura Adams Armer's *Waterless Mountain* (1931).

Ansel Adams' most explicit effort to turn his photography to more critical, social documentary purposes was *Born Free and Equal* (1944), in which he recorded the lives of Japanese-Americans interned during World War II at Manzanar in the Sierra Nevada. A number of critics have concluded that Adams' photographs are too optimistic to generate an understanding of Manzanar — he directed the camera out toward the mountains surrounding Manzanar (which he believed served as a source of inspiration for the Japanese-Americans) more often than he conveyed the privations of the camp. However, it was there that the severity of the California desert landscape came into Adam's purview, and he would increasingly return to the desert over the next decade to define it as a place of majesty rivaling Yosemite.

In *The Land of Little Rain* (1950), Adams returned to the work of his early collaborator, Mary Austin (who had died in 1934), both to celebrate a kind of forgotten landscape, and to protest environmental destruction. Originally published in 1903, Austin's text describes the land and natural beauty of the

Owens Valley in southeastern California — just before the growth of Los Angeles in the late nineteenth century forced the diversion of water from the region east of the Sierra Nevada. The increased demand for water by this large metropolis at the edge of the desert destroyed the fragile ecology of the Owens Valley, and an agriculturally viable, though arid land, became a barren desert. Adams had been on the board of the Sierra Club since 1934 and had participated vigorously in efforts to protect the Sierras. In *The Land of Little Rain*, he paired selections from Austin's text with his own current photographs of the region to demonstrate the pressing need for conservation. This episode forcefully focused Adams' sense of advocacy and inspired him to combine his mastery of dramatic composition with the social commitment he had acquired in the 1930s and his lifelong devotion to nature.

By the 1950s and 1960s, technology, water reclamation, and settlement seemed to have gained an upper hand in the arid West, and the remaining desert wilderness became an important focus of conservationists, who enlisted the photographic book as a persuasive medium. In the 1960s, the Sierra Club began its line of exhibition-format books, beginning with *This Is the American Earth* (1960) by Ansel Adams and the editor-author Nancy Newhall. This book grew out of an influential, traveling Sierra Club exhibition of 1955, organized by Adams and Newhall to deliver a powerful conservation message. The book embraces the American landscape as a valuable inheritance to be treasured for its aesthetic, physical, and spiritual qualities. Adams defined his editorial position in a letter to David Brower, editor of the Sierra Club publication: "We must bear in mind that this is a poetic concept, blending the emotional effects of the images and the words into a unique single expression."[4] *This Is the American Earth* was one of the most popular photographic books of its time. The success of the book and the Sierra Club's use of photographic publications to call attention to endangered lands encouraged further publications. In what would become a memorial to a drowned landscape, *The Place No One Knew: Glen Canyon on the Colorado* (1963) featured color photographs taken by Eliot Porter a year before the canyon was dammed to create Lake Powell. Sent to every member of Congress, and published in several editions, *The Place No One Knew* publicized what would be seen by environmentalists as an enormous loss.[5]

MAY CASTLEBERRY

1. Mary Street Alinder and Andrea Gray Stillman, eds., *Ansel Adams: Letters and Images 1916–1984* (Boston: Little, Brown and Company, 1988), p. 39.

2. Lanier Graham, "The Art of Frederick Sommer, Part I: Recent Work, Elective Affinities," *Image*, 33 (Winter 1990–91) p. 47.

3. Lange's influence on Adams is thoroughly explored in Sandra S. Phillips, "Ansel Adams and Dorothea Lange: A Friendship of Differences," *Ansel Adams/New Light: Essays on His Legacy and Legend* (San Francisco: The Friends of Photography, 1993).

4. David Featherstone, "This Is the American Earth: A Collaboration by Ansel Adams and Nancy Newhall," *Ansel Adams/New Light: Essays on His Legacy and Legend* (San Francisco: The Friends of Photography, 1993), p. 68.

5. For further references to Eliot Porter and the Glen Canyon project, see Chuck Hagen, "Land and Landscape," *Aperture*, no. 120 (Summer 1990), pp. 16–20.

Ansel Adams
North House (Hlauuma)
From *Taos Pueblo*, 1930
Gelatin silver print on Dassonville paper
Collection of Hans P. Kraus, Jr.

TAOS PUEBLO

ANNE HAMMOND

In the 1920s, a passionate interest in Native American culture of the Southwest had developed among Europeans and Americans. The quest for a culture with an all-pervading spirituality brought to New Mexico the New York socialite Mabel Dodge Luhan, writers Mary Austin and D.H. Lawrence, and also Carl Gustav Jung, the famous psychoanalyst. In the spring of 1927, Ansel Adams drove with Albert Bender, the San Francisco philanthropist and collector, from San Francisco to Santa Fe to meet Mary Austin, who had made a considerable reputation as a novelist and nature writer. Reviewers of her *The Land of Little Rain* (1903), about the Southwest, had ranked her with John Muir and Henry David Thoreau. When they met in 1927, Mary Austin was nearly sixty years old, and Ansel Adams was twenty-five.

Adams seems to have proposed to Bender the idea of a portfolio about the Southwest; Bender then promised his financial support and suggested that Adams ask Austin to contribute the text. In late April 1928, Adams wrote to tell her how excited he was about "the Acoma Portfolio" they had talked about.[1] But their first choice, Acoma Pueblo, presented difficulties. In the summer of 1928, the Fox Corporation hired the filmmaker Robert Flaherty to produce a film, which was never completed, about pueblo life in Acoma. Another movie was subsequently produced there (*Redskin*) by Paramount in 1929. Austin feared this might raise Acoma's expectations of high fees for photography. She offered the alternative of Zuni, with its landscape interests of Thunder Mountain and Inscription Rock.[2] Finally, Taos Pueblo, with which she had a personal connection through Mabel Dodge Luhan, her rival for cultural leadership in New Mexico, was chosen.

During their three-month stay with Mary Austin in 1929, Adams and his wife, Virginia, visited Luhan at her ranch, Los Gallos, in Taos. Luhan had known everyone of any artistic or intellectual reputation in New York before she decided to move to New Mexico in 1916. She had been told by an occultist that the spirit world had elected her to be the bridge between Indian and white cultures, and she took steps to fulfill this destiny by taking as her lover a Taos Indian, Antonio Luhan (originally Lujan), who had first worked as her chauffeur. It was he who went to the governor of the pueblo to plead the case for Austin and Adams' project.[3] The conditions under which Adams was permitted to photograph in Taos Pueblo included a fee[4] and a presentation copy of the book, which the members of the pueblo wrapped in deerskin and placed in their kiva for safekeeping.

Although the photographs and the plates were produced independently, Adams and Austin would surely have conferred to some extent about the Taos book. But it was not until a year after he had read Austin's manuscript in the autumn of 1929 that Adams selected and sequenced his photographs. Austin recommended that on future collaborations they should work in closer consultation: "I think that we can do a little better next time by getting together on the subject before we begin."[5]

In a time of great economic instability, immediately after the stock market crash of October 1929, Adams was understandably nervous about pricing the book and judging the size of the edition for maximum sales. He offered two proposals to Mary Austin in April 1930:

Here are the comparative specifications on the two propositions regarding the book:

1. 250 copies @ $50 will require the sale of 90 copies to meet the material cost of the edition.

2. 100 copies @ $75 will require the sale of 45 copies to meet the material cost of the edition.

I am strongly advised to work on the second plan: while I will not make as much as I would were the entire edition of 250 copies sold, I would be in a much safer position, and assured of almost complete distribution of the 100 copies.[6]

Despite these worries about the state of the market, Adams and Austin decided to print one hundred copies and sell them at $75 apiece. In 1930, when the average American income was around $1,300 per year, and $75 was the price of a new washing machine, *Taos Pueblo* was a very expensive book. The edition nevertheless sold out in two years.[7] The success of the book was a major factor in Adams' decision to abandon his aspiration to become a concert pianist and to devote himself to a career as a serious photographer.

The job of printing went to Edwin and Robert Grabhorn, who had just printed *Poems by Robinson Jeffers* (1928) for the Book Club of California, to which Adams had contributed the portrait frontispiece. The Grabhorns had difficulty printing *Taos Pueblo* because of the unusually large page size and a curling paper

Ansel Adams
Church at Ranchos de Taos
From *Taos Pueblo*, 1930
Gelatin silver print on Dassonville paper
Collection of Hans P. Kraus, Jr.; courtesy Ansel Adams Publishing Trust,
Carmel, California

Ansel Adams
South House (Hlaukwima)
From *Taos Pueblo*, 1930
Gelatin silver print on Dassonville paper
Collection of Hans P. Kraus, Jr.; courtesy Ansel Adams Publishing Trust,
Carmel, California

stock, which resulted in typeset sheets that were not quite straight. The binder refused to accept the job under these conditions, so the book was reset and printed on a larger trade press owned by William Eveleth.[8] The paper was made to order by Crane and Company, with half the stock delivered to the Grabhorn Press for the printing of the text, and the other half to William E. Dassonville, who coated the paper with a silver bromide emulsion on which Adams made his photographic enlargements.[9] Adams recalled in later years that the entire stock of paper should have been soaked before printing, because after its coating with photographic emulsion and the processing procedures, the photographically printed pages took on a slightly different texture from the typographic pages in the book.[10]

The image of a harmonious and poetic life in the pueblos was widely disseminated by anthropologists, poets, and painters. Marsden Hartley had been brought to New Mexico by Mabel Dodge Luhan in 1918. In his writings, he encouraged American artists to turn for inspiration to their own history and landscape, rather than look to European models. Hartley presented the Native American (the "Red Man") as "the one truly indigenous religionist and esthete of America."[11] The Indian was for him the ideal of an artist true to himself and his culture, completely in tune with the natural world. Luhan also succeeded in drawing D.H. Lawrence to Taos in 1922, as someone who could express the potential of Taos for a new world culture. Lawrence described Taos as "rather like one of the old monasteries. When you go there you feel something final. There is an arrival. The nodality still holds good."[12]

Taos as spiritual center also attracted C.G. Jung in 1925. Sitting with a chief of the Taos Indians on the fifth story of one of the main house clusters of the pueblo, he learned that the people of Taos climbed to their housetops, microcosms of their sacred mountain, in order to help their father the sun cross the sky each day. The ascending structure of Taos Pueblo reflected this spiritual necessity — the Indians' perceived responsibility for the perpetuation of the natural order.[13] *North House (Hlauuma) and Taos Mountain* relates a relatively small and apparently fragile building to the mountain's strength and permanence. The adobe architecture of the pueblos had always been associated with sacred landscape forms.[14]

In *North House (End View)*, Adams chose to exploit the cubism of the stepped-back stories and their connecting ladders. During the period of his work in Taos, Adams was becoming aware of the influence of post-Cubist abstraction as exemplified in the work of John Marin, whom Adams met there in 1929. In both Marin's and Andrew Dasburg's work, a geometric interpretation of form was applied to the landscape and to the buildings of the pueblos.[15] Austin, however, saw the adobe cubes as a demonstration of the native development of Pueblo buildings: "the pyramidal house-heap was shaped out of tribal necessities" (p. 8). By "house-heap" she implied a quality of organic growth typical of Pueblo Indian architecture. For her the buildings represented the "Mother Hive" (p. 14).

On the basis of its description in Austin's text as "deep-rooted, grown-from-the-soil" (p. 4), Adams included as the final plate *Church at Ranchos de Taos,* despite the fact that it was not actually part of Taos Pueblo. Here, Adams' interest in angular composition transforms the large masses of adobe into a mountainous pyramid with sphinxlike animal haunches. The church, photographed at a low angle from the rear, embodies the pueblo and the mountain in a single subject, and by purposely not showing the front entrance, the church is taken out of its Spanish Catholic context. However, Adams and Austin were not Native American purists. They accepted the synthesis of Indian and Spanish traditions in the Southwest. While at work on *Taos Pueblo,* they were simultaneously engaged on another collaboration: a book on the Spanish colonial arts of the region written by Austin and her friend Frank Applegate and illustrated with photographs of applied and decorative arts and crafts by Adams. Despite all Mary Austin's efforts she failed to find a publisher for it before her own death in 1934.

1. Ansel Adams to Mary Austin, April 28, 1928, Mary Austin Collection, Huntington Library, San Marino, California. Unless otherwise noted, further references to the Adams-Austin correspondence are to this collection.

2. Mary Austin to Ansel Adams, July 5, 1928.

3. Ansel Adams, "Conversations with Ansel Adams," interview conducted by Ruth Teiser and Catherine Harroun in 1972, 1974, and 1975, Regional Oral History Office, Bancroft Library, University of California at Berkeley, 1978, p. 172. (hereafter referred to as "Conversations"). Mabel changed Lujan (the original Spanish) to Luhan, to avoid the constant misspelling of the name by her friends. Tony Lujan was Adams' subject for plate III, *A Man of Taos.*

4. In "Conversations," conducted in the mid-1970s, Adams thought he remembered paying $100 (p. 178), but in his *Autobiography* (Boston: Little, Brown and Company, 1985), p. 90, the payment is recorded as $25.

5. Mary Austin to Ansel Adams, January 2, 1931.

6. Ansel Adams to Mary Austin, April 4, 1930.

7. Mary Austin to Ansel Adams, January 13 and March 13, 1931. Austin was not happy about the high cost of *Taos Pueblo* and tried very hard to find a publisher in New York to print a cheaper edition (as the first of a proposed series on the pueblos, including Zuni, Hopi, and Acoma), but she failed. A reasonably priced reprint of the book has never been produced. The facsimile edition, published by New York Graphic Society in 1977, sold for $375.

8. Elinor Raas Heller and David Magee, *Bibliography of the Grabhorn Press, 1915–1940* (San Francisco: Alan Wofsy Fine Arts, 1975), p. 78.

9. The printing papers Dassonville produced (Adams was especially fond of "Charcoal Black" which he used until 1933) had become so popular among photographers by 1924 that Dassonville gave up his studio work to become a full-time photographic paper manufacturer.

10. "Conversations," p. 176.

11. Marsden Hartley, "The Red Man," in Hartley, *Adventures in the Arts* (New York: Boni and Liveright, 1921; repr. New York: Hacker Art Books, 1972), pp. 13–24.

12. D.H. Lawrence, "Taos," *The Dial,* 74 (March 1923), pp. 251–54.

13. C.G. Jung, *Memories, Dreams, Reflections* (London: Collins, 1963; repr. 1974), p. 280.

14. Vincent Scully, *Pueblo: Mountain, Village, Dance* (New York: Viking Press 1972; repr. 1975), p. 9.

15. See Marin, *Dance of the Santo Domingo Indians* (1929), in Charles C. Eldredge, Julie Schimmel, and William H. Truettner, *Art in New Mexico, 1900–1945,* exh. cat. (Washington, D.C.: National Museum of American Art, 1986), fig. 103, p. 95; Dasburg, *El Rito,* in Sharyn Rolfsen Udall, *Modernist Painting in New Mexico 1913–1935* (Albuquerque: University of New Mexico Press, 1984), fig. 22, p. 61.

WATERLESS MOUNTAIN

PETER E. PALMQUIST

The Navajo called Laura Adams Armer "the woman who wears the turquoise" and "hard-working woman." She was the first white woman to have a sand painting prepared in her honor and the first permitted to film the sacred Mountain Chant ceremony (1928) for distribution as a feature-length movie. She was also a respected painter and photographer for many years before she turned her hand to writing. Her first book, *Waterless Mountain* (1931), was published when she was fifty-seven years old. It received both the Newbery Medal and the Longmans, Green & Company's prize for juvenile fiction.

Anthropologist Alfred L. Kroeber, in a blurb on the *Waterless Mountain* dust jacket, succinctly describes Armer's unique contribution to American juvenile literature: "*Waterless Mountain* is a direct, simple story, movingly told. It is human, it is good Indian and authentic Navajo. Like [Oliver] LaFarge's *Laughing Boy*, it shows that we have entered a time when the Indian is no longer a dummy to hang our own romanticism on, but an interest and appeal in himself as he really is."

Congratulated on the success of her book, Armer reflected, "I've been writing books in my mind for the last thirty-five years. *Waterless Mountain* was merely the first one I put down on paper."[1]

Unlike most books chosen for the "Perpetual Mirage" exhibition, *Waterless Mountain* is less a "photographic book" and more a derivative of a photographer's preoccupation with both photography and painting; ultimately it is the spiritual combination of these two media with the written word. After more than two decades of exhibition photography, where Armer had remained tied to the photographic conventions of the era, she now felt empowered to employ her camera to record situations which she subsequently translated into thematic "illustrations" for an increasingly wide audience. In the case of *Waterless Mountain*, this meant finding a more spiritual vehicle that would appeal to a juvenile audience.

Both the dust jacket and frontispiece illustration for *Waterless Mountain* are clearly photographic in vision and impact, and only after a more detailed examination do we realize that it is actually a painting. Moreover, the painting was itself based on a composite of two different photographs, both taken by Armer. The first is an overview and the second a close-up image of the foreground figures. The composite, thus formed, was a perfect counterpoint to Armer's emerging literary style.

Six other books by Armer, all with Southwestern themes, followed: *Dark Circle of Branches* (1933); *Cactus* (1934); *Southwest* (1937); *Farthest West* (1939); and her autobiography, *In Navajo Land* (1962), which was published shortly before her death in 1963 at age eighty-nine. (*The Forest Pool*, published in 1938, featured a Mexican theme.)

Armer's life journey stands as a fascinating preface to the genesis of *Waterless Mountain* and deserves a brief profile. Laura May (Adams) Armer (1874–1963) was born in Sacramento, California, the youngest of three children. Her father had been a farmer-turned-carpenter who had tried his hand at gold mining, but his luck was bad; he also broke his leg and his claim was jumped. Her mother achieved recognition as the seamstress who made the elegant rose brocade wedding dress worn by Mrs. Leland Stanford. As a child, Laura was considered "puny" and "dreamy" and was doted on by her mother. A photograph of Laura at an early age shows her with a strong, almost masculine look, a determined scowl in her large, protuberant eyes, and blonde corkscrew curls. By age sixteen, Armer had shown a penchant for sketching and painting, and her uncle provided money for her to enter the San Francisco School of Art, which she then attended for six years.

Following her graduation from art school, Armer established a photography studio in San Francisco, where she catered to members of California high society. She also exhibited successfully in Photographic Salons well into the 1920s.[2] In the spring of 1902 she and her sister visited the Southwest for the first time: "There at Tucson and in the Catalina Mountains I was first inoculated with the desert delirium."[3] Upon her return she wrote articles illustrated with her photographs for *Sunset* and *Overland Monthly*. She married classmate Sidney Armer (1871–1962), who later achieved fame as the highest paid commercial illustrator in California.[4] They had already known each other for at least eight years, yet the marriage was an uneasy partnership. Laura claimed to trace her heritage back to *the* presidential Adamses, while

Laura Adams Armer
Canyon de Chelly, Carrying Her Rugs to the Trading Post, c. 1925
Wheelwright Museum of the American Indian, Santa Fe

Laura Adams Armer
Frontispiece from Armer, *Waterless Mountain*, 1931
Collection of Peter E. Palmquist

Sidney was a Jew. He was also a socialist. Throughout their life together, Sidney was as accommodating as Laura was demanding, yet in the end their artistic partnership was far closer than either would have dared to admit.

Their son Austin was born in 1903 (an infant daughter died in 1905). Laura doted on Austin, and he became the nude child pictured in many of her art photographs until, at age sixteen, he finally rebelled.

Following her marriage, Laura abandoned her San Francisco studio and moved her darkroom to her home with Sidney in Berkeley. Here she continued her art photography and in 1904 won four awards in the Kodak Competition. In 1905 she illustrated Theodore Elden Jones' book *Leaves From an Argonaut's Note Book* and in 1906 traveled on assignment to Tahiti.[5]

In 1923, Armer returned to the Southwest. She had already heard of the Navajo song concerning "Dawn Boy," a child of the White Corn wandering in the House of Happiness: "and it was the song of Dawn Boy that decided the route of our vacation in June, 1923. We left Berkeley in a Buick touring car, Sidney and I, our twenty-year-old son Austin, and Paul Louis Faye, a friend who had lived among the Navajos. . . . We were prepared to camp out in a dry country. The running board of the car held canteens of water and a lunch box. A trunk on the rear stowed a gasoline camp stove with pots and pans. Sleeping bags and ethnological reports filled half the back seat. Cameras and canned goods reposed at our feet. . . ."[6]

It was on this trip that Armer purchased her famed turquoise earrings. She saw some that she wanted and asked Faye what she should pay for them. "If they are heart's desire, pay what equals heart's desire." Since few white women wore turquoise at this time, Armer's chance purchase gave her an entry to the Navajo and frequently provided the turning point in times of delicate negotiations.

February 1924 found Laura "armed with paint, brushes, canvas, and cameras" as she prepared to capture the scenes at Sunset Post and Oraibi. She also met Lorenzo Hubbell, of the Hubbell Trading Post, who was to exert a profound influence on her life for the next fifteen years (he became her mentor, arranged her trips into Navajo areas, and helped fund her 1928 film, *The Mountain Chant*). In hopes of meeting local Indians, she agreed to teach an art class in the nearby government school; she had forty Hopi boys and girls in her first class. The following year she requested that Hubbell find her a retreat where she could paint and photograph in solitude. Hubbell took her to Blue Canyon, where she set up her canvases and paints in two tiny tents. As Hubbell left, he remarked, "If this moon place is not wild enough for you, send word to Oraibi and I will try to find you what you want." Asked if she did not feel lonely, "staying week after week in the canyon," she replied, "Here with Navajos I am not hampered by trivialities, but I have learned that one must win his own place in the spiritual world, painfully and alone. . .The Promised Land lies on the other side of a wilderness."[7]

Her biggest challenge, namely, that no woman could be admitted to sacred native ceremonies, was met in Armer's characteristic head-on fashion: "Tell them not to think of me as a woman, but as an artist."[8] Likewise, when the Navajo objected to her photographing or copying their sand paintings, she asked what exactly was sacred. Learning that the "sprinkling of pollen" was the forbidden ingredient, she convinced the elders that perhaps it would be no violation to photograph the sand paintings *sans* pollen. She eventually recorded more than one hundred sand paintings with her camera and paint brush.[9]

Even more remarkable was her ability to arrange for filming the Mountain Chant ceremony. With no previous filmmaking experience, Armer wrote, directed, edited, produced, and marketed the entire project. She even convinced Lorenzo Hubbell to make a major capital investment in the film. Since some of the public showings were narrated by Navajos in native tongue, *The Mountain Chant* is considered to be the first "all Indian" motion picture "in an aboriginal language."[10]

Marketing *The Mountain Chant* was another matter entirely. Armer traveled to Hollywood, hired an agent, and embarked on a roller-coaster life of hope and disappointment. Everyone agreed that Armer's film was a fine example of "Art" but not marketable as such. On October 18, 1928, Armer wrote to Lorenzo Hubbell: "I'm not a success as a salesman. . .everything is business, graft, politics, pull, cringing slavery. You can't realize until you come here [to Hollywood]. Its a gimme gimme attitude. Sorry, but its one woman against millions of businessmen."[11] Nonetheless, despite the obvious lack of a public forum, her film was rather widely viewed. Private showings before the Section of Anthropology and Psychology of the New York Academy of Sciences, the Explorer's Club, and at the University of Pennsylvania were but three of many venues. Armer's struggle to promote the film commercially, however, was making her ill, and in desperation she retreated increasingly into her writing. In the winter of 1931, she lived in a furnished apartment in Winslow, Arizona, while working on her second book, *Dark Circle of Branches*.

In April 1932 Armer described her journey eastward to receive the Newbery Medal: "I was living in the wilderness of the Navajo and Hopi country, seventy-eight miles from the railroad. In the Hopi village of Oraibi, a sand storm raged for four days before I left. . . . Traveling by train across New Mexico, through Texas to New Orleans. . .I had time to think about the Newbery

Laura Adams Armer
Canyon de Chelly, c. 1925
Wheelwright Museum of the American Indian, Santa Fe

Medal. . .that I, as a genuine amateur in the field of literature, had never heard of the Newbery Medal."[12]

Laura had yet another reason to exult: "It was during the depression years, when *The Waterless Mountain* saved us from going hungry, that I received in Winslow a check for $2000 from my publishers. Mr. Hubbell introduced me to the banker, to have it cashed. The banker's remark I have never forgotten: 'The whole damned country isn't worth $2000.' That pleased me very much, showing the difference in points of view of the materialist and the dreamer. That is what I am. . . ."[13] More writing followed. In 1935, *Southwest*, which she wrote and ilustrated, was published. "Southwest mythology," she wrote, "centers about the Almighty Sky, the endless one, who bears the stars upon his back at night and makes a trail of beauty for the Sun Bearer by day." She also put herself into the manuscript, in passages such as: "This is the Hard-working Woman who paints on paper," or "He smiled back at the Hard-working Woman with the soft white hair like downy breast feathers of the eagle."[14]

The Trader's Children (1937) is also highly autobiographical. Laura refers to herself as "Aunt Mary," to Sidney as "Uncle Joe," and describes how they built an eight-sided house where they "could draw and paint and study." She was later sued by one of the subjects described in the book for "demeaning his character." The suit was settled for $750 and discontinuance of the book.[15]

Armer disavowed that she ever had mystical leanings toward the Indians, but a *New York Times* reviewer spoke of her as "being naturally a pagan mystic." Her son, Austin, added these words concerning his mother's religious tendencies: "My mother had no religious background that I know of, altho she mentioned some ancestors in New York were Unitarians. . .awe of the natural and supernatural — faith in miracles — profound belief in extrasensory perception, etc., she had aplenty."[16]

Although Laura and Sidney had lived apart for much of the Depression (Sidney found work in Detroit), they continued to intertwine their art. Laura's books, for example, were illustrated in one of three ways: by Sidney alone, by Laura alone, or by the two working together. In the case of *Waterless Mountain*, there are four illustrations by Laura, one by both Laura and Sidney, and the remainder by Sidney.[17] As previously mentioned, the dust jacket and frontispiece illustration actually reproduce a painting by Laura, based on a composite of two of her photographs.

After 1936, Laura no longer visited the Southwest as part of her work. Unable to establish ownership of the eight-sided studio that she had built on the reservation, she was forced to consolidate her life and return to California. In 1938, her book *The Forest Pool* was recognized as the most distinguished picture book of that year. The book was illustrated, in color, with her paintings.[18] Her remaining years were spent writing — including work on a 50,000-word manuscript about sand painting[19] — and reminiscing about the Southwest and art generally.

In March 1960, Laura received a telephone call from a man planning to give a talk on *Waterless Mountain* at Fresno University. He wanted to know if it had sold 50,000 copies. To which Laura replied, "I couldn't tell him off-hand but would count up my royalty statements for 30 years. I think they show a satisfactory number. Man said he didn't know whether I was dead or alive."[20] The following day she checked her accounts, confirming, with ill-suppressed glee, that *Waterless Mountain* had indeed sold in excess of 50,000 copies.

The following month she noted that a recording had just been released of *Waterless Mountain* and that her "yearly" statement from Longmans indicated that one hundred copies had already been sold: "It is [now] thirty years ago that I wrote it." She further noted, "When I was in New York some years ago certain enthusiasts said to me: 'Longmans, Green & Co. have published two masterpieces for children, *Robinson Crusoe* and *Waterless Mountain*.' I should be blushing to write this, but I confess I felt somewhat exhilarated. . . ."[21]

1. *Publisher's Weekly*, April 30, 1932, pp. 1878–79, quoted in Laverne Mau Dicker, "Laura Adams Armer: California Photographer," *California Historical Quarterly*, 56 (Summer 1977), p. 136. Laura was also fond of recalling an early premonition: "Don't worry. . .when you are an old woman you will write what you fail to paint."

2. For Armer's growing authority in the field of photography, see her article, "The Picture Possibilities of Photography," published in *Overland Monthly*, 36 (September 1900), pp. 241–45. Armer was an exhibitor at the San Francisco Photographic Salons of 1901, 1902, and 1903, and active in numerous salons in the early 1920s. Most of her salon photographs were Pictorialist portraits or views of San Francisco, especially the waterfront and Chinatown. A collection of her photographic negatives is located at the Wheelwright Museum, Santa Fe, New Mexico. Collections of vintage photographs are found at the Wheelwright Museum, the California Historical Society, and The Oakland Museum.

3. Laura Armer to Eugene L. Conrotto, December 27, 1859, quoted in Eugene L. Conrotto, "Armer: Letters," MA thesis (Stanislaus: California State College, 1978), p. 297. Conrotto was the editor of *Desert Magazine*, and in 1960 he published a ten-part series of articles by Armer on the Southwest. Conrotto's thesis was built around the letters exchanged between himself and Armer in connection with these articles.

4. Sidney Armer developed logos and advertising symbols for many manufacturers, including Albert's Flapjack Mix, "Miss Sun Maid" (the raisin girl), Hill's Brothers "Turk," the Del Monte shield, and various designs for the Morse Seed Company. In later life, Sidney was very successful with his water-

color paintings of California wildflowers, which were regularly published by the Richfield Oil Company.

5. Laura provided eight full-page illustrations for Jones' book. They are presumed to be photographic, or at least based on photographs. She had been commissioned by the passenger agent of the Oceanic Steamship Company to take a series of photographs for promotional purposes. Unfortunately, the agent did not have authority to make this commission and she was not paid for her work.

6. Laura Adams Armer, *In Navajo Land* (New York: David McKay Company, 1962), p. 18.

7. Ibid., p. 52.

8. Ibid., p. 65.

9. See Conrotto, "Armer: Letters," pp. 471–72. "When the 76th [sandpainting copy] was finished the Navajos christened her, The Woman Who Works Very Hard." A number of Armer's painted illustrations are at the University of California, Berkeley. A sound recording of her descriptions of the meaning of these sand paintings is thought to exist.

10. A copy of *The Mountain Chant* is held by the Wheelwright Museum, Santa Fe, New Mexico. For an account of the production of this film, see Laura Adams Armer, "The Crawler, Navajo Healer," *The Masterkey*, 27 (January – February 1953), pp. 5–10.

11. Laura Adams Armer to Lorenzo Hubbell, October 18, 1928, Manuscript Division, University of Arizona, Tucson.

12. "Armer, Laura Adams," *Contemporary Authors*, 13 (1978), p. 6.

13. Conrotto, "Armer: Letters," p. 304.

14. Ibid., p. 242.

15. Alberta Armer, *Working Hands* (Published by the author, 1981), pp. 110–11.

16. Conrotto, "Armer: Letters," p. 244.

17. Of the plate opposite p. 26, Laura wrote (ibid., p. 499): "We both did it. The deer are mine and the background is Sidney's."

18. *The Forest Pool* followed Laura's visit to Mexico. The illustrations, reproduced in color, very much reflect the influence of painter Diego Rivera.

19. Present whereabouts unknown.

20. Conrotto, "Armer: Letters," pp. 321–22.

21. Ibid., pp. 330–31.

CHARIS WILSON AND EDWARD WESTON:
CALIFORNIA AND THE WEST

SUSAN DANLY

*"People who see the deserts only from main highways or train windows often suppose them to be monotonous wastes,
but the California deserts, like the rest of the state, contain a great variety of subject matter.
The photographer who wants to really see the desert must go prepared to forsake main traveled roads
for twisting sandy tracks and boulder-strewn dry washes. Only by traveling the deserts' own roads will he find
the wealth of material they have to offer. From sandstone concretions around the Salton Sea to yuccas and granite piles on the Mojave
to the badlands of Death Valley – there is enough material to keep a hundred photographers busy for years to come."* [1]

— Edward Weston

For Edward Weston, the real challenge of desert photography was in capturing the diversity of what he called its "Life." In early April 1937, with a grant from the Guggenheim Foundation (the first ever awarded to a photographer), Weston set off to record the desert landscape as part of a larger project — "the making of a series of photographic documents of the west." His use of the words "photographic documents" in the context of American art produced during the Great Depression, is particularly relevant for this two-year period of intensive photographic production, from 1937 to 1939. The decade of the 1930s had already seen a burgeoning of documentary photography all across America, from images of urban poverty made by the New York Film and Photo League to the scenes of devastated Dust Bowl farms and the haggard faces of migrant laborers made by the Farm Security Administration photographers in the Midwest and Far West. With a disclaimer that his own work "was not at all documentary in the present popular sense of the word," Weston went on to describe his goals for the Guggenheim project: "My work this year as in the past has been directed toward photographing Life. I have not been concerned with making records, cataloguing subject matter. Rather I have tried to sublimate my subject matter, to reveal its significance and to reveal Life through it." [2]

The result was *California and the West*, published in 1940, a book which combines a selection of Weston's Guggenheim photographs with a text written by Charis Wilson, who accompanied

Edward Weston
Zabriskie Point, Death Valley, 1938
From Weston, *California and the West*, 1940
Gelatin silver print, 7½ x 9½ (19.1 x 24.1)
Center for Creative Photography, The University of Arizona, Tucson

Edward Weston
Yucca, Mojave Desert (Joshua Tree, Mohave Desert), 1937
From Weston, *California and the West*, 1940
Gelatin silver print, 9½ x 7½ (24.1 x 19.1)
Center for Creative Photography, The University of Arizona, Tucson

· 125 ·

Edward Weston
Yucca, Wonderland of Rocks, 1937
From Weston, *California and the West,* 1940
Gelatin silver print, 9½ x 7½ (24.1 x 19.1)
Center for Creative Photography, The University of Arizona, Tucson

Weston on his travels. Wilson, then in her early twenties, was a close friend who had first modeled for the photographer in 1934. It was she who encouraged Weston to apply for the Guggenheim grant, helped him draft the application, and kept a daily logbook of his work. Her notes, filled with the day-to-day details of their lives and the photographic project, eventually became the text for the book.[3] And it is that text, in combination with the images, that breathes real life into this publication. Wilson's prose provides narrative structure in the form of a free-spirited travelogue, and it sheds light on the humanist side of Weston's photography. Wilson, whose father was a writer,[4] later married Weston and, during their years together from 1934 to 1945, often acted as the ghost writer for his articles on photography.[5] Knowledgeable about his working methods and frequently more articulate about his subjects, Wilson managed to convey the sense of adventure and camaraderie that characterized their travels. Her writings about the difficulties of photographing in the desert are especially vivid and are critical for a modern reader in recapturing the texture of American life in the 1930s.

Wilson and Weston had begun planning the work schedule and budget for the Guggenheim project months before the grant was awarded. In describing the equipment needed for the project, Weston wrote: "The first and most important item was a car." Then he went on to list his photographic equipment: an 8 x 10 Century Universal Camera, tripod, focusing cloth, lenses and filters, and twelve film holders. To augment the award of $2,000, the couple also arranged with *Westways*, the magazine of the Southern California Auto Club, to produce additional photographs in exchange for money to buy a reliable automobile that could take them through the deserts and mountains of California. Their brand-new Ford may have been a luxury, but their meager camping supplies were spartan — canned vegetables, dried fruits, cheese, crackers, honey, and nut butter. Throughout their 22,000 miles of travel over the next two years, they slept in sleeping bags on the ground, cooked with a small two-burner camp stove, and hauled water in a five-gallon desert waterbag. The editor at *Westways*, Phil Hanna, provided Wilson and Weston with another critical tool for their travels, maps of some of the more obscure and virtually inaccessible areas of the California desert. Armed with Hanna's directions, they set off for Death Valley in late April 1937, hoping to photograph the desert before the temperature made it impossible.

Death Valley presented a special challenge to the photographer, both physically and aesthetically. The desert lacked the abundant flora and fauna that Weston was used to photographing on the California coast at Carmel. His first photographs on the Guggenheim trip, close-up views of plants, emphasized the textures of plant forms against the backdrop of bulging boulders in the manner of his studies of kelp against the rocks at Point Lobos. Some plant studies, such as the view of a Joshua tree taken in raking light from a low vantage point, even suggest the format that Weston had used in earlier portraits, such as the image of Diego Rivera shown with his head thrown back, enframed by blank sky.

But when Weston entered Death Valley, he was immediately confronted with a wide, sweeping view, devoid of plant life, that required a different approach to landscape photography. The desert offered a vast panorama of folded mountain ranges, wind-eroded canyons, and flat, unarticulated basins. The sharp contrast of light and shade would prove to be a key factor in providing the means to distinguish form, space, and scale in the desert. Even Charis Wilson's first description of Death Valley is written with the tonal vocabulary of a black-and-white photograph:

North and south the valley seemed to extend to infinity – harsh barefaced mountain hemming in the narrow trough. More than a mile below us, spread over the valley's width, lay a glistening salt bed, with tapering ribbons of white extending from its sides. The dazzling white lake was bordered with a fringe of feathery grey that melted into a background of deep chocolate brown. At the base of the cliff we stood on, the neat arc of an alluvial fan was rimmed by a fine black line which we presently realized was a highway. Across the valley rose the seamed scared wall of the Panamints, with seeping curves of vast alluvial aprons at its base and a sparkling coat of snow on its peaks.[6]

Ironically, as Wilson noted in her text, good light was often hard to come by in the desert, and Weston had to work hard to find the right lighting conditions amidst the wind and rain storms, overcast days, and the ever present blowing clouds of dust and sand. In addition, his search for good vantage points was often hindered by the lack of paved roads and the poorly marked trails that were barely passable, even in the four-wheel drive truck provided by Don Curry, the Park geologist in Death Valley. Wilson described their fruitless ascent of Butte Valley in the Panamint Range at the west side of the valley:

Half a life time of jolting and banging and we came suddenly onto a comparatively smooth roadbed. The hills opened out and we could see, a mile or so away, a long bunker-shaped mass of dark rock. It had stripes along its side, to be sure – black and white stripes possibly – but of such a subdued nature as to attract little attention. This was the wonder-butte we had almost, literally, broken our necks to see. Undoubtedly, it was a fine specimen geologically; photographically it was just a butte. The next day we gave up. A close dirty sky shut down over the valley, locking in the humidity.[7]

Edward Weston
Badwater, Death Valley, 1938
From Weston, *California and the West*, 1940
Gelatin silver print, 7¹¹⁄₁₆ x 9⅝ (19.3 x 24.5)
Center for Creative Photography, The University of Arizona, Tucson

Edward Weston
Concretions, Salton Sea, 1938
From Weston, *California and the West*, 1940
Gelatin silver print, 7½ x 9½ (18.9 x 24.1)
Center for Creative Photography, The University of Arizona, Tucson

Edward Weston
Dead Man, Colorado Desert, 1937
From Weston, *California and the West*, 1940
Gelatin silver print, 7½ x 9½ (19.1 x 24.1)
Center for Creative Photography, The University of Arizona, Tucson

In addition to providing information about the photographic conditions, Wilson's narrative adds the essential element of human drama to the story of the Guggenheim project. For one of the most startling images included in the book, *Dead Man, Colorado Desert*, Weston photographed the body of a drifter that they discovered near Carrizo, east of San Diego. But without Wilson's text, which explains how they stumbled on the drifter's hand-scrawled message for help and his worldly possessions bundled up in a bandanna, the man has no real identity. His head and body lie on the parched ground like the sandstone concretions that Weston photographed at the Salton Sea. The real pathos of his existence comes not from the photograph, but through the written description of the man:

He lay on his back between the trees, half on a light piece of tarpaulin; a short, emaciated man with close-cropped hair and a stubble of red beard. His faded blue jacket and once-white shirt were open across his chest; his worn corduroy pants were ripped and roughly mended; long underwear showed under the torn cuffs. One battered shoe was off, lying near the small bare foot. His open eyes stared straight up. One hand rested lightly on his chest, the other lay at his side with the thumb and middle finger pressed together. Beside him stood a half-full bottle of fresh milk, a can of water with KY stamped on it, and a small bundle done up in a blue bandanna with a pencil through the knot.[8]

Here was a man whose lonesome death in the desert is further underscored by the other images of abandonment that fill this book — the crumbling buildings at Leadfield in Death Valley, or the ruins of the rhyolite mines in Nevada. But for Weston the idea of abandonment was only one element in the varied "Life" of the desert.[9] The physical challenge of photographing in the desert — confronting the constant heat, wind, and blowing grit — only seemed to sharpen his resolve to capture the desert's elusive beauty. It was far more difficult for him to marshal the primal forces of the natural world for a panoramic picture than it was to focus on its details. The powerful geologic forces conveyed in his photographs of the Panamints or the elemental simplicity of water and sky in his view of Badwater, seem to transcend the everyday worries of the Depression. But it is only in the combination of Weston's transcendent view of nature and Wilson's text about the ordinary details of human life that this book achieves its true sense of proportion and purpose. Their combined experience of the American desert was the first and perhaps most essential step in capturing what Weston called the "sublimated" character of California and the West. Desert life provided a formal and human perspective on the other distinctive regions of the state through which they journeyed — the fogbound seacoast, the snow-capped peaks of the Sierras, the rolling farmland of northern California, and the varied wilderness of Yosemite. The desert encouraged Weston to see the big picture, one that included traces of human existence as well as nature's overpowering forces.

1. Edward Weston, "Photographing California," *Camera Craft*, 46 (February 1939), p. 64.

2. Ibid., p. 56.

3. Wilson's unpublished manuscript, "Journal of Guggenheim Year 1937–1938," is in the collection of the Huntington Library, San Marino, California, along with five hundred prints made in 1940 from negatives made on the trip. For a discussion of those photographs, see Susan Danly, "Edward Weston's Gift to the Huntington Library," in *Edward Weston in Los Angeles*, exh. cat. (San Marino, California: Huntington Library, 1986), pp. 39–63.

4. Harry Leon Wilson (1867–1939) was the author of *Ruggles, Bunker, and Merton: Three Masterpieces of Humor* (Garden City, New York: Doubleday & Company, 1935).

5. For a more detailed discussion of Wilson's contribution as both a critical resource and a writer, see Karen E. Quinn's essay in *Weston's Westons: California and the West*, exh. cat. (Boston: Museum of Fine Arts, 1994), pp. 19–37.

6. *California and the West*, p. 18.

7. Ibid., p. 22.

8. Ibid., p. 43.

9. For an especially cogent essay on the paradigm of the desert as "deserted landscape," see P. Reyner Banham, *Scenes in America Deserta* (Cambridge, Massachusetts: The MIT Press, 1989).

Dorothea Lange
Dust Bowl, 1938
From Lange and Taylor,
An American Exodus: A Record of Human Erosion, 1939
Gelatin silver print, 10⅜ x 13⁵⁄₁₆ (26.4 x 33.8)
The Oakland Museum, California; Dorothea Lange Collection, Gift of Paul S. Taylor

Accompanied by the following text:
"It's made good one time. Of course everyone thinks maybe it'll come back."
— Coldwater District, Texas, June 17, 1938

AN *AMERICAN EXODUS* AS
A DOCUMENTARY MILESTONE

ROBERT COLES

No question, social observers and journalists have been journeying into poor neighborhoods, rural and urban, for generations, and in so doing have connected their written reports to a visual effort of one kind or another. Henry Mayhew's sensitively rendered *London Labour and the London Poor* (1861), which describes work done in the nineteenth century in London, was accompanied by the drawings of George Cruikshank, the well-known English illustrator — as if such an inquiry called for a pictorial response. When George Orwell's *The Road to Wigan Pier* was first published (1937), its text was supplemented by photographs, poorly reproduced, their maker unacknowledged — yet, surely some who read Orwell's provocative and suggestive text were grateful for a glimpse of the world this great essayist had visited under the auspices of the New Left Book Club.

By the 1930s, under the auspices of the Farm Security Administration, and especially Roy Stryker, who had a keen sense of the relationship between politics and public awareness, a number of photographers were roaming the American land eager to catch sight of, then, through their cameras, catch hold of (document) a country struggling mightily with the consequences of the Great Depression — in the words of President Franklin Delano Roosevelt (1937) "one-third of a nation ill-housed, ill-clad, ill-nourished." So it is that Russell Lee and Ben Shahn and Arthur Rothstein and Walker Evans and Marion Post Wolcott, and not least Dorothea Lange became part of a great photographic and cultural moment — the camera as an instrument of social awareness, and yes, political ferment.

Though some photographers place great store in the titles they attach to the pictures they take, or write some comments that will help locate the viewer, give him or her a sense of where the scene is, provide, even, a bit of context (how the person taking the picture happened to be at a particular place at a particular time), most photographers are content to let their work stand very much on its own, a silent confrontation, as it were, for us all too wordy folk, for whom language (in the form of abstractions and recitations) can sometimes become an obstacle rather than a pathway to the lived truth of various lives. But Dorothea Lange's work in the 1930s, quite able, of course, to stand on its own,

became part of something quite unique and important — and that connection (her photographs, the statements of some of the men and women whose pictures she took, and the text of the labor economist Paul Taylor) would become a major achievement in the annals of "field work," of social science research, of public information as rendered by a photographer and an academic (who, in this case, happened to be husband and wife).

It is possible to take much for granted as one goes through the pages of the 1939 edition of *An American Exodus* (it was re-issued in 1969 with a foreword by Paul Taylor, then still alive — Dorothea Lange had died in 1965). The pictures are still powerful, even haunting, yet some of them have become absorbed in an American iconography of sorts — the one titled *The Road West, U.S. 54 in Southern New Mexico*, for instance, or the one taken in the Texas Panhandle in 1938 that shows a woman in profile, her right hand raised to her brow, her left to her neck: a portrait of perplexity if not desperation. That woman is quoted as saying "If you die, you're dead — that's all," and we, over half a century later, are apt to forget that in the 1930s there was no solid tradition of interviewing those who are the subjects of a photographic study, linking what someone has to say to her or his evident circumstances as rendered by the camera. Again and again Dorothea Lange asked questions, wrote down what she heard (or overheard). Her sharp ears were a match for her shrewd and attentive eyes, and she knew to let both those aspects of her humanity connect with the people she had come to understand.

Meanwhile, her husband was daring to do an original kind of explorative social science. He was accompanying her; he was learning about the people, the locales she was photographing — how much people got for picking crops, and how much they paid for living in a migratory labor camp, and more broadly, what had happened in the history of American agriculture from the earliest years of this century to the late 1930s. This was a study, after all, of a nation's fast-changing relationship to its land — a major shift both in land usage and population: from the old South and the Plains states, to California and Arizona, and from small farms or relatively genteel plantations to so-called factory-farms that now utterly dominate our grain and food (and animal) pro-

Dorothea Lange
Grain Elevators, Barbed Wire, and Gang Plows on the High Plains, 1937–38
From Lange and Taylor,
An American Exodus: A Record of Human Erosion, 1939
Gelatin silver print, 9¹⁵⁄₁₆ x 6¹⁵⁄₁₆ (25.2 x 17.6)
The Oakland Museum, California; Dorothea Lange Collection,
Gift of Paul S. Taylor

duction. A combination of the economic collapse of the 1930s and the disastrous drought of that same time dislodged hundreds of thousands of Americans, some of whom sought jobs in cities, but many of whom embarked on the great trek westward, the last of the major migrations in that direction. For Paul Taylor, such an economic disaster was also a human one, and he knew how to do justice to both aspects of what was, really, a drastic, urgent crisis for humble small-farm owners or sharecroppers or tenant farmers or field hands. Taylor wanted to let his fellow citizens know the broader social and economic and historical facts and trends that had culminated in the 1930s "exodus"; Lange wanted us to see the world being left, the world being sought, and attend the words of the participants in what was a tragedy (for some), an opportunity (for others).

Although these two observers and researchers concentrated on the largely white families who departed the plains because that once enormously fertile expanse had become scorched earth, we are also asked to remember the Delta of the South, parts of Mississippi and Louisiana and Arkansas and, by implication, the especially burdensome life of blacks, whose situation, in the 1930s, even for progressives, was far less a subject of concern than it would become a generation later, in the 1960s. The New Deal, be it remembered, was very much sustained, politically, by the (white) powers of the South, and black folk then, as now, on the very bottom of the ladder, were not even voters. Nevertheless, Lange and Taylor paid them heed, and did so prophetically — took us with them to the cities, to Memphis: another exodus, that of millions of such people from the old rural South to its urban centers, or more likely, to those up North.

Also, prophetically, these two original-minded social surveyors were at pains to attend what we today call the environment — what happens to the land, the water, that human beings can so cavalierly, insistently take for granted. In picture after picture, we see not only human erosion — people becoming worn and vulnerable — but the erosion of the American land: farmland devastated not only by the bad luck of a serious drought, but by years and years of use that became abuse. It was as if the prodigal land had been deemed beyond injury or misfortune — until, naturally, it turned out to be otherwise. Suddenly the parched land said no to a people, to a nation, and suddenly the roads that covered that land bore an unprecedented kind of traffic: human travail on the move.

But Lange and Taylor go further; give us more to think about than the tragedy of the Dust Bowl, which had become a major event in a nation already reeling from the collapse of its entire (manufacturing, banking) economy. Some of the pictures of California (the promised land!) tell us that new misfortunes, even catastrophes, would soon enough follow what had taken place in Oklahoma and Texas and Kansas and Nebraska and the Dakotas. The lush Imperial Valley, where thousands came in hope, yet again, of using their hands, their harvesting savvy, to pick crops, make a living, was already in the 1930s becoming a scene of litter, a place where the land had to bear another kind of assault, different from a succession of plantings that aren't rotated, but are planned in advance with consideration of what the earth needs as well as what it can enable. The debris, the junk that covers some of the California land, was no doubt given us by Lange so that we would see how disorganized and bewildered and impoverished these would-be agricultural workers had become, their down-and-out, even homeless lives documented: the bare land all they had in the way of a place to settle, to be as families, at least for awhile. Yet, we today know how common such sights are across the nation — how those who live under far more comfortable, even affluent circumstances have their own ways of destroying one or another landscape, defacing fields, hills, valleys that might otherwise be attractive to the eye as an aspect of nature untarnished.

These pictures remind us, yet again, that tragedies have a way of becoming contagious, that one of them can set in motion another, that the temptation to solve a problem quickly (let those people cross the country fast, and find much-needed work fast) can sometimes be costly, indeed. There is something ever so desolate about the California land in Lange's pictures — even though that land, nevertheless, welcomed the people who flocked to it with jobs, with the hope that goes with work. Environmental problems to this day plague parts of California, among other Western states (and those of the East, too, of course) — problems that have to do with the way both land and water are used. A half century ago, Lange and Taylor more than hinted at those problems, even as, again, they gave us a peek at the urban crisis we would be having, come a decade or two, when they followed some of the South's black tenant farmers into the ghettos of a major city, Memphis.

Also important and prophetic was the manner in which this project was done — informally, unpretentiously, inexpensively, with clear, lucid language and strong, direct, compelling photographs. For some of us, who still aim to learn from people out there in that so-called "field," this particular piece of research stands out as a milestone: it offers us a guiding sense of what was (and presumably still is) possible — the direct observation of people interested in learning firsthand from other people, without the mediation of statistics, theory, and endless elaborations of

Dorothea Lange
Dust Bowl (Abandoned Dust Bowl Farm), 1937
From Lange and Taylor,
An American Exodus: A Record of Human Erosion, 1939
Gelatin silver print, 9⅝ x 13⅜ (24.4 x 34)
The Oakland Museum, California; Dorothea Lange Collection,
Gift of Paul S. Taylor

Accompanied by the following text:
"Section after section dried up and blowed away."
— Refugee in California
Dallam County, Texas. June 1937

"IF YOU DIE, YOU'RE DEAD—THAT'S ALL"

Texas Panhandle. 1938

Dorothea Lange
Page spread from Lange and Taylor
An American Exodus: A Record of Human Erosion, 1939
Library Collection, Whitney Museum of American Art, New York

so-called "methodology." Here were a man and a woman, a husband and a wife, who drove across our nation with paper and pen, with a camera; who had no computers and "punch cards" and questionnaires and "coding devices," no tape recorders, even, or audio-visual apparatus, no army of research assistants "trained" to obtain "data." Here were two individuals who would scorn that all too commonly upheld tenet of today's social science research, the "value-free" attitude. They were, rather, a man and a woman of unashamed moral passion, of vigorous and proudly upheld subjectivity, anxious not to quantify or submit what is seen to conceptual assertion, but to notice, to see and hear, and in so doing, to feel, then render so that others, too, would know in their hearts as well as their heads what it is that happened at a moment in American history, at a place on the American subcontinent. Here,

finally, the camera came into its own as a means of social and even economic and historical reflection. These pictures, in their powerfully unfolding drama, in their manner of arrangement and presentation and sequencing, tell us so very much, offer us a narrative sense of where a social tragedy took place, and how it shaped the lives of its victims. This is documentary study at its revelatory best — pictures and words joined together in a kind of nurturing interdependence that makes the old aphorism that the whole is greater than the sum of its parts ring true once more.

An American Exodus turned out to be not only a wonderfully sensitive, compellingly engaging documentary study, but it challenged others to follow suit, to do their share in taking the measure, for good and bad, of our nation's twentieth-century fate. Dorothea Lange was not only an energetic, ambitious photogra-

Homeless family, tenant farmers in 1936. Cut from the land by illness, driven to the road by poverty, they walk from county to county in search of the meagre security of relief.

Atoka County, Oklahoma. June 16, 1938

HIGHWAY TO THE WEST

"They keep the road hot a goin' and a comin'."
"They've got roamin' in their head."

U S 54 in southern New Mexico

Dorothea Lange
Page spread from Lange and Taylor,
An American Exodus: A Record of Human Erosion, 1939
Library Collection, Whitney Museum of American Art, New York

pher, she was a moral pilgrim of sorts, ever ready to give us a record of human experience that truly matters: our day-to-day struggles as members of a family, of a neighborhood, of a nation, to make do, to take on life as best we can, no matter the obstacles presented us. So with Paul Taylor — a social scientist who dared pay a pastoral regard to his ordinary fellow citizens, even as he mobilized a prophetic kind of inquiry into the larger forces at work on them, on their nation. We can do no better these days, over a half century after their book appeared, to look at it not only as an aspect of the past (a remarkable social record, an instance of careful collaborative inquiry on the part of a photographer, and an essayist and companion-investigator), but as a summons to what might be done in the years ahead, what very much needs to be done: a humane and literate kind of social inquiry.

Laura Gilpin
The Gate, Laguna, N.M., 1924
From Gilpin, *The Pueblos: A Camera Chronicle*, 1941
Platinum print, 9¼ x 7⅝ (23.5 x 19.4)
Amon Carter Museum, Fort Worth, Texas; Gift of the artist

THE PUEBLOS

RINA SWENTZELL

Laura Gilpin, like Frank Waters and other writers and photographers of the early 1900s, saw the powerful beauty and strength of place in the Southwest. They felt that the canyons, rocks, and shrubs of this beautiful and harsh place reverberated a significance which included human existence and gave it meaningfulness. Laura Gilpin sensed "the deep roots of the long past centuries" in such a way that "other parts of the country felt shallow by comparison."[1] *The Pueblos: A Camera Chronicle* (1941) was an effort to illustrate her response to the place and people of the Southwest. Her life story is parallel to that of Frank Waters, who also lived in Colorado Springs before coming into Arizona and New Mexico, and who also tried to describe that power of place and its significance to human life.

In some of the photographs in *The Pueblos* that focus on the natural landscape (pp. 45 and 113), Gilpin captured the exacting and exuberant power contained in the clouds, mesas, and piñon trees. That power of natural forms and forces was something that Gilpin acknowledged and could align herself with in order to photograph moments of its beauty and strength.

Her photographs of the Pueblo people, however, do not communicate their essence as full and complex human beings. She sensed the power of the place but did not understand the soul of the Pueblo people or their relationship with the place, although Martha Sandweiss writes that "the relationship between people and land in terms of potential to sustain domestic life" was important to Gilpin.[2] Sandweiss also claims that men of that era focused on the West as a place of inviolate pristine beauty.[3] Gilpin did photograph many domestic moments, such as the mother and child on p. 87 of *The Pueblos*. The subject, most likely, would not have been chosen by a man, but even for Gilpin the photograph illustrates the universal connection between mother and child rather than one which gives us an insight into the Pueblo people and their specific relationships. Although her photographs show a genuine respect for the Pueblo people and a strong desire to be in connection with *her* Indian subjects, she portrays them the way she thinks they ought to be — Sandweiss gives an example of her photographing a Zuni woman from the knees up, for instance, because she was not wearing the usual white moccassin-leggings.[4]

Gilpin had been told by other writers that the relationship between Pueblo people and the land was special and spiritually

Laura Gilpin
Acoma Water Hole (Acoma, New Mexico), 1939
From Gilpin, *The Pueblos: A Camera Chronicle*, 1941
Amon Carter Museum, Fort Worth, Texas; Bequest of Laura Gilpin

Laura Gilpin
Square Tower House, Mesa Verde National Park, Colorado, 1926
From Gilpin, *The Pueblos: A Camera Chronicle*, 1941
Gelatin silver print, 9½ x 7¹¹⁄₁₆ (24.1 x 19.5)
Amon Carter Museum, Fort Worth, Texas; Bequest of Laura Gilpin

significant. Non-native people such as D.H. Lawrence, Mary Austin, and Frank Waters had written about Pueblo culture, often describing it as a product of the Indian's sensitivity to the place. Like Gilpin, however, these writers never found the appropriate words to describe that interaction. Gilpin posed Pueblos against adobe walls (p. 101), adobe buildings (pp. 109, 117), architectural features (pp. 111, 85), and rock walls (p. 115). They are presented as part of the physical setting but their peculiar humanness is absent. They are not involved in life and are obviously stifled by the meagerness of their posed activities. They remain separate from the land, the photographer, and us.

The photographs of architecture are beautiful and reflect the undeniable patterning of built and natural forms (pp. 37, 95). Gilpin shows the built forms as extensions of cliffs, mesas, and rocks (pp. 27, 35, 41, 46) and illustrates the sensitivity of the builders to the spirit of the place, its elements, and forms. The builders appear as statuesque figures, with no emotion in their far-off gazing eyes. It was typical of the 1920s and 1930s to describe native Pueblo people as enshrouded in a spiritualism which was unattainable by the non-Indian. There was a need, it seems, on the part of non-Indian writers, painters, and photographers, to have people in the world who were beyond corruption by Western technology and values. Consequently, Indian people were removed from life, objectified, and romanticized. Their humanness was erased.

Gilpin, in a way uncharacteristic of her era, uses archaeology and scientific theories to try to explain the mystical Pueblo people. She begins her introduction by saying that "It is only in recent years that we have begun to realize the thrilling and amazing history that the archaeologists are unfolding for us. . . ."[5] The book, a camera chronicle, is divided into the archaeological periods of Pueblo history. Gilpin moved from the early basketmaker to historic times with text and photographs, but the first photograph in the text is of an archaeologist, Dr. Frank Roberts, "at work on a dig in northern Colorado." She goes on to explain that "the modern archaeologist works with extreme scientific precision and skill."[6]

This was an era of utmost optimism in the power of science. Science could unfold the past, and define the future, and solve the problems of the world. Everything, including nature, was within the domain of science. Scientific information was essential to the belief that nature and the world could be understood through logical and rational processes.

Gilpin unconsciously accepted and worked off these premises, not so much in her personal life as in her work. She could not relate directly to the Pueblo people whom she was photographing, but rather had to overlay scientific-archaeological information to validate her very human interest in a different group of people. She was also typical of the romanticists coming into the Southwest during that era, who wanted to find alternatives to the Western scientific mode of understanding.

In a later book, *The Enduring Navaho* (1968), Gilpin did show a more intuitive understanding of another group of native people, probably because, as Sandweiss suggests, she had more intimate times among the Navajos. She developed these connections through her friend Elizabeth Foster, who was a nurse on the Navajo reservation for many years. Gilpin's photographs assume no specific cultural knowledge about the Navajos, but do show us nongeneralized Indians. Such specificity, I think, was not possible with *The Pueblos* because her contact with the people had been superficial.

Yet I believe that Gilpin could have had a deep connection with the Pueblo people because her own rural lifestyle was based on a value system that encouraged taking care of and nurturing others. Her father, Frank Gilpin, became very dependent on her, emotionally and financially, after her mother's death. She took care of him for sixteen years. Shortly after her father's death, her friend Elizabeth Foster became an invalid, and she was Foster's primary caretaker for the next twenty-six years. Gilpin remained loyal and respectful while caring for each in turn. She was obviously hard-working, tenacious, and self-motivated.

Pueblo people were, during those years, also tenacious, hard-working, and nurturing. Their industriousness was obvious from the number of stone and adobe ruins throughout the Southwest. Houses were in constant repair and renewal. Villages were built and left after a generation or less. The Pueblos were tenacious in their love for the land and in their persistence to live and be one with the often harsh and dry place they depended on for survival. Nurturing was seen as an essential part of life. In songs and stories, the people asked for love, as in the following Tewa prayer:

Northward Lake ones
Those of you who are Corn-silk Old Women
Here you have come
We lay our lives out
So that we may be loved. . . .
For that we ask

The Pueblos, then, acknowledged the human need for reciprocal love and care. The Corn-silk Old Women were those who dwelt under the Lake of the North, and it was through them that the people were connected with other simultaneous worlds below. Love and consideration were also asked of the clouds, winds, and other natural forces. Without the winds bringing the clouds which brought rain, the corn would not sprout and grow. The Pueblos knew that they had a responsibility to love and care in return. The human need for love was seen as identical to the wind's need for acknowledgment, consideration, and love. Without love and consideration from the forces of nature, the Pueblo people could not survive.

It was here that the romantic non-Indians of the 1920s–1930s diverged from the native peoples. The non-Indians, given their cultural development, could intellectually appreciate and express love for nature but could not feel a reciprocal relationship with the sun, clouds, and winds. Nature could be captured through the camera for its beauty, but living within it and depending on it for survival was an alien concept. It was quaint to see the Indians run through the community space of the pueblo to generate human energy that would be directed toward the sun — who needed energy to continue his daily route across the sky. But it was almost impossible for the non-Indians to empathize with the Pueblos' sense of urgency that the sun would disappear without their help. Science assured non-Indians that the sun was beyond human influence. Independence from nature was part of the American-Western sensibility of the era. Indeed, this separation was necessary if one were to live in the human-centered Western world fostered by science. Although the romantics who moved into the Southwest felt an alienation from American society, they could not attain the oneness with nature that came with survival dependency. Nature was not viewed as a flowing, interactive force, and people were not seen as part of that flow, but rather as units, specialists and experts who could study other people objectively.

Laura Gilpin's rational mind treated Pueblo people as subjects of scientific study, and yet her intuitive self sensed them as people from whom deep, essential ways of being with the living earth could be learned. She saw nature as a pristine beauty and the Pueblo people as mystical beings living in elegant harmony within their natural surroundings. This she shows us in *The Pueblos*. Yet she also sensed something deeper in the Pueblo world which does not come through in the book. She sensed that there was power and significance in the long-term and interdependent relationship between the native people and the land.

1. Martha A. Sandweiss, *Laura Gilpin: An Enduring Grace*, exh. cat. (Fort Worth, Texas: Amon Carter Museum, 1986), p. 12.

2. Ibid., p. 11.

3. Ibid., p. 12.

4. Ibid., p. 44.

5. Laura Gilpin, *The Pueblos: A Camera Chronicle* (New York: Hastings House, 1941), p. 9.

6. Ibid., p. 13.

Ansel Adams
East of Death Valley, California, 1941
From Austin and Adams, *The Land of Little Rain*, 1950
Gelatin silver print, 7½ x 9¼ (19.1 x 23.5)
Ansel Adams Publishing Rights Trust, Carmel, California

Accompanied by the following text:
"East away from the Sierra, south from Panamint and Amargosa, east and south many an uncounted mile, is
the Country of Lost Borders."

THE LAND OF LITTLE RAIN

ANNE HAMMOND

As a member of the board of the Sierra Club from 1934 on, Ansel Adams witnessed the club's evolution in the 1940s from a hiking and climbing organization to one that promoted nature as ecological community rather than as recreational commodity. In 1936, he represented the Sierra Club at a conference of National and State Parks in Washington, D.C., where he showed congressmen his portfolio of photographs of the wilderness landscapes of the Kings Canyon area of the Sierra Nevada in order to further the campaign for a National Park. On this same occasion, Adams met Secretary of the Interior Harold L. Ickes,[1] who had been encouraging the change in environmental attitudes from utilitarian anthropocentrism to valuation of wilderness for its own sake.

In 1934, Ickes had already convened a National Parks Conference in Washington and registered his intent to preserve as much wilderness as possible. The highest function of a National Park was to serve as "the great outdoor temple."[2] The Wilderness Society, founded in 1935 by environmental preservationists Robert Marshall, Robert Sterling Yard, and Aldo Leopold, was also heralding wilderness not only as an essential resource for the human experience of solitude, but as a fundamental ecological web of life.

In the years leading up to *The Land of Little Rain,* Adams, as a board member, may well have participated in the Sierra Club's change of its statement of purpose in 1951: rather than rendering the Sierra wilderness accessible, the goal of the club would now be to preserve it.[3] As his notion of publishing *The Land of Little Rain* began to take shape, he was reminded of the fragility of environmental victories by the attempt in 1948 by the City of Los Angeles to encroach upon the resources of Kings Canyon, despite the area's status as a National Park. Also that year, the Upper Basin Compact, which proposed to make waters of the Colorado River available to four Western states, threatened to flood the empty canyons of Dinosaur National Monument in Utah with a dam and reservoir at Echo Park. A conservation war was declared against government and corporate interests by the Sierra Club and Wilderness Society.[4]

In 1949, Adams arranged with the publisher Houghton Mifflin to reprint the whole of the 1903 text of the book *The Land of Little Rain* by the famous nature writer Mary Austin (1868–1934). The new edition would include forty-eight photographs, paired with quotations from this and other Austin books.

Adams described the book, published in 1950, as a sequel to *Yosemite and the Sierra Nevada* (1948), in which excerpts from the writings of John Muir had appeared in a similar arrangement with sixty-four Adams photographs.[5]

In the chapter "Land of Little Rain" in her autobiography, *Earth Horizon* (1932), Mary Austin described how the rapid growth of the agricultural industry in nineteenth-century Southern California had increased the thirst of Los Angeles for water from the Sierra Nevada until the water rights of the Owens Valley region were finally bought up by the National Bureau of Reclamation in 1906. In the summer of 1944, Ansel and his wife, Virginia, took Nancy Newhall on a trip through the Owens Valley. (In 1955 Adams and Newhall would curate an exhibition about the need for environmental preservation called "This Is the American Earth," which was published as a book in 1960 and hailed as "the most important announcement the Sierra Club has ever made.")[6] On this trip, Adams wanted to show Newhall the devastating effects on the now barren terrain that had resulted from the permitted diversion of the valley's natural resources.[7]

Mary Austin's story of the betrayal of Owens Valley was undoubtedly the primary motivation for Adams' depiction of the region as nearly derelict. When Austin's text first appeared as a series of magazine articles in the 1890s, these lands east of the Sierra Nevada were already dry and inhospitable. When the streams running into it were diverted, many farms failed completely from lack of irrigation.

Adams was no stranger to the landscape of the Southwest. In 1930, he had collaborated with Austin on *Taos Pueblo,* a book of photographs and text about a Pueblo Indian village in New Mexico, but he reprinted *The Land of Little Rain* in 1950 primarily as a setting for his photographs. Adams first assembled photographs he had made in the early 1940s of the region near Owens Valley, east of the Sierra Nevada, and then, in the spring of 1949, he made an expedition into the desert to take an additional twenty-two images.

The excerpts Adams selected from *The Land of Little Rain* do not serve as accurate captions for the photographs — as he says in his introductory note, they are not "literal legends to a pictorial catalogue of the land of little rain." Taking additional texts from two other Austin sources, *California, the Land of the Sun* (1914) and *Earth Horizon,* he also took considerable liberties with the order

Ansel Adams
Watercourse in the Tungsten Hills
From Austin and Adams, *The Land of Little Rain*, 1950
Ansel Adams Publishing Rights Trust, Carmel, California

Accompanied by the following text:
"... by the creek where it wound toward the river against the sun
and sucking winds."

Ansel Adams
*Alkali Flat, Alabama Hills and Sierra Nevada in Distance (Mount Whitney
Third Summit from Left)*
From Austin and Adams, *The Land of Little Rain*, 1950
Ansel Adams Publishing Rights Trust, Carmel, California

Accompanied by the following text:
"The whole Sierra along the line of faultage has the contour of a wave
about to break . . . and rears its jagged crest above the abrupt desert shore."

and structure of the quotations, often abridging and recombining sentences to enhance their effect.[8] In many of the spreads of picture and text, he attempted to match the essence of Austin's metaphors with his own photographic tropes. For example, plate 45 is opposite the text, "The whole Sierra along the line of fault-age has the contour of a wave about to break. . .and rears its jagged crest above the abrupt desert shore." Adams here joined together two sentences from *California, the Land of the Sun* (p. 150), in which, incidentally, this wave motif appears repeatedly. By means of a low camera angle, Adams created a perceptual illusion, turning the desert plain and snowy peak into an image of a cresting wave.

While preparing *The Land of Little Rain*, Adams was also producing for Houghton Mifflin *My Camera in the National Parks* (1950), whose introduction stresses the importance of wilderness preservation within the National Parks. He quotes Whitman, borrows turns of phrase from John Muir, and describes the geomorphic aspects of mountain ranges as "primal gestures of the earth." In plate 14 of *The Land of Little Rain*, the "gesture" is one of volatile but inexorable evolutionary process — Austin's text presents the hills as "squeezed up out of chaos" and "aspiring to the snow-line." Adams' commitment to the primeval scene or the untouched natural environment embraced the spiritual values of Muir and Whitman as well as principles of geological change. In his own note to *The Land of Little Rain* he wrote (p. 110): "once the habits of mountain-loving and desert-hating are broken down through experience, the grand unity of the land of little rain becomes apparent." It is just as necessary to be desert-loving as mountain-loving if we are to recognize that the unique life of the desert is complementary to that of mountains in the macrocosm of nature.

The plates in *The Land of Little Rain* can be divided into two categories. One group represents the primeval natural scene deserving of wilderness preservation, and consists of about twenty-five images, including mountainous landscapes, eroded rock forms, weathered branches, and crazed and glistening alkali flats. Another group represents lands altered and inhabited by man, which therefore require resource conservation. There are some twenty-three photographs of roadways and railways passing through sagebrush and sand. The images present pastoral life under desert conditions — sheep herds in clouds of dust, bleached animal bones, a lone windmill, a sand fence, and an oasis of cottonwood and poplar trees. Within this category are also pictures that represent the cultural components of the region — portraits of a European-American miner, a Paiute man, and a young Mexican boy, a ruined building of adobe bricks, a piece of weathered wood with a crude calendar scratched onto it, and a desert

Ansel Adams
Basin Peak and the Buttermilk County Road
From Austin and Adams, *The Land of Little Rain*, 1950
Ansel Adams Publishing Rights Trust, Carmel, California

Accompanied by the following text:
"This is the nature of that country."

Ansel Adams
New York Butte (Inyo Range) and Rocks of the Alabama Hills
Photoengraving from Austin and Adams, *The Land of Little Rain*, 1950
Ansel Adams Publishing Rights Trust, Carmel, California

gravesite. Adams' choice of subjects in this last group did follow Austin's text, which had included stories about the region's Native American tribes, white American prospectors and mule-team drivers, and Mexican-American communities. The tri-racial complexion of Southwestern life was for Austin one of the region's most distinctive features.

In *The Land of Little Rain*, Adams offered a bifocal and potentially conflicting vision — a conservationist account of a region deprived of water, and a preservationist message of the grander unity of nature as a whole. The photographs show us what might have been prevented in terms of agricultural loss if local interests had managed to resist the larger economic de-mands of the state, but Adams also crusaded for the preservation of pure wilderness, a cause often viewed as remote and idealistic compared to social concerns for water rights. It was the ancient lakebeds and sand-sculpted rocks of the eastern Sierra, unchanged for centuries, which qualified this desert as authentic wilderness.

Ansel Adams
Desert Bones
From Austin and Adams, *The Land of Little Rain*, 1950
Ansel Adams Publishing Rights Trust, Carmel, California

1. Ickes was instrumental in securing Adams' commission from the Department of the Interior to photograph the National Parks and Monuments for a series of murals in 1941–42.

2. T.H. Watkins, *Righteous Pilgrim: The Life and Times of Harold L. Ickes 1874–1952* (New York: Henry Holt & Co., 1990), p. 550.

3. Michael P. Cohen, *The History of the Sierra Club 1892–1970* (San Francisco: Sierra Club Books, 1988), p. 100.

4. Ibid., pp. 144–49.

5. Ansel Adams to Nancy Newhall, February 15, 1949, The Ansel Adams Publishing Rights Trust, Carmel, California.

6. David Brower, *For Earth's Sake: The Life and Times of David Brower* (Salt Lake City, Utah: Peregrine Smith Books, 1990), p. 192.

7. Malin Wilson, "Walking on the Desert in the Sky," in *The Desert Is No Lady: Southwestern Landscapes in Women's Writing and Art* (New Haven and London: Yale University Press, 1987), p. 53.

8. When he was interviewed years later, Adams made a point of stating that the text of the original book was printed in its entirety in the 1950 reprint. Ansel Adams, "Conversations with Ansel Adams," interview conducted by Ruth Teiser and Catherine Harroun in 1972, 1974, and 1975, Regional Oral History Office, Bancroft Library, University of California at Berkeley, 1978, p. 559.

Laura Gilpin
Storm from La Bajada Hill, New Mexico, 1946
From Gilpin, *The Rio Grande, River of Destiny . . .*, 1949
Gelatin silver print, 20 x 24 (50.8 x 61)
Amon Carter Museum, Fort Worth, Texas; Gift of the artist

GILPIN'S RIO GRANDE AS SEEN
BY ANOTHER

JOHN R. CHÁVEZ

The Rio Grande, River of Destiny: An Interpretation of the River, the Land, and the People is the full title of Laura Gilpin's 1949 photographic book about one of North America's great arid regions. Taking a geographical approach, Gilpin depicts the river, in black-and-white pictures, from its origin in the Rocky Mountains to its mouth at the Gulf of Mexico. Seemingly, the book falls naturally into three major divisions corresponding to the river's drainage area: "The Source" in Colorado, "Midstream" in New Mexico, and "The Border," between Texas and Mexico.[1]

At the source of the Rio Grande, Gilpin begins with mountainous landscapes gradually occupied by cattle, sheep, and Anglo-American cowboys. As the river widens, these motifs merge with shots of meadows, log cabins, and a small town, the habitat of fishermen, miners, and lumberjacks. As Gilpin and the river enter the San Luis Valley, farms and adobe buildings appear, signaling a change to agriculture and Hispanic culture. At midstream, below the gorge in northern New Mexico, the natural landscape recedes into the background, and culture moves to the fore as Gilpin focuses on Pueblo and Hispanic life. South of Albuquerque, the river is surrounded by desert and sky, an irrigated cottonfield stretching into the horizon. On the border, industrial cityscapes of El Paso contrast with shots of traditional rural Mexico, the latter increasing as Gilpin moves into the remote country of the Big Bend. South of the confluence of the Pecos and Rio Grande, Gilpin photographs bridges, revealing the water joins even as it separates Texas and Mexico. Finally, at the delta, the river meets the sea, and the commercial importance of both is evident through pictures of ships in port.[2]

As we can see, throughout *The Rio Grande* Gilpin seeks to relate the river to the human activity it shapes. Through pictures and text, she narrates brief histories of the river's peoples, attempting to present these from different perspectives. At the same time she seeks to place these peoples in a positive light, the same light in which she sees nature itself. Though occasionally critical of the destruction inflicted by humans against one another and the environment, Gilpin's photographs and commentary are generally benevolent. In this she reflects the optimism of the years immediately after World War II. Despite her agreement

with Ansel Adams — that objective photography be used in the interpretation of human geography — the negative side of American society is barely discernible in Gilpin's work. And despite her disagreement with the popular aesthetics of magazines such as *Look* and *Life*, Gilpin manifests the same popular social optimism found in those magazines. Moreover, her own upbringing in the provincial, pro-development, Anglo-American West undercuts the critical positions she does take concerning environmental, but especially cultural, issues.[3]

Although Gilpin's forte is the interpretation of the physical environment, in *The Rio Grande* she ventures into cultural interpretation[4] and unintentionally substantiates the belief that objectivity in such study is unlikely. While focusing on the landscape, particularly the stream itself, Gilpin's pictures and narratives usually allude to the relationship between nature and the region's various cultures. Because of this, her illustrations, with their historical and cultural commentary rooted in Anglo-American tradition, invite comparison and criticism from other ethnic perspectives. As the objects of much of her study, Indians doubtless see Gilpin's pictures of themselves and their landscape in a different light. Certainly, Mexican-Americans have their own distinct visions of the land.

When Gilpin produced *The Rio Grande* in the 1940s, landscape photography was a field dominated by those who could afford the training, equipment, and travel necessary for the endeavor. Indeed, as a woman, Gilpin herself constantly had to overcome financial constraints to sustain her career and produce the books on which her reputation rests. Shortages and rationing during and immediately after World War II made *The Rio Grande* an even more difficult project to complete; nonetheless, the book was published in 1949. If a well-born, professionally trained Anglo-American photographer had such difficulties reaching publication,[5] it should be no surprise that photographic work by the region's socially disadvantaged Mexican-American population did not reach the same level. Although people of Mexican descent took pictures as amateurs and even as professionals, their work remained and remains relatively unknown. Because of this, images of the land and its meaning for Mexican-

Americans are perhaps better apprehended through their literature.

Facing fewer financial obstacles than those affecting Mexican-American photographers, writers of Mexican descent appeared in significant numbers, though only after 1965. Until that year, occasional stories and poems by Mexican-Americans went into print in marginal newspapers and magazines, with one or two books enjoying ephemeral lives in the mainstream commercial press. That began to change with César Chávez's grape boycott and the advent of the Chicano civil rights movement. The movement inspired a cultural renaissance; dance, music, drama, painting, as well as literature burst into production. During the 1970s, the quantity of literary work increased dramatically though generally still through small publishers. While photography by Chicanos also made an appearance, landscape photographs were limited.[6] As a result, one of the major themes of the movement — the relationship of Chicanos to the Southwest — was explored primarily through literary imagery. Indeed, within the Southwest, the Rio Grande and its surroundings proved to be a frequent object of description by Chicano writers. We can thus draw insightful comparisons between passages from Chicano literature and the illustrations and comments of Laura Gilpin's *Rio Grande*.

While Gilpin's southeasterly geographical approach seems culturally neutral in that Anglo settlement moved west and Hispanic settlement north, her direction permits her to begin in the predominantly Anglo areas of her native Colorado.[7] Such a direction would less likely occur to a Mexican-American photographic explorer, who would more probably begin in Brownsville and head upriver in search of its source. Historically, of course, the pattern of Hispanic settlement did not follow the river from mouth to source, but rather went from El Paso to Colorado and spread along the Rio Grande between Laredo and Port Isabel. Without a unified purpose similar to Gilpin's, the landscape images of Chicano writers naturally represent scattered points along the river. By following Hispanic settlement patterns generally, however, we can compare the Chicano images to Gilpin's as they intersect with the landscape.

Roughly halfway between the Rio Grande's source and its mouth, the city of El Paso serves as a good starting point for a comparison between the visions of Gilpin and those of Chicano writers. In a series of four photographs, Gilpin illustrates the modern urban area, stressing industrialization and excluding more traditional scenes north of the Rio Grande boundary between Mexico and the United States. First, she depicts a train crossing the river with smokestacks behind it; second, she takes a panoramic shot of the metropolitan area; and then she moves to a copper refinery and a cement factory. Though acknowledging the

historical significance of the river — noting, for instance, the crossing of conquistador Juan de Oñate — the images of modernity predominate: "Here is a copper refinery, where red-hot molten copper is poured into molds amidst rising steam. . . ."[8]

By contrast, Estela Portillo Trambley, author of *Rain of Scorpions*, mythologizes the landscape, preferring to see the land "behind the houses and the smelter." Within her narrative an Indian storyteller comments:

Indians and Mexicans have the. . .blood of the earth. . . . clustered in the valleys of the big river and where the earth was dry and parched by the sun, they followed the tall cliffs looking for water and food, and when they found it, some stayed behind and carved the mountain for their home.

Looking to the pre-industrial past, Portillo Trambley identifies the arid landscape with its Indian and mestizo peoples. These peoples drank from the river and planted their crops in soil irrigated by the waters, making lives for themselves in the process. The "new order of steel and concrete" created by Anglo capitalists displaced traditional lives, sometimes creating chaos "like the twister of the desert." Portillo Trambley's social criticism regarding El Paso's industrial development contrasts sharply with Gilpin's optimistic vision. While Gilpin mildly criticizes environmental abuse at the end of *The Rio Grande*, clearly she writes prior to the major environmental and ethnic concerns raised in the 1960s.[9]

Indeed, the most important difference between Gilpin and other Chicano authors, including Portillo Trambley, is the place of Mexican-Americans in the Rio Grande landscape. In her book, Gilpin acknowledges, "With more than half of its population of Mexican blood, El Paso is international in character." However, Gilpin accepts an ethnic distinction commonly made in the Southwest of the 1940s, but less accepted by the 1970s, certainly not by those in the Chicano movement. Regarding New Mexico's Mesilla Valley, just north of El Paso, Gilpin remarks, "Here one feels the transition from the Spanish-American of the Santa Fe area, whose lineage came direct from Spain, to the Mexican who has come across the border seeking work and higher wages in the United States."[10] Pictures of farm workers picking cotton in the valley accompany this remark.

The notion that the Hispanics of northern New Mexico are somehow more Spanish and consequently less Indian than those farther south is rejected by most Chicano writers. For example, in *Tortuga*, by novelist Rudolfo Anaya, two characters, whom Gilpin might have identified as "Spanish Americans," define their ancestry in relation to the Rio Grande's Jornada del Muerto just north of the Mesilla. To one character the desolate valley, also photographed by Gilpin, is not a journey of death, but "a journey of life. Our forefathers have wandered up and down this river valley for a long, long time. First the Indians. . .then others came but they all stopped here. . . ."[11] Anaya, a native of New Mexico, sees his people as mestizo, tied to the land primarily through their Indian ancestry. This tie for Chicano writers makes the Rio Grande and the Southwest an indigenous homeland in a way not recognized by Gilpin and other Anglo-Americans.

Of course, Gilpin, like other devotees of the Rio Grande, especially admires northern New Mexico, "the land containing America's oldest history." This heavily Pueblo and Hispanic cultural area forms the core of her book. "The Heritage of Spain" is the title of her section on the Mexican-American subculture of New Mexico. The section begins with a photograph of La Conquistadora, the statue of the Virgin Mary that accompanied the Spanish on their re-conquest of the province in the early 1690s. The dozen pictures that follow stress the distinctive architecture, crafts, and occupations of the area's Spanish-speaking inhabitants.[12] While all this compliments the inhabitants, with its emphasis on their venerable traditions, it remains elitist for its stress on foreign European, rather than native Indian influences. Despite the conflict between Indian and Spaniard over the centuries, the same process of biological and cultural intermixing that occurred in central Mexico occurred in New Mexico, creating a mestizo population and culture appropriately called "Mexican." Over time, entire Pueblo villages merged with Spanish-speaking colonists who were often already mestizos from earlier interbreeding with Indians farther south. Chicano writers of the 1970s would recognize and take pride in their heritage from the conquered as well as the conqueror.

In his novel *Heart of Aztlán*, set in Albuquerque and the villages of northern New Mexico, Rudolfo Anaya seeks to reestablish the ties between the Indian, "Spanish-American," and Mexican traditions severed at the turn of the century by Anglo intellectuals and artists interested in the Southwest. Concerned with the traumatic uprooting of New Mexican villagers by economic hardship, Anaya portrays their "new life in the bigger cities of Las Vegas, Santa Fe, [and] Albuquerque." The life of his protagonist becomes a search for the ties to "the sacred land" lost in his move to an Albuquerque barrio. In developing his theme, Anaya applies the ancient myth of Aztlán, the Aztecs' land of origin, often placed in the Southwest among the Pueblos. "We are the fruit of the people who wandered from the mythical land of Aztlán, the first people of this land who wandered south in search of a sign," sings a balladeer to his barrio neighbors.[13] Thus the ancient Aztecs wandered south in search of the sign that would tell them where to found Mexico City, a sign now gracing

Laura Gilpin
Boy on Donkey, n.d.
Photoengraving from Gilpin, *The Rio Grande, River of Destiny . . .*, 1949
Amon Carter Museum, Fort Worth, Texas; Bequest of Laura Gilpin

Laura Gilpin
Sotol Plant, n.d.
From Gilpin, *The Rio Grande, River of Destiny . . .* , 1949
Amon Carter Museum, Fort Worth, Texas; Bequest of Laura Gilpin

the Mexican flag. In this way, Anaya links the local Spanish-speaking New Mexicans not only to their own Indian past, but to their identity with the Mexican nation from which they were severed in 1848. Clearly, the Mexican-American writers who came out of the Chicano movement envisioned the Rio Grande Valley and the entire Southwest in a way Anglo-Americans such as Laura Gilpin had not. The region was their homeland not primarily because of their colonial, Spanish heritage, but because of their Indian and Mexican roots.

The issue of the Mexican-Americans' place in the landscape becomes even more apparent as the visions of other Chicano writers intersect with Gilpin's along the Rio Grande border between Texas and Mexico. According to Gilpin, "In Presidio [two hundred miles southeast of El Paso] old adobe walls are softened by the feathery leaves of the salt cedar, or tamarisk, and time seems of little importance." Though recognizing the Hispanic presence, she depicts a stereotypically idyllic and somnolent landscape, suggesting its inhabitants have few cares in the world. By contrast, in *El diablo en Texas*, Aristeo Brito describes a more ominous scene: "I would like to frame it for an instant, like a painting, but long shadows populate my mind, shadows that whisper in my ear that Presidio is very far from heaven."[14] In his novel, Brito narrates the somber tale of a nineteenth-century Mexican journalist and lawyer struggling to recover land lost by his people in the area. Indeed, conflict between Texans and Mexicans over land along the Rio Grande border dates back to the 1830s.

Though bypassing the issue in Presidio, Gilpin acknowledges the hostilities southeast of Laredo in the lower Rio Grande Valley: "conflicts along the border were legion. Raids of retaliation moved back and forth, instigated first by one side, then by the other." However, she follows with an account of the Mier expedition which ended with the execution of dozens of Anglo-Texans; no mention is made of the innocent Mexican families driven from San Antonio by Anglo-Americans during the same period. Her photograph of the international bridge at Roma supports her statement that by the 1940s life had "settled into a quiet routine with friendly intercourse across the Rio Grande."[15] The Good Neighbor Policy in effect at that time had helped maintain favorable relations between the United States and Mexico; however, by the 1970s issues such as immigration once again created tension, not only between the two countries, but between the ethnic groups.

The central icon of that hostility is, of course, the Alamo, included in Gilpin's book despite its location over 150 miles from the Rio Grande. In her accompanying narrative, Gilpin relates the events in traditional pro-Anglo fashion: "the gallant defenders had fought to the last man against the overwhelming force of

Santa Ana's [sic] army."[16] She makes no mention of the Texas Mexicans who defended the Alamo alongside Bowie and Crockett; moreover, she was certainly unaware that Crockett and several others surrendered, rather than fighting to the end as myth would have it. Finally, she pays little attention to Mexico's fear of losing its territorial integrity. These flaws were common to the 1940s, when Gilpin produced *The Rio Grande*, but the 1970s, as we have seen, brought challenges to the perspective she represented.

A Chicano professor in Joseph V. Torres-Metzgar's novel, *Below the Summit*, refutes that perspective bluntly: "Texans remember the Alamo — and remember the Alamo — and remember the Alamo — when it should have been cut down long ago and forgotten"; indeed, "Texans revered the Alamo and praised it and nearly prayed to it." Unfortunately, that memory was usually inaccurate, one-sided, and selective. While Santa Anna did slaughter hundreds of Texans there and at Goliad, vengeance was fully gained at San Jacinto and throughout the Texas Revolution, in which many more Mexican than Texan troops died. Nonetheless, partly because of the Alamo, Mexicans and Mexican-Americans continued to experience prejudice and discrimination for generations after 1836. In his *Generaciones y semblanzas*, Rolando Hinojosa-S. recounts daily life in the small towns and cities of the lower Rio Grande Valley from Laredo to Brownsville, though under fictitious place-names. In predominantly Mexican-American communities, his characters lead their lives, avoiding discrimination as much as possible but constantly aware of their subordinate status in a conquered land. Nevertheless, they await a better destiny: "the day will come when *la raza* [the Mexican-American people] will live in Belken County like it did before these bastards came here."[17]

Obviously, the images of the Rio Grande landscape projected by Chicano authors in the 1970s contrast sharply with those of Laura Gilpin and other Anglo-Americans in the 1940s. Though mildly critical of the damage done to the environment, Gilpin's photographs and narratives portray relations among the region's ethnic groups as tranquil. While recognizing historical conflict, she ignores its continuation. Moreover, her interpretations, though kindly disposed toward Indian and mestizo peoples, clearly derive from the dominant Anglo-American perspective. Though ostensibly an art book of benign photography, *The Rio Grande, River of Destiny* cannot escape the centuries of continuing conflict in the region.[18] Chicano literature serves to remind us that the Rio Grande remains a contested landscape. Even in the nineties, despite improved trade between the United States and Mexico, conflict over issues such as immigration indicates that the destiny of Mexican-Americans remains tied to the landscape.

1. Laura Gilpin, *The Rio Grande, River of Destiny: An Interpretation of the River, the Land, and the People* (New York: Duell, Sloan and Pearce, 1949), p. 3.

2. Ibid., pp. 4, 14–15, 22–23, 26, 28–29, 32, 33, 35, 37, 41, 55, 60, 71, 95, 110, 139, 141, 150, 163–65, 168–69, 175-79, 205, 208, 228, 235.

3. Milan Hughston, lecture on Gilpin's *Rio Grande*, unpublished transcript, pp. 3–5, 15.

4. Ibid., 13.

5. Martha A. Sandweiss, *Laura Gilpin: An Enduring Grace* (Fort Worth, Texas: Amon Carter Museum, 1986), pp. 19–20, 76, 80.

6. For a Mexican-American photographic collection produced in the 1980s, see Steven A. Yates, *Retratos Nuevomexicanos: A Collection of Hispanic New Mexican Photography*, exh. cat. (Taos, New Mexico: Millicent Rogers Museum, 1987).

7. Gilpin, *The Rio Grande*, p. 3, and Sandweiss, *Laura Gilpin*, p. 13.

8. Gilpin, *The Rio Grande*, pp. 162–65.

9. Estela Portillo Trambley, "Rain of Scorpions," in *Rain of Scorpions and Other Writings* (Berkeley, California: Tonatiuh International, 1975), pp. 116–17, and Gilpin, *The Rio Grande*, p. 236.

10. Ibid., pp. 163, 151.

11. Ibid., p. 141, and Rudolfo A. Anaya, *Tortuga* (Berkeley, California: Editorial Justa Publications, 1979), p. 4.

12. Gilpin, *The Rio Grande*, pp. 65, 106, 109–20.

13. Rudolfo A. Anaya, *Heart of Aztlán* (Berkeley, California: Editorial Justa Publications, 1976), pp. 4, 83.

14. Gilpin, *The Rio Grande*, pp. 178–79, and Aristeo Brito, *El diablo en Texas: Literatura chicana* (Tucson, Arizona: Editorial Peregrinos, 1976), p. i, my translation.

15. Gilpin, *The Rio Grande*, p. 208.

16. Ibid., pp. 155, 159.

17. Joseph V. Torres-Metzgar, *Below the Summit* (Berkeley, California: Tonatiuh International, 1976), p. 164, and Rolando Hinojosa-S., *Generaciones y semblanzas*, trans. Rosaura Sánchez (Berkeley, California: Editorial Justa Publications, 1977), p. 150.

18. Gilpin, *The Rio Grande*, p. 236.

Eliot Porter
Pool and Reflections, Grand Gulch, San Juan River, Utah, May 23, 1962, 1962
From Porter, *The Place No One Knew: Glen Canyon on the Colorado*, 1963
Dye-transfer print, 8⅛ x 10⅜ (21 x 26.4)
Amon Carter Museum, Fort Worth, Texas; Bequest of Eliot Porter

THE PLACE NO ONE KNEW

MARC REISNER

"In Cathedral Canyon, beyond a series of immense, vaulted bends, we come to a sudden closing in of the walls
where the floor disappears into a water-filled trough no wider than a man's body.
Swimming through is a dreamlike adventure. Shivering, we glide along like seals, chin deep in the water,
through still depths into an inscrutable solitude."

— Eliot Porter, *The Place No One Knew*

Nature took a hundred and fifty million years to make Glen Canyon. Humans, playing God, erased it in a decade.

In 1963, when the Bureau of Reclamation closed the gates of Glen Canyon Dam in Utah and the reservoir behind it began to fill, *The New York Times* did not consider this a newsworthy event. The dedication of Hoover Dam twenty-eight years earlier had brought ten thousand people, including the President of the United States, to a desolate, scorched backwater in the desert Southwest, but by the 1960s the erection of such a giant dam was an almost quotidian event. It was mightily significant for those who, in the short term, stood to be enriched, but Americans, collectively speaking, greeted the permanent loss of another river or canyon stretch with a yawn, or perhaps just a shrug.

There were in those days no environmental impact statements demanded by a National Environmental Policy Act. There was no Wild and Scenic Rivers Act. There was no Endangered Species Act. Any such law might have stopped the construction of Glen Canyon Dam, which is why many members of Congress representing Western states want to get rid of such laws — and, in the current congressional climate, may succeed.

The American West, which has been my home since I left New York City nineteen years ago, is a landscape of lonely forested ranges and vast pale deserts. It is also a landscape of sprawling new suburbs spawned by older suburbs and of electrifying green pastures watered by aqueducts. More than anything it is a land of wide-open hypocrisy and a fierce, rugged, stalwart socialism.

Water trickles through the roots of it. Except for a sliver of the coastal Northwest, America west of Kansas is uniformly more arid than its other-worldly Eastern counterpart. A year's worth of rain in Las Vegas is a month's worth in New York. In most years, San Francisco, a full-fledged semi-desert, sees no rainfall for six months; it is sustained by distant snowmelt collected behind a dam — the only large dam ever built inside a National Park. Los Angeles, on the threshold of true deserthood while it emulates Miami, lies in its dry basin with three huge river-fed catheters hooked to its nose.

Without its dams — there are thousands — the American West would be little more inhabited than the Sahara or Mongolia. In 1857, one of the region's early explorers, Lieutenant Joseph Christmas Ives, having struggled for weeks against the Colorado River's current through the pitiless Sonoran Desert, issued a proclamation upon turning back toward the Sea of Cortez. "It seems intended by Nature," Ives inscribed in his journal, "that the Colorado River, along the greater portion of its lonely and majestic way, shall be forever unvisited and undisturbed...I cannot conceive of a more worthless and impracticable region than the area we now find ourselves in." As that despondent thought (for Ives' mission had been to encourage settlement) nailed itself down, the lieutenant was standing a few miles from the site of modern Las Vegas, whose population grows by five thousand each month.

Major John Wesley Powell, who floated in the river's opposite direction — from Wyoming to what has become Lake Mead — returned somewhat more sanguine than Ives. You could settle the West, Powell concluded, if you captured its flowing water and made it flow elsewhere. Nearly all the region was too dry to raise crops, Powell told a nation of farmers. California, lacking summer rainfall, was even drier than it looked. (California was where everyone wanted to go.) But even if you diverted all the water out of Utah's meager streams, you could farm about three percent of the state — a chunk slightly larger than Rhode Island. It was worth trying, Powell concluded, only if the federal government was allowed to assume such a costly and perilous undertaking.

Powell's famous treatise on Western climate and irrigation was regarded by Western members of Congress as an unconscionable slight against their great, great, greater-than-great states — and as barely camouflaged socialism. Westerners then loathed federalism even more than they profess to now. But it soon

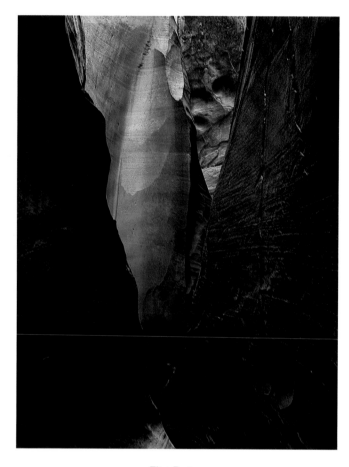

Eliot Porter
Dungeon Canyon, Glen Canyon, Utah, 1961
From Porter, *The Place No One Knew: Glen Canyon on the Colorado*, 1963
Dye-transfer print, 13¼ x 10¼ (33.7 x 26)
Amon Carter Museum, Fort Worth, Texas; Bequest of Eliot Porter

Eliot Porter
Pools in the Narrows, Bridge Canyon, Glen Canyon, Utah,
September 5, 1962, 1962
From Porter, *The Place No One Knew: Glen Canyon on the Colorado*, 1963
Dye-transfer print, 10¼ x 8⁹⁄₁₆ (26 x 20.8)
Amon Carter Museum, Fort Worth, Texas; Bequest of Eliot Porter

Eliot Porter
Pool in Upper Hidden Passage, Glen Canyon, Utah, August 27, 1961, 1961
From Porter, *The Place No One Knew: Glen Canyon on the Colorado,* 1963
Dye-transfer print, 10⅝ x 8⁵⁄₁₆ (26.2 x 20.7)
Amon Carter Museum, Fort Worth, Texas; Bequest of Eliot Porter

Eliot Porter
Dungeon Canyon, Glen Canyon, Utah, August 29, 1961, 1961
From Porter, *The Place No One Knew: Glen Canyon on the Colorado,* 1963
Dye-transfer print, 10⅝ x 8⅛ (27 x 20.6)
Amon Carter Museum, Fort Worth, Texas; Bequest of Eliot Porter

Eliot Porter
Lichen, Glen Canyon, Utah, August 24, 1961, 1961
From Porter, *The Place No One Knew: Glen Canyon on the Colorado,* 1963
Dye-transfer print, 8¼ x 10⅚ (21 x 26.8)
Amon Carter Museum, Fort Worth, Texas; Bequest of Eliot Porter

became obvious that states, counties, and least of all private enterprise couldn't build dams in the yawning canyons of this geologically infant landscape, and what was obvious turned tragic when a privately built Eastern dam collapsed during a deluge and caused the Johnstown flood. The disappearance of Johnstown, Pennsylvania, was an event of monumental significance for the arid West, for it stiffened the resolve of federalists such as Theodore Roosevelt to have the government build dams.

Roosevelt, the former police commissioner of New York City, was instrumental, above all others, in creating the Bureau of Reclamation, which was to become the godfather of arid America, in 1902. The Bureau's early dams were relatively small and its successes were quiet ones — a few thousand acres of desert settled and irrigated here and there. But the next Roosevelt saw the Bureau differently: it could employ tens of thousands, and resettle millions at a time when the West lay prostrate under the Great Depression and the Dust Bowl. Under FDR, the five largest structures on earth were erected almost at once; they were all dams, and they were all Western dams. As Hoover, Bonneville, Shasta, Fort Peck, and Grand Coulee rose magisterially from their river canyons, the Bureau — which is to say, the federal government — assumed awe-inspiring importance to the Western states. Hoover Dam watered and illuminated Los Angeles, the fastest-growing city in history. Grand Coulee and Bonneville transformed the Northwest from a forested wilderness into an industrial empire mainlining cheap hydroelectricity to crank out battleships and airplanes. Shasta turned California's searing Central Valley into the most productive stretch of continuous farmland in the world.

Among all Western rivers, the Colorado was to become the Bureau's obsession; it is the only river of significance in a landscape almost as large as the original thirteen states. The Bureau and its client region wanted nothing less than utter control: no flowing water was to remain anywhere. Upriver from Lake Mead, dams comparable in size to Hoover would be built in the Grand Canyon, in Glen Canyon, at Echo Park and Flaming Gorge on the Green River, the Colorado's main tributary, and at countless sites on smaller tributaries all over the place.

Among all these potential new dams, the ones to be built in the Grand Canyon attracted the most critical attention; the dam that would drown Glen Canyon attracted much less. The reason is offered by Porter's title, which is as apt as book titles get: since Powell's party had floated rapturously through Glen Canyon almost a hundred years earlier, only a few thousand people had visited the place. That did not make it less of a place. Battered and haunted by huge upriver rapids created by unyielding upthrusts of gneiss, Powell had drifted into Glen Canyon's languorous current almost tearful with relief. For the next two hundred miles,

Southwestern sandstone frosted itself over the hard Precambrian bedrock. The malleable sandstone formed, amid no rapids, a canyon landscape incomparably beautiful. It was a canyon of intimate proportions, almost claustrophobic at times, nothing like the stupendous amphitheater downriver. Glen Canyon was intricately folded, mysteriously chasmed, brazenly colored and striped, and, where springs burst or seeped from walls, tropically lush. Under chiaroscuro and moonlit skies, Powell, encamped in arcadian glens, groped perfervidly for appropriate place names. He came up with Music Temple, Mystery Canyon, Little Eden, Moonlight Creek, Dungeon Canyon, Balanced Rock Canyon, Star Bar — all the places that survive in Eliot Porter's book as photographs.

When the inundation of Glen Canyon was first proposed, the population within a hundred-mile radius would have fit inside a Third Avenue high rise. The nearest paved road was hours away. Aside from the itinerant jack Mormon, sheepherder, or early river rat who had experienced the place — and a few conservationists, like David Brower, who had not, or not yet — the canyon lacked a constituency. Echo Park, a bright, meadowed chasm along the Green River, was better visited, so a minor lobby coalesced around it. Glen Canyon was drowned through a horsetrade: it was simply swapped for Echo Park, which would be spared. Brower and the Sierra Club, who were pretty much the corporeity of the environmental lobby, helped orchestrate the deal. In his poignant forward to *The Place No One Knew*, Brower flagellates himself for it — as he still does.

Floyd Elgin Dominy, initials FED, of scabrous vocabulary and hard-boiled will, was Brower's archenemy in the Colorado River wars. As Commissioner of Reclamation, he produced his own coffee-table book, featuring Lake Powell and his dam, and in the foreword, which he wrote himself, he managed to capture an era: "Dear God: Did you cast down two hundred miles of canyon and mark: 'For poets only'? Multitudes hunger for a lake in the sun." Actually, the giant houseboat reservoir was almost an afterthought. The real purpose of Glen Canyon Dam is to generate hydroelectricity. Sold at premium peak-hour rates to air-condition Phoenix and Salt Lake City, the power revenues subsidize desert farmers for whom already-subsidized water is not enough. For some of them, the whole river, even though they use most of it, still isn't enough. The ultimate purpose of the Grand Canyon dams — which Brower and the Sierra Club, with some help from *The Reader's Digest* and *My Weekly Reader*, barely managed to stop — would have been to generate even more hydroelectric power revenues to finance an aqueduct hooking the Colorado to a more generous river, like the Columbia or the Snake.

Those were days when Americans were enthralled by anything big or bigger. They were years when the rugged-individualist West, without admitting or even knowing it, was growing hopelessly addicted to federal beneficence in the form of dams, cheap water, and hydropower subsidies. The addiction persists and is still fed, but the national frame of mind that permitted Glen Canyon Dam and offended Powell's ghost has passed into history.

So has Glen Canyon.

TRANSFORMATION AND REASSESSMENT, 1960–1996

Robert Adams
Motel, 1970
From Adams, *The New West . . .* , 1974
Gelatin silver print, 5⅞ x 5¹⁵⁄₁₆ (14.9 x 15.1)
Whitney Museum of American Art, New York; Purchase, with funds from
the Photography Committee 96.12

pp. 158–59: Tan Hawaiian with Tanya (detail)
Cover illustration from Venturi, Brown, and Izenour, *Learning from
Las Vegas*, 1972

Robert Adams
Along Interstate 25, 1968–71
From Adams, *The New West . . .* , 1974
Gelatin silver print, 5½ x 5⅞ (14 x 14.9)
Collection of Sondra Gilman and Celso Gonzalez-Falla

Linda Connor
Spanish Entering the Canyon de Chelly, Arizona, 1982
From Dingus et al., *Marks in Place: Contemporary Responses to Rock Art*, 1988
Contact print on printing-out paper, toned with gold chloride,
8 x 10 (20.3 x 25.4)
Collection of the artist; courtesy Howard Greenberg Gallery, New York

Linda Connor
Hands, Canyon de Chelly, 1982
From Dingus et al., *Marks in Place: Contemporary Responses to Rock Art*, 1988
Contact print on printing-out paper, toned with gold chloride,
8 x 10 (20.3 x 25.4)
Collection of the artist; courtesy Howard Greenberg Gallery, New York

Lee Friedlander
Sonoran Desert, 1995
Gelatin silver print, 20 x 16 (50.8 x 40.6)
Collection of the artist; courtesy Fraenkel Gallery, San Francisco, and Robert Miller Gallery, New York

Lee Friedlander
Sonoran Desert, 1995
Gelatin silver print, 20 x 16 (50.8 x 40.6)
Collection of the artist; courtesy Fraenkel Gallery, San Francisco, and Robert Miller Gallery, New York

Photographic publishing by the sixties and seventies had begun to consider the landscape of the American West clearly altered, if not scarred, by explosive postwar growth. Partly in reaction to the sentimentality of older views of pristine nature — now widely published in anodyne posters and calendars — younger photographers, acknowledging the Western landscape they actually inhabited, began to document more common sites: sprawling suburbs, roadside signage, and empty tracts of land.

One of the most significant departures from the wilderness aesthetic was the updated genre of the "road book." No longer isolated as an unmapped territory or a "strange corner of our country," the desert West had by now been firmly integrated into the US by a network of interstate highways, most notably Route 66. With the automobile, anyone could traverse the country in air-conditioned, individual comfort, and the desert became advertising's favorite backdrop for the automobile. Unlike the pioneering explorers of the Great Surveys, or even Edward Weston and Charis Wilson during their travels in California and the West, photographers began to cross the arid lands with an ease and a speed that required little accommodation with the place.

In presenting a mobile, restless America, no book was more influential than Robert Frank's *The Americans* (1955), a record of a cross-country journey, of a passage through a great American desert.[1] Robert Venturi, Denise Scott Brown, and Steven Izenour's *Learning from Las Vegas* (1972) considers a city built to catch the attention of a passing motorist: an oasis in the raw desert has become a glittering urban stop on the road and the object of a now classic architectural survey. *Royal Road Test* (1967) by Edward Ruscha, Patrick Blackwell, and Mason Williams also uses the mentality of the road to show a test drive in which a typewriter is flung from a speeding car to the desert floor. A filmlike succession of captioned photographs identifies a Royal typewriter, a "test driver" (Edward Ruscha), and each and every piece of the typewriter after it has been thrown from a speeding Buick Le Sabre. As a consumer object, *Royal Road Test* suggests something between a typing manual and an automobile guide, enlisting every photograph, every caption, and a consistently deadpan style to make the reader aware of the book as a unified work of art. Like the twenty-six photographs in Ruscha's *Gasoline Stations* (1962), the inexpensively published and artist-designed *Royal Road Test* is characteristic of the "artist's book" genre that emerged in the 1960s with Ruscha, a Los Angeles-based Pop artist, as one of its leaders.

Recent books serve to remind us that, whether seen as a test site for cars or nuclear weapons, the desert continues to attract and preserve human debris. In so doing, they restate an earlier understanding of the desert as both wasteland and memorial, an understanding best expressed in Mark Twain's *Roughing It* (1872): "The desert was one prodigious graveyard. And the log-chains, wagon tires, and rotting wrecks of vehicles were almost as thick as the bones. I think we saw log-chains rusting there in the desert to reach across any state in the Union."[2]

By the 1970s, Robert Adams, Lewis Baltz, and other photographers who were identified with the

"New Topographics" school of photography presented inhabited lands as the aesthetic rivals to the untouched natural landscape.[3] Robert Adams' *The New West, Landscapes Along the Colorado Front Range* (1974) links a series of closely related views of the sprawling suburbs along the Colorado Front Range, creating an unsentimental vision of the latest wave of settlement and construction in the West. Its repetitive structure focuses our attention on the minutiae that comprise a local scene and also helps to define Adams' idea of the "centerless" landscape of the American West.

In the past two decades, a number of photographers have been increasingly lured by wastelands and empty spaces — or by what Walker Evans once called the "enchantment . . . of the aesthetically rejected subject."[4] Perhaps stimulated by the entropic spaces defined by novelist Thomas Pynchon and earth artist Robert Smithson in the 1960s, these photographers began to look at the wasted peripheries of modern cities, as seen here in Lewis Baltz's *Nevada* (1978). Joe Deal observes the banal (yet, by implication, precarious) suburban life along the San Andreas Fault Line in Southern California in his portfolio *The Fault Zone* (1981).

Others, far less neutral in their assessments of exploitation of the land, have presented a searing indictment of military testing in the West. Richard Misrach and Myriam Weisang Misrach's *Bravo 20: The Bombing of the American West* (1990) offers, in sequenced photographs of bombed-out lands and explanatory text, a somewhat satirical proposal to turn a contaminated Nevada test site into a National Park. *Bravo 20* recalls the persuasive intent and the heightened emotional register of the earlier Sierra Club books, even as it proposes to turn a now despoiled desert space into a tourist site.[5] More recent books present a more optimistic environmental awareness: photographer Mark Klett and ethnobotanist Gary Nabhan consider the ways diverse communities might thrive in the Sonoran desert in *Desert Legends* (1994); while writer-photographer Leslie Marmon Silko and photographer Lee Marmon's *Rain* (1996) describes continuing traditions in the Pueblo cultivation of the landscape of home.

Photographic books of the last two decades also reflect a heightened consciousness of the cumulative photographic tradition in the West, a consciousness that was intensified by museum exhibitions of nineteenth-century Survey photographs.[6] The organized, collectivist survey of the Western landscape resurfaced in *Second View: The Rephotographic Survey Project* (1984). This project, organized by Mark Klett, JoAnn Verburg, and others, looked back on the exact sites of those "first" images to show them as they appeared one hundred years after the Great Surveys. This historically mindful approach is evident in *Marks in Place: Contemporary Responses to Rock Art* (1988), with its studies of ancient pictographs made by Linda Connor, John Pfahl, and others; in Robert Adams' *From the Missouri West* (1980); and in Peter Goin's *Tracing the Line* (1987), which follows the old nineteenth-century survey lines taken after the Mexican-American War.

All these books show that a dialogue now exists between contemporary photographers and those

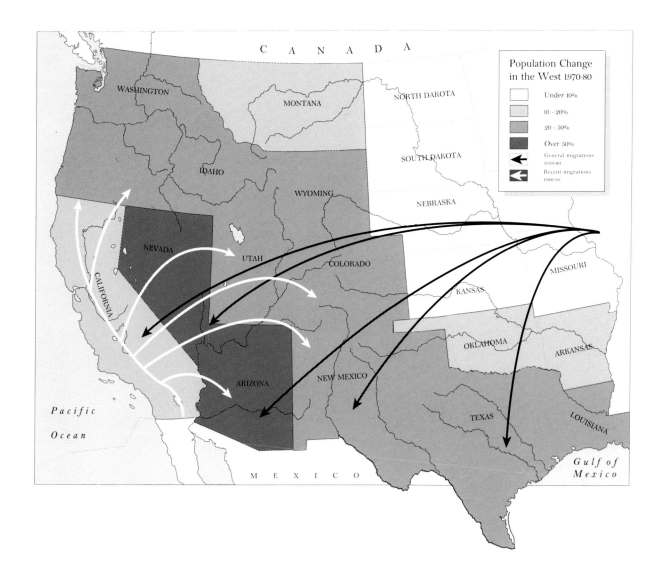

who previously framed the Western landscape. But it is also clear that the terms of the conversation with the landscape have changed over the last century. Some of the more ironic photographs by Len Jenshel, Alex Harris, and others reveal — in scenes of the Grand Canyon, Mojave Desert, or Canyon de Chelly shot through the glass of a car windshield or a hotel window — that the detached experience of looking at a photographic book about the American West may be closer to our actual experience of the place than it ever was before.

MAY CASTLEBERRY

1. Though beyond the scope of this exhibition, *The Americans* and other photographic books documenting larger American tours became much more common as it became easier for individuals to traverse the entire country by car.

2. Mark Twain, *Roughing It* (New York and London: Harper & Brothers Publishers, 1913), I, pp. 136–37.

3. That such a school of photography existed was proposed in the exhibition "New Topographics: Photographs of a Man-Altered Landscape," held at the International Museum of Photography at George Eastman House, Rochester, New York, in 1975.

4. "I lean towards the enchantment, the visual power, of the aesthetically rejected subject"; Walker Evans, "The Thing Itself Is Such a Secret and So Unapproachable," *Yale Alumni Magazine* (February 1974). Thanks to Elaine Reichek for bringing this reference to my attention.

5. For further exploration of the contradictions or possibilities of environmental advocacy in photography, see Vicky Goldberg, "A Terrible Beauty," *Art News*, 90 (Summer 1991), pp. 106–13; Miwon Kwon, "The Pleasures of Nature in Ruins," *Documents*, 1 (Fall–Winter 1992), pp. 20–26; Andrew Ross, "How to Occupy Your Own Country," *Documents*, 1 (Fall–Winter 1992), pp. 12–19; Rebecca Solnit, *Savage Dreams* (San Francisco: Sierra Club Books, 1995).

6. These photographs have been held and valued as historical artifacts in collections such as the Beinecke Rare Book and Manuscript Library at Yale, the Boston Public Library, and the Missouri Historical Society for many decades. It is in more recent decades that this work has been championed, collected, and widely exhibited as art. The exhibition "Era of Exploration: The Rise of Landscape Photography in the American West, 1860–1885," organized in 1977 for the Albright-Knox Art Gallery, Buffalo, and The Metropolitan Museum of Art, New York, by Weston J. Naef in collaboration with James N. Wood, offered the first major endorsement from the museum world. Earlier advocacy by Ansel Adams, Beaumont Newhall, and many others contributed to the greater exposure and understanding of nineteenth-century Western photographs in a museum context.

LEARNING FROM LAS VEGAS: MIRAGE OF MIRAGES

LISA PHILLIPS

The Las Vegas strip is a unique American phenomenon — a flashy, glittering wonderland of neon signs, casinos, motels, and gas stations rising abruptly out of the barren Nevada desert. Anyone who has approached Las Vegas at night knows the power of that vista — it is breathtaking and transfixing.

Extremes and paradox define the Las Vegas experience. First there is the dramatic contrast between the stark, natural beauty of the desert landscape and the artificial, electric urban oasis. Then there is the disparity between outside and inside. The ersatz city can be hallucinogenic and beautiful from a distance; its more troubling aspects are revealed up close. Las Vegas is about both dreams and their dissolution.

Developed by greedy promoters and populated by Mafia racketeers, showgirls, croupiers, pimps, and FBI agents, Las Vegas was created with one thing in mind: to sell dreams for cash. The appeal to the American dream of striking it rich, hitting the big time, has made Las Vegas the number one tourist destination in America. Every day buses and planes discharge thousands of visitors, who are herded into one of the clock-free casino caverns to spend their hard-earned money at blackjack or the slot machines and maybe take in a show. Las Vegas is above all a commercial center — a strip that advertises itself.

This is precisely what architects Robert Venturi, Denise Scott Brown, and Steven Izenour found so compelling about Las Vegas. It represents the pinnacle of a certain kind of American vernacular expression: roadside architecture. For Venturi, Brown, and Izenour, the Las Vegas strip offered rich territory for analysis. Like the Pop artists before them, they advocated learning from vernacular images, images driven by commerce, in order to alter and enrich high culture.

In 1968, they conducted an architecture study at Yale University to research Las Vegas, which led to the publication in 1972 of their seminal tract, *Learning from Las Vegas*. Now regarded as one of the most important architectural studies of the century, the book stirred a great deal of debate and controversy when it first appeared. The architects were accused of cultural slumming, of succumbing to the lowest common denominator, to the most vulgar embodiment of base values. But they were praised by others for approaching Las Vegas' manipulative strategies, its "architecture of persuasion" with open eyes in order to gain insight from its rich use of symbols. It was the publication of *Learning from Las Vegas* that catapulted Venturi, Brown, and Izenour into the public eye.

Learning from Las Vegas is a detailed analysis of the city's commercial values, commercial methods, and heraldic symbolism. It was the first time that architects looked at the commercial landscape and introduced it into architecture. *Learning from Las Vegas* signaled the authors' engagement with popular culture and more specifically with the phenomenon of automobile culture and its role in urban development. Their approach throughout was interdisciplinary and sociological, but they looked at the architecture in a semiotic, structuralist sense.

The large-format book is full of color photographs, charts, maps, drawings, and graphs analyzing casinos, signs, gas stations, wedding chapels, and automobile rental offices. Venturi, Brown, and Izenour used a full set of taxonomic charts and comparative maps to study architectural features and patterns of movement and activity. They created a map to show every written word on the strip in proportional scale. Borrowing from Pop artist Edward Ruscha's earlier photomontage of the Sunset Strip in Los Angeles, they made a continuous photographic elevation of the Vegas strip. The architecture of Las Vegas is shown to be an agglomeration of styles and eclectic accumulations: from Egyptian pyramids, Roman forums, and Moroccan casbahs to frontier lodges and space-age fantasies.

Elaborate studies were made of seven big casinos: the Sahara, the Riviera, the Stardust, Caesar's Palace, The Dunes, Aladdin, and the Tropicana. Among the things examined were interior and exterior architectural features — fronts, sides, backs, aerial views, entrances, roofs, parking, pedestrian spaces, oases, fountains,

Physiognomy of a Typical Casino Sign
Offset lithograph from Venturi, Brown, and Izenour, *Learning from Las Vegas,* 1972

foliage, signs, and sculptures. Linkages were established, similarities shown, and certain features revealed as consistent with the casino's repertoire of symbols.

Perhaps most important, the architects concluded that billboards were not negative intrusions in the landscape; they were, rather, a twentieth-century form of heraldic symbolism with a lineage extending back to Egyptian pylons, Roman triumphal arches, and medieval cathedral facades. They placed this new American popular vernacular in the context of historical monuments — monuments loaded with communicative symbolism. The signs function sculpturally and pictorially during the day and as a play of lights at night. They are mixed-media events (words, pictures, shapes, lights) which contain different scales for close-ups and for distance. Perpendicular to the highway, they compete to persuade and inform. *Learning from Las Vegas* recognized these signs as a new kind of building that responds to speed, mobility, and car culture.

The architects viewed Las Vegas as a commercial oasis — a liberated pleasure zone like Disneyland, Hadrian's Villa, or Xanadu. It is fanciful, light, full of illusion and fantasy. In the end, the team found its architecture honest — forthright in stating itself as pleasure, entertainment, commerce — in contrast to the puritanical and bombastic creations of late modernism, which claimed to be pure but actually represented the ego.

Learning from Las Vegas' critique of modernism was initiated in Robert Venturi's earlier important polemic, *Complexity and Contradiction in Architecture* (1966). In refuting modernism's claims of pure functionalism, *Learning from Las Vegas* considers how modernist heroes like Le Corbusier and Mies van der Rohe also had definite iconographic preferences and had, in fact, been inspired by industrial vernacular forms such as factories and grain elevators.

Learning from Las Vegas embraces eclecticism, the ugly, the ordinary, and above all, ornament. Venturi, Brown, and Izenour advocated a democratic approach to architecture — one that would confront and combine divergent values. Theirs is an architecture for a pluralist society that merges the values of various classes in a single dialogue. In demonstrating how buildings and their urban context are critically interdependent, *Learning from Las Vegas* significantly increased interest in "popular" forms and in the languages of subcultures.

Lately, the Las Vegas of the sixties and seventies has become the object of popular nostalgia, as evidenced in the recent films *Casino* and *Leaving Las Vegas*. The old tawdry "Sin City" is fast disappearing, transformed into a corporate theme park of family-value fun. Today, *Learning from Las Vegas* is also not without its nostalgic charm and appeal — it is a book about a legendary time and place — a man-made desert oasis that inspired a revolution in architecture.

Map of Las Vegas Strip Showing Heraldic Symbolism (detail)
Offset lithograph from Venturi, Brown, and Izenour,
Learning from Las Vegas, 1972

Robert Adams
Edge of San Timoteo Canyon, San Bernardino County, California, 1978
From Adams, *From the Missouri West*, 1980
Gelatin silver print, 16 x 20 (40.6 x 50.8)
Collection of the artist; courtesy Fraenkel Gallery, San Francisco,
and Howard Greenberg Gallery, New York

FROM THE MISSOURI WEST

ADAM D. WEINBERG

"And God called the dry land Earth."
— Genesis 1:10

"We animate what we can, and we see only what we animate."
— Ralph Waldo Emerson, *Experience*

The act of naming is an act of familiarization. Naming a feature of a landscape, especially a landscape as daunting and inhospitable as the American desert West, was a way of personalizing and domesticating it. And until something has been labeled it is difficult to progress to the more complex tasks of describing, organizing, and systematizing.

When the four great geographic and geological surveys of the West were born after the Civil War, one of the first, albeit unofficial, tasks of the survey members was to name what they saw. While each survey had its own scientific specialty, their most important collective responsibility was to map the land: to provide accurate, detailed geographical and topographical information about the vast, largely unexplored regions of the desert West for social, economic, and military purposes. For their maps, the surveyors occasionally used existing Indian names or names provided by settlers; but frequently they named or renamed the geographical features themselves. Sometimes the appellations were simply descriptive of the visual features of a particular canyon, mesa, or mountain. Other times they bestowed the name of survey members, family members, or helpful politicians.

The survey photographers who accompanied the explorers and scientists made pictures that recorded the land as it was being named and charted. Their images were pictorial catalogues of the lands being explored, providing identification photographs for the government, scientists, and the great majority of American people who had not seen and perhaps would never see the sights themselves. Frequently, the vantage points first established by the survey photographers were those that would be used again and again by other contemporary photographers as well as by later generations — including, in our century, the scenic overlooks which dot the highways of the Western landscape, and the typical landscape postcards displayed in drugstore racks. These viewpoints were repeated not simply because they were the most accessible, the most informational, or the most scenic, but be-

cause the repetition of an established viewpoint was a ritual, a deed of visual recognition. Photographing, like naming and mapping, was a form of acclimatization. It helped make the terra cognita.

It is against this backdrop of the named and the known, first established by the survey photographers, that the pictures of Robert Adams and other photographers of his generation must be understood. The endless repetition of the standard landscape view obscures what was fresh in the early survey photography, creating visual clichés and denying the present state of the land itself, our use and abuse of it. The popular conception of the Western landscape today remains that of a pure, unadulterated, and spectacular place. In his essay "In the Twentieth-Century West," Adams addressed the destruction of the landscape of the West and discussed some of the attitudinal shifts that would be necessary for its preservation:

Someday. . .we will go back to naming places as they are. It is probably too much to hope for the frankness that gave early Colorado place names like Lye and Oil Can, but it was those hard names that neutralized skepticism about the sweet ones like Maybell and Pleasant Plains, and this lesson in the value of candor may yet be learned. At least there will come a time when we stop naming places for lake shores that aren't there, and attaching to names eastern suffixes like "glen" and "green." And if we call places by names that are accurate, we may ultimately find it easier to live in them.[1]

In a similar fashion, Adams' photographs offer a lesson in the value of candor. Adams has resolutely and intuitively discovered a visual unnaming process. His pictures make fresh what we think we have seen and know. He rediscovers the known landscape and returns it to a state similar to that found by the survey photographs: strange, unknown, and unnamed.

It is Adams' references to survey photography that make *From the Missouri West* (1980) a milestone. In the afterword, Adams relates his own picture making to the nineteenth-century

Robert Adams
Nebraska State Highway 2, Box Butte County, Nebraska, 1978
From Adams, *From the Missouri West*, 1980
Gelatin silver print, 16 x 20 (40.6 x 50.8)
Collection of the artist; courtesy Fraenkel Gallery, San Francisco,
and Howard Greenberg Gallery, New York

Robert Adams
Quarried Mesa Top, Pueblo County, Colorado, 1978
From Adams, *From the Missouri West*, 1980
Gelatin silver print, 16 x 20 (40.6 x 50.8)
Collection of the artist; courtesy Fraenkel Gallery, San Francisco,
and Howard Greenberg Gallery, New York

exploration of the West and his family's connection to its settlement (his grandfather made panoramic photographs of the Dakota prairies). He also cautions: "As a 'survey' this one is not literally a cross section of the West, nor is it a catalogue of what is unusual there."[2] Indeed, the Missouri River, which defines a Western territory comprising more than half of the continental United States, is treated in the course of only forty-seven photographs, of which twenty were made in Colorado, eight in California, seven each in Wyoming and Oregon, two in South Dakota, and one each in Nebraska, Utah, and Arizona — the other Western states through which the Missouri flows are not even represented.

Nevertheless, *From the Missouri West* can claim a definitive kinship with the tradition of survey photography. The title of the book itself suggests that Adams, in survey fashion, *is* dealing with a larger idea of the West. The Missouri River, known to every schoolchild as the route first scouted by Lewis and Clark with considerable help from the Shoshone Indian woman Sakajawea, is the literal and metaphorical jump-off point for his exploration. His precisely rendered black-and-white — but predominantly gray — images, exquisitely printed in duotone, are generally organized in a sequential fashion from the Missouri westward — the first image having been made in South Dakota and the last in Oregon. Unlike typical survey publications, Adams' pictures are not accompanied by diagrams or maps, and they include little text: an epigraphic quote, a three-paragraph postscript, and most important, following the photographs, a list of descriptive captions. The language of the captions echoes a surveyor's crisp descriptions, which give the location and/or directional point of view (e.g., "Northeast from Flagstaff Mountain, Boulder County, Colorado"). However, the minimal amount of text paradoxically serves to underline the "scientific and informational purity" of the pictures themselves. Their seemingly prosaic, unpictorial character gives them the semblance of images made for the purpose of data alone.

Most significantly, by purposefully separating the titles from the images, Adams does not merely make claims for formal purity and photographic self-sufficiency, but also allows the images to float freely, disconnected from the specifics of location. The images exist in isolation — one image to a spread — or juxtaposed with one another, thus enabling them to symbolically and poetically conjure a larger image of the West rather than the very limited geographical area being photographed.

Robert Adams' stylistic approach is the true testament of his link to nineteenth-century survey photography. Adams has cultivated a style which perhaps achieves its apotheosis in *From the Missouri West*. It is a style which at first appears to be randomly composed, emotionally distanced, and for the most part downright unpicturesque. In photographs such as *Eucalyptus Along Interstate 10, San Bernardino County* it is difficult to ascertain the subject or know if there is a subject at all. A cursory examination shows a conifer tree, cropped dramatically at the top, clumsily bisecting the image. On the left, a palm tree gracelessly fronts several other trees while a minute man-made structure establishes a nearly nonexistent background. On the right, a few branches from a eucalyptus tree are visually and oddly detached from their source. A small plant (or is it the top of a large tree?) hovers in an indeterminate middle ground. An almost invisible mountain range seems like a willfully feeble attempt to suggest a background.

The lack of a singular, clearly established subject recurs time and again and in various guises throughout *From the Missouri West*. Is the subject of *South from Rocky Flatts, Jefferson County, Colorado* the tire tracks in the foreground? A rather unimposing, unscenic geological formation smack in the middle ground? The highway fences, telephone poles, and cars sneaking in from the right? The distant, partially blocked mountains in the background? Or the large featureless band of white which signifies a sky? Adams' frequent use of cloudless skies pointedly recalls the typically blank skies of the survey photographs, which were caused by the technical limitations of the wet-plate collodion process. Adams' "new topographical" approach, with its matter-of-fact, meta-scientific distance, recalls the fresh, earnest, and sometimes awkward views made by his survey predecessors. He skillfully and subtly plays with the would-be objective and the sometime seemingly nonselective character of survey photography and uses it to his own subjective ends. As he wrote: "At their best the [nineteenth-century] photographers accepted limitations and faced space as the antitheatrical puzzle it is — a stage without a center. The resulting pictures have an element almost of banality about them, but it is exactly this acknowledgment of the plain surface to things that helps legitimize the photographer's difficult claim that the landscape is coherent."[3] Adams' pictures acknowledge, as did those of survey photographers, that a component of landscape photography is the acceptance of what is visually ordinary. Through this acceptance we may not only transcend aesthetic conventions, but also perhaps expand our perception of the social and economic consequences of overdevelopment in the desert West.

In contrast, Adams' more immediate predecessor, Ansel Adams, who also admired the work of survey photographers, did not accept the ordinary as a photographic restriction. He largely sought the extraordinary in the Western landscape — the extraordinary sky, reflection, tree, or geological formation. He endowed

Robert Adams
Cottonwoods Below Lonetree Reservoir, Larimer County, Colorado, 1977
From Adams, *From the Missouri West*, 1980
Gelatin silver print, 16 x 20 (40.6 x 50.8)
Collection of the artist; courtesy Fraenkel Gallery, San Francisco,
and Howard Greenberg Gallery, New York

Robert Adams
South from Rocky Flatts, Jefferson County, Colorado, 1978
From Adams, *From the Missouri West*, 1980
Gelatin silver print, 16 x 20 (40.6 x 50.8)
Collection of the artist; courtesy Fraenkel Gallery, San Francisco,
and Howard Greenberg Gallery, New York

Robert Adams
Bulldozed Water Hole, Weld County, Colorado
Offset lithograph from Adams, *From the Missouri West,* 1980

Robert Adams
Clear-cut and Burned, East of Arch Cape, Oregon, 1976
From Adams, *From the Missouri West,* 1980
Gelatin silver print, 16 x 20 (40.6 x 50.8)
Collection of the artist; courtesy Fraenkel Gallery, San Francisco,
and Howard Greenberg Gallery, New York

each subject with a pictorial ideality while suppressing common-place reality. For this reason, Ansel Adams' photographs often feed the clichés of the West as a virgin wilderness consisting primarily of spectacular sites. In his photographs for *From the Missouri West,* Robert Adams reinvents antitheatrical, visual indirection. Instead of fortifying reality through technical wizardry and aggrandizing a singular, clearly comprehensible subject as Ansel Adams does, Robert Adams embraces contradiction. In formal terms, his images lack a central, not to mention spectacular, subject. In conceptual terms they lack obvious, simply explicable meaning.

Robert Adams, although he admires the work of Ansel Adams, subverts the approach of his predecessor. As a result, his work is closer to that of nineteenth-century survey photographers. Yet his photographs put even greater emphasis on the notion of banality. He reinvents what is picturesque in order to better conform to his own experience of an adulterated, violated, and regulated wilderness. In comparing *Alkali Lake, Albany County, Wyoming,* for example, to a similarly conceived photograph by Timothy O'Sullivan made in 1868 of Hot Springs, Smokey Valley, we see some shared sensibilities. Both artists clearly admire the irresistible, open expanse of land and sky. Both present relatively small, self-contained, puddle-shaped bodies of water in an arid environment. Both have set up their cameras in places that seem to some degree arbitrary and show a rather commonplace type of subject. Neither site is especially spectacular (similar photographs were made of a variety of small lakes, sink-holes, and hot springs throughout the West by both photographers). However, there is a crucial difference between the two images. In O'Sullivan's photographs, the positive though humble significance of the human being (in this case represented by the team and wagon, although typically indicated by a single minute figure) is central to the visual and conceptual sense of the picture. A certain grandeur is established by the horses and wagon in relation to the overwhelming scale of the land and sky. The caption for this picture could well read "Behold what we have seen!" Adams' picture also depicts a symbol of humankind, an almost imperceptibly small fence which laterally divides the photograph, subtly separating the lake and the viewer from the land beyond. The caption here might read "Behold what we have wrought!" The human presence here is largely negative. We are not just admirers naming and picturing what we see for the first time. We are interlopers who must undo or unname what is there, who must imagine what once was, what we have lost. What at first glance may seem beautiful in its unremarkable, flatfooted simplicity is tinged with sadness. As the epigraph to *From the Missouri*

West, quoted from Loren Eiseley, reads, "Nothing is lost, but it can never be again as it was."

While Adams' picture is not without hope, it does not represent the promise inherent in O'Sullivan's image. What is hopeful in Adams's picture is not merely the diminutive dimension of human incursion into the land — which seems to futilely fence in what is boundless — but also his reinvention of the landscape, what he called a landscape of "candor." *From the Missouri West* presents a view that is in keeping with our time. It is neither wistfully nostalgic nor wishfully optimistic. Through his photographs, Adams has discovered a visual name for unspectacular places previously thought unworthy of naming. By defamiliarizing a West we think we know, he has named a West we are obligated to confront.

1. Robert Adams, *Why People Photograph: Selected Essays and Reviews* (New York: Aperture, 1994), pp. 166–67.

2. Robert Adams, *From the Missouri West* (New York: Aperture, 1980), afterword.

3. Adams, *Why People Photograph*, p. 146.

Lewis Baltz
Fluorescent Tube, 1978
From Baltz, *Nevada,* 1978
Gelatin silver print, 6⅜ x 9½ (16.2 x 24.1)
Janet Borden, Inc., New York

TERMINAL DOCUMENTS:
THE EARLY DESERT OF LEWIS BALTZ

ROBERT A. SOBIESZEK

"The break, the disenchantment of the spherical world instead of the flat one.
On a sphere, to leave one point is already to begin to move toward it! The sphere is monotony. The poles are merely a fiction."[1]
— Victor Segalen, "Essay on Exoticism"

The landscape underwent rather grave changes between 1956 and 1979. Between the release of John Ford's desert epic *The Searchers* and that of Andrei Tarkovsky's post-apocalyptic film *Stalker*, the landscape was increasingly perceived with far more than a simple loss of innocence and only a bit less than a complete surrender to cynicism. Of course, the real landscape during these years was progressively scarred, mutilated, poisoned, sterilized of all life forms, and made, over the course of a couple of decades, to truly resemble T.S. Eliot's "stony rubbish" filled with "broken images."[2] But, much more important, our very idea of the landscape (and "landscape" after all is nothing but a perception) changed utterly and without, it would seem, redemption. In that nearly quarter of a century, a "death of nature" (*pace* Bill McKibben) took place in which the classic laws of thermodynamics were turned upside down, the notion of natural sublimity was reduced to the literary trope it had always been, and the idea that there was a nature apart from human culture and alteration was rendered preposterous. It is within this change, this fundamentally radical shift in perceiving the landscape that Lewis Baltz's *Nevada*, a series of fifteen black-and-white photographs made in 1977 and a monograph published by Castelli Graphics in 1978, may be located.

Between 1956 and 1979, a new order of landscape had taken hold of the imagination. In literature and drama, it was as if Eliot's fabled wasteland had completely displaced sylvan pastorals and Edenic backdrops. One has only to think of Samuel Beckett's desolate stage sets, J.G. Ballard's terminal deserts of both physical and psychic dissolution, or Stephen King's depiction of a ruined, post-apocalyptic landscape where the ultimate battle between good and evil is waged in the Nevada desert. In painting and other visual arts, a similar trajectory away from the pastoral and toward the apocalyptic took place in these years. Here, one has only to picture the blackened, burnt, and despoiled panoramas of Anselm Keifer or Robert Smithson's strategies of reclaiming strip mines and industrial quarries. Smithson's theories of an entropic universe in which everything is "confounded into a unitary chaos" and "seemed to contain *ruins in reverse*,"[3] are, in fact, markedly similar to the landscape dynamics articulated in fiction of the period by those who "found in entropy or the measure of disorganization for a closed system an adequate metaphor."[4] Photographically, traditional Luminist landscapes and grand operatic vistas of scenic wonders were suddenly replaced by topographic documents of a "man-altered landscape," littered with housing developments, mobile-home parks, and anonymous industrial structures.[5] Bracketed, as it were, by the release of Ford's *The Searchers* at the beginning and by Tarkovsky's *Stalker* in 1979 at the end, the landscape of this period shifted from one kind of desert to another. Ford's desert of the American West, a vast dry void in which anything is possible and nature remains the one transcendent constant,[6] had been transformed into Tarkovsky's irradiated desert of shallow lagoons lined with rusting scrap and rotting detritus and endless paths through overgrown weeds and collapsing structures where nothing is constant.[7]

Nevada, produced toward the end of this period, stands at a significant juncture in Baltz's work. It is not merely a suite of minimally cool images of similar types of buildings or a set of formal typologies, as was Baltz's former series — *The Tract Houses* (1969–71) or *The New Industrial Park Near Irvine, California* (1975). *Nevada* is far broader in what it encompasses. Nor does it exhibit the exploded perspectives and multiple viewpoints of his later studies of single, discrete sites such as *San Quentin Point* (1981–83) or the monumental *Candlestick Point* (1984–88) — *Nevada* is too synoptic and abbreviated in its scope. As in the earlier works, Baltz's highly refined and clinical, if now seemingly unordered, vision carefully detailed his subject: a portion of bulldozed earth, various housing developments, a few newly completed houses, certain architectural details, and a roadside bar at night. That they are all taken

Lewis Baltz
Hidden Valley, Looking South, 1978
From Baltz, *Nevada*, 1978
Gelatin silver print, 6⅜ x 9½ (16.2 x 24.1)
Janet Borden, Inc., New York

somewhere in a Western state is the only thing apparently connecting these disparate images. As in the work that preceded it, some of the facades and front yards depicted in *Nevada* have something of the deadpan severity of a Donald Judd sculpture or the wry irony of an Edward Ruscha photograph of the 1960s.

The panoramic views in *Nevada*, on the other hand, exhibit a romantic landscape sensibility not unlike Timothy O'Sullivan's, the nineteenth-century photographer of Arizona's Colorado River and Nevada's Carson Desert. Like O'Sullivan in the 1870s, Baltz carefully measures the vastness of the terrain by such devices as a glimpse of a far horizon spotted just over a closely seen rocky tor; and, like his forerunner, he calibrates the extent of civilization's incursion into the wilderness by portraying freshly built settlements harbored within shadowed valleys.

Measurement and calibration are what this kind of landscape photography is ultimately all about; both O'Sullivan and Baltz assume the same tasks, but to radically different ends that are summarized in two single images. In 1871, O'Sullivan photographed a rock abraded by blowing sands near Fortification Rock in Arizona. Next to the boulder, over which a flat valley and distant hills are viewed, O'Sullivan carefully placed an everyday glass bottle and what appears to be a metal cup: two scales of a measurable certainty in an otherwise incalculable vastness. In the fourth plate of *Nevada*, Baltz photographs a fluorescent lighting tube, found lying on the ground at a construction site, which had been repeatedly run over and smashed by vehicular traffic. Instead of providing the document with any inherently stable criterion of measure, Baltz deliberately occludes any certainty since there is no practical way of telling what the original length of the tube had been. The fact that Baltz titles the print only as *Fluorescent Tube* and does not offer any hint of the subject's geographic location, as he does in each of the other fourteen images, only buttresses the indeterminacy of the document.

Baltz attempts in *Nevada* nothing short of constructing a new vocabulary for landscape photography, a vocabulary that had been already outlined by novelist William S. Burroughs and artist Robert Smithson, but that had not as yet been fully worked out in photography. It was a formal vocabulary of sorts, reflecting Burroughs' "infinity of variety at the information level, sufficient to keep so-called scientists busy forever exploring the 'richness of nature.'"[8] It was also a strategy for picturing a landscape from multiple vantage points, indeterminable perspectives, and positions that are alternatively within and exterior to the principal subject; a strategy suggestive of Smithson's "infinite camera" that was "somewhere between the still and the movie camera,"[9] and somewhat akin to that used by Ruscha in his *Sunset Strip* of 1966. In *Nevada* Baltz's focus is no longer on the sterile architecture of an equally sterile late-century environment, but on an entropic *terrain vague* where what is built is merged with what is unbuilt, where "sprawl" and "blight" have become the picturesque norm, where the positions of observer and inhabitant are confounded, and where past and present are intermingled.

Baltz's later claim that "it might be more useful, if not necessarily more true, to think of photography as a narrow, deep area between the novel and film"[10] may be instructive at this point. The concept of an indeterminable, fluid view of nature (or the world) had led Smithson to postulate the "infinite camera" and an "open landscape" "which embodies multiple views, some of which are contradictory, whose purpose is to reveal a clash of angles and orders within a sense of simultaneity" and thereby shatter "any predictable frame of reference."[11] A similar kind of thinking led Baltz to *Nevada* and to his update, as it were, of Lady Elizabeth Eastlake's contention in 1857 that photography was positioned somewhere between descriptive narrative and pictorial depiction.[12] In *Nevada*, Baltz documented the dismal and utterly banal building sites that were suddenly being strewn about the Western desert in long shots and close-ups, under noonday glare and nighttime mysteries, and all in a montaged sequence of pictorial "events" that suggests an overlapping of beginnings and ends, ground breaking and finished landscaping, the construction process itself and the after-hours respite at a bar. Here, as in the finest filmic or novelistic montage (not to mention life in general), narrative sequences are indeterminate, time and space are nonlinear, and any causal relationships are shattered or exploded.

In the late twentieth century, the greed of expansion and development has saturated the desert landscape and turned it into a new kind of graveyard, one of the spirit if not always the body and one filled with mounds of debris whose source, whether construction or ruination, is seldom clear. The French critic Paul Virilio paraphrased the German philosopher Walter Benjamin's metaphor of explosion, with its ensuing "debris projected over great distances":

These distances, however, are no longer situated in any depth of field or "perspective". . . . We now have an open system, in which no one can find any perceptible, objective limits. It is a field of constitutive dispersal. It is a world of dispersed, or scattering, structures whose amplitude. . . we can no longer measure. . . .[13]

Baltz tries to depict precisely such an unmeasurable, explosive dispersal of structures in *Nevada*, and he discovers the analogue for this metaphor in a composite view of venal activity scattered across some forlorn corners of the Nevada desert. In 1978, Stephen King situated the climax of *The Stand* in Las Vegas,

Lewis Baltz
Model Home, Shadow Mountain, 1978
From Baltz, *Nevada*, 1978
Gelatin silver print, 6⅜ x 9½ (16.2 x 24.1)
Janet Borden, Inc., New York

Lewis Baltz
New Construction, Shadow Mountain, 1978
From Baltz, *Nevada*, 1978
Gelatin silver print, 6⅜ x 9½ (16.2 x 24.1)
Janet Borden, Inc., New York

Lewis Baltz
Night Construction, Reno, 1978
From Baltz, *Nevada*, 1978
Gelatin silver print, 6⅜ x 9½ (16.2 x 24.1)
Janet Borden, Inc., New York

the ultimate paradigm of desert development, and ended it with a thermonuclear explosion that does not disperse as much as vaporize and whose aftermath produced "the most spectacular sunset Stu had ever seen in his life."[14] In *Nevada*, published the same year, Baltz gave us a penultimate view of this wasteland in black-and-white images.

Once thought to "blossom like a rose" following development in the last century,[15] the desert of the American West has become, for Baltz and others, the backdrop for a lingering, inescapable entropy occasioned by avarice and some sort of Manifest Destiny. But Baltz's vision is not in the service of any anti-development propaganda, as some have claimed,[16] nor of any politics except those encompassing a personal coming to terms with viewing the present world landscape, which has become progressively one of uncertain "continuums and conjunctions of affects,"[17] as opposed to one of linear certainty and logical clarity. To deal with such a landscape, Baltz redefined documentary photography and its approach to landscape at precisely the same time he came to understand that what was generally thought of as "landscape" no longer existed. Incapable, as it were, of escaping the spherical world where everything is the same, Baltz began in *Nevada* to fashion a flattened and deadly earnest trajectory across the desert in search of new images and new ways of having them have meaning. After *Nevada*, his work became increasingly convolved within even deeper explorations of the incessant entropy that surrounds us and with the greater demands placed on the contemporary artist to unearth, as it were, those broken images from the waste-strewn barrens, stony rubbish, and unitary chaos we call life at the end of the century.

1. Victor Segalen, "Essay on Exoticism," trans. Richard Howard, *Normal*, 13 (Winter 1987), p. 61.

2. T. S. Eliot, "The Waste Land," in *The Complete Poems and Plays: 1909–1950* (New York: Harcourt, Brace & World, 1962), p. 38.

3. Robert Smithson, "A Tour of the Monuments of Passaic, New Jersey," in Nancy Holt, ed., *The Writings of Robert Smithson: Essays with Illustrations* (New York: New York University Press, 1979), pp. 53–54; cf. also Robert A. Sobieszek, *Robert Smithson: Photo Works*, exh. cat. (Los Angeles: Los Angeles County Museum of Art, 1993), p. 27.

4. Thomas Pynchon, "Entropy" (1960), in *Slow Learner: Early Stories* (New York: Little, Brown and Company, 1984), p. 88.

5. Cf. William Jenkins, *New Topographics: Photographs of a Man-Altered Landscape*, exh. cat. (Rochester, New York: International Museum of Photography at George Eastman House, 1975).

6. Cf. Jane Tompkins, "Language and Landscape: An Ontology for the Western," *Artforum*, 28 (February 1990), p. 97.

7. The author is grateful to Anniliese Varaldiev for bringing this movie to his attention.

8. William S. Burroughs, *Nova Express* (New York: Grove Press, 1964; repr. New York: Grove Press, Evergreen Edition, 1992), p. 49.

9. See Sobieszek, *Robert Smithson: Photo Works,* p. 32.

10. Lewis Baltz, *Rule Without Exception*, ed. Julia Brown Turrell, exh. cat. (Des Moines: Des Moines Art Center, 1990), p. 77.

11. Robert Smithson, "Art Through the Camera's Eye," in Eugenie Tsai, *Robert Smithson Unearthed: Drawings, Collages, Writings* (New York: Columbia University Press, 1991), p. 91.

12. Lady Elizabeth Eastlake, "Photography," reprinted in Beaumont Newhall, *On Photography: A Source Book of Photo History in Facsimile* (Watkins Glen, New York: Century House, 1956), p. 101.

13. Paul Virilio, *The Lost Dimension*, trans. Daniel Moshenberg (New York: Semiotext(e), 1991), p. 72.

14. Stephen King, *The Stand* (New York: Doubleday and Company, 1978; repr. New York: New American Library, 1980), p. 769.

15. C.W. Dana, writing in 1856, cited in Hans Huth, *Nature and the American: Three Centuries of Changing Attitudes* (Berkeley and Los Angeles: University of California Press, 1957), p. 131.

16. See Estelle Jussim and Elizabeth Lindquist-Cock, *Landscape as Photograph* (New Haven and London: Yale University Press, 1985), p. 147.

17. Gilles Deleuze and Félix Guattari, *A Thousand Plateaus: Capitalism and Schizophrenia*, trans. Brian Massumi (Minneapolis: University of Minnesota Press, 1987), p. 162.

Richard Misrach
Active Eagle's Nest, 1986
From Misrach, *Bravo 20: The Bombing of the American West*, 1990
Dye-coupler print cold-mounted on rag board, 30 x 38 (76.2 x 96.5)
Collection of the artist; courtesy Robert Mann Gallery, New York

RICHARD MISRACH'S *BRAVO 20*: *THE BOMBING OF THE AMERICAN WEST*

TERRY TEMPEST WILLIAMS

"The landscape was magnificent. I was surrounded by the vast expanse of the alkali flat, which acted like a great reflector of light.
As the sun broke the horizon, Lone Rock cast its shadow across the landscape.
Like a strange animation it began shrinking. The sky, the colors, the atmosphere, were cool and brilliant.
The landscape boasted the classic beauty characteristic of the desert.
It was also the most graphically ravaged environment I had ever seen.
I found myself at the epicenter, the heart of the apocalypse. Alone, no sounds, no movement. No buildings, no roads. No indication of life,
no promise of civilization. Only the smell of rusted metal. Bombs and lifeless holes. Side by side were great beauty and great horror."

— RICHARD MISRACH

Richard Misrach understands the desert as a landscape of paradox, especially the deserts of the American West. Bravo 20 is a bombing range. It is public land used by the United States Navy for more than three decades without authorization. Each day bombs batter this desert just outside Fallon, Nevada.

This is a story of a landscape ravaged by war, a war fought inside the military mind and imagination. It is one story in a much larger narrative rooted in the ideology of the cold war culture which includes Alamogordo, New Mexico, where the world's first nuclear test was conducted by the United States government on July 16, 1945. Names and places like Hanford, Washington; Rocky Flats, Colorado; Dugway, Utah; the Idaho National Energy Laboratory; the Barry M. Goldwater Air Force Range in Arizona; and of course, the Nevada Nuclear Test Site where the Department of Energy tested atomic bombs continuously from 1951 to 1992 — all serve as tangible reminders that this story of environmental degradation in the name of national security is not an abstraction but an open wound in the landscapes and lives of those who live here.

The photographs of Richard Misrach in *Bravo 20: The Bombing of the American West* allow us to bear witness to what has largely remained hidden, secret. We walk through surreal territory where the carcasses of fish and the remnants of bombs mirror one another. It is an aesthetic of deprivation, a land of little water, a land of little conscience. Artifacts of death and destruction remain. Through Misrach's eye we see twice, what is on the ground and what is buried in our history.

SEVEN IMAGES FROM *BRAVO 20*

Partially Buried Bomb

The rusty ordnance appears as an arrowhead left among the scree. As a species we have always evolved through our weaponry. Early desert dwellers worked pieces of flint into hunting points by striking rock against rock with the careful control of their hands. What hand, whose fingers pushed the button that opened the hatch that allowed this bomb to fall, explode, and rupture silence?

Active Eagle's Nest

A piece of machinery is left in the desert, painted in military camouflage. It is seen by eagles. Two eagles build a nest in this metal tree. Eggs are laid, hatched. Young birds are fed. Rabbits are sacrificed in the bellies of birds. There is life among the wreckage.

Overturned Armored Personnel Carrier

A white-starred tank is overturned. Blue sky above. Desert pavement below. The teeth of tank treads are turned upward on the sand like vertebrae, bones used by the wind as whistles.

Bomb Crater and Standing Water (Orange)

It is water. It is blood. It is the wound from which we are asked to drink.

Crater and Destroyed Convoy

It is water. It is blood. It is the wound from which we are asked to drink twice.

Richard Misrach
Partially Buried Bomb, 1986
From Misrach, *Bravo 20: The Bombing of the American West*, 1990
Dye-coupler print cold-mounted on rag board, 30 x 38 (76.2 x 96.5)
Collection of the artist; courtesy Robert Mann Gallery, New York

Richard Misrach
Overturned Armored Personnel Carrier, 1986
From Misrach, *Bravo 20: The Bombing of the American West*, 1990
Dye-coupler print cold-mounted on rag board, 30 x 38 (76.2 x 96.5)
Collection of the artist; courtesy Robert Mann Gallery, New York

Lone Rock (Dawn)

A mound appears on the horizon in the first light of day. It rises from the desert like a fist.

Shadow of Lone Rock (Afternoon)

The light of day deepens, stretching the shadow of Lone Rock almost to the horizon. A path is created, a way to walk around the craters of war.

From these photographs of the real, Richard Misrach moves us into a landscape of the imagined: *Bravo 20 National Park*. It is a proposal of reclamation, serious in its intention, playful in its presentation, encompassing plan, site architectural drawings, project cost estimates, and ideas for park concessions. Inside gift shops, one could purchase "maps of radioactive landfills, national trajectories of nuclear clouds, nuclear materials transportation routes" along with "Bombs Away" T-shirts, mugs, tote bags, and bumper stickers.

Misrach creates a complete and appropriate vision for the reinvention of our military wastelands, "the first environmental memorial," a way to heal both the physical and psychological abuses rendered on the deserts of the American West. These scarred, poisoned, and forgotten terrains become places of pilgrimage where we remember the wrongs that have been committed on behalf of armed beliefs. *Bravo 20 National Park* enters the registry of the Sacred.

Misrach writes, "In 1986. . .two civilians, Doc Bargen and Richard Holmes, went before Congress and said, 'Look there are thousands of unexploded live bombs that have been buried beneath the sands over the years and we can't decontaminate them. It would cost millions of dollars and would be only 95 percent effective.' And so, given that the Navy could not clean it up, Congress passed the Military Lands Withdrawal Act of 1986, which gave the Navy authorization to resume bombing for fifteen years, until the year 2001."

The countdown begins.

These photographs are not without personal reference. I live in the Great Basin Desert where the military has written its scarred history on the face of this landscape. The *Enola Gay* apprenticed here, with her pilots dropping bombs outside Wendover, Nevada, for target practice. And the Dugway Proving Ground is on the other side of the mountain range I look at each day; Salt Lake City is only a stone's throw away. The sun sets with a memory of military abuse. As residents, we hear about these stories but rarely see the evidence.

This summer, I witnessed the evidence. I flew above the West Desert with a pilot who worked at the Tooele Army Depot. He knew the ground below us and he knew the minds and mys-

Richard Misrach
Crater and Destroyed Convoy, 1986
From Misrach, *Bravo 20: The Bombing of the American West*, 1990
Dye-coupler print cold-mounted on rag board, 30 x 38 (76.2 x 96.5)
Collection of the artist; courtesy Robert Mann Gallery, New York

Richard Misrach
Shadow of Lone Rock (Afternoon), 1986
From Misrach, *Bravo 20: The Bombing of the American West*, 1990
Dye-coupler print cold-mounted on rag board, 30 x 38 (76.2 x 96.5)
Collection of the artist; courtesy Robert Mann Gallery, New York

Richard Misrach
Lone Rock (Dawn), 1986
From Misrach, *Bravo 20: The Bombing of the American West*, 1990
Dye-coupler print cold-mounted on rag board, 30 x 38 (76.2 x 96.5)
Collection of the artist; courtesy Robert Mann Gallery, New York

teries behind these war game maneuvers. I will never forget the barracks below, white concrete tombs that still housed the wet eye bombs decades old. They looked like coffins left above ground by funeral directors who never found the time to bury them because no families claimed or mourned their remains.

A few miles beyond, there are dunes. Deep holes appear as sunbursts, sand radiating in all directions. The pilot told me this was where bombs were being destroyed, part of the SALT II agreement. Soviet witnesses have stood and watched their demise.

"Here — " I thought to myself. "Just a few miles from my home, my home and a million others."

And beyond the dunes, the structure which creates, manufactures, and tests chemical warfare spreads out on the desert among the sage and pronghorn antelopes. All three entities were in view. Pools of toxic residue glistened in unearthly colors of magenta and chartreuse. I witnessed our shadow like a raven as we crossed over the site. I was beginning to get sick from the motion, emotion, as the plane kept circling over this military playground. We returned back to Tooele airstrip. Feet on the ground. I lowered my head and walked back to the tiny terminal for a drink of water, hoping it would settle both my stomach and my nerves.

It is disorienting, disquieting to realize what our public lands are being asked to absorb. Their physical abuse is our own. Unless we see them, feel them, take their pain into our own bodies and create measures to heal the wounds of war, we will continue to support, as Myriam Weisang Misrach reports in her impassioned text, "military training done in the name of national security that overrides both human rights and the laws of the United States." We will remain complicit to a "closed society one that places peace last and an ideology of war first."

There is a another vantage point in the Nevada desert that mirrors the Lone Rock of Doc Bargen and Dick Holmes. It is a keyhole in the Goshute Mountains where the curvature of the earth can be seen. Today, as it has perhaps always been, it is a funnel of flight where migrating hawks soar through without ever flapping their wings. Goshawk, Cooper's hawk, sharp-shinned hawk, kestrel, merlin, golden eagle, red-tail, and Swainson's hawk are just some of the individuals who follow this route. Below them is this great desert. The *Enola Gay* flew this territory fifty years ago. In the silence and grace of their migrations, I wonder what these birds must feel as sonic booms jar their concentration, force them to veer abruptly left or right of their ancestral paths. What must they think as they look down and see target debris and standing water (orange)? Surely they have perched at one time or another on the "Tower Bull's Eye" that stands in the Bravo 20 terrain that Misrach photographed as a scaffolding for the wind. I feel such shame in the presence of these magnificent birds for the way we have misused our power and our imagination. We have copied the gift of flight without remembering the source of our inspiration.

Bravo 20: The Bombing of the American West is a visual act of civil disobedience. Misrach is a photographer for our time because he is not afraid to tell the truth of what he sees. He has set his artistic gaze on the Nuclear West and created a work of beauty. When Rainer Maria Rilke wrote, "Beauty is the beginning of terror," he must have been anticipating the cantos of Richard Misrach.

William Henry Jackson
Eroded Sandstones, Monument Park, 1873
and
JoAnn Verburg
Eroded Sandstones, Woodman Road, Colorado Springs, Colorado, 1977
From Klett et al., *Second View: The Rephotographic Survey Project*, 1984
Gelatin silver prints, 10 x 16 (25.4 x 40.6)
Rephotographic Survey Project, Tempe, Arizona

SECOND VIEW:
A SEARCH FOR THE WEST THAT EXISTS ONLY IN PHOTOGRAPHS

THOMAS W. SOUTHALL

Second View: The Rephotographic Survey Project[1] is a startling record of a century of change in the American West and a revelation of how photography has been used to mold perceptions of the region. Between 1977 and 1979, the Rephotographic Survey Project located and rephotographed more than 120 sites originally photographed by Timothy O'Sullivan, William Henry Jackson, and other pioneering photographers employed by the government and railroad surveys in the 1860s and 1870s. Building on earlier before/after studies, in particular a procedure geologist Harold Malde developed to establish visual benchmarks, the RSP painstakingly matched original vantage points and even duplicated the seasonal light and time of day.

Just as the original nineteenth-century surveys' seductive views of exotic landscapes generated excitement about the West, the RSP provided fascinating documents of what these lands had become. The pairs of old and new photographs presented in *Second View* reveal countless dramatic changes — virgin valleys transformed into huge reservoirs by dammed rivers, open fields replaced by sprawling towns, and bizarre geysers now fenced in by walkways crowded with tourists.

Examination of the paired views and the evidence of change or lack of change can be almost hallucinatory. One reviewer, John Carter, commented, "My first reaction was that it was like looking through a stereoscope, where the third dimension that was added was temporal rather than spatial. It is not unlike looking around a corner, but rather than seeing new vistas of space, one sees old vistas of time. The effect is jarring."[2]

The visual manifestation of time is especially evident in the book's frontispiece of dramatically eroded rock columns in Monument Park, Colorado which effectively suggests the two types of time and change, natural and man-made, present throughout the paired images. The almost incomprehensible scope of geologic time measured in thousands, even millions, of years is suggested by the small shift of a boulder that had broken apart and moved a few inches over the last century on the path of erosion that will eventually turn it into sand and dust. In contrast, the effects of people significantly appear more brutal and inexplicable, as indicated by the decapitation of the head of the ancient eroded rock, which the RSP photographers learned may have been removed by locals for use as a coffee table or decoration for a country club driveway.[3]

Perhaps even more surprising were paired views that contradicted pessimistic assumptions about the detrimental effects of inhabitation. Numerous scenes showed amazingly little change or actually suggested improvement or rejuvenation, such as the RSP 1979 image of the barren desert landscape that showed no evidence of the huge Gould and Curry mining buildings that had been the subject of O'Sullivan's 1868 view. Many of these paired views not only challenged assumptions about environmental damage, but also, as revisionist Western historian Patricia Limerick has pointed out, challenge Western myths of unbridled booming prosperity by showing that our experience of the land was also a story of failure, disappointment, and depletion of resources. Limerick wrote: "Perhaps most important to me and my colleagues in western American history, the Rephotographic Survey Project rested on the idea that western American history was a continuous, running story. . . . Intentionally or not, the Rephotographic Survey Project rejected the abstract, shifty definition of the West as frontier, and saw the West as a set of solid and continuous places. The project by its very nature assumed a connection between the western present and the western past."[4]

The seductive game of measuring change or lack thereof, however, is just the most basic and literal insight provided by the RSP and *Second View*. Compared to other key photographic books on the West, *Second View: The Rephotographic Survey Project* stands in a special position because its real subject is actually less the Western landscape than the very nature of photography itself.

By following in the footsteps of photographers a hundred years earlier, the RSP uncovered a wealth of information about how their nineteenth-century predecessors worked and how their photographs represented the landscape. In her introductory essay, JoAnn Verburg described how often the RSP photogra-

Timothy O'Sullivan
Quartz Mill Near Virginia City, 1868
and
Mark Klett
Site of the Gould and Curry Mine, Virginia City, Nevada, 1979
From Klett et al., *Second View: The Rephotographic Survey Project*, 1984
Gelatin silver prints, 8 x 20 (20.3 x 50.8)
Rephotographic Survey Project, Tempe, Arizona

phers were surprised by their experience of a site, compared to what they had expected from the hundred-year-old photograph. Sometimes it might be the addition of different senses — smells and sounds, or landscape features and human activity that lay just outside of the camera view. In other cases, the shock was discovering how radically the photographer's selection of vantage point had manipulated the scene. The book's cover is one of the most dramatic distortions the RSP found — A. J. Russell's vantage point had transformed an insignificant niche in a cliff into a dramatically threatening "hanging rock." These discoveries provided tangible evidence that even though the nineteenth-century survey photographers may not have been formally trained as artists, they were masterful picture makers capable both of adding drama to conventional scenes and interpretive perspective to seemingly objective documents.

The reconstruction of the photographers' activities was especially fascinating because it provided an entirely new methodology and a wealth of evidence with which to understand how the photographers worked, what their goals and intentions might have been, and how their work might have been used and interpreted both in their time and today. While much previous art historical study of photographs of the American West has tended to take the work out of context and celebrate the formal beauty of

individual pictures, *Second View* helps reestablish the original context of these works by reconstructing different photographers' series and working procedures. Although the nineteenth-century photographers left few written records to explain their goals and intentions, by retracing their activities, the RSP provided an invaluable new tool for identifying the critical and often very subjective choices made by their predecessors, including selection of subjects, point of view, and even use of light and shadow.

Second View presents numerous discoveries that give a better idea of the shared as well as the divergent ways their predecessors worked, including how far they ventured from well-worn routes and their diverse approaches to similar subjects. *Second View* also found evidence of scientific intent, such as O'Sullivan's triangulated sets of views, which followed geographic mapping methods. Assumptions about the exact scientific intentions and usefulness of these photographs were also challenged by photographs such as that depicting Witches Rocks, which RSP photographer Rick Dingus discovered had been photographed by O'Sullivan using a tilted camera. This vantage point may have added to the drama of the scene, but the appearance of uplifted geologic activity could also lead to incorrect scientific interpretations.

For the most part, the RSP's documentation can only challenge previous interpretations and raise significant new ques-

A.J. Russell
Hanging Rock, Foot of Echo Cañon, 1867–68
and
Rick Dingus
Hanging Rock, Foot of Echo Canyon, Utah, 1978
From Klett et al., *Second View: The Rephotographic Survey Project*, 1984
Gelatin silver prints, 8 x 20 (20.3 x 50.8)
Rephotographic Survey Project, Tempe, Arizona

tions, and the RSP is careful about drawing conclusions based on partial evidence. In fact, the greatest contribution of *Second View* may be that it poses more questions than it answers. In this way, *Second View* is more akin to the reports of the earlier nineteenth-century surveys, which were largely compilations of raw, undigested data, than to the more narrowly focused picture books of the 1970s and 1980s, such as the Sierra Club publications, with their clearly stated themes and missions.

Even in design, *Second View* is closer to the dry nineteenth-century scientific reports than to contemporary art monographs. While well printed and clearly laid out, the book primarily has the appearance of being a report, not a coffeetable surrogate for the experience of the landscape or a tightly organized argument about what the West is or should be. This is a book that is meant to be mined, to inspire and stimulate thought. The photographs are straightforwardly presented and treated as information, not the celebration of a glorious landscape.

The expansive meaning of this project is suggested, but far from exhausted, by the essays that accompany the paired pictures. JoAnn Verburg's text identifies the goals of the project and provides a colorful account of the surprises and personal experiences of the photographers. However, many of her observations also reflect a lack of self-awareness: "We however who began with no ambition to make a realistic survey of the West, got one. Unlike our predecessors, we did not take what we thought would be appealing shots. Instead, we did a survey of a survey. In the century between their work and ours, natural and manmade changes had left marks on the sites. Trees and bushes as well as houses and antennae have spoiled many of the compositions made by the earlier workers, and have given us a number of views that seem aesthetically weak or of dull or ugly subjects. Our representation of the West is less the result of what we noticed or preferred than of what we found — changed or not — at predetermined points. So, ironically, our survey did what theirs purported to do: to show the West without shaping it to our own artistic purposes."[5]

Mark Klett's essay on the methodology of the RSP provides a firm scientific explanation of the procedures that clearly benefits from the author's undergraduate background as a geologist. His outline of the exact techniques of the RSP is essential to understand the conclusions that might be drawn from the work, and also provides clear instructions to future workers who may want to continue the process and add to the record.

Paul Berger's provocative essay concentrates on the question of how time is recorded in photography by discussing the RSP work in the tradition of photographic studies of time, from Muybridge, Marey, and Bragaglia to recent photographic explo-

Timothy O'Sullivan
Tertiary Conglomerates, Weber Valley, Utah, 1869
and
Rick Dingus
Witches Rocks, Weber Valley, Utah, 1978
From Klett et al., *Second View: The Rephotographic Survey Project*, 1984
Gelatin silver prints, 8 x 20 (20.3 x 50.8)
Rephotographic Survey Project, Tempe, Arizona

rations of time, including Eve Sonneman's diptychs and other "rephotography" projects by Bill Ganzel and Frank Gohlke. While Berger's essay analyzes how photographs translate and embody time symbolically, his essay does not attempt to address the full range of issues suggested by the RSP's work.

Berger's discussion of Frank Gohlke's understated views of tornado destruction in Wichita Falls, Texas, in 1979, paired with views of the rebuilt site a year later, is especially illuminating because it goes beyond the issue of time and establishes the critical connection between the RSP and the new approaches to vernacular, human-transformed landscapes that characterized the work of the 1970s New Topographic photographers. Gohlke was one of many emerging photographers, including Robert Adams, Joe Deal, Nick Nixon, Lewis Baltz, Bernd and Hilla Becher, among others, whose work was brought together in the seminal "New Topographics" exhibition organized at the Eastman House by Bill Jenkins in 1975, just a few years before the inception of the RSP. Although the term New Topographics is a somewhat awkward label for photographers as divergent as Robert Adams and the Bechers, these photographers were united by a shared interest in the occupied, common landscape, rather than the pristine wilderness characteristic of classic landscape photographers like Ansel Adams and Eliot Porter. Ansel Adams lamented the incursion of jet plane trails in his skies and retouched out graffiti he

felt marred views of otherwise pristine nature, but the New Topographic photographers consciously embraced these subjects. The RSP provided a third alternative: to simply accept and record human intrusion whenever it appeared in predetermined sites. By concentrating on the "vernacular" landscape, as defined by J.B. Jackson and other landscape historians, the New Topographic photographers encouraged a new understanding of nature that includes all our surroundings, even the most humble backyard of a tract house or sprawl of a suburban mall.

While the New Topographic photographers rediscovered undervalued, common landscapes, the RSP explored similar territory by showing what had become of landscapes that might once have been considered wilderness, but now had experienced at least a century of human activity. Many changes and losses documented by the RSP are obviously to be lamented, but their photographs also suggest that human occupation does not necessarily have to be destructive, radical, or uncontrolled. In fact the RSP's refusal to draw predictable negative conclusions about the evidence of people in their photographs makes the project all the more useful to critics and contemporary commentators reevaluating our relationship with the land.

The RSP is also allied with New Topographics concerns in their exploration of photographic style and their attempts to develop a "styleless" photography. Jenkins' introduction to the

Timothy O'Sullivan
Rock Formations, Pyramid Lake, Nevada, 1867
and
Mark Klett
Pyramid Isle, Pyramid Lake, Nevada, 1979
From Klett et al., *Second View: The Rephotographic Survey Project*, 1984
Gelatin silver prints, 8 x 20 (20.3 x 50.8)
Rephotographic Survey Project, Tempe, Arizona

New Topographics exhibition catalogue frankly acknowledges that "the main problem at the center of this exhibition is one of style,"[6] an ironic observation on a gathering of photographers who aspire to "subdue the intrusion of style in the picture."[7] In many ways, the RSP's mechanical duplication of predetermined vantage points, light, and time makes their approach even closer to Deal's goal of a "minimum of interference" by the photographer.[8] The RSP explores similar stylistic issues that concern the New Topographic photographers, but JoAnn Verburg's comment about achieving a true sense of objectivity indicates a misunderstanding of the impossibility of this exercise — unlike the New Topographic photographers, who only aspire to "the *appearance* of neutrality."[9]

If the failure of *Second View* to exhaust the meaning and significance of the RSP's findings seemed a shortcoming to some reviewers, it is also the strength of the book. It is a "report," as the authors declared, in many ways a gathering of raw, undigested data, like the reports of their predecessors, which was meant to be open to different uses and interpretations. We might lament the RSP's failure to follow up on many of the implications and questions raised by their experiences — in particular, if they were so often surprised by their experiences on the site and the peripheral views beyond the predetermined frames of their predecessors, why didn't they include some of those expansive views in their

report? However, the extended contribution of *Second View* may be the excellent foundation it provided for future work by both the participants and other photographers. Rick Dingus, for example, joined with other photographers to examine the traces ancient cultures left on the landscape in *Marks in Place: Contemporary Responses to Rock Art* (1988), a book of Indian rock art. Mark Klett's personal work in the Southwest, published in *Revealing Territory* (1992), especially builds on his experiences with the RSP and includes numerous photographs that have either symbolic references to his predecessors, or are even rephotographs he made with greater freedom than he had as part of the RSP — including, for example, a broader view and more subjective interpretation of the scene. The careful before/after methodology established by the RSP has been successfully employed by numerous subsequent rephotography projects, including John R. Charlton's views of the Colorado River in Donald L. Baars' *The Canyon Revisited: A Rephotography of the Grand Canyon* (1994), and Peter Goin's study of Lake Tahoe in *Stopping Time: A Rephotographic Survey of Lake Tahoe* (1992). The issues identified by *Second View* also continue to be explored by New Topographic photographers and numerous followers, including a group of photographers known for their involvement with the project "Water in the West."

Second View should be valued especially for the questions it raises about the nature of photographic documents and how they control our way of thinking about the land. Ultimately, we have to question whether the West has been well served by the beautiful photographs that often were treated as substitutes for firsthand knowledge of the land. We have to wonder if selective views, no matter how well intentioned, beautiful, and seductive, can lead to distorted thinking and wrong decisions if they are mainly used for propaganda and promotion. Despite its unassuming presentation and seemingly simple before/after methodology, *Second View*

is truly a seminal work that raises fascinating questions about what the West was, what it is now, and what its future might be. As a work of photographic documentation and art, its importance and influence are already well established, but its greatest significance in the long distinguished history of photographic publications on the West may be the way it illuminates the transformative power of the photographic document and suggests that the West we have come to know and accept may ironically only really exist in the pages of books.

1. Mark Klett, Ellen Manchester, JoAnn Verburg, Gordon Bushaw, and Rick Dingus, with an essay by Paul Berger, *Second View: The Rephotographic Survey Project* (Albuquerque: University of New Mexico Press, 1984).

2. John E. Carter, "Book Reviews," *Annals of Iowa* 49 (Winter–Spring 1988), p. 288.

3. The actual source of these and many other changes in the landscape may be beyond factual documentation and the RSP avoids presenting speculation as fact. This pair of photographs, like many others, raises interesting questions about whether rephotography provides actual scientific evidence or serves a more symbolic, speculative function.

4. Patricia Nelson Limerick, "Second Views and Second Thoughts: Mark Klett and the Re-exploration of the American West," in *Revealing Territory: Photographs of the Southwest by Mark Klett* (Albuquerque: University of New Mexico Press, 1992), pp. 12, 13.

5. JoAnn Verburg, "Between Exposures," in *Second View*, pp. 9–10.

6. William Jenkins, *New Topographics: Photographs of a Man-Altered Landscape*, exh. cat. (Rochester, New York: International Museum of Photography at George Eastman House, 1975), p. 5.

7. Ibid., p. 6.

8. Ibid.

9. Ibid.

CATALOGUE OF WORKS

WITH BIOGRAPHIES BY JULIE L. MELLBY

Ansel Adams
Self-Portrait, 1936
Gelatin silver print
Ansel Adams Publishing Rights Trust, Carmel, California

ANSEL ADAMS

BORN: 1902, SAN FRANCISCO
DIED: 1984, CARMEL, CALIFORNIA

Ansel Adams studied to be a concert pianist, but abandoned music in 1927 when his first portfolio of photographs was published. The same year, Adams met and began collaborating with writer Mary Austin on the book *Taos Pueblo* (1930). A second project was never completed, although Adams later published Austin's *The Land of Little Rain* (1950), accompanied by his photographs. A member of the Sierra Club since 1919, Adams joined its board of directors in 1932, and his book *Sierra Nevada* (1938) was used to persuade Congress to establish the Kings Canyon National Park. Together with Edward Weston and others, Adams formed Group f/64 (1932), which rejected the Pictorial style of photography, and opened the Ansel Adams Gallery in San Francisco to exhibit the group's work.

In 1940, Adams directed California's first major photography exhibition, "The Pageant of Photography," and then in New York helped found The Museum of Modern Art's photography department, serving as vice-chairman from 1940 to 1942. He collaborated with writer-curator Nancy Newhall on seven books, including the first of the Sierra Club's exhibit format series *This Is the American Earth* (1960). Adams was the recipient of the Presidential Medal of Freedom (1980) and had retrospective exhibitions at both The Metropolitan Museum of Art, New York (1974), and The Museum of Modern Art, New York (1979).

BOOKS:

Taos Pueblo
Photographs by Ansel Adams, essay by
Mary Austin
San Francisco: The Grabhorn Press, 1930 [ii, 62]
pp.; 17½ x 13 (44.5 x 33)
12 original photographs ranging in size from
6 x 8⅜ (15.2 x 21.3) to 9 x 6⁷⁄₁₆ (22.9 x 16.4) are
printed on special uncoated silver bromide
paper produced by Will Dassonville of San
Francisco; typography and printing by the
Grabhorn Press; binding by Hazel Dreis
The original, leather-bound edition of 100
copies plus 8 artist's copies sold for $75 each.
Copy 1: Center for Creative Photography,
The University of Arizona, Tucson
Copy 2: DeGolyer Library, Southern Methodist
University, Dallas
Copy 3: Collection of Hans P. Kraus, Jr.

Born Free and Equal: Photographs of the Loyal Japanese-Americans at Manzanar Relocation Center, Inyo County, California
By Ansel Adams
New York: US Camera, 1944
112 pp.; 11 x 8¼ (28 x 20)
65 black-and-white reproductions of
photographs by Adams
Copy 1: Center for Creative Photography,
The University of Arizona, Tucson
Copy 2: Collection of Hans P. Kraus, Jr.

The Land of Little Rain
Text by Mary Austin, photographs by Ansel
Adams, introduction by Carl Van Doren
Boston: Houghton Mifflin Company [printed at
The Riverside Press], 1950
xviii, 133 pp.; 10¼ x 8¼ (26 x 21)
48 black-and-white reproductions of
photographs by Adams
Copy 1: Library Collection, Whitney Museum
of American Art, New York
Copy 2: Center for Creative Photography,
The University of Arizona, Tucson

Winter Storm, Mount Tom, Sierra Nevada
no. 29, 1950
Printer's proof from *The Land of Little Rain*,
11 x 16¼ (28 x 41.2)
Center for Creative Photography,
The University of Arizona, Tucson

"Death Valley," *Arizona Highways* 29, no. 10
(October 1953), pp. 16–35
By Nancy Newhall and Ansel Adams
14 x 11 (36 x 28)
Amon Carter Museum Library, Fort Worth,
Texas
From its beginnings in the twenties until the
present day, *Arizona Highways* has published
work by the finest photographers depicting the
Western landscape. One of the first large-format
magazines to make extensive use of color,
Arizona Highways did not limit itself geographi-
cally to the state of Arizona. Adams' and
Newhall's work in Death Valley was published
one year later in an expanded format.

Death Valley
Photographs by Ansel Adams, story by Nancy
Newhall, guide by Ruth Kirk, maps drawn by
Edith Hamlin
San Francisco: 5 Associates, 1954
55 pp.; 12¼ x 9¼ (31 x 23.5)
23 black-and-white and 10 color reproductions
of photographs by Adams
Copy 1: Library Collection, Whitney Museum
of American Art, New York
Copy 2: Center for Creative Photography,
The University of Arizona, Tucson

PHOTOGRAPHS:

East of Death Valley, California, 1941
Published in *The Land of Little Rain*
Gelatin silver print, 7½ x 9¼ (19.1 x 23.5)
Center for Creative Photography,
The University of Arizona, Tucson

Saltflats Near Ballarat, California, c. 1941
Published in *The Land of Little Rain*
Gelatin silver print, 10½ x 13½ (26.7 x 34.3)
Center for Creative Photography,
The University of Arizona, Tucson

The Owens Valley, Bishop Region, from the Buttermilk Country, California, c. 1943
Published in *The Land of Little Rain*
Gelatin silver print, 7½ x 9½ (19 x 24.1)
Center for Creative Photography,
The University of Arizona, Tucson

Lone Pine Peak and Mt. Whitney, from Lone Pine, California, 1944
Published in *Born Free and Equal* and *This Is the American Earth*
Gelatin silver print, 12⅞ x 18⅜ (32.7 x 46.7)
The Museum of Modern Art, New York
Gift of the photographer

Mount Williamson, Sierra Nevada from Manzanar, California, 1944
Variation of image published in *The Land of Little Rain*
Gelatin silver print, 7⁹⁄₁₆ x 9⁵⁄₁₆ (19.2 x 23.6)
The Museum of Modern Art, New York
Gift of David H. McAlpin

Sunrise, Mount Tom, Sierra Nevada, California, 1948
Published in *The Land of Little Rain*
Gelatin silver print, 15½ x 19½ (39.4 x 49.5)
Center for Creative Photography,
The University of Arizona, Tucson

Manly Beacon, from Golden Canyon, Death Valley, California, c. 1948
Published in *Death Valley*
Gelatin silver print, 10½ x 13¼ (26.7 x 33.7)
Center for Creative Photography,
The University of Arizona, Tucson

Near Zabriskie Point, Death Valley, California, n.d.
Published in *Death Valley*
Gelatin silver print, 10¾ x 13½ (27.3 x 34.3)
Center for Creative Photography,
The University of Arizona, Tucson

ROBERT ADAMS

BORN: 1937, ORANGE, NEW JERSEY

Robert Adams received a PhD (1965) in English from the University of Southern California. He is the recipient of two NEA Fellowships (1973 and 1978), two Guggenheim Fellowships (1973 and 1980), the Charles Pratt Memorial Award (1987), and an award from the MacArthur Foundation (1994). His publications include *The New West* (1974), *Denver* (1977), *Prairie* (1978), *From the Missouri West* (1980), *Beauty in Photography* (1981), *Our Lives and Our Children* (1984), *Summer Nights* (1985), *Los Angeles Spring* (1986), and *Perfect Times, Perfect Places* (1988). Adams' first one-artist show was held at The Museum of Modern Art, New York (1971), and a retrospective exhibition and catalogue, *Robert Adams: To Make It Home* (1989), were prepared by the Philadelphia Museum of Art. Adams lives and works in Longmont, Colorado.

BOOKS:

The New West, Landscapes Along the Colorado Front Range
Written and photographed by Robert Adams, foreword by John Szarkowski
Boulder, Colorado: Colorado Associated University Press, 1974
xii, 120 pp.; 9½ x 10¼ (24.1 x 26)
56 black-and-white reproductions of photographs by Adams
Collection of the artist

From the Missouri West
By Robert Adams
New York: Aperture, 1980
[60] pp.; 9½ x 11½ (24.1 x 29.2)
59 black-and-white reproductions of photographs by Adams
Library Collection, Whitney Museum of American Art, New York

PHOTOGRAPHS:

Along Interstate 25, 1963
Published in *The New West*
Gelatin silver print, 5¼ x 5¾ (13.3 x 14.6)
Collection of the artist; courtesy Fraenkel Gallery, San Francisco, and Howard Greenberg Gallery, New York

Along Interstate 25, 1968
Published in *The New West*
Gelatin silver print, 5⁹⁄₁₆ x 5¹³⁄₁₆ (14.1 x 14.8)
Whitney Museum of American Art, New York; Purchase, with funds from the Photography Committee 96.10

Farm Road and Cottonwood South of Raymer, 1968
Published in *The New West*
Gelatin silver print, 6 x 6 (15.2 x 15.2)
Whitney Museum of American Art, New York; Purchase, with funds from the Photography Committee 96.11

Along Interstate 25, 1968–71
Published in *The New West*
Gelatin silver print, 5½ x 5⅞ (14 x 14.9)
Collection of Sondra Gilman and
Celso Gonzalez-Falla

Pikes Peak, 1969
Published in *The New West*
Gelatin silver print, 5¾ x 5⅞ (14.6 x 14.9)
Collection of the artist; courtesy Fraenkel Gallery, San Francisco, and Howard Greenberg Gallery, New York

Motel, 1970
Published in *The New West*
Gelatin silver print, 5⅞ x 6 (14.9 x 15.2)
Whitney Museum of American Art, New York; Purchase, with funds from the Photography Committee 96.12

Sunday School, a Church in a New Tract, Colorado Springs, 1970
Published in *The New West*
Gelatin silver print, 5½ x 6 (14 x 15.2)
Collection of the artist; courtesy Fraenkel Gallery, San Francisco, and Howard Greenberg Gallery, New York

Newly Completed Tract House, Colorado Springs, 1974
Published in *The New West*
Gelatin silver print, 14 x 11 (35.6 x 27.9)
Collection of the artist; courtesy Fraenkel Gallery, San Francisco, and Howard Greenberg Gallery, New York

Northeast from Flagstaff Mountain, Boulder County, Colorado, 1975
Published in *From the Missouri West*
Gelatin silver print, 16 x 20 (40.6 x 50.8)
Collection of the artist; courtesy Fraenkel Gallery, San Francisco, and Howard Greenberg Gallery, New York

Cottonwoods Below Lonetree Reservoir, Larimer County, Colorado, 1977
Published in *From the Missouri West*
Gelatin silver print, 16 x 20 (40.6 x 50.8)
Collection of the artist; courtesy Fraenkel Gallery, San Francisco, and Howard Greenberg Gallery, New York

Alkali Lake, Albany County, Wyoming, 1978
Published in *From the Missouri West*
Gelatin silver print, 16 x 20 (40.6 x 50.8)
Collection of the artist; courtesy Fraenkel Gallery, San Francisco, and Howard Greenberg Gallery, New York

Edge of San Timoteo Canyon, San Bernardino County, California, 1978
Published in *From the Missouri West*
Gelatin silver print, 16 x 20 (40.6 x 50.8)
Collection of the artist; courtesy Fraenkel Gallery, San Francisco, and Howard Greenberg Gallery, New York

Nebraska State Highway 2, Box Butte County, Nebraska, 1978
Published in *From the Missouri West*
Gelatin silver print, 16 x 20 (40.6 x 50.8)
Collection of the artist; courtesy Fraenkel Gallery, San Francisco, and Howard Greenberg Gallery, New York

South from Rocky Flatts, Jefferson County, Colorado, 1978
Published in *From the Missouri West*
Gelatin silver print, 16 x 20 (40.6 x 50.8)
Collection of the artist; courtesy Fraenkel Gallery, San Francisco, and Howard Greenberg Gallery, New York

Quarried Mesa Top, Pueblo County, Colorado, 1978 and 1990
Published in *From the Missouri West*
Gelatin silver print, 16 x 20 (40.6 x 50.8)
Collection of the artist; courtesy Fraenkel Gallery, San Francisco, and Howard Greenberg Gallery, New York

Laura Adams Armer, n.d.
The Wheelwright Museum of the American Indian, Santa Fe

LAURA MAY (ADAMS) ARMER
BORN: 1874, SACRAMENTO, CALIFORNIA
DIED: 1963, VACAVILLE, CALIFORNIA

In the 1890s, Laura Adams opened a private studio in San Francisco, specializing in portrait photography, and gained a reputation as one of the most successful professional photographers in the Bay Area. She advocated Pictorialism, teaching classes for women in her studio and publishing an article entitled "The Picture Possibilities of Photography" (1900). Although she announced her retirement when she married illustrator Sidney Armer, in fact she continued to photograph, finally closing her studio in 1923. That year, Armer took her first trip to the Navajo reservation, and she returned annually for the next thirteen years to study Navajo music and folklore. Her appreciation for Native American customs can be seen in her documentary film and in the numerous children's books

she wrote and illustrated with her husband, winning a Newbery Medal (1932) and a Caldecott Medal (1939).

BOOKS:

Waterless Mountain
By Laura Adams Armer, illustrated by Sidney Armer and Laura Adams Armer
New York, Toronto: Longmans, Green and Company, 1931
xi, 212 pp.; 9½ x 7½ (24.1 x 19.1)
16 black-and-white reproductions of photographs by Laura Adams Armer and Sidney Armer; frontispiece is a reproduction of a painting inspired by two photographs by Laura Adams Armer
Copies 1 and 2: Collection of Peter E. Palmquist

MARY HUNTER AUSTIN
BORN: 1868, CARLINVILLE, ILLINOIS
DIED: 1934, SANTA FE, NEW MEXICO

Mary Hunter was transplanted at the age of twenty from her native Midwest to a homestead on the edge of the Mojave Desert. In 1891, she married Stafford Wallace Austin and moved to Owens Valley, where he became the manager of a vineyard. When the business failed, Austin went to work to support her husband. Her only child, a daughter, was born the same year that her first short story appeared in the *Overland Monthly* (1892).

Austin met the charismatic journalist Charles Lummis and left her husband to pursue her writing under Lummis' encouragement. Back in Owens Valley, Austin completed a series of desert stories entitled *The Land of Little Rain* (1903). The book has special poignancy because in 1906, shortly after its release, the Los Angeles Water District diverted the Owens River to irrigate Los Angeles and the Valley's farms were destroyed.

Austin later settled in New York City, where she frequented the salon of Mabel Dodge (Luhan) and became active in women's rights. In 1924, she moved back to Santa Fe and built her final home, Casa Querida. The house was a frequent destination for visitors, among them Ansel Adams, who collaborated with Austin on *Taos Pueblo* (1930). A second collaboration was cut short by Austin's death in 1934.

BOOKS
see Ansel Adams, *Taos Pueblo,* and *The Land of Little Rain*

(CHARLES) LEWIS BALTZ
BORN: 1945, NEWPORT BEACH, CALIFORNIA

Lewis Baltz began developing and printing photographs at the age of twelve. He received a BFA (1969) from the San Francisco Art Institute and an MFA (1971) from the Claremont Graduate School. Baltz is the recipient of two NEA Fellowships (1973 and 1977), a Guggenheim Fellowship (1976), a US-UK Bicentennial Exchange Fellowship (1980), and the Charles Pratt Memorial Award (1991). His numerous monographs include *The New Industrial Park Near Irvine, California* (1975), *Nevada* (1978), *Park City* (1980) with Gus Blaisdell, and *Rond de Nuit* with Olivier Boissiere (1992). Baltz currently lives and works in France.

BOOKS:

Nevada
By Lewis Baltz
New York: Castelli Graphics, 1978
17 pp.; 8½ x 10½ (21.6 x 26.7)
15 black-and-white reproductions of photographs by Baltz
Library Collection, Whitney Museum of American Art, New York

Park City
By Lewis Baltz and Gus Blaisdell
Albuquerque: Artspace Press; New York: Castelli Graphics, 1980
246 pp.; 10¾ x 11¼ (27.3 x 28.6)
102 black-and-white reproductions of photographs by Baltz
Copies 1 and 2: Library Collection, Whitney Museum of American Art, New York

PHOTOGRAPHS:

B Street, Sparks, 1978
Published in *Nevada*
Gelatin silver print, 6⅜ x 9½ (16.2 x 24.1)
Janet Borden, Inc., New York

Fluorescent Tube, 1978
Published in *Nevada*
Gelatin silver print, 6⅜ x 9½ (16.2 x 24.1)
Janet Borden, Inc., New York

Hidden Valley, Looking South, 1978
Published in *Nevada*
Gelatin silver print, 6⅜ x 9½ (16.2 x 24.1)
Janet Borden, Inc., New York

Hidden Valley, Looking Southwest, 1978
Published in *Nevada*
Gelatin silver print, 6⅜ x 9½ (16.2 x 24.1)
Janet Borden, Inc., New York

Lemmon Valley, Looking North, 1978
Published in *Nevada*
Gelatin silver print, 6⅜ x 9½ (16.2 x 24.1)
Janet Borden, Inc., New York

Lemmon Valley, Looking Northeast, 1978
Published in *Nevada*
Gelatin silver print, 6⅜ x 9½ (16.2 x 24.1)
Janet Borden, Inc., New York

Lemmon Valley, Looking Northwest Toward Stead, 1978
Published in *Nevada*
Gelatin silver print, 6⅜ x 9½ (16.2 x 24.1)
Janet Borden, Inc., New York

Mill Street, Reno, 1978
Published in *Nevada*
Gelatin silver print, 6⅜ x 9½ (16.2 x 24.1)
Janet Borden, Inc., New York

Model Home, Shadow Mountain, 1978
Published in *Nevada*
Gelatin silver print, 6⅜ x 9½ (16.2 x 24.1)
Janet Borden, Inc., New York

Mustang Bridge Exit, Interstate 80, 1978
Published in *Nevada*
Gelatin silver print, 6⅜ x 9½ (16.2 x 24.1)
Janet Borden, Inc., New York

Nevada 33, Looking West, 1978
Published in *Nevada*
Gelatin silver print, 6⅜ x 9½ (16.2 x 24.1)
Janet Borden, Inc., New York

New Construction, Shadow Mountain, 1978
Published in *Nevada*
Gelatin silver print, 6⅜ x 9½ (16.2 x 24.1)
Janet Borden, Inc., New York

Night Construction, Reno, 1978
Published in *Nevada*
Gelatin silver print, 6⅜ x 9½ (16.2 x 24.1)
Janet Borden, Inc., New York

Reno–Sparks, Looking South, 1978
Published in *Nevada*
Gelatin silver print, 6⅜ x 9½ (16.2 x 24.1)
Janet Borden, Inc., New York

US 50, East of Carson City, 1978
Published in *Nevada*
Gelatin silver print, 6⅜ x 9½ (16.2 x 24.1)
Janet Borden, Inc., New York

ADOLPH F.A. (FRANCIS ALPHONSE) BANDELIER
BORN: 1840, BERN, SWITZERLAND
DIED: 1914, SEVILLE, SPAIN

Bandelier lived in Switzerland until 1848, when he and his family joined his father in Illinois. In 1855, Bandelier returned to Switzerland to study geology at the University of Bern until he was forced to rejoin his family in Illinois in the late 1850s. For the next twenty years, Bandelier worked in the family banking business. At night, he pursued his own interest in pre-Columbian culture, publishing several articles that brought him to the attention of ethnologist Lewis Henry Morgan. Morgan arranged for Bandelier to research Native Americans of the American Southwest, and in 1880, Bandelier discovered the ancient cliff dwellings at Frijoles Canyon.

To supplement his small salary, Bandelier wrote scientific articles and one novel, *Die Koshare,* set in prehistoric times at the ancient ruins in Frijoles Canyon. This was later published in English under the title *The Delight Makers* (1890). A second volume, prepared in collaboration with journalist-photographer Charles Lummis, was never completed. After Bandelier's death, Lummis used his 1890 photographs for a second edition of *The Delight Makers* (1916), released to honor Bandelier in the same year that Frijoles Canyon was renamed Bandelier National Park.

BOOKS:
see Lummis, *The Delight Makers*

William H. Bell, c. 1860s
Detail of stereograph
Library of Congress, Washington, D.C.

WILLIAM H. BELL
BORN: 1830, LIVERPOOL, ENGLAND
DIED: 1910, PHILADELPHIA

William H. Bell (frequently confused with Dr. William A. Bell) was born in England but raised in Pennsylvania. He opened a photography gallery in Philadelphia, where he earned a repu-

tation as a daguerreotypist. During the Civil War, Bell served as chief photographer for the Army Medical Museum in Washington, D.C., and in 1872 was called back into service by the War Department to substitute for Timothy O'Sullivan as photographer for the US Geographical Surveys West of the 100th Meridian under Lieutenant George Wheeler. Reproductions of photographs by Bell and O'Sullivan were published in Wheeler's final report (1874).

BOOKS:
see O'Sullivan, *Photographs*

PHOTOGRAPHS:

Perched Rock, Rocker Creek, Arizona, 1872
Published in *Photographs Showing Landscapes, Geological and Other Features, of Portions of the Western Territory of the United States, Obtained in Connection with Geographical and Geological Explorations and Surveys West of the One Hundredth Meridian, Seasons of 1871, 1872, and 1873*
Albumen print, 10⅞ x 8 (27.6 x 20.3)
The Denver Art Museum; Funds from Mr. and Mrs. George G. Anderman, Nancy Lake-Benson, Florence R. and Ralph L. Burgess Trust, Collectors' Choice 1990, J. Rathbone Falck, General Service Foundation, Mr. and Mrs. William D. Hewit, Mr. and Mrs. Edward H. Leede, Pauline A. and George R. Morrison Trust, Jan and Frederick Mayer, Ginny Williams, Estelle Wolf, anonymous donors, and the generosity of our visitors, with additional support from the voters who created the Scientific and Cultural Facilities District

JULIUS BIEN
BORN: 1826, HESSE-CASSEL, GERMANY
DIED: 1909, NEW YORK

Trained in Germany, Julius Bien established a small printing business in New York City (1848), later specializing in complex scientific and artistic work. Once acclaimed for his lithography, Bien turned to map-making and received the prestigious commission from the Secretary of War to engrave the maps for the twelve-volume *Reports of Explorations and Surveys, to Ascertain the Most Practicable and Economical Route for a Railroad from the Mississippi River to the Pacific Ocean. Made Under the Direction of the Secretary of War in 1853–5, According to Acts of Congress of March 3, 1853, May 31, 1854, and August 5, 1854* (1853–55). An active partner in the production of the albums he published, Bien lobbied the California State Legislature for support of J.D.

Whitney's geological survey and published the monumental *The Yosemite Book* (1868), with original albumen prints by Carleton Watkins. Wishing to replicate this eloquent volume, F.V. Hayden hired Bien to produce *Sun Pictures of Rocky Mountain Scenery* (1870), with photographs by A.J. Russell. A friend of Clarence King, Bien worked closely with him to raise the money for the printing of his *Report of the Geological Exploration of the Fortieth Parallel* (1870–80), comprised of seven volumes and an atlas. Bien's finest work can be seen in the panoramic views of Clarence Dutton's *Atlas to Accompany the Monograph on the Tertiary History of the Grand Cañon District* (1882), drawn from photographs by John Hillers.

BOOKS:
see Hillers, Jackson, O'Sullivan

WILLIAM BLACKMORE
BORN: 1827, SALISBURY, ENGLAND
DIED: 1878, SALISBURY, ENGLAND

William Blackmore was a London solicitor and speculator who promoted the commercial development of the American West. With the help of a survey by government geologist F.V. Hayden, Blackmore published *Colorado: Its Resources, Parks, and Prospects as a New Field for Emigration* (1869), in which he reproduced articles by explorers, officials, and tourists encouraging settlement in his Western properties. He accompanied Hayden's first expedition to Yellowstone in 1872, supplementing the government funding for William H. Jackson's photography equipment. Blackmore's speculations eventually failed and he went bankrupt, committing suicide in 1878. His collection of photographs became the basis for the Smithsonian Institution's Native American collection, and his personal accomplishments are remembered at the Blackmore Museum in Salisbury, England.

BOOKS:

Colorado: Its Resources, Parks, and Prospects as a New Field for Emigration, with an Account of the Trenchara [sic] and Costilla Estates, in the San Luis Park
By William Blackmore
London: Sampson Low, Son, and Marston, 1869
217 pp.; 11 x 8¼ (28 x 21)
8 mounted albumen prints
DeGolyer Library, Southern Methodist University, Dallas

DAVID (ROSS) BROWER
BORN: 1912, BERKELEY, CALIFORNIA

David Brower's long association with the Sierra Club (founded in 1892 by John Muir) began with membership in 1933. He moved to Yosemite in 1935 to manage the Park's publicity department, working closely with photographer Ansel Adams. When Brower became an editor for the University of California Press, he served on the Sierra Club's board and, in 1952, was named the Club's first executive director.

In this post, Brower began a publishing campaign to promote wilderness conservation, successfully challenging the building of dams in Dinosaur National Monument with special issues of the *Sierra Club Bulletin* and the book *This Is Dinosaur* (1955). He initiated the Club's exhibit format series with *This Is the American Earth* (1960), published together with Adams and Nancy Newhall, followed by *In Wilderness Is the Preservation of the World* (1962), with Eliot Porter. Although successful, Brower's political lobbying resulted in the Sierra Club's loss of tax-exempt status, which intensified its financial difficulties and eventually led to Brower's resignation in 1969. Brower went on to found the John Muir Institute and Friends of the Earth, and continues to champion the conservation of our natural resources.

BOOKS:
see Hyde, Porter

GORDON BUSHAW
BORN: 1947, COLFAX, WASHINGTON

Gordon Bushaw graduated from the University of Washington in 1971 with a BS in mathematics and since 1973 has been teaching mathematics at Central Kitsap High School in Silverdale, Washington. During the summers of 1977–79, he worked with the Rephotographic Survey Project, and his photographs were included in its exhibition and catalogue *Second View* (1984). Bushaw continues to exhibit throughout the Northwestern United States.

BOOKS:
see Klett, *Second View*

PHOTOGRAPHS:

Fissure, Steamboat Springs, Nevada, 1979
Diptych with Timothy O'Sullivan's *Untitled,* 1869
Published in *Second View*
Gelatin silver prints, 8 x 20 (20.3 x 50.8)
Rephotographic Survey Project, Tempe, Arizona

Hot Springs, Dixie Valley, Nevada, 1979
Diptych with Timothy O'Sullivan's *Hot Springs, Smokey Valley,* 1868
Published in *Second View*
Gelatin silver prints, 8 x 20 (20.3 x 50.8)
Rephotographic Survey Project, Tempe, Arizona

FREDERICK (HASTINGS) CHAPIN
BORN: 1852, LAFAYETTE, INDIANA
DIED: 1900, HARTFORD

A prosperous Hartford businessman, Frederick Chapin was also an early member of the Appalachian Mountain Club (founded in 1876) and often traveled to Boston for the Club's meetings and activities. He made his first trip to the Rocky Mountains in 1886 and published a series of articles in the Club's journal, *Appalachia*, detailing his expeditions to the West. These reports were drawn together and published by the Club as *Mountaineering in Colorado* (1889), illustrated by Chapin's own photographs.

In the summer of 1889, Chapin visited and photographed the ancient cliff dwellings at Mesa Verde, and published an illustrated paper of his findings in *Appalachia* the following spring. This article received such enthusiastic response that, after a second visit, Chapin wrote and illustrated *The Land of the Cliff-Dwellers* (1892). Although his work was eclipsed in 1893 by Swedish geologist Gustaf Norden-skiöld's scientific study of Mesa Verde, Chapin's book remains the first published examination of that site.

BOOKS:

The Land of the Cliff-Dwellers
By Frederick H. Chapin
Boston: Appalachian Mountain Club, W.B. Clarke and Company, 1892
ix, 188 pp.; 7¾ x 5½ (19.7 x 14)
67 black-and-white reproductions of photographs by Chapin
Library Collection, Whitney Museum of American Art, New York

J. Smeaton Chase, n.d.
Palm Springs Historical Society, California

J.(JOSEPH) SMEATON CHASE
BORN: 1864, LONDON
DIED: 1923, BANNING, CALIFORNIA

J. Smeaton Chase emigrated to the United
States in 1890, settling in Los Angeles, where
he worked as a Resident Settlement Worker
of the Bethlehem Institutional Church. Chase
spent much of his free time traveling on horseback throughout California with his friend,
artist Carl Eytel. At the age of forty-seven
Chase wrote his first book, *Yosemite Trails*
(1911). Chase was also an amateur photographer, and his work was used to illustrate
John Van Dyke's popular book *The Desert*
(1916), as well as Chase's own *California
Desert Trails* (1919).

BOOKS:

*The Desert: Further Studies in Natural
Appearances*
By John Charles Van Dyke, with illustrations
from photographs by J. Smeaton Chase
New York: Charles Scribner's Sons, c. 1918
xxii, 233 pp.; 8 x 5¾ (20.3 x 14.6)
32 black-and-white reproductions and one
photoengraving from photographs by Chase
Copies 1 and 2: Library Collection,
Whitney Museum of American Art, New York

California Desert Trails
By J. Smeaton Chase, with illustrations from
photographs by the author and an appendix of
plants, also hints on desert traveling
Boston, New York: Houghton Mifflin Company,
1919
xvi, 387 pp.; 9 x 6 (23 x 15)
35 black-and-white reproductions of photographs
by Chase
Copy 1: Special Collections, The University of
Arizona, Tucson
Copy 2: Library Collection, Whitney Museum of
American Art, New York

*Our Araby: Palm Springs and the Garden of
the Sun*
By J. Smeaton Chase, with illustrations from
photographs by the author
Pasadena: Star-News Publishing Company, 1920
83 pp.; 7 x 4¾ (17.8 x 12.1)
Map, 9 black-and-white reproductions of
photographs by Chase
Special Collections, The University of Arizona,
Tucson

PHOTOGRAPHS:

In Thousand-Palm Cañon, n.d.
Published in *California Desert Trails,* 1919
Gelatin silver print, 3³⁄₁₆ x 5½ (8.1 x 14)
Palm Springs Desert Museum, California

A Sidewinder Ready for Business, n.d.
Published in *California Desert Trails,* 1919
Gelatin silver print, 3¼ x 5½ (8.3 x 14)
Palm Springs Desert Museum, California

Sunset and the Sentinel, n.d.
Published in *The Desert,* 1918
Gelatin silver print, 3⅛ x 5½ (7.9 x 14)
Palm Springs Desert Museum, California

R.D. CLEVELAND
DATES UNKNOWN

R.D. Cleveland was an amateur photographer.
His photographs illustrate *Che! Wah! Wah!,* the
record of an 1883 trip by the Montezumas Club,
a group of Eastern Railroad freight agents, from
Chicago to Chihuahua, Mexico.

BOOKS:

*Che! Wah! Wah! or, the Modern Montezumas
in Mexico*
By George G. Street
Rochester: E.R. Andrews, 1883
113 pp.; 10¾ x 7¼ (27.3 x 18.4)
Map, 33 mounted albumen photographs by
R.D. Cleveland, woodcuts from sketches by the
author
Copy 1: DeGolyer Library, Southern Methodist
University, Dallas
Copy 2: Special Collections, The University of
Arizona, Tucson

LINDA CONNOR
BORN: 1944, NEW YORK

Linda Connor received a BFA (1967) from
the Rhode Island School of Design, where
she studied photography with Harry Callahan,
and an MS (1969) from the Illinois Institute
of Technology, where she studied with Aaron
Siskind. Since 1969, she has taught at the San
Francisco Art Institute while still lecturing
and traveling throughout the world. Connor
was awarded an NEA Fellowship (1976) and a
Guggenheim Fellowship (1979) to complete
her book *Solos* (1979). She was a member of
the National Endowment for the Arts-sponsored photographic survey project "Marks
and Measures: Pictographs and Petroglyphs
in a Modern Art Context," later published as
*Marks in Place: Contemporary Responses to Rock
Art* (1988). The catalogue *Spiral Journey* (1990)
was published to accompany a retrospective
exhibition of Connor's photography at the
Museum of Contemporary Photography in
Chicago.

BOOKS:

*Marks in Place: Contemporary Responses
to Rock Art*
Photographs by Linda Connor, Rick Dingus,
Steve Fitch, John Pfahl, and Charles Roitz,
essays by Polly Schaafsma and Keith Davis,
foreword by Lucy R. Lippard
Albuquerque: University of New Mexico
Press, 1988
xii, 133 pp.; 8¾ x 11½ (22.2 x 29.2)
104 black-and-white and color reproductions of
photographs by Connor, Dingus, Fitch, Pfahl,
and Roitz
Library Collection, Whitney Museum of
American Art, New York

PHOTOGRAPHS:

Bighorn Sheep, Three Rivers, New Mexico,
1982
Published in *Marks in Place*
Contact print on printing-out paper, toned with
gold chloride, 8 x 10 (20.3 x 25.4)
Collection of the artist; courtesy Howard
Greenberg Gallery, New York

Hands, Canyon de Chelly, Arizona, 1982
Published in *Marks in Place*
Contact print on printing-out paper, toned with
gold chloride, 8 x 10 (20.3 x 25.4)
Collection of the artist; courtesy Howard
Greenberg Gallery, New York

Kachina Kiva, Utah, 1982
Published in *Marks in Place*
Contact print on printing-out paper, toned with
gold chloride, 8 x 10 (20.3 x 25.4)
Collection of the artist; courtesy Howard
Greenberg Gallery, New York

Spanish Entering Canyon de Chelly,
Arizona, 1982
Published in *Marks in Place*
Contact print on printing-out paper, toned with
gold chloride, 8 x 10 (20.3 x 25.4)
Collection of the artist; courtesy Howard
Greenberg Gallery, New York

Spanish Alphabet, Inscription Rock,
New Mexico, 1983
Published in *Marks in Place*
Contact print on printing-out paper, toned with
gold chloride, 8 x 10 (20.3 x 25.4)
Collection of the artist; courtesy Howard
Greenberg Gallery, New York

Comet Panel, Arizona, 1986
Published in *Marks in Place*
Contact print on printing-out paper, toned with
gold chloride, 8 x 10 (20.3 x 25.4)
Collection of the artist; courtesy Howard
Greenberg Gallery, New York

Edward S. Curtis
Self-Portrait, 1899
Archives of The Pierpont Morgan Library, New York

EDWARD S. (SHERIFF) CURTIS
BORN: 1868, NEAR WHITEWATER, WISCONSIN
DIED: 1952, LOS ANGELES
___

In 1867, Edward S. Curtis opened his own
commercial photography business in Seattle,
specializing in portraits and romantic landscapes. Railroad tycoon E.H. Harriman hired
Curtis as official photographer for an expedition to Alaska in 1899. By 1900, he had resolved
to devote his life to photographing Native
Americans and made his first photographic
trip to the Southwest. Between 1900 and 1905,

he took photographs for his proposed publication *The North American Indian.* Having exhausted his personal funds, Curtis sent a traveling
exhibition of his work to the East and secured
the patronage of New York banker J. Pierpont
Morgan. The first volume of *The North American
Indian* was published in 1907, and over the next
twenty-odd years Curtis struggled with publication delays and fund-raising until the last volume
was finally published in 1930. During the 1930s,
Curtis suffered a nervous breakdown and remained relatively inactive for the rest of his life.

BOOKS:

*The North American Indian; Being a Series of
Volumes Picturing and Describing the Indians
of the United States, and Alaska*
Written, illustrated, and published by Edward S.
Curtis, edited by Frederick Webb Hodge, fore-
word by Theodore Roosevelt, field research
conducted under the patronage of J. Pierpont
Morgan, photogravures by John Andrew and
Son, Boston
Seattle: E.S. Curtis; Cambridge: The University
Press, 1907–09; Norwood, Massachusetts:
Plimpton Press, 1907–30
20 vol.; 13 x 9¾ (33 x 24.8); issued with 20 portfo-
lios of loose photogravure plates with one leaf of
captions; gravures are printed either on vellum
12 x 16 (30.5 x 40.6) or tissue 13 x 16½ (33 x 41.9)
Copies 1, 2, and 3 [vol. 1, vol. 2, vol. 12]: The
Pierpont Morgan Library, New York
Copy 4 [vol. 1]: Yale Collection of Western
Americana, Beinecke Rare Book and Manuscript
Library, Yale University, New Haven,
Connecticut

The Flute of the Gods
By Marah Ellis Ryan, illustrated by Edward S.
Curtis
New York: Frederick A. Stokes Company, 1909
vii, 338 pp.; 8½ x 5¾ (21.6 x 14.6)
24 reproductions of photographs by Edward S.
Curtis
Ryan's book is a fictionalized treatment of Hopi
mythology and culture. At least three separate
editions were published in 1909, with differing
numbers and sequences of illustrations.
Copy 1: Library Collection, Whitney Museum of
American Art, New York
Copy 2: Special Collections, The University of
Arizona, Tucson

PHOTOGRAPHS:

Acoma and Enchanted Mesa, 1904
Gelatin silver print, 5¾ x 7¾ (14.7 x 19.7)
Centre Canadien d'Architecture/Canadian
Centre for Architecture, Montreal

Acoma Belfry
Published in *The North American Indian: Large
Plates Supplementing Volume XVI,* 1907–30
Photogravure, 13 x 16½ (33 x 41.9)
The Pierpont Morgan Library, New York

Cañon de Chelly–Navaho, 1904
Published as a photogravure in *The North
American Indian: Large Plates Supplementing
Volume I,* 1907–30
Platinum print, 16⅛ x 20⅝ (41 x 52.4)
Collection of Christopher G. Cardozo

A Feast Day at Acoma
Published in *The North American Indian: Large
Plates Supplementing Volume XVI,* 1907–30
Photogravure, 13 x 16½ (33 x 41.9)
The Pierpont Morgan Library, New York

Water Carriers, c. 1904
Gelatin silver print, 5⁷⁄₁₆ x 7⅝ (14 x 19.5)
Yale Collection of Western Americana, Beinecke
Rare Book and Manuscript Library, Yale
University, New Haven, Connecticut

The Apache
Published in *The North American Indian: Large
Plates Supplementing Volume I,* 1907–30
Photogravure, 16½ x 13 (41.9 x 33)
The Pierpont Morgan Library, New York

Loitering at the Spring
Published in *The North American Indian: Large
Plates Supplementing Volume XII,* 1907–30
Photogravure, 13 x 16½ (33 x 41.9)
The Pierpont Morgan Library, New York

ROBERT DAWSON
BORN: 1950, SACRAMENTO, CALIFORNIA
___

Robert Dawson received an MA in interdisciplinary studies from San Francisco State University in 1979 and spent the next three years
photographing the evaporation of California's
Mono Lake. Together with Steve Johnson, he
founded the Great Central Valley Project, which
culminated in 1993 with a book and traveling
exhibition. Since 1983, Dawson has been co-
director with Ellen Manchester of the Water
in the West Project, a consortium of seven
photographers who document water issues in
the West with such books as *Arid Waters* (1992),
with Peter Goin. Dawson lives and teaches in
the San Francisco Bay Area.

BOOKS:
see Goin, *Arid Waters*

PHOTOGRAPHS:

The Needles, Pyramid Lake, Nevada, 1990
Published in *Arid Waters*
Gelatin silver print, 16 x 20 (40.6 x 50.8)
Collection of the artist

JOE DEAL
BORN: 1947, TOPEKA, KANSAS

Joe Deal received a BFA (1970) from the Kansas
City Art Institute, Missouri, and an MA (1974)
and MFA (1978) from the University of New
Mexico, Albuquerque. He served as director
of exhibitions at the International Museum of
Photography, George Eastman House (1975–76),
and was included in the museum's influential
exhibition *New Topographics* (1975). He has received a Guggenheim Fellowship (1984) and
two NEA Fellowships (1977 and 1980). An assistant professor of art at the University of California, Riverside, from 1976 to 1988, Deal now
teaches at Washington University in St. Louis,
Missouri.

BOOKS:

Joe Deal: Southern California Photographs,
1976–86
Foreword by J.B. Jackson; essays by Mark
Johnstone and Edward Leffingwell
Albuquerque: The University of New Mexico
Press in association with the Los Angeles
Municipal Art Gallery, 1992
147 pp.; 10¼ x 11¼ (26 x 28.6)
68 black-and-white reproductions of
photographs by Deal
Library Collection, Whitney Museum of
American Art, New York

PHOTOGRAPHS:

Colton, California, 1978
Published in the portfolio *The Fault Zone* (1981)
and in *Southern California Photographs*
Gold-toned gelatin silver print, 14 x 14
(35.6 x 35.6)
Collection of the artist

Indio, California, 1978
Published in the portfolio *The Fault Zone* (1981)
and *Southern California Photographs*
Gold-toned gelatin silver print, 14 x 14
(35.6 x 35.6)
Collection of the artist

Palm Springs, California, 1979
Published in the portfolio *The Fault Zone* (1981)
Gold-toned gelatin silver print, 14 x 14
(35.6 x 35.6)
Collection of the artist

Soboba Hot Springs, California, 1979
Published in the portfolio *The Fault Zone* (1981)
and in *Southern California Photographs*
Gold-toned gelatin silver print, 14 x 14
(35.6 x 35.6)
Collection of the artist

FREDERICK S. (SAMUEL) DELLENBAUGH
BORN: 1853, McCONNELSVILLE, OHIO
DIED: 1935, NEW YORK

Frederick Dellenbaugh was working as an illustrator for Albert C. Ives' monthly magazine *Our
Leisure Moments* when, at the age of seventeen,
Major John Wesley Powell hired him as an artist
for the US Geographical and Geological Survey
of the Rocky Mountain Region. From 1871 to
1873, Dellenbaugh drew some of the first maps
of the Grand Canyon area and later published a
history of his adventures in *Romance of the
Colorado River* (1902) and *A Canyon Voyage*
(1908). He went on to study painting in New
York, Munich, and Paris, often returning to the
Southwest to paint desert scenes.

BOOKS:

*The Grand Cañon of Arizona, Through the
Stereoscope: The Underwood Patent Map
System Combined with Eighteen Original
Stereoscopic Photographs*
Explanatory notes edited by F.S. Dellenbaugh
New York, London: Underwood & Underwood,
c. 1904, 1906
64 pp.; 6½ x 4 (16.5 x 10.1)
Map, 18 stereographic views of the Grand
Canyon, with extensive descriptive notes on the
back of each card
Originally published in 1900, numerous reprints
Yale Collection of Western Americana,
Beinecke Rare Book and Manuscript Library,
Yale University, New Haven, Connecticut

RICK DINGUS
BORN: 1951, APPLETON CITY, MISSOURI

A free-lance photographer since 1972, Rick
Dingus received his MA (1977) and MFA
(1981) from the University of New Mexico,
Albuquerque. He is the recipient of an NEA/
Mid-America Art Alliance Regional Fellowship (1987) and three Ford Foundation grants
(1977–79). His work as a member of the Rephotographic Survey Project (1978–79) led to
his book *The Photographic Artifacts of Timothy
O'Sullivan* (1982) and the survey's publication
Second View (1984). Dingus was one of five photographers included in the National Endowment
for the Arts-sponsored survey project and exhibition "Marks and Measures: Pictographs and
Petroglyphs in a Modern Art Context," later
published as *Marks in Place: Contemporary Responses to Rock Art* (1988). Since 1982, he has
lived in Lubbock, Texas, teaching at Texas
Tech University.

BOOKS:

see Klett, Conner

PHOTOGRAPHS:

The Drumstick, Weber Valley, Utah, 1978
Diptych with Timothy O'Sullivan's *Conglomerate
Column, Weber Valley*, 1869
Published in *Second View*
Gelatin silver prints, 10 x 16 (25.4 x 40.6)
Rephotographic Survey Project, Tempe,
Arizona

*Hanging Rock, Foot of Echo Canyon,
Utah*, 1978
Diptych with A.J. Russell's *Hanging Rock,
Foot of Echo Cañon*, 1867–68
Published in *Second View*
Gelatin silver prints, 8 x 20 (20.3 x 50.8)
Rephotographic Survey Project, Tempe,
Arizona

STEVE FITCH
BORN: 1949, TUCSON, ARIZONA

Steve Fitch received a BA (1971) in anthropology from the University of California, Berkeley, and began working as a photography instructor at Berkeley's ASUC Studio, along with Richard Misrach. Fitch received two NEA Fellowships (1973, 1975) to complete his book *Diesels and Dinosaurs* (1976) before returning to school. He received an MA (1978) in photography from the University of New Mexico, Albuquerque, and taught at the University of Colorado, Boulder (1979–85). Fitch was one of five photographers asked to participate in the National Endowment for the Arts–sponsored survey project "Marks and Measures: Pictographs and Petroglyphs in a Modern Art Context" and the subsequent publication *Marks in Place: Contemporary Responses to Rock Art* (1988). He currently teaches in Santa Fe, New Mexico, where he works in neon sculpture.

BOOKS:

Diesels and Dinosaurs: Photographs from the American Highway
By Steve Fitch, designed by Steve Fitch and Roger Minick
Berkeley: Long Run Press, 1976
[84] pp.; 11¼ x 9¼ (28.6 x 23.5)
50 black-and-white reproductions of photographs by Fitch
Library Collection, Whitney Museum of American Art, New York

see also Connor, *Marks in Place*

PHOTOGRAPHS:

Hit the Rim Loaded, 1972
Published in *Diesels and Dinosaurs*
Gelatin silver print, 9 x 10⅞ (22.9 x 27.6)
Collection of the artist

LEE FRIEDLANDER
BORN: 1934, ABERDEEN, WASHINGTON

Lee Friedlander began photographing in 1948, free-lancing for such magazines as *Esquire, Collier's,* and *Art in America*. He is the recipient of three Guggenheim Fellowships (1960, 1962, and 1977) and an NEA Fellowship (1972). His many publications include *Self-Portrait* (1970), *Photographs of Flowers* (1975), *The American Monument* (1976), and *Flowers and Trees* (1981). The photographs in this exhibition are from his forthcoming book on the Sonoran Desert. Friedlander lives and works in New City, New York.

PHOTOGRAPHS:

Sonoran Desert, 1992
Gelatin silver print, 20 x 16 (50.8 x 40.6)
Collection of the artist; courtesy Fraenkel Gallery, San Francisco, and Robert Miller Gallery, New York

Sonoran Desert, 1994
Gelatin silver print, 20 x 16 (50.8 x 40.6)
Collection of the artist; courtesy Fraenkel Gallery, San Francisco, and Robert Miller Gallery, New York

Sonoran Desert, 1994
Gelatin silver print, 20 x 16 (50.8 x 40.6)
Collection of the artist; courtesy Fraenkel Gallery, San Francisco, and Robert Miller Gallery, New York

Sonoran Desert, 1995
Gelatin silver print, 20 x 16 (50.8 x 40.6)
Collection of the artist; courtesy Fraenkel Gallery, San Francisco, and Robert Miller Gallery, New York

Sonoran Desert, 1995
Gelatin silver print, 20 x 16 (50.8 x 40.6)
Collection of the artist; courtesy Fraenkel Gallery, San Francisco, and Robert Miller Gallery, New York

Sonoran Desert, 1995
Gelatin silver print, 20 x 16 (50.8 x 40.6)
Collection of the artist; courtesy Fraenkel Gallery, San Francisco, and Robert Miller Gallery, New York

CAROLE GALLAGHER
BORN: 1950, BROOKLYN, NEW YORK

Carole Gallagher received an MA (1976) from Hunter College in New York City. In 1979, after reading declassified documents of the Atomic Energy Commission, Gallagher became interested in the people, known as downwinders, whose lives were affected by the nuclear tests of the 1950s. She moved to Utah in 1983 and for the next ten years, sponsored by the Utah State Historical Society, she interviewed and photographed downwinders of the Nevada Test Site. Her work resulted in a book, *American Ground Zero* (1993), and an exhibition at the International Center of Photography, New York, in 1994.

BOOKS:

American Ground Zero: The Secret Nuclear War
By Carole Gallagher, foreword by Keith Schneider
Cambridge, Massachusetts: The MIT Press; Lunenburg, Vermont: The Stinehour Press, 1993
xxxiii, 427 pp.; 10¼ x 10¼ (26 x 26)
Maps, 118 black-and-white reproductions of photographs by Gallagher, with additional reproductions of photographs by Dorothea Lange and others
Library Collection, Whitney Museum of American Art, New York

ALEXANDER GARDNER
BORN: 1821, PAISLEY, SCOTLAND
DIED: 1882, WASHINGTON, D.C.

Alexander Gardner's reputation as a commercial photographer began after he emigrated to the United States in 1856 and found a job at the New York studio of Mathew Brady. Gardner moved to Washington, D.C., and managed a new branch of Brady's studio until 1862 or 1863, when he left to open a studio of his own. *Gardner's Photographic Sketch Book of the War* (1866) was published following the Civil War and included work by Timothy O'Sullivan and other photographers who had joined Gardner's studio.

In 1867, the Kansas Pacific Railroad began a campaign to acquire congressional support for the extension of the railroad from Kansas to California. They initiated a survey, with Gardner as the official photographer (1867–73), of the proposed route along the 35th parallel. The resulting photographs were published by Gardner in stereographs and an album of prints entitled *Across the Continent on the Kansas Pacific Railroad (Route of the 35th Parallel)* (1869). Twenty autotype plates by Gardner were included in the official report by William J. Palmer, *Report of Surveys Across the Continent in 1867–'68 on the Thirty-Fifth and Thirty-Second Parallels, for a Route Extending the Kansas Pacific Railway to the Pacific Ocean at San Francisco and San Diego* (1869), and several images were used by survey member Dr. William A. Bell for his account of the expedition, *New Tracks in North America* (1869).

PHOTOGRAPHS:

Cañada de las Uvas, or Tejon Pass in Sierra Nevada, California, 1,690 Miles West of Missouri River, 1867
Published in *Across the Continent on the Kansas Pacific Railroad (Route of the 35th Parallel)*
Albumen print, 5⅞ x 8 (14.9 x 20.3)
Missouri Historical Society, St. Louis

*El Moro, or Inscription Rock, Western
New Mexico, 1,000 Miles West of Missouri
River,* 1867
Published in *Across the Continent on the Kansas
Pacific Railroad (Route of the 35th Parallel)*
Albumen print, 5⅞ x 8 (14.9 x 20.3)
Missouri Historical Society, St. Louis

*On the Great Plains, Kansas, 294 Miles West of
Missouri River,* 1867
Published in *Across the Continent on the Kansas
Pacific Railroad (Route of the 35th Parallel) and
Report of Surveys Across the Continent in 1867–'68
on the Thirty-Fifth and Thirty-Second Parallels, for a
Route Extending the Kansas Pacific Railway to the
Pacific Ocean at San Francisco and San Diego*
Albumen print, 5⅞ x 8 (14.9 x 20.3)
Missouri Historical Society, St. Louis

*Partridge Creek, Western Base of Mogoyon
Range, Arizona; Mescal Plant in Foreground,
1,280 Miles from Missouri River,* 1867
Published in *Across the Continent on the Kansas
Pacific Railroad (Route of the 35th Parallel)*
Albumen print, 5⅞ x 8 (14.9 x 20.3)
Missouri Historical Society, St. Louis

*"Westward the Course of Empire Takes Its
Way," Laying Track, 300 Miles West of
Missouri River,* 1867
Published in *Across the Continent on the Kansas
Pacific Railroad (Route of the 35th Parallel) and
Report of Surveys Across the Continent in 1867–'68
on the Thirty-Fifth and Thirty-Second Parallels, for a
Route Extending the Kansas Pacific Railway to the
Pacific Ocean at San Francisco and San Diego*
Albumen print, 5⅞ x 7⅞ (14.9 x 20)
Missouri Historical Society, St. Louis

*Zuni Indians Near Border of New Mexico, on
Western Slope of Sierra Madre, 1,035 miles from
Missouri River,* 1867
Published in *Across the Continent on the Kansas
Pacific Railroad (Route of the 35th Parallel)*
Albumen print, 5¹⁵⁄₁₆ x 8 (15.1 x 20.3)
Boston Public Library, Print Department

*The Mojave Desert, in the Great Basin,
California, Sierra Nevada in the Distance, 1,650
Miles from the Missouri River,* 1867–68
Published in *Across the Continent on the Kansas
Pacific Railroad (Route of the 35th Parallel) and
Report of Surveys Across the Continent in 1867–'68
on the Thirty-Fifth and Thirty-Second Parallels, for a
Route Extending the Kansas Pacific Railway to the
Pacific Ocean at San Francisco and San Diego*
Albumen print, 5¹⁵⁄₁₆ x 8¹⁄₁₆ (15.1 x 20.3)
Boston Public Library, Print Department

Two Races at Fort Mojave, Arizona, 1867–68
Published in *Across the Continent on the Kansas
Pacific Railroad (Route of the 35th Parallel)*
Albumen print, 5¹⁵⁄₁₆ x 8 (15.1 x 20.3)
Boston Public Library, Print Department

*Yucca Tree, "Spanish Bayonet," on the Great
Basin, Southern California, Sierra Nevada in
the Distance, 1,670 Miles from the Missouri
River,* 1867–68
Published in *Across the Continent on the Kansas
Pacific Railroad (Route of the 35th Parallel)*
Albumen print, 5¹⁵⁄₁₆ x 8 (15.1 x 20.3)
Boston Public Library, Print Department

*Crossing of the Sierra Nevadas, California,
Techapa Pass, California, 1,720 Miles West of
the Missouri River,* 1868
Published in *Across the Continent on the Kansas
Pacific Railroad (Route of the 35th Parallel) and
Report of Surveys Across the Continent in 1867–'68
on the Thirty-Fifth and Thirty-Second Parallels, for
a Route Extending the Kansas Pacific Railway to
the Pacific Ocean at San Francisco and San Diego*
Albumen print, 5¹⁵⁄₁₆ x 8 (15.1 x 20.3)
Boston Public Library, Print Department

Fred E. Mang, Jr.
Laura Gilpin and Her Famous Shiprock, c. 1972
Gelatin silver print
Amon Carter Museum, Fort Worth, Texas

LAURA GILPIN

BORN: 1891, COLORADO SPRINGS, COLORADO
DIED: 1979, SANTA FE, NEW MEXICO

Following the advice of her mentor, Gertrude
Käsebier, Laura Gilpin attended the Clarence
White School in New York (1916–18). Returning
to Colorado Springs, she opened a commercial
photography studio and in 1925 established the
Gilpin Publishing Company, for which she
wrote, illustrated, and published *The Pikes Peak
Region* (1926) and *The Mesa Verde National Park*
(1927). During the 1920s, she began photographing the daily life of Native Americans, later
publishing *The Pueblos* (1941) and *The Enduring
Navaho* (1968). Gilpin moved to Santa Fe in 1945
and began photographing the Rio Grande
River; *The Rio Grande, River of Destiny,* which
she wrote as well as designed, was published in

1949. A commercial photographer for over sixty
years, Gilpin received, at the age of eighty-four, a
Guggen-heim Fellowship to make hand-coated
platinum prints. She donated her estate to the
Amon Carter Museum, which organized a retrospective of her work in 1986.

BOOKS:

*The Mesa Verde National Park: Reproductions
from a Series of Photographs by Laura Gilpin*
By Laura Gilpin
Colorado Springs, Colorado: The Gilpin
Publishing Company, 1927
[22] pp.; 11¼ x 8¼ (28.6 x 21)
19 black-and-white reproductions of photographs
by Gilpin
Copy 1: Library Collection, Whitney Museum of
American Art, New York
Copy 2: Amon Carter Museum Library, Fort
Worth, Texas

The Pueblos: A Camera Chronicle
By Laura Gilpin
New York: Hastings House, 1941
124 pp.; 9¾ x 7½ (24.8 x 19.1)
Maps, 76 black-and-white reproductions of
photographs by Gilpin
Copy 1: Library Collection, Whitney Museum of
American Art, New York
Copy 2: Amon Carter Museum Library, Fort
Worth, Texas
The Pueblos was Gilpin's first full-length book.
It included photographs made from the 1920s
to 1941. She divided the text into archaeological
periods and asked her friend Jesse Nusbaum of
Santa Fe's Laboratory of Anthropology to check
her text for accuracy. Contemporary reviews saw
in Gilpin's book a mixture of scholarly text and
appealing photographs that helped describe the
"special lure" of the Southwest. The original
price was $3.

Pictorial Postcards of the Southwest
By Laura Gilpin
Set no. 9: Canyon de Chelly, Arizona
Santa Fe: Laura Gilpin, c. 1946
Postcards, 5½ x 3½ (14 x 9)
5 collotype postcards after photographs by
Gilpin
Amon Carter Museum Library, Fort Worth,
Texas
This set of postcards was no. 9 in a series that
Gilpin began publishing in 1937. Earlier sets
were devoted to her Navajo and Pueblo series,
followed by postcards of Chimayo, Ranchos de
Taos Church, San Ildefonso, and Taos Pueblo.

The Rio Grande, River of Destiny: An Interpretation of the River, the Land, and the People
By Laura Gilpin
New York: Duell, Sloan and Pearce, 1949
xii, 244 pp.; 10¾ x 8¼ (27.3 x 21)
Maps, 229 black-and-white reproductions of photographs by Gilpin
Copy 1: Library Collection, Whitney Museum of American Art, New York
Copies 2 and 3: Amon Carter Museum Library, Fort Worth, Texas

PHOTOGRAPHS:

Balcony House, Mesa Verde, 1924
Published in *The Mesa Verde National Park* and *The Pueblos*
Platinum print, 9⅜ x 7½ (23.8 x 19)
Amon Carter Museum, Fort Worth, Texas; Bequest of Laura Gilpin

The Gate, Laguna, N.M., 1924
Published in *The Pueblos*
Platinum print, 9¼ x 7⅝ (23.5 x 19.4)
Amon Carter Museum, Forth Worth, Texas; Gift of the artist

House of the Cliff Dwellers, Mesa Verde, Colorado, 1925
Published in *The Mesa Verde National Park* and *The Pueblos*
Platinum print, 9½ x 7⁹⁄₁₆ (24.1 x 19.2)
Amon Carter Museum, Fort Worth, Texas; Bequest of Laura Gilpin

Navaho Study at Mesa Verde (Prayer), 1925
Published in *The Mesa Verde National Park* and *The Pueblos*
Waxed platinum print, 14 x 18 (35.6 x 45.7)
Amon Carter Museum, Fort Worth, Texas; Bequest of Laura Gilpin

Round Tower, Cliff Palace (Mesa Verde, Colorado), 1925
Published in *The Mesa Verde National Park* and *The Pueblos*
Hand-coated platinum print, 9⁹⁄₁₆ x 7⅝ (24.3 x 19.4)
Amon Carter Museum, Fort Worth, Texas; Bequest of Laura Gilpin

Square Tower House, Mesa Verde National Park, Colorado, 1926
Published in *The Mesa Verde National Park* and *The Pueblos*

Gelatin silver print, 9½ x 7¹¹⁄₁₆ (24.1 x 19.5)
Amon Carter Museum, Fort Worth, Texas; Bequest of Laura Gilpin

Storm from La Bajada Hill, New Mexico, 1946
Published in *The Rio Grande, River of Destiny*
Gelatin silver print, 20 x 24 (50.8 x 61)
Amon Carter Museum, Fort Worth, Texas; Gift of the artist

The Rio Grande Yields Its Surplus to the Sea, 1947
Published in *The Rio Grande, River of Destiny*
Gelatin silver print, 15¹³⁄₁₆ x 9¹³⁄₁₆ (40.2 x 24.9)
Amon Carter Museum, Fort Worth, Texas; Gift of the artist

PETER GOIN
BORN: 1951, MADISON, WISCONSIN

After receiving an MA (1975) and an MFA (1976) from the University of Iowa, Peter Goin moved to Nevada, where he teaches photography and video at the University of Nevada at Reno. His publications include *Tracing the Line: A Photographic Survey of the Mexican-American Border* (1987), *Nuclear Landscapes* (1991), and *Stopping Time: A Rephotographic Survey of Lake Tahoe* (1992). Goin collaborated with photographer Robert Dawson on the Pyramid Lake and the Water in the West projects, serving as editor and photographer for their book *Arid Waters: Photographs from the Water in the West Project* (1992).

BOOKS:

Tracing the Line: A Photographic Survey of the Mexican-American Border
By Peter Goin
Reno, Nevada: Peter Goin, 1987
[85] leaves of plates, [5] leaves of text, 10½ x 14 (26.7 x 35.6)
85 mounted gelatin silver prints by Goin
Copy 1: Library Collection, Whitney Museum of American Art, New York
Copy 2: Yale Collection of Western Americana, Beinecke Rare Book and Manuscript Library, Yale University, New Haven, Connecticut

Arid Waters: Photographs from the Water in the West Project
Edited by Peter Goin, text by Ellen Manchester
Reno: University of Nevada Press, 1992
x, 88 pp.; 9½ x 10 (24.1 x 25.4)
Black-and-white reproductions of photographs

by Laurie Brown, Gregory Conniff, Robert Dawson, Peter Goin, Terry Evans, Wanda Hammerbeck, Mark Klett, and Martin Stupich; with additional reproductions of historic photographs
Library Collection, Whitney Museum of American Art, New York

EMMET GOWIN
BORN: 1941, DANVILLE, WEST VIRGINIA

Emmet Gowin studied photography with Harry Callahan at the Rhode Island School of Design, where he received an MFA in 1967. A meeting with Frederick Sommer that same year proved influential to his work, and their friendship still continues. Gowin was the recipient of a Guggenheim Fellowship (1975) and two NEA Fellowships (1977 and 1980) which funded travels to photograph in Europe and the American Southwest. Gowin has taught photography from 1967–71 at the Dayton Art Institute and from 1973 to the present at Princeton University. In recent years, he has explored the use of aerial photography to capture the American landscape. He is currently at work on a book about the American West which will feature the photographs in this exhibition.

PHOTOGRAPHS:

Mining Exploration, Near Silver City, Nevada, 1988
Gelatin silver print, 9⅝ x 9¾ (24.4 x 24.8)
Collection of the artist; courtesy PaceWildensteinMacGill Gallery, New York

Pivot Agriculture, Near the Grand Coulee Dam, Washington, 1989
Gelatin silver print, 9⁹⁄₁₆ x 9¹¹⁄₁₆ (24.3 x 24.6)
Collection of the artist; courtesy PaceWildensteinMacGill Gallery, New York

Edge of the Salton Sea, California, 1990
Gelatin silver print, 9⁷⁄₁₆ x 9⅗₆ (24 x 24.3)
Collection of the artist; courtesy PaceWildensteinMacGill Gallery, New York

Mining Exploration and Bomb Disposal Site, Tooele, Army Depot, Tooele, Utah, 1991
Gelatin silver print, 9⁹⁄₁₆ x 9¹¹⁄₁₆ (24.3 x 24.6)
Collection of the artist; courtesy PaceWildensteinMacGill Gallery, New York

KAREN HALVERSON
BORN: 1941, SYRACUSE, NEW YORK

Karen Halverson received a BA (1963) in philosophy from Stanford University, an MA (1965) in the history of ideas from Brandeis University, and a second MA (1975) in anthropology from Columbia University before beginning her career as a photographer. She became an instructor at the International Center of Photography in New York City, then moved to California to teach photography at the University of Southern California. Her work was included in the 1992 exhibition and catalogue *Between Heaven and Home: Contemporary American Landscape Photography*. She currently lives and works in Studio City, California.

BOOKS:

Confronting Nature in Los Angeles, Mulholland: 1993
Book dummy, 10 x 12 (25.4 x 30.5)
Collection of the artist; courtesy Janet Borden, Inc., New York

PHOTOGRAPHS:

Mulholland near Durand Drive, Los Angeles, California, March 15, 1993, 1993
Fujicolor print, 12 x 36 (30.5 x 91.4)
Collection of the artist; courtesy Janet Borden, Inc., New York

ALEX HARRIS
BORN: 1949, ATLANTA

Educated at the Phillips Andover Academy and Yale University, Alex Harris collaborated with Robert Coles on the book *The Old Ones of New Mexico* (1974). A Guggenheim Fellowship (1979–80) allowed him to continue his photography of New Mexico, leading to an invitation to join the New Mexico Survey Project (1982–84) sponsored by the National Endowment for the Humanities. The result was Harris' book *The Essential Landscape* (1985). Harris serves as director of the Center for Documentary Photography at Duke University, where he also teaches. His monographs include *River of Traps* (1990), with William DuBuys, and *Red White Blue and God Bless You* (1994).

BOOKS:

The Essential Landscape: The New Mexico Photographic Survey
Essays by J.B. Jackson; editor, Steven A. Yates; photographers: Thomas F. Barrow, Miguel Gandert, Alex Harris, Paul Logsdon, Joan Myers, Anne Noggle, Mary Peck, Bernard Plossu, Edward Ranney, Meridel Rubenstein, Richard Wickstrom, and Richard Wilder
Albuquerque: University of New Mexico Press, 1985
vii, 147 pp.; 9¾ x 10¾ (24.8 x 27.3)
Black-and-white and color reproductions of photographs by survey photographers
Amon Carter Museum Library, Fort Worth, Texas

Red White Blue and God Bless You: A Portrait of Northern New Mexico
By Alex Harris
Albuquerque: University of New Mexico Press, in association with the Center for Documentary Studies, Duke University, 1992
127 pp.; 10½ x 11½ (26.7 x 29.2)
6 black-and-white and 79 color reproductions of photographs by Harris
Library Collection, Whitney Museum of American Art, New York

PHOTOGRAPHS:

Sombrillo, New Mexico, Looking South from Ben Vigil's 1952 Chevrolet, August, 1986
Published in *Red White Blue and God Bless You*
Ektacolor print, 16 x 20 (40.6 x 50.8)
Collection of the artist; courtesy Bonni Benrubi Gallery, New York

FRED HARVEY
BORN: 1835, LONDON
DIED: 1901, LEAVENWORTH, KANSAS

Fred Harvey came to the United States at the age of fifteen and found a job washing dishes in a New York restaurant. After several successful occupations, the entrepreneurial Harvey approached the Atcheson, Topeka & Santa Fe Railroad with a proposal to provide meals for its passengers. His dining rooms became famous, as did the waitresses, or Harvey Girls, who served in them. Harvey Houses were soon opened along the entire length of the AT&SF, and gallery shops were added to sell Southwestern art, as well as prints and photographs created by professional Harvey artists. A printing house was established to publish books, brochures, and postcards promoting tourism in the Southwest.

Harvey died of cancer in 1901, but the Fred Harvey Company continued to grow. El Tovar, the most successful of the Harvey hotels, was built at the rim of the Grand Canyon in 1904 and soon expanded into an entire village. In the 1920s, automobile tours known as South-west Indian Detours were organized to visit sites not accessible by train, using Harvey Girls as guides. The partnership with the Santa Fe Railroad continued until 1968, and many Harvey Houses still exist today.

BOOKS:
see Moon, Peabody

Dr. Hayden on the Trail, n.d.
The Bancroft Library, University of California, Berkeley

F.V. (FERDINAND VANDEVEER) HAYDEN
BORN: 1828, WESTFIELD, MASSACHUSETTS
DIED: 1887, PHILADELPHIA

A Civil War surgeon and experienced geologist, F.V. Hayden was named professor of mineralogy and geology at the University of Pennsylvania in 1865. When Nebraska was granted statehood in 1867, Hayden was put in charge of a geological survey of Nebraska, reporting to the Interior Department's General Land Office. In 1869, Hayden's growing organization was renamed the Geological and Geographical Survey of the Territories of the United States and transferred to the Interior Secretary's office.

As one method of assuring continued government funding for his explorations, Hayden hired the renowned printer Julius Bien to produce *Sun Pictures of Rocky Mountain Scenery* (1870), with thirty of A.J. Russell's photographs from *The Great West Illustrated* (1869). Hayden convinced photographer W.H. Jackson to accompany his survey in 1870 without salary. In 1871, Jackson, with artist Thomas Moran, documented the survey's exploration of the headwaters of the Yellowstone River. Hayden's lobbying, along with Jackson's photographs, helped persuade Congress and President Grant to make Yellowstone America's first National Park in 1872. Hayden's survey became the best known of all the Western expeditions at the time and received the largest appropriations until it was discontinued in 1879 by the same law that established the US Geological Survey.

BOOKS:
see Jackson, Russell

F.J. (FRANK JAY) HAYNES

BORN: 1853, SALINE, MICHIGAN
DIED: 1921, ST. PAUL, MINNESOTA

As a young man, F.J. Haynes traveled around rural Michigan, selling chromolithographs from a horse-drawn view-wagon. In 1876, he opened a studio in Moorhead, Minnesota, and received commissions from the Northern Pacific Railroad, which named Haynes their official photographer in 1881. That same year, Haynes visited Yellowstone National Park for the first time and acquired the first franchise for a photography studio inside the Park. In 1883, in addition to his work for the NPRR, Haynes became the official photographer of Yellowstone and superintendent of its art department. His images of the park became internationally famous and when President Arthur planned an excursion there, Haynes was asked to accompany and photograph the journey, later published as *Journey Through the Yellowstone National Park and Northwestern Wyoming* (1883).

BOOKS:

Journey Through the Yellowstone National Park and Northwestern Wyoming, 1883, Photographs of Party and Scenery Along the Route Traveled, and Copies of the Associated Press Dispatches Sent Whilst en Route. The Party: Chester A. Arthur, President of the United States [and others]. *Escort: Troop G., Fifth Cavalry, Captain E.M. Hayes, Lieutenant H. De H. Waite*
By F.J. Haynes
n.p., 1883
43 pp. and 44 leaves of plates; 10½ x 15 (26.7 x 38.1)
104 mounted albumen prints by Haynes
The Denver Art Museum

JOHN KARL HILLERS

BORN: 1843, BRINKUM, GERMANY
DIED: 1925, WASHINGTON, D.C.

Passing through Salt Lake City in 1871, Civil War veteran and teamster John (originally Johann) Hillers chanced to meet Major John Wesley Powell, who hired him as a boatman for Powell's second Colorado River expedition. Powell employed a series of photographers, E.O. Beaman, Walter Clement Powell, and James Fennemore, for whom Hillers volunteered to help carry equipment in return for photography lessons. By 1873, Hillers was an accomplished photographer and remained with Powell as his official photographer until 1879, when the US Geographical and Geological Survey of the Rocky Mountain Region was discontinued by the same law that established the US Geological Survey. Powell became director of the Bureau of Ethnology and appointed Hillers as its photographer. When Powell was also named director of the US Geological Survey in 1881, Hillers became its chief photog-rapher, serving both departments until he retired in 1900.

BOOKS:

"The Cañons of the Colorado,"
Scribner's Monthly 9, no. 3 (January 1875): pp. 293–310
By Major J.W. Powell
9 x 6 (23 x 15.2)
Illustrations from photographs by Hillers and Beaman
Yale Collection of Western Americana, Beinecke Rare Book and Manuscript Library, Yale University, New Haven, Connecticut

Exploration of the Colorado River of the West and Its Tributaries. Explored in 1869, 1870, 1871, and 1872 under the Direction of the Secretary of the Smithsonian Institution
By John Wesley Powell
Washington, D.C.: Government Printing Office, 1875
xi, 291 pp.; 11¾ x 9½ (29.8 x 24.1)
Map, 80 engravings from photographs by Hillers and E.O. Beaman. Thomas Moran redrew some of the photographs
Library, Denver Museum of Natural History

Houses and House-Life of the American Aborigines
By Lewis Henry Morgan
Contributions to North American Ethnology, vol. 4
Washington, D.C.: Government Printing Office, 1881
xiv, 281 pp.; 11¾ x 9¼ (29.8 x 23.5)
4 heliotypes of photographs by Hillers
Copy 1: Library Collection, Whitney Museum of American Art, New York
Copy 2: William Reese Company, New Haven, Connecticut

Tertiary History of the Grand Cañon District with Atlas
By Clarence E. Dutton
Monographs of the United States Geological Survey, vol. 2
Washington, D.C.: Government Printing Office, 1882
xiv, 264 pp.; 12¼ x 9½ (31.1 x 24.1)
4 heliotypes of photographs by Hillers, printed by Julius Bien
This volume was published with an oversize atlas illustrated by Thomas Moran and William Henry Holmes.
Copy 1: Private collection
Copy 2: Special Collections, The University of Arizona, Tucson

PHOTOGRAPHS:

Shini-mo, Altar from the Brink of Marble Canyon, Colorado River, c. 1875
Albumen print, 13¼ x 9¾ (34 x 25)
George Eastman House, Rochester

Hopi Pueblo of Walpi, First Mesa, Arizona, 1876
Published in *Houses and House-Life of the American Aborigines*
Albumen print 9¾ x 12¹⁵⁄₁₆ (25 x 32.8)
Centre Canadien d'Architecture/Canadian Centre for Architecture, Montreal

The Grand Canyon, To-Ro-Wip Valley, Colorado River, 1879
Albumen print, 13 x 9¾ (33 x 24.8)
Hallmark Photographic Collection, Hallmark Cards, Inc., Kansas City, Missouri

Pueblo de Santo Domingo, New Mexico, 1880
Published in *Houses and House-Life of the American Aborigines*
Albumen print, 9⅝ x 12¹⁵⁄₁₆ (24.7 x 32.9)
Centre Canadien d'Architecture/Canadian Centre for Architecture, Montreal

Pueblo de Taos, North, New Mexico, 1880
Published in *Houses and House-Life of the American Aborigines*
Albumen print, 9⅞ x 12¹⁵⁄₁₆ (25.1 x 32.5)
Centre Canadien d'Architecture/Canadian Centre for Architecture, Montreal

WILLIAM T. (TEMPLE) HORNADAY
BORN: 1854, PLAINFIELD, INDIANA
DIED: 1937, STAMFORD, CONNECTICUT

A naturalist and radical wildlife conservationist, William Hornaday worked his way through Iowa State Agricultural College as a self-taught taxidermist for the college museum. He was appointed chief taxidermist of the United States National Museum (1882–90), where he developed the first department of living animals and created a National Zoological Garden under the auspices of the Smithsonian Institution. In 1896, Hornaday became the first director of the New York Zoological Gardens (later known as the Bronx Zoo), where he remained until his retirement in 1926.

BOOKS:

Camp-fires on Desert and Lava
By William T. Hornaday, photographically illustrated by Dr. Daniel Trembly MacDougal, Mr. John M. Phillips, and the author, with two new and original maps by Godfrey Sykes, geographer to the expedition
New York: Charles Scribner's Sons, 1908
366 pp.; 9¼ x 6¼ (23.5 x 16)
Maps, 65 black-and-white and color reproductions of photographs by MacDougal, Phillips, and Hornaday
Copy 1: Library Collection, Whitney Museum of American Art, New York
Copy 2: Library, Denver Museum of Natural History

PHILIP HYDE
BORN: 1921, SAN FRANCISCO

Philip Hyde left the United States Army Air Force in 1945 and returned to school, studying photography with Ansel Adams, Minor White, and others at the California School of Fine Arts (1947–50). An active supporter of the American wilderness, Hyde joined the Sierra Club in 1949, and his photographs have often been used in its posters, calendars, and books, such as *The Last Redwoods* (1963), *Navajo Wildlands* (1967), and *Mountain and Desert* (1973). Hyde lives and works in Taylorville, California.

BOOKS:

Drylands: The Deserts of North America
Photographs and text by Philip Hyde, introduction and notes on plants and animals of the North American deserts by David Rains Wallace
A Yolla Bolly Press Book
San Diego: Harcourt Brace Jovanovich, 1987
173 pp.; 13¼ x 14¾ (33.7 x 37.5)
95 color reproductions of photographs by Hyde, drawings by Vincent Lopez
Library Collection, Whitney Museum of American Art, New York

PHOTOGRAPHS:

White Domes, Valley of Fire, Nevada, 1970 (1987 print)
Published in *Drylands*
Ektacolor print, 15 x 13¼ (38.1 x 33.7)
Collection of the artist

WILLIAM HENRY JACKSON
BORN: 1843, KEESEVILLE, NEW YORK
DIED: 1942, NEW YORK

Following the Civil War, William Henry Jackson settled in Omaha and, with two of his brothers, opened a photography studio in 1868. While photographing along the newly completed Union Pacific Railroad in 1870, Jackson met government geologist F.V. Hayden, who convinced him to accompany the US Geological Survey of the Territories as a freelance photographer. In 1871, Jackson was hired as the Survey's official photographer, and spent the next seven summers with Hayden. Jackson's images of Yellowstone were sent to members of Congress and influenced the decision to designate Yellowstone as our first National Park in 1872. *The Mount of the Holy Cross,* taken in 1873 in Colorado, is one of Jackson's best-known photographs.

Returning to private life in 1879, Jackson opened the W.H. Jackson Photography and Publishing Company in Denver. He joined the Detroit Photographic Company in 1898 and continued with the organization until its bankruptcy forced him to retire in 1924. Jackson moved to New York City but left retirement in 1935 to complete a set of murals, now in the Interior Department's Museum, and other art for the National Park Service.

BOOKS:

Bulletin of the United States Geological and Geographical Survey of the Territories: 1874 and 1875. Bulletin No. 1, Second Series, 1875
By F.V. Hayden
Washington, D.C.: Government Printing Office, 1875
211 pp.; 9 x 5½ (23 x 14)
Maps, 2 heliotypes and illustrations from drawings by Jackson
Geology Library, Yale University Library, New Haven, Connecticut

Descriptive Catalogue of the Photographs of the United States Geological Survey of the Territories, for the Years 1869 to 1875, Inclusive
Second Edition
Department of the Interior, United States Geological Survey of the Territories, Miscellaneous Publications no. 5
By William Henry Jackson
Washington, D.C.: Government Printing Office, 1875
80 pp.; 9 x 5¾ (23 x 14.6)
14 illustrations from photographs by Jackson
Originally published in 1874
Collection of Charles Schwartz (2nd edition)

[*Rocky Mountain Views*]
By William Henry Jackson
S.l.: s.n., c. 1881
[195] pp.; 5¼ x 8½ (13.3 x 21.6)
195 mounted gelatin silver prints by Jackson, all images are titled and numbered
Copy 1: Yale Collection of Western Americana, Beinecke Rare Book and Manuscript Library, Yale University, New Haven, Connecticut
Copy 2: Collection of Charles Schwartz

The Cañons of Colorado: From Photographs by W.H. Jackson
Denver, Colorado: Frank S. Thayer, [c. 1900]
8¼ x 5½ (21 x 14) unfolds to 8¼ x 84 (21 x 213.4)
Accordion binding with 16 tinted black-and-white reproductions of photographs by Jackson
Library, Denver Museum of Natural History

PHOTOGRAPHS:

The Cañon of the Mancos, c. 1874–75
Albumen print, 9¾ x 13 (24.8 x 33)
Collection of Charles Schwartz

Great Cañon of the Colorado, near Peach Springs, c. 1885
Albumen print, 13¼ x 9⅞ (34 x 25.4)
George Eastman House, Rochester

The Grand Canyon of Arizona from O'Neill Point, 1902
Albumen print from a negative by H.G. Peabody, 16¾ x 39¼ (42.5 x 99.7)
Private collection

Castellated Rocks near Monument Park, n.d.
Published in *Bulletin of the United States Geological and Geographical Survey of the Territories: 1874 and 1875. Bulletin No. 1, Second Series,* 1875
Albumen print, 14½ x 21 (36.8 x 53.3)
Yale Collection of Western Americana, Beinecke Rare Book and Manuscript Library, Yale University, New Haven, Connecticut

GEORGE WHARTON JAMES
BORN: 1858, GAINSBOROUGH, ENGLAND
DIED: 1923, SAN FRANCISCO

George Wharton James emigrated to the United States in 1881. He worked as a Methodist minister in Nevada and California until a public scandal in 1889 forced him to leave his church and his family. It was during a self-imposed exile from California that James first visited the Grand Canyon, where he returned each summer for the rest of his life. In 1892, he found work as a publicity agent for a tourist hotel near Pasadena and successfully published souvenir booklets and tourist guides promoting Southern California. He organized tours to the Grand Canyon and other Southwestern locations, publishing *In & Around the Grand Canyon* (1900) as well as a companion guidebook, *The Grand Canyon of Arizona, How to See It* (1911). Although James was an amateur photographer, he often traveled with professionals such as George L. Rose, C.C. Pierce, and F.H. Maude, using their work in his books and articles. In 1901, James sold many of his own photographs to Pierce, who appropriated and copyrighted them, leaving the question of authorship obscured even today. James was assistant editor of the *Craftsman* (1904–05), editor of *Out West* (1912–14), and the author of more than forty-two books.

BOOKS:

In & Around the Grand Canyon: The Grand Canyon of the Colorado River in Arizona
By George Wharton James
Boston: Little, Brown, and Company, 1900
xxiv, 341 pp.; 8¾ x 6¼ (22.2 x 16)
100 black-and-white reproductions of photographs by James and other photographers

identified in the captions; includes a bibliography and guide to photographing the Grand Canyon. Originally published in 1900; later editions included folding maps and "Practical Hints to Tourists."
Copy 1: Library Collection, Whitney Museum of American Art, New York (1901 edition)
Copy 2: Library, Denver Museum of Natural History (1913 edition)

The Wonders of the Colorado Desert (Southern California): Its Rivers and its Mountains, its Canyons and its Springs, its Life and its History, Pictured and Described
By George Wharton James, with upwards of three hundred pen-and-ink sketches from nature, by Carl Eytel
Boston: Little, Brown, and Company, 1906
2 vol.; 9 x 6¼ (23 x 16)
Maps, 29 black-and-white reproductions of photographs by James
Special Collections, The University of Arizona, Tucson

Arizona the Wonderland: The History of its Ancient Cliff and Cave Dwellings, Ruined Pueblos, Conquest by the Spaniards; Jesuit and Franciscan Missions, Trail Makers and Indians; a Survey of its Climate, Scenic Marvels, Topography, Deserts, Mountains, Rivers and Valleys; a Review of its Industries; an Account of its Influence on Art, Literature and Science; (and Some Reference to What it Offers of Delight to the Automobilist, Sportsman, Pleasure and Health Seeker)
By George Wharton James
Boston: The Page Company, 1917
xxiv, 478 pp.; 9¾ x 6¾ (24.7 x 17.1)
Map, 48 black-and-white and 12 color reproductions of photographs by James and others
Special Collections, The University of Arizona, Tucson

LEN JENSHEL
BORN: 1949, BROOKLYN, NEW YORK

Len Jenshel received a BFA (1975) from The Cooper Union in New York City. He is the recipient of an NEA Fellowship (1978), an award from the New York State Council on the Arts (1978), and a Guggenheim Fellowship (1980). He has taught at The Cooper Union, New York University, the School of Visual Arts, and the International Center of Photography, all in New York City, where he continues to live and work.

BOOKS:

Travels in the American West: Photographs by Len Jenshel
Washington, D.C., London: Smithsonian Institution Press in association with Constance Sullivan Editions, 1992
61 pp.; 10 x 8½ (25.4 x 21.6)
27 color reproductions of photographs by Jenshel
Library Collection, Whitney Museum of American Art, New York

PHOTOGRAPHS:

Dante's Point–Death Valley National Park, California, 1990
Published in *Travels in the American West: Photographs by Len Jenshel*
Chromogenic print, 15 x 22 (38.1 x 55.9)
Yancey Richardson Gallery, New York

CHARLES GRANVILLE JOHNSON
DATES UNKNOWN

Charles Granville Johnson lived in Arizona from 1863 to 1868. While there, he produced the photographs and texts for *The Territory of Arizona,* an ambitious study originally projected for publication in twenty-five parts. In 1868 Johnson moved to San Francisco, where three parts of the *The Territory of Arizona* were published a year later. Two parts focus on steamboating efforts on the Colorado River and one part on Cocopah Indian life on the lower Colorado. Later correspondence about the publication indicates that Johnson had moved to Tombstone, Arizona, by 1897.

BOOKS:

The Territory of Arizona, Embracing a History of the Territory; Its Mineral, Agricultural, and Commercial Advantages; Its Climate and Boundaries; and the Great Colorado of the Pacific. Beautifully Illustrated with Actual Photographs of the Country, the Rivers, the Towns, the Cities and the Different Indian Tribes
By Charles Granville Johnson
San Francisco: Vincent Ryan & Co., 1869
32 pp.; 12¹/₁₆ x 9¾ (31 x 25)
5 mounted albumen prints
DeGolyer Library, Southern Methodist University, Dallas

Clarence King in the Act of Climbing a Mountain, c. 1869
The Bancroft Library, University of California, Berkeley

CLARENCE KING
BORN: 1842, NEWPORT, RHODE ISLAND
DIED: 1901, PHOENIX

Clarence King graduated in 1862 from Yale's Sheffield Scientific School and volunteered (1863–66) for J.D. Whitney's Geological Survey of California. At the age of twenty-four, King traveled to Washington, D.C., to propose a mapping and resource-assessment of a 100-mile swath that flanked the route of the transcontinental railroad between the Sierra Nevadas and the western Rocky Mountains. King and his backers convinced Congress and the War Department to appropriate funds for the US Geological Exploration of the 40th Parallel for the Corps of Engineers. King's hiring of a photographer, Timothy O'Sullivan, to document his expeditions, was an important precedent for subsequent federal surveys.

At the end of the survey's initial three years, King's friend from the Whitney survey, photographer Carleton Watkins, substituted briefly for O'Sullivan, who returned in 1872 to complete King's field documentation. Julius Bien printed the *Report of the Geological Exploration of the Fortieth Parallel* (1870–80), published in seven large quarto volumes. The next-to-last volume was King's own synthesis—*Systematic Geology* (1878). King's survey completed its operations and went out of existence in 1879, two months before Congress and President Hayes replaced the territorial surveys led by Hayden, Powell, and Wheeler with the US Geological Survey. King served as the USGS' first director. He set high standards for appointments to and work by the new agency's staff, before resigning in 1881 to enter private business.

BOOKS:
see O'Sullivan, *Systematic Geology*

MARK KLETT
BORN: 1952, ALBANY, NEW YORK

Mark Klett earned a BS (1974) in geology from St. Lawrence University and an MFA (1977) in photography from the State University of New York, Buffalo, before joining the US Geological Survey as a field assistant (1977–79). With Ellen Manchester and photographer JoAnn Verburg, Klett conceived and founded the Rephotographic Survey Project in 1977, funded by Polaroid and the National Endowment for the Arts, to retrace the work of nineteenth-century American photographers. Together with two other photographers, Klett completed the project in 1984 with the publication of *Second View*. Klett has received four NEA Fellowships (1979, 1982, 1984, and 1993) and was named photographer of the year by the Friends of Photography (1993). He is currently manager of the Photography Collaborative Facility at Arizona State University, Tempe.

BOOKS:

Second View: The Rephotographic Survey Project
By Mark Klett, chief photographer; Ellen Manchester, project director; JoAnn Verburg, project coordinator; Gordon Bushaw and Rick Dingus, project photographers; essay by Paul Berger
Albuquerque: University of New Mexico Press, 1984
ix, 211 pp.; 9¼ x 12½ (23.4 x 31.8)
Maps, 142 black-and-white reproductions of photographs by Gordon Bushaw, Rick Dingus, and Mark Klett, 121 black-and-white reproductions of photographs by nineteenth-century survey photographers, and 4 black-and-white reproductions of photographs by others
Library Collection, Whitney Museum of American Art, New York

Traces of Eden: Travels in the Desert Southwest
Photographs by Mark Klett, essay by Denis Johnson, critical text by Peter Galassi
A Polaroid Book
Boston: David R. Godine, 1986
[44] pp.; 9½ x 11½ (24 x 29.2)
16 black-and-white and color reproductions of photographs by Klett
Library Collection, Whitney Museum of American Art, New York

Revealing Territory, Photographs of the Southwest
By Mark Klett, essays by Patricia Nelson Limerick and Thomas W. Southall
Albuquerque: University of New Mexico Press, 1992
170 pp.; 7½ x 12¼ (24 x 31)
115 black-and-white reproductions of photographs by Klett
Library Collection, Whitney Museum of American Art, New York

Desert Legends: Re-Storying the Sonoran Borderlands
Stories by Gary Paul Nabhan, photographs by Mark Klett
New York: Henry Holt and Company, 1994
[6], [vi], 207 pp.; 9¼ x 10¾ (24 x 28)
56 black-and-white reproductions of photographs by Klett
Library Collection, Whitney Museum of American Art, New York

PHOTOGRAPHS:

Monument Rock, Canyon de Chelly National Monument, Arizona, 1978
Diptych with Timothy O'Sullivan's Cañon de Chelle . . . , 1873
Published in *Second View*
Gelatin silver prints, 8 x 20 (20.3 x 50.8)
Rephotographic Survey Project, Tempe, Arizona

Pyramid Isle, Pyramid Lake, Nevada, 1979
Diptych with Timothy O'Sullivan's *Rock Formations, Pyramid Lake, Nevada,* 1867
Published in *Second View*
Gelatin silver prints, 8 x 20 (20.3 x 50.8)
Rephotographic Survey Project, Tempe, Arizona

Site of the Gould and Curry Mine, Virginia City, Nevada, 1979
Diptych with Timothy O'Sullivan's *Quartz Mill Near Virginia City,* 1868
Published in *Second View*
Gelatin silver prints, 8 x 20 (20.3 x 50.8)
Rephotographic Survey Project, Tempe, Arizona

Car Passing Snake, Eastern Mojave Desert, 1983
Published in *Traces of Eden*
Gelatin silver print, 16 x 20 (40.6 x 50.8)
Collection of the artist

Night Storm, Glendale, Arizona, 1993
Published in *Desert Legends*
Gelatin silver print, 16 x 20 (40.6 x 50.8)
Collection of the artist

Saguaro with Shirt at the U.S.-Mexican Border, 1993
Published in *Desert Legends*
Gelatin silver print, 20 x 16 (50.8 x 40.6)
Collection of the artist

Second Tank at Tinajas Atlas, Where Many Died Trying to Find Water, 1993
Published in *Desert Legends*
Gelatin silver print, 16 x 20 (40.6 x 50.8)
Collection of the artist

ERNEST KNEE
BORN: 1907, MONTREAL
DIED: 1982, SANTA FE, NEW MEXICO

Ernest Knee was a self-taught Canadian photographer who moved to the American Southwest to recover from rheumatic fever. Living in Santa Fe, he gained a reputation for his expertise with large-format cameras. He formed friendships with local artists such as Gustave Baumann, Andrew Dasberg, and Randall Davey, serving as photographer of their work. Besides still photography, Knee worked in motion pictures and in the 1930s made one short film, *A Day in Santa Fe,* and produced two others, *Santa Fe, N.M.* (1942, also published as a book) and *Old Mexico* (1950).

BOOKS:

Santa Fe, New Mexico
By Ernest Knee
New York: Hastings House, 1942
101 pp.; 9¼ x 6¼ (23.5 x 16)
120 black-and-white reproductions of photographs by Knee
Library Collection, Whitney Museum of American Art, New York

ELLSWORTH L. (LEONARDSON) KOLB
BORN: 1876, SMITHFIELD, PENNSYLVANIA
DIED: 1960, LOS ANGELES

Searching for adventure, Ellsworth Kolb came to the Grand Canyon in 1901, followed the next year by his brother, Emery (1881–1976). Their plans to open a photography studio were hindered when they found that all concessionaire contracts had been given to the Santa Fe Rail-road-Fred Harvey coalition. Undaunted, they opened the Kolb Studio in a tent pitched on private property at the Canyon's rim and operated in the Canyon successfully for more than seventy-five years. Their darkroom was built four and one-half miles down in the Canyon at the closest source for running water. Each day, they photographed tourists, ran to the darkroom, developed the prints, and ran back before the tourists had finished hiking the Canyon's trails.

To satisfy the demand for scenic views of the Grand Canyon, the Kolbs produced a booklet of hand-colored lithographic prints taken from their photographs, which went into numerous reprints. In 1913, Emery took over the studio and Ellsworth moved to Los Angeles, where he wrote *Through the Grand Canyon from Wyoming to Mexico* (1914), a journal of the Kolb brothers' journey down the Green and Colorado Rivers in 1911. After Emery's death, the Kolb Studio was saved from demolition by the Historic Sites Act; it remains at its original location, used as a bookstore and information center.

BOOKS:

Through the Grand Canyon from Wyoming to Mexico
By E.L. Kolb, with a foreword by Owen Wister, with 72 plates from photographs by the author and his brother
New York: The Macmillan Company, 1914
xx, 344 pp.; 8¾ x 6¾ (22.2 x 17.1)
72 black-and-white reproductions, and a color frontispiece, of photographs by Ellsworth and Emery Kolb
Reprinted numerous times; the 1930 and subsequent editions included 76 reproductions
Copy 1: Library Collection, Whitney Museum of American Art, New York
Copy 2: Special Collections, The University of Arizona, Tucson

DOROTHEA LANGE
BORN: 1895, HOBOKEN, NEW JERSEY
DIED: 1965, BERKELEY, CALIFORNIA

Born Dorothea Margaretta Nutzhorn, Lange took her mother's maiden name while studying photography with Clarence White at Columbia University (1917–18). She settled in San Francisco, where she opened a studio in 1919, marrying Western painter Maynard Dixon the following year. In 1935, she began working with Paul Taylor (whom she later married) for the California Emergency Relief Administration, transferring to Roy Striker's Historical Section under the Resettlement Administration (later the Farm Security Administration) along with other photographers such as Walker Evans, Ben Shahn, and Arthur Rothstein. Many of Lange's FSA photographs were used to illustrate Archibald MacLeish's poem "The Land of the Free" (1938) and a collaboration between Lange and Taylor, *An American Exodus* (1939). Lange was the first woman to receive a Guggenheim Fellowship in photography (1941) but relinquished it when World War II was declared. Her career as a freelance photographer continued into the 1960s; she died shortly before a retrospective exhibition of her work opened at The Museum of Modern Art, New York.

BOOKS:

An American Exodus: A Record of Human Erosion
By Dorothea Lange and Paul Schuster Taylor
New York: Reynal and Hitchcock, 1939
158 pp.; 10¼ x 7¾ (26 x 19.7)
Illustrated with black-and-white reproductions of photographs by Lange, supplemented with photographs from the Oklahoma Historical Society, Arthur Rothstein, Horace Bristol, Ron Partridge, Otto Hagel, and others. Original price was $2.75.
Copies 1 and 2: Library Collection, Whitney Museum of American Art, New York
Copy 3: Collection of Charles Schwartz
Copy 4: Private collection

PHOTOGRAPHS:

Dust Bowl (Abandoned Dust Bowl Farm), 1937 (1995 print)
Published in *An American Exodus*
Gelatin silver print, 9⅝ x13⅜ (24.4 x 34)
The Oakland Museum, California; Dorothea Lange Collection, Gift of Paul S. Taylor

Grain Elevators, Barbed Wire, and Gang Plows on the High Plains, 1937–38 (1995 print)
Published in *An American Exodus,* p. 90
Gelatin silver print, 9¹⁵⁄₁₆ x 6¹⁵⁄₁₆ (25.2 x 17.6)
The Oakland Museum, California; Dorothea Lange Collection, Gift of Paul S. Taylor

Abandoned Farm, 1938 (1995 print)
Published in *An American Exodus,* p. 92
Gelatin silver print, 10⅜ x 13¼ (26.3 x 33.7)
The Oakland Museum, California; Dorothea Lange Collection, Gift of Paul S. Taylor

Dust Bowl, 1938 (1995 print)
Published in *An American Exodus,* p. 96
Gelatin silver print, 10⅜ x 13⁹⁄₁₆ (26.4 x 35.4)
The Oakland Museum, California; Dorothea Lange Collection, Gift of Paul S. Taylor

Dust Bowl Farmyard, 1938 (1995 print)
Published in *An American Exodus,* p. 100
Gelatin silver print, 9⅝ x13⅜ (24.4 x 34)
The Oakland Museum, California; Dorothea
Lange Collection, Gift of Paul S. Taylor

Homeless Family, Oklahoma, 1938 (1995 print)
Published in *An American Exodus,* p. 64
Gelatin silver print, 10⅜ x 13¹⁵⁄₁₆ (26.4 x 35.4)
The Oakland Museum, California; Dorothea
Lange Collection, Gift of Paul S. Taylor

*The Road West, U.S. 54 in Southern New
Mexico,* 1938 (1995 print)
Published in *An American Exodus,* p. 65
Gelatin silver print, 6¹⁵⁄₁₆ x 9¹⁵⁄₁₆ (17.6 x 25.2)
The Oakland Museum, California; Dorothea
Lange Collection, Gift of Paul S. Taylor

Woman of the High Plains, Texas Panhandle,
1938 (1995 print)
Published in *An American Exodus,* p. 101
Gelatin silver print, 13⅛ x 10⅜ (33.3 x 26.4)
The Oakland Museum, California; Dorothea
Lange Collection, Gift of Paul S. Taylor

JUNGJIN LEE
BORN: 1961, TAE-KU, KOREA

———————

Jungjin Lee received a BFA (1984) from Hong-ik
University, Seoul, and worked for several years
as a documentary photographer before moving
to New York in 1988. She received her MA (1991)
from New York University, and the following
year published her first book, *The American
Deserts* (1992). Lee currently divides her time
between New York and Korea.

BOOKS:

The American Deserts
Photographs by Jungjin Lee
[Seoul, Korea: Shigak Publications, 1992]
[50] pp.; 14¼ x 10 (36 x 25)
32 reproductions of photographs by Lee
Library Collection, Whitney Museum of
American Art, New York

PHOTOGRAPHS:

Untitled, The American Desert, 1992
Published in *The American Deserts*
Sensitized photo emulsion on rice paper, 37 x 25
(94 x 63.5)
Collection of the artist; courtesy
PaceWildensteinMacGill Gallery, New York

Untitled, The American Desert, 1992
Published in *The American Deserts*
Sensitized photo emulsion on rice paper, 37 x 25
(94 x 63.5)
Collection of the artist; courtesy
PaceWildensteinMacGill Gallery, New York

PAUL LOGSDON
BORN: 1931, GREENVILLE, KENTUCKY
DIED: 1989, SANTA FE, NEW MEXICO

———————

In 1976, after twenty years as a military jet pilot,
Paul Logsdon retired from the Air Force and
began a second career as an aerial photographer. He said he visualized his Cessna 150 airplane
as a very tall tripod. Flying the plane and using
a hand-held camera, Logsdon photographed
Southwestern landscapes and ruins for magazines such as *National Geographic, Scientific
American*, and the *Albuquerque Journal.* In 1982,
Logsdon was invited to participate in the New
Mexico Photographic Survey and his work was
included in its publication *The Essential Landscape* (1985).

BOOKS:
see Harris, *Essential Landscape*

PHOTOGRAPHS:

*Indian Community, Navajo Settlement, San
Juan Basin,* 1982
Published in *Essential Landscape*
Cibachrome II print, 14 x 19 (35.6 x 48.3)
Museum of Fine Arts, Museum of New Mexico,
Santa Fe; from the New Mexico Photographic
Survey Project/NEA

Ruins–Chetro Ketl, Chaco Canyon, 1982
Published in *Essential Landscape*
Cibachrome II print, 15 x 19 (38.1 x 48.3)
Museum of Fine Arts, Museum of New Mexico,
Santa Fe; from the New Mexico Photographic
Survey Project/NEA

Bob Miller
*Charles Lummis and Theodore Roosevelt at Occidental College,
Los Angeles,* 1911
The Southwest Museum, Los Angeles

CHARLES F. (FLETCHER) LUMMIS
BORN: 1859, LYNN, MASSACHUSETTS
DIED: 1928, LOS ANGELES

———————

A catalyst for cultural development in Southern
California, Charles Lummis was a tireless promoter of the Southwest (a term he popularized).
He attended Harvard University (1877–80), paying his tuition in part through the sale of 14,000
hand-printed copies of his *Birch Bark Poems*
(1879). In 1884, Lummis began walking from
Cincinnati to Los Angeles, writing a weekly
letter to the *Los Angeles Times* along the way.
One hundred and forty-three days later he
arrived and became the *Times*' first city editor.
In 1892, he published a collection of his letters
in *A Tramp Across the Continent.*

Lummis suffered a paralytic stroke in 1887
and moved to New Mexico to convalesce, where
he met archaeologist Adolph Bandelier. He
served as photographer for Bandelier's ethnographic studies of the Pueblo Indians and, after
Bandelier's death, used his photographs to
illustrate a second edition of Bandelier's novel
The Delight Makers (1916). Lummis became the
editor (1894–1905) of the illustrated magazine
Land of Sunshine (later called *Out West*) and
developed it into an important outlet for
Southwestern photographers. He published
more than 450 books, articles, and stories, and
attracted a following that included author Mary
Austin, painter Maynard Dixon, and President
Theodore Roosevelt. He helped found The
Southwest Museum, Los Angeles (1907), which
preserves his collection of Native American
artifacts as well as his personal library.

BOOKS:

The Land of Poco Tiempo
By Charles F. Lummis
London: Sampson Low, Marston, & Company,
1893
vii, 310 pp.; 9½ x 6¼ (24.1 x 16)
38 illustrations from photographs by Lummis
Copy 1: Library, Denver Museum of Natural
History (1928 edition)
Copy 2: Special Collections, The University of
Arizona, Tucson

Land of Sunshine 4, no. 3 (February 1896)
Los Angeles: Land of Sunshine Publishing
Company, 1894–1901
9 x 6½ (23 x 16.5)
Under the editorship of Charles Lummis, the
journal went from being a booster publication
for local real estate and chamber of commerce
interests to a serious regional literary journal.
Special Collections, The University of Arizona,
Tucson

The Delight Makers
By Adolph F. Bandelier, with an introduction by
Charles F. Lummis
New York: Dodd, Mead and Company, 1918
xvii, 490 pp.; 8½ x 5¾ (21.6 x 14.6)
18 black-and-white reproductions of photographs
by Lummis and Frederick C. Hicks
First published without illustrations in 1890,
archaeologist Bandelier's book is a fictionalized
treatment of the inhabitants of the ancient ruins
of Frijoles Canyon, New Mexico. This 1918 edition is a second printing of the second edition,
first published in 1916 with reproductions of
photographs by Lummis
Copy 1: Library Collection, Whitney Museum of
American Art, New York
Copy 2: Special Collections, The University of
Arizona, Tucson

*Mesa, Cañon and Pueblo, Our Wonderland of
the Southwest, Its Marvels of Nature, Its
Pageant of the Earth Building, Its Strange
Peoples, Its Centuried Romance*
By Charles F. Lummis
New York, London: The Century Company, 1925
xvi, 517 pp.; 8½ x 5¾ (21.6 x 14.6)
Map, black-and-white reproductions of pho-
tographs by Lummis, A.C. Vroman, Ben
Wittick, and others
Copy 1: Library Collection, Whitney Museum of
American Art, New York
Copy 2: Library, Denver Museum of Natural
History
Copy 3: Special Collections, The University of
Arizona, Tucson

SKEET McAULEY
BORN: 1951, MONAHANS, TEXAS

Skeet McAuley received his MFA (1978) from
Ohio State University and taught photography at
the University of North Texas (1981–93). He
received two NEA Fellowships (1984 and 1986),
which allowed him to spend his summers photographing Native Americans with a large-format
camera. This project culminated in an exhibition
at the Amon Carter Museum and
the publication entitled *Sign Language* (1989).
McAuley currently lives and works in Los
Angeles.

BOOKS:

*Sign Language: Contemporary Southwest Native
America*
By Skeet McAuley, introduction by N. Scott
Momaday, contributions by Luci Tapahonso,
Mike Mitchell, and Martha A. Sandweiss
New York: Aperture Foundation, 1989
78 pp.; 9½ x 11½ (24.1 x 29.2)
49 color reproductions of photographs by
McAuley
Library Collection, Whitney Museum of
American Art, New York

RICHARD MISRACH
BORN: 1949, LOS ANGELES

Richard Misrach is the recipient of four NEA
Fellowships (1973, 1977, 1984, and 1992), a Gug-
genheim Fellowship (1979), and a Distinguished
Career in Photography award (1994) from the
Los Angeles Center for Photographic Studies.
In addition, he has the distinctive honor of hav-
ing a street in the Mojave Desert named for him.
His numerous books include *Desert Cantos* (1987),
Bravo 20: The Bombing of the American West
(1990), and a photographic book of strobe-lit
cacti in Saguaro NationalPark (1979), intention-
ally published without title, text, or pagination.

BOOKS:

Desert Cantos
By Richard Misrach, essay by Reyner Banham
Albuquerque: The University of New Mexico
Press, 1987
106 pp.; 9 x 12 (23 x 30.5)
Maps, 55 color reproductions and 9 color text
figures from photographs by Misrach
Library Collection, Whitney Museum of
American Art, New York

Bravo 20: The Bombing of the American West
By Richard Misrach, with Myriam Weisang
Misrach
Baltimore, London: The John Hopkins
University Press, 1990
xv, 133 pp.; 9 x 12 (23 x 30.1)
Maps, 36 color reproductions of photographs by
Misrach
The Friends of Photography circulated an exhi-
bition in conjunction with this book, 1990–91
Library Collection, Whitney Museum of
American Art, New York

PHOTOGRAPHS:

Active Eagle's Nest, 1986
Published in *Bravo 20*
Dye-coupler print cold-mounted on rag board,
30 x 38 (76.2 x 96.5)
Collection of the artist; courtesy Robert Mann
Gallery, New York

"School Bus" Target, 1986
Published in *Bravo 20*
Dye-coupler print cold-mounted on rag board,
30 x 38 (76.2 x 96.5)
Collection of the artist; courtesy Robert Mann
Gallery, New York

Bombs, Destroyed Vehicles, and Lone Rock, 1987
Published in *Bravo 20*
Dye-coupler print cold-mounted on rag board,
30 x 38 (76.2 x 96.5)
Collection of the artist; courtesy Robert Mann
Gallery, New York

Navy Fence, 1987
Published in *Bravo 20*
Dye-coupler print cold-mounted on rag board,
30 x 38 (76.2 x 96.5)
Collection of the artist; courtesy Robert Mann
Gallery, New York

Waiting, Edward's Air Force Base, 1987
Published in *Desert Cantos*
Chromogenic print mounted on paperboard,
37¹⁵⁄₁₆ x 47¹¹⁄₁₆ (96.4 x 121.1)
Whitney Museum of American Art, New York;
Purchase, with funds from the Photography
Committee 93.73

FREDERICK I. (INMAN) MONSEN
BORN: 1865, BERGEN, NORWAY
DIED: 1929, PASADENA, CALIFORNIA

———

Frederick Monsen's family emigrated to the United States in 1868 and he grew up on the Utah frontier. Learning photography from his father, Monsen worked on several government expeditions, including the US-Mexico Boundary Geological Survey in 1886 and the Yosemite National Park Survey in 1896. Beginning in 1893 and continuing until his death, Monsen presented illustrated lectures with his own photographs and lantern slides. An early experimenter in camera and print technology, he was the first professional to use flexible film and a hand-held camera, which he took on trips to New Mexico to photograph Native Americans. He published a series of articles in *The Craftsman* (1906–07) describing his success with hand-held, semi-concealed cameras, which prompted George Eastman to invite Monsen on an all-expense-paid trip to the Southwest. Two years later, they made the journey and Eastman published a booklet, ostensibly written by Monsen, advocating the use of the new Kodak camera, called *With a Kodak in the Land of the Navajo* (1909).

BOOKS:

With a Kodak in the Land of the Navajo
Text and illustrations by Frederick I. Monsen
Rochester: Eastman Kodak Company, [1909]
32 pp.; 6¼ x 4¼ (16 x 10.8)
Black-and-white reproductions of photographs by Monsen
Special Collections, The University of Arizona, Tucson

CARL MOON
BORN: 1879, WILMINGTON, OHIO
DIED: 1948, PASADENA, CALIFORNIA

———

Carl (originally Karl) Moon moved to Albuquerque in 1903 and opened a photography studio, specializing in portraits of Native Americans. After three years, he was given a small exhibition at New York's Museum of Natural History, which led to an exhibition at the White House and annual shows for several years in Washing-ton's newly opened National Museum. Moon became the official photographer for the Santa Fe Railroad and for the Fred Harvey Company. The SFRR moved Moon to the Grand Canyon in 1907 and built him a studio at the Canyon's rim. Here he devoted the next seven years to creating the Fred Harvey Collection of South-west Indian Pictures. Moon moved to Pasadena in 1914 to pursue his own work and attempted to produce a limited-edition handmade portfolio of Native

American portraits. By 1935, ten were finished but the asking price of $3,500 was prohibitive and few sold. Moon spent his last years collaborating with his wife, Grace (Purdie) Moon, on children's books about Southwest Indian life.

BOOKS:

Roads to Yesterday, Along the Indian Detour
[By Carl Moon]
Fred Harvey, n.d.
[31] leaves of plates; 9¾ x 13 (24.8 x 33)
30 tipped-in reproductions of sepia-tinted photographs attributed to Carl Moon while working for the Fred Harvey Company
Copy 1: Special Collections, The University of Arizona, Tucson
Copy 2: Collection of Charles Schwartz

JOAN MYERS
BORN: 1944, DES MOINES, IOWA

———

Although Joan Myers received an MA (1966) in musicology from Stanford University, during the 1970s she became interested in non-silver photographic processes. She moved to Santa Fe and in 1980 was asked to join the New Mexico Photographic Survey. This project, funded by the National Endowment for the Arts, allowed twelve photographers to document the subject of their choice within the state. Myers chose to photograph the Santa Fe Trail, at that time unmarked and unused for more than a century. She continued the project on her own in four adjoining states, traveling more than 15,000 miles during the next three years. The result was an exhibition that toured for three years and the book *Along the Santa Fe Trail* (1986). Myers continues to live and work in New Mexico.

BOOKS:

Along the Santa Fe Trail
Photographs by Joan Myers, essay by Marc Simmons
Albuquerque: University of New Mexico Press, 1986
xxi, 184 pp.; 10 x 8½ (25.4 x 21.6)
Map, 55 black-and-white reproductions of photographs by Myers
Library Collection, Whitney Museum of American Art, New York

see also Harris, *Essential Landscape*

PHOTOGRAPHS:

Round Mound, New Mexico, 1982
Published in *Essential Landscape*
Platinum-Palladium photograph with hand-coloring, 9¾ x 12⅛ (24.8 x 30.8)
Museum of Fine Art, Museum of New Mexico, Santa Fe; from the New Mexico Photographic Survey Project/NEA

PATRICK NAGATANI
BORN: 1945, CHICAGO

———

The son of Japanese-American parents, Patrick Nagatani was born shortly after his parents were released from a United States internment camp and only days after the bombing of Hiroshima. Both events later influenced his photography. Nagatani received a BFA (1968) from California State University and taught high school for ten years before completing his MA (1980) at the University of California, Los Angeles. The recipient of two NEA Fellowships (1984 and 1992), Nagatani worked as associate professor of art at Loyola Marymount University and, since 1987, has worked at the University of New Mexico, Albuquerque.

BOOKS:

Nuclear Enchantment: Photographs by Patrick Nagatani
Essay by Eugenia Parry Janis
Albuquerque: University of New Mexico Press, 1991
138 pp.; 9¼ x 12¼ (23.5 x 31.1)
Maps, 40 color reproductions of photographs by Nagatani
Library Collection, Whitney Museum of American Art, New York

NANCY (PARKER) NEWHALL
BORN: 1908, LYNN, MASSACHUSETTS
DIED: 1974, JACKSON, WYOMING

———

Nancy Parker was studying painting at the Art Students League in New York City when she met and married photo-historian Beaumont Newhall in 1936. When Beaumont Newhall enlisted in the Air Force (1943), Nancy Newhall took over as acting curator of photography for his newly created photography department at The Museum of Modern Art, New York. Over the next three years, she curated fifteen exhibitions, including major retrospectives of the work of both Paul Strand and Edward Weston. Nancy Newhall is credited with having had a special talent for integrating images and text, and many of her twenty-two books involved collaborations with an artist. Ansel Adams worked together with Newhall on seven books, most notably the landmark classic of conservationism, *This Is the American Earth*, published by the Sierra Club in 1960.

BOOKS:
see Adams, *Death Valley*

Gustaf Nordenskiöld, c. 1890
Mesa Verde National Park, Colorado

GUSTAF E.A. NORDENSKIÖLD
BORN: 1868, STOCKHOLM
DIED: 1895, MORSIL STATION, SWEDEN

Gustaf Nordenskiöld, descended from a prominent family of Swedish-Finns, studied mineralogy and geology at the University of Uppsala, Sweden. He contracted tuberculosis during an expedition to the Arctic, and went south to improve his health, eventually coming to the United States. When he arrived in Colorado in 1891, he only intended to spend a week at the ranch of Richard Wetherall, who gave tours of the cliff dwellings at Mesa Verde.

Enthralled by the ruins, Nordenskiöld remained for over two months, carefully excavating, photographing, and mapping many of the rooms and collecting Anasazi artifacts. He was arrested when he tried to ship the artifacts home to Sweden, but the charges were dismissed when it was discovered that there were no laws against such appropriations. Nordenskiöld returned to Stockholm and produced *The Cliff Dwellers of the Mesa Verde* (1893), a monumental study of the architecture and archaeology of Mesa Verde. His visit influenced the passage of the American Antiquities Act in 1906 and the designation of Mesa Verde as a National Park the same year.

BOOKS:

The Cliff Dwellers of the Mesa Verde, Southwestern Colorado, Their Pottery and Implements
By G. Nordenskiöld, translated by D. Lloyd Morgan
Stockholm, Chicago: P.A. Norstedt & Söner, 1893
174 pp., 15 x 11 (38 x 28)
Maps, autotype and gravure plates, color and black-and-white lithographs from photographs by Nordenskiöld, frontispiece is an autotype portrait of Nordenskiöld, heliotypes from photographs by Charles Westphal, appendix of human remains by G. Retzius. Published in Swedish as *Ruiner af Klippboningar i Mesa Verde's Cañons* (Stockholm, 1893)
Copies 1 and 2: Private collection
Copy 3: Amon Carter Museum Library, Fort Worth, Texas
Copy 4: Kline Library, Yale University, New Haven, Connecticut

BARBARA NORFLEET
BORN: 1926, LAKEWOOD, NEW JERSEY

Barbara Norfleet received an MA (1950) and a PhD (1951) from Radcliffe College/Harvard University in psychology. She has received several awards for her photography, including two NEH Fellowships (1975 and 1977), a Guggenheim Fellowship (1984), two NEA Fellowships (1982 and 1984), and the Aaron Siskind Award (1991). Currently, Norfleet holds the positions of curator of photography at the Carpenter Center for the Visual Arts as well as senior lecturer in visual and environmental studies, both at Harvard University. The photographs in this exhibition are from her forthcoming book on military test sites.

PHOTOGRAPHS:

Naval Weapons Testing Base: 45 Square Miles (Abandoned in 1974 Because of Total Contamination), Salton Sea, CA (No. 35), 1989
Selenium-toned gelatin silver print, 11¼ x 16¾ (28.6 x 42.6)
Collection of the artist

Naval Weapons Testing Base: 45 Square Miles (Abandoned in 1974 Because of Total Contamination), Salton Sea, CA (No. 40), 1989
Selenium-toned gelatin silver print, 11¼ x 16¾ (28.6 x 42.6)
Collection of the artist

JESSE L. (LOGAN) NUSBAUM
BORN: 1887, GREELEY, COLORADO
DIED: 1975, SANTA FE, NEW MEXICO

Jesse Nusbaum's parents were members of the original Horace Greeley Colony, organized in the 1870s, where Jesse was raised. His father taught him construction and he taught himself photography. While teaching at the Las Vegas Normal School, Nusbaum spent his summers on archaeological explorations of Mesa Verde with Edgar Hewett. When Hewett was named the first director of the Museum of New Mexico in Santa Fe (1909), he hired Nusbaum to supervise the restoration of the Palace of Governors (the oldest public building in the United States). In 1921, Nusbaum became superintendent of Mesa Verde and devoted the next thirty-seven years to the development and maintenance of this National Park. He constructed the Park's first museum (1924) with the financial assistance of John D. Rockefeller and was named consulting archaeologist (1927) by the Secretary of the Interior. Nusbaum's son Deric grew up inside the park and *Deric in Mesa Verde* is a twelve-year-old boy's story of his adventures there.

BOOKS:

Deric in Mesa Verde
By Deric Nusbaum, with a foreword by Stephen T. Mather
New York: G.P. Putnam's Sons, 1926
xii, 166 pp.; 8¼ x 5¾ (21 x 14.6)
22 black-and-white reproductions of photographs by Jesse Nusbaum and others, sketches by Eileen Nusbaum
Special Collections, The University of Arizona, Tucson

TIMOTHY H. (HENRY) O'SULLIVAN
BORN: 1840, IRELAND OR STATEN ISLAND, NEW YORK
DIED: 1882, STATEN ISLAND, NEW YORK

As a teenager, Timothy O'Sullivan joined the New York studio of photographer Mathew Brady, moving with the studio to Washington, D.C., where he worked under Alexander Gardner. When Gardner left to establish his own gallery in 1862, O'Sullivan went along and the images they took during the Eastern campaigns can be seen in Gardner's *Photographic Sketch Book of the [Civil] War* (1866).

In 1867, Clarence King invited O'Sullivan to join the US Geological Exploration of the 40th Parallel; for three seasons, O'Sullivan photographed geological features, landscapes, and industrial sites along the proposed route for the Central Pacific Railroad through Nevada and Utah. He left the West briefly in 1870 to join an expedition to the Isthmus of Darien (Panama) but returned the following year, this time assigned to Lieutenant George Wheeler's US Geographical Surveys West of the 100th Meridian. In 1872, O'Sullivan participated in the King survey's last field work; Wheeler hired Philadelphia photographer William Bell to replace O'Sullivan. In 1873, O'Sullivan rejoined Wheeler's survey and traveled through New Mexico and Arizona, where his famous views of Canyon de Chelly were taken. After several years in the private sector, O'Sullivan was hired by King in 1879 as the US Geological Survey's photographer. O'Sullivan was named chief photographer for the United States Treasury Department in 1880, but he resigned after only five months and died of tuberculosis soon after.

BOOKS:

Photographs Showing Landscapes, Geological and Other Features, of Portions of the Western Territory of the United States, Obtained in Connection with Geographical and Geological Explorations and Surveys West of the One Hundredth Meridian, Season of 1871
By Lieut. Geo. M. Wheeler, Corps of Engineers, U.S. Army
[Washington, D.C.: n.p., c. 1871]
1 leaf, 35 plates; 20 x 17 (50.8 x 43.2)
Lithographed title page is followed by 35 albumen prints mounted on sheets with imprint of the War Department, Corps of Engineers and plate number.
The Metropolitan Museum of Art, New York; Purchase, Joseph Pulitzer Bequest and Horace W. Goldsmith Foundation Gift, 1986
This is a variant edition of the official publication: *Photographs Showing Landscapes, Geological and Other Features, of Portions of the Western Territory of the United States, Obtained in Connection with Geographical and Geological Explorations and Surveys West of the One Hundredth Meridian, Seasons of 1871, 1872, and 1873.*

Photographs Showing Landscapes, Geological and Other Features, of Portions of the Western Territory of the United States, Obtained in Connection with Geographical and Geological Explorations and Surveys West of the One Hundredth Meridian, Seasons of 1871, 1872, 1873, and 1874

By 1st Lieut. Geo. M. Wheeler, Corps of Engineers, US Army; Julius Bien, lithographer
[Washington, D.C.: n.p., c. 1875]
[51 pp.]; 16 x 22 (40.6 x 56)
A lithographed title page is followed by 25 albumen prints (4 from 1871, 2 from 1872, 9 from 1873, and 10 from 1874) mounted on sheets with imprint of the War Department, Corps of Engineers and plate number. A descriptive text is printed on each facing page.
Yale Collection of Western Americana, Beinecke Rare Book and Manuscript Library, Yale University, New Haven, Connecticut
This is a variant edition of the official publication *Photographs Showing Landscapes, Geological and Other Features, of Portions of the Western Territory of the United States, Obtained in Connection with Geographical and Geological Explorations and Surveys West of the One Hundredth Meridian, Seasons of 1871, 1872, and 1873* [1 leaf, 50 plates; 16 x 21½ (40.6 x 54.6) Lithographed title page is followed by 50 albumen prints mounted on sheets with imprint of the War Department, Corps of Engineers and plate number. Each season is numbered independently: 1871 (O'Sullivan) numbered 1–16; 1872 (Bell) numbered 1–15; and 1873 (O'Sullivan) numbered 1–19], 50 sets of which were published c. 1975.

Descriptive Geology
By Arnold Hague and S.F. Emmons
Report of the Geological Exploration of the Fortieth Parallel, vol. 2
Washington, D.C.: Government Printing Office, 1877
xiii, 890 pp.; 11¾ x 9¾ (30 x 24.8)
26 lithographs, reproductions of photographs by O'Sullivan, and printed by Julius Bien
DeGolyer Library, Southern Methodist University, Dallas

Systematic Geology
By Clarence King
Report of the Geological Exploration of the Fortieth Parallel, vol. 1
Washington, D.C.: Government Printing Office, 1878
xii, 803 pp.; 11¾ x 9 (30 x 23)
Also called *Professional Paper of the Engineer Department, U.S. Army, no. 18*
"Illustrated by XXVIII plates and XII analytical geological maps, and accompanied by a geological and topographical atlas."—t.p.
"All the illustrations of this volume were executed by Julius Bien, the chromo-lithographs after studies by Gilbert Munger, plates in black after photographs by T.H. O'Sullivan," (p. ix).

Copy 1: DeGolyer Library, Southern Methodist University, Dallas
Copy 2: William Reese Company, New Haven, Connecticut

PHOTOGRAPHS:

The "Pyramid" and Tufa Knobs, Pyramid Lake, Nevada, 1868
Photolithograph after this photograph published in *Systematic Geology*
Albumen print, 7¹³⁄₁₆ x 10⅝ (19.8 x 26.9)
George Eastman House, Rochester

Tufa Rocks, Pyramid Lake (Nevada), 1868
Photolithograph after this photograph published in *Systematic Geology*
Albumen print, 8½ x 11½ (21.6 x 29.2)
Gilman Paper Company, New York

Volcanic Ridge, Trinity Mountains (Nevada), 1868
Photolithograph after this photograph published in *Systematic Geology*
Albumen print, 8 x 10¾ (20.3 x 27.3)
Gilman Paper Company, New York

Volcanic Ridge, Trinity Mountains (Nevada), 1868
Photolithograph after this photograph published in *Systematic Geology*
Albumen print, 8¾ x 11½ (22.2 x 29.2)
Gilman Paper Company, New York

Black Cañon, Colorado River, from Camp 8, Looking Above, 1871
Published in *Photographs Showing Landscapes, Geological and Other Features, of Portions of the Western Territory of the United States, Obtained in Connection with Geographical and Geological Explorations and Surveys West of the One Hundredth Meridian, Seasons of 1871, 1872, and 1873*
Albumen print, 8 x 10⅞ (20.3 x 27.6)
The Denver Art Museum

Black Cañon, Colorado River, Looking Above from Camp 7, 1871
Published in *Photographs Showing Landscapes, Geological and Other Features, of Portions of the Western Territory of the United States, Obtained in Connection with Geographical and Geological Explorations and Surveys West of the One Hundredth Meridian, Seasons of 1871, 1872, and 1873*
Albumen print, 8 x 10⅞ (20.3 x 27.6)
The Denver Art Museum

Bluff Opposite Big Horn Camp, Black Cañon, Colorado River, 1871
Published in *Photographs Showing Landscapes, Geological and Other Features, of Portions of the Western Territory of the United States, Obtained in Connection with Geographical and Geological Explorations and Surveys West of the One Hundredth Meridian, Seasons of 1871, 1872, and 1873*
Albumen print, 8 x 10⅞ (20.3 x 27.6)
The Denver Art Museum

Cereus Giganteus, Arizona, 1871
Published in *Photographs Showing Landscapes, Geological and Other Features, of Portions of the Western Territory of the United States, Obtained in Connection with Geographical and Geological Explorations and Surveys West of the One Hundredth Meridian, Seasons of 1871, 1872, and 1873*
Albumen print, 11 x 8 (28 x 20.3)
Hallmark Photographic Collection, Hallmark Cards, Inc., Kansas City, Missouri

Entrance to Black Cañon, Colorado River from Above, 1871
Published in *Photographs Showing Landscapes, Geological and Other Features, of Portions of the Western Territory of the United States, Obtained in Connection with Geographical and Geological Explorations and Surveys West of the One Hundredth Meridian, Seasons of 1871, 1872, and 1873*
Albumen print, 8 x 10⅞ (20.3 x 27.6)
The Denver Art Museum

Wall in the Grand Cañon, 1871
Published in *Photographs Showing Landscapes, Geological and Other Features, of Portions of the Western Territory of the United States, Obtained in Connection with Geographical and Geological Explorations and Surveys West of the One Hundredth Meridian, Seasons of 1871, 1872, and 1873*
Albumen print, 10⅞ x 8 (27.6 x 20.3)
Private collection

Ancient Ruins in the Cañon de Chelle, N.M., 1873
Published in *Photographs Showing Landscapes, Geological and Other Features, of Portions of the Western Territory of the United States, Obtained in Connection with Geographical and Geological Explorations and Surveys West of the One Hundredth Meridian, Seasons of 1871, 1872, and 1873*
Albumen print, 10¾ x 7⅞ (27.3 x 20)
Hallmark Photographic Collection, Hallmark Cards, Inc., Kansas City, Missouri

Cañon de Chelle, N.M., 1873
Published in *Photographs Showing Landscapes, Geological and Other Features, of Portions of the Western Territory of the United States, Obtained in Connection with Geographical and Geological Explorations and Surveys West of the One Hundredth Meridian, Seasons of 1871, 1872, and 1873*
Albumen print, 8 x 10⅞ (20.3 x 27.6)
Hallmark Photographic Collection, Hallmark Cards, Inc., Kansas City, Missouri

Old Mission Church, Zuni Pueblo, New Mexico, 1873
Published in *Photographs Showing Landscapes, Geological and Other Features, of Portions of the Western Territory of the United States, Obtained in Connection with Geographical and Geological Explorations and Surveys West of the One Hundredth Meridian, Seasons of 1871, 1872, and 1873*
Albumen print, 10⅞ x 8 (20.3 x 27.5)
Centre Canadien d'Architecture, Montreal

Shoshone Falls, Snake River, 1874
Published in *Photographs Showing Landscapes, Geological and Other Features, of Portions of the Western Territory of the United States, Obtained in Connection with Geographical and Geological Explorations and Surveys West of the One Hundredth Meridian, Seasons of 1871, 1872, 1873, and 1874*
Albumen print, 7⅞ x 10¾ (20 x 27.3)
Hallmark Photographic Collection, Hallmark Cards, Inc., Kansas City, Missouri

HENRY G. (GREENWOOD) PEABODY

BORN: 1855, ST. LOUIS, MISSOURI
DIED: 1951, GLENDORA, CALIFORNIA

Henry Peabody graduated from Dartmouth College (1876) and worked as a commercial photographer in Boston until 1900 when he moved his business to California and started to specialize in Southwestern landscapes. Over his sixty-year career, Peabody worked in every photographic process from daguerreotype to 35mm color film, and published fourteen books, including *Glimpses of the Grand Canyon of Arizona* (1902), *Bryce Canyon National Park* (1932), and *Zion National Park* (1932). His popularity led William H. Jackson to hire him as a photographer for the Detroit Publishing Company, the largest postcard firm in the United States, and it is for these scenic views that Peabody is best known.

PHOTOGRAPHS:

Acoma Pueblo/Old Church at Pueblo of Acoma, 1902
Published by the Detroit Publishing Company
Chromolithograph, 7 x 9 (17.8 x 22.9)
Christopher Cardozo, Inc., Minneapolis

A Cactus Garden in California, 1902
Published by the Detroit Publishing Company
Chromolithograph, 7 x 9 (17.8 x 22.9)
Christopher Cardozo, Inc., Minneapolis

The Grand Canyon of Arizona from O'Neill Point, 1902
Published by the Detroit Publishing Company
Albumen print, 16¾ x 39¼ (42.5 x 99.7)
Private collection

On the Zig Zags, Bright Angel Trail, Grand Canyon, Arizona, 1902
Published by the Detroit Publishing Company
Chromolithograph, 7 x 9 (17.8 x 22.9)
Christopher Cardozo, Inc., Minneapolis

MARY PECK

BORN: 1952, MINNEAPOLIS, MINNESOTA

Mary Peck studied photography at Utah State University, graduating in 1974, when she moved to Santa Fe to work as an assistant to Paul Caponigro (1974–76) and to Laura Gilpin (1977–79). Peck began photographing eastern New Mexico and the Texas Panhandle region, which led to an invitation in 1982 to join the New Mexico Survey Project funded by the National Endowment for the Arts. An award from the Texas Historical Foundation allowed her to extend the Texas portion of her work and finish her contribution to the book *Contemporary Texas* (1986). Peck now lives and works in Port Angeles, Washington.

BOOKS:

Chaco Canyon: A Center and Its World
Photographs by Mary Peck, essays by Stephen H. Lekson, John R. Stein, Simon J. Ortiz, design by Eleanor Caponigro
Santa Fe: Museum of New Mexico Press, 1994
80 pp.; 9½ x 12¾ (24.1 x 32.4)
Maps, 38 black-and-white reproductions of photographs by Peck, with reproductions of historic photographs, including three aerial photographs by Charles A. Lindbergh from the School of American Research Collections, Museum of New Mexico
Library Collection, Whitney Museum of American Art, New York

see also Harris, *Essential Landscape*

PHOTOGRAPHS:

Chaco Canyon, 1990
Published in *Chaco Canyon*
Gelatin silver print, 9 x 27 (22.9 x 68.6)
Collection of the artist

Chaco Canyon, Peñasco Blanco, 1990
Published in *Chaco Canyon*
Gelatin silver print, 9 x 27 (22.9 x 68.6)
Collection of the artist

Chaco Canyon, Pueblo Bonito, 1990
Published in *Chaco Canyon*
Gelatin silver print, 9 x 27 (22.9 x 68.6)
Collection of the artist

EDNA BRUSH PERKINS
BORN: 1880, CLEVELAND
DIED: 1930, CLEVELAND

An active leader in Ohio's women's suffrage
movement, Edna Brush married physician
Roger Perkins (1905), with whom she raised four
children. A painter and musician, Perkins spent
time in New York studying aesthetic dancing;
her paintings received honorable mention in a
number of American museum exhibitions. She
also had a fervent zeal for adventure. She
climbed the Jungfrau in Switzerland and traveled by caravan into the Sahara Desert. In 1919,
she and her friend Charlotte Jordan spent a
frustrating weekend attempting to cross Death
Valley by car. One year later, they returned with
a wagon, maps, and enough supplies to last
through a month-long adventure in the Mojave
Desert. Two books came of her travels: *The
White Heart of Mojave* (1922) and *A Red Carpet
on the Sahara* (1925).

BOOKS:

*The White Heart of Mojave: An Adventure
with the Outdoors of the Desert*
By Edna Brush Perkins
New York: Boni and Liveright Publishers, 1922
229 pp.; 9 x 6 (23 x 15.3)
Map, 8 black-and-white reproductions from pho-
tographs attributed to Perkins
Library Collection, Whitney Museum of
American Art, New York

JOHN PFAHL
BORN: 1939, NEW YORK

John Pfahl received an MA (1968) from Syracuse
University in America's first graduate-level
program in color photography. He immediately
joined the faculty at the Rochester Institute of
Technology where he taught until 1977 and
began his *Altered Landscape Series.* He has
received two Creative Artists Public Service
grants (1975 and 1979) and an NEA Fellowship
(1977). Pfahl was one of five photographers asked
to participate in the National Endowment for
the Arts Survey Project "Marks and Measures:
Pictographs and Petroglyphs in a Modern Art
Context," later published as *Marks in Place:
Contemporary Responses to Rock Art* (1988). A
retrospective exhibition of Pfahl's work, entitled
"A Distant Land," toured the country in 1990.

BOOKS:
see Conner, *Marks in Place*

PHOTOGRAPHS:

*Abiquiu Reservoir, "Horses and Men on
Horseback . . . ,"* 1984
Published in *Marks in Place*
Chromogenic color print, 14 x 11 (35.6 x 28)
Janet Borden, Inc., New York

*Abiquiu Reservoir, ". . . Large Spear Points and
Some Feathered Shaft,"* 1984
Published in *Marks in Place*
Chromogenic color print, 14 x 11 (35.6 x 28)
Janet Borden, Inc., New York

Caroline Poole
Photoengraving from *A Modern Prairie Schooner . . . ,* 1919
Private collection

CAROLINE B. (BOEING) POOLE
BORN: C. 1885, DETROIT, MICHIGAN
DIED: 1932, SANTA FE, NEW MEXICO

The daughter of aircraft magnate William
Boeing, Caroline (sometimes called Carolyn)
Boeing married West Point Academy graduate
John Poole in 1907. At his retirement from the
Army, the Pooles moved to Pasadena, where
they became active in many philanthropies.
Caroline Poole was especially interested in
Native American arts and crafts and assembled
a large collection of Indian baskets. She also
collected fine press bindings and was an amateur photographer, illustrating and publishing
at least one book, *A Modern Prairie Schooner on
the Transcontinental Trail* (1919), about a car trip
to the desert. On a trip to visit her son, who was
attending school outside Santa Fe, Poole died;
in her memory, her husband donated her collection of 2,400 Native American baskets to The
Southwest Museum, Los Angeles, along with a
new wing to house them.

BOOKS:

*A Modern Prairie Schooner on the
Transcontinental Trail: The Story of a
Motor Trip*
By Caroline Poole
San Francisco: privately printed, 1919
53 pp.; 11¾ x 8½ (30 x 21.6)
32 tipped-in black-and-white reproductions of
photographs by Poole
250 copies were printed by John Henry Nash of
San Francisco
Copy 1: Collection of Victoria Dailey
Copy 2: Private collection
Copy 3: Special Collections, The University of
Arizona, Tucson

ELIOT (FURNESS) PORTER
BORN: 1901, WINNETKA, ILLINOIS
DIED: 1990, SANTA FE, NEW MEXICO

Harvard-educated Eliot Porter received his MD (1929) and went on to a research and teaching position in a Harvard laboratory. Porter's interest in photography, particularly the photography of birds, was encouraged by Alfred Stieglitz and Ansel Adams. After a one-artist exhibition at Stieglitz's An American Place (1938–39) in New York, Porter resigned from teaching to concentrate on his art. He began experimenting with Kodak's new Kodachrome color film, receiving two NEA Fellowships (1941 and 1946) for this work, which was exhibited at The Museum of Modern Art, New York (1943), by Nancy Newhall.

Porter moved to Santa Fe in 1946 and concentrated on landscape photography. He began an association with David Brower and the Sierra Club, together publishing the books and posters for which he is best known. Their second collaboration, *The Place No One Knew* (1963), is an elegy for the Glen Canyon area at the Utah-Arizona border, photographed only months before a new dam flooded the Canyon. Porter went on to publish more than twenty books, including his obsession of half a century, *Birds of North America: A Personal Selection* (1972). His numerous exhibitions include the first one-artist show of color photography ever held at The Metropolitan Museum of Art (1979).

BOOKS:

The Place No One Knew: Glen Canyon on the Colorado
By Eliot Porter, edited with a foreword by David Brower
San Francisco: Sierra Club, 1963
170 pp.; 13¾ x 10½ (36 x 27)
Map, 72 color reproductions of photographs by Porter
Copy 1: Library Collection, Whitney Museum of American Art, New York
Copy 2: Amon Carter Museum Library, Fort Worth, Texas

PHOTOGRAPHS:

Dungeon Canyon, Glen Canyon, Utah, August 29, 1961, 1961
Published in *The Place No One Knew*
Dye-transfer print, 10⅝ x 8⅛ (27 x 20.6)
Amon Carter Museum, Fort Worth, Texas;
Bequest of Eliot Porter

Lichen, Glen Canyon, Utah, August 24, 1961, 1961
Published in *The Place No One Knew*
Dye-transfer print, 8¼ x 10⁹⁄₁₆ (21 x 26.8)
Amon Carter Museum, Fort Worth, Texas;
Bequest of Eliot Porter

Pool in Upper Hidden Passage, Glen Canyon, Utah, August 27, 1961, 1961
Published in *The Place No One Knew*
Dye-transfer print, 10⅝ x 8¹⁵⁄₁₆ (27 x 22.7)
Amon Carter Museum, Fort Worth, Texas;
Bequest of Eliot Porter

Terraces in Brook, Aztec Creek, Forbidden Canyon, Utah, August 28, 1961, 1961
Published in *The Place No One Knew*
Dye-transfer print, 8⅜ x 10¼ (21.3 x 26)
Amon Carter Museum, Fort Worth, Texas;
Bequest of Eliot Porter

Balanced Rocks, Balanced Rock Canyon, Glen Canyon, Utah, September 6, 1962, 1962
Published in *The Place No One Knew*
Dye-transfer print, 10⅜ x 8³⁄₁₆ (26.4 x 20.8)
Amon Carter Museum, Fort Worth, Texas;
Bequest of Eliot Porter

Pool and Reflections, Grand Gulch, San Juan River, Utah, May 23, 1962, 1962
Published in *The Place No One Knew*
Dye-transfer print, 8⅛ x 10⅜ (21 x 26.4)
Amon Carter Museum, Fort Worth, Texas;
Bequest of Eliot Porter

Pools in the Narrows, Bridge Canyon, Glen Canyon, Utah, September 5, 1962, 1962
Published in *The Place No One Knew*
Dye-transfer print, 10¼ x 8³⁄₁₆ (26 x 20.8)
Amon Carter Museum, Fort Worth, Texas;
Bequest of Eliot Porter

Water Seeps, Glen Canyon, Utah, September 1962, 1962
Published in *The Place No One Knew*
Dye-transfer print, 8¹¹⁄₁₆ x 8⅛ (22.1 x 20.6)
Amon Carter Museum, Fort Worth, Texas;
Bequest of Eliot Porter

John Wesley Powell, Leader of the US Geographical and Geological Survey of the Rocky Mountain Region, n.d. National Archives, Washington, D.C.

JOHN WESLEY POWELL
BORN: 1834, MOUNT MORRIS, NEW YORK
DIED: 1902, HAVEN, MAINE

Largely self-taught in the natural sciences, John Wesley Powell studied briefly at Oberlin College and schools in Illinois. He volunteered for service during the Civil War, lost his right arm at Shiloh, and saw combat again at Vicksburg and Nashville. After the war, Major Powell became professor of geology at Illinois Wesleyan (now Bloomington University), where he began organizing summer expeditions to the Rocky Mountains. In 1869, with private funds and government rations, Powell formed an expedition to explore the Green and Colorado Rivers by boat. Ten men spent three months under treacherous conditions; in the end only six survived.

Powell immediately sought government aid for a second, more scientific examination in 1871 of the Colorado River and its tributaries. He hired a succession of photographers—E.O. Beaman, Walter Clement Powell, James Fennemore, and finally John Hillers—to document his survey. Powell's account of his two voyages was published as *Exploration of the Colorado River of the West and Its Tributaries* (1875, revised and enlarged as *Canyons of the Colorado,* 1895). His survey, initially under the aegis of the Smithsonian Institution, was transferred to the Interior Department in 1874 as the second division of F.V. Hayden's organization, and then as the US Geographical and Geological Survey of the Rocky Mountain Region. His interest in land use and government land laws led to the publication of *Report on the Lands of the Arid Regions of the United States* (1878), which presented his plan for irrigation in the West. In 1879, Powell became the first director of the Bureau of American Ethnology and, in 1881, succeeded Clarence King as director of the US Geological Survey, where he served for thirteen years.

see Hillers, *Exploration*

EDWARD RANNEY
BORN: 1942, CHICAGO

Edward Ranney's interest in the Incan and Mayan cultures led to a Fulbright Fellowship (1964) and an NEA Fellowship (1974) to travel and photograph in Peru. Ranney received a Guggenheim Fellowship (1977–78) to photograph the New Mexico landscape. These awards were followed in 1982 by an invitation to join the National Endowment for the Arts-funded New Mexico Survey Project, which culminated in the exhibition and publication *The Essential Landscape* (1985). Ranney currently lives and works in Santa Fe.

BOOKS:
see Harris, *The Essential Landscape*

PHOTOGRAPHS:

Star Axis, New Mexico, 8/12/82, 1982
Published in *The Essential Landscape*
Gelatin silver print, 12¼ x 18 (31.1 x 45.7)
Collection of the artist

Star Axis, New Mexico, Looking North, 1/6/83, 1983
Published in *The Essential Landscape*
Gelatin silver print, 6⅜ x 9 (16.2 x 23)
Collection of the artist

Star Axis, New Mexico, Looking North, 1/7/83, 1983
Published in *The Essential Landscape*
Gelatin silver print, 5⅞ x 9 (14.9 x 23)
Collection of the artist

EDWARD RUSCHA
BORN: 1937, OMAHA

Ed Ruscha served eight years in the US Navy before leaving in 1964 to pursue a career as an artist. He was the recipient of a National Council on the Arts Award (1967) and a Guggenheim Fellowship (1971). Ruscha has used photography primarily to create a series of books, including *Twentysix Gasoline Stations* (1962), *Some Los Angeles Apartments* (1965), *The Sunset Strip* (1966), *Royal Road Test* (1967), and *A Few Palm Trees* (1970). He lives and works in Los Angeles.

BOOKS:

Royal Road Test
By Mason Williams, Edward Ruscha, and Patrick Blackwell
Los Angeles: Mason Williams and Edward Ruscha, 1967
[52] pp.; 9½ x 6¼ (24.1 x 16)
Spiral bound with black-and-white reproductions of photographs by Patrick Blackwell
Copies 1 and 2: Library Collection, Whitney Museum of American Art, New York

A.J. (ANDREW JOSEPH) RUSSELL
BORN: 1830, NUNDA, NEW YORK
DIED: 1902, BROOKLYN, NEW YORK

Captain A.J. Russell was the first Civil War officer officially appointed as a photographer when he was assigned to document the activities of the United States Military Railroad Construction Corps (1862–65). After the war, Russell became the official photographer for the Union Pacific Railroad and led a group of photographers who traveled with the construction crew. He is best known for his photograph of the completion of the transcontinental railroad at Promontory Point, Utah (1869).

While in Utah, Russell met Clarence King, director of the US Geological Exploration of the 40th Parallel, and spent several weeks photographing with this government survey before returning to New York City. Russell's railroad photographs were published by the Union Pacific Railroad as *The Great West Illustrated* (1869), intended as the first of a series of portfolios. The following year, government geologist F.V. Hayden used thirty of these photographs for his *Sun Pictures of Rocky Mountain Scenery* (1870). Russell opened a studio in New York and throughout the 1870s worked for *Frank Leslie's Illustrated Newspaper* as a photojournalist; he retired in Brooklyn in 1891.

BOOKS:

The Great West Illustrated in a Series of Photographic Views Across the Continent; Taken Along the Line of the Union Pacific Railroad West from Omaha, Nebraska, with an Annotated Table of Contents Giving a Brief Description of Each View; Its Peculiarities, Characteristics, and Connection with the Different Points on the Road, vol. 1
By A.J. Russell
New York: Union Pacific Railroad Company, 1869
12 pp., 50 leaves of plates, 13¼ x 19¼ (33.7 x 49)

50 mounted albumen photographs by Russell
Union Pacific Museum, Omaha; this copy is also called *Jabbleman Album, The Great West Illustrated*

Sun Pictures of Rocky Mountain Scenery, With a Description of the Geographical and Geological Features, and Some Account of the Resources of the Great West; Containing Thirty Photo-Graphic Views Along the Line of the Pacific Railroad, From Omaha to Sacramento
By F.V. Hayden, photographs by Andrew J. Russell, essay by J.S. Newberry
New York: Julius Bien, 1870
vii, 150 pp.; 12½ x 10¼ (31.8 x 26)
30 mounted albumen prints by Russell; smaller versions of the plates in *The Great West Illustrated*
DeGolyer Library, Southern Methodist University, Dallas

PHOTOGRAPHS:

Bitter Creek Valley, Panoramic, 1868
Published in *The Great West Illustrated*
Albumen print, 13 x 16 (33 x 40.6)
Union Pacific Museum, Omaha

Castle Rock, Green River, 1868
Published in *The Great West Illustrated*
Albumen print, 13 x 16 (33 x 40.6)
Union Pacific Museum, Omaha

Embankment, East of Granite Canyon (Granite Canyon, from the Water Tank), 1868
Published in *The Great West Illustrated*
Albumen print, 13 x 16 (33 x 40.6)
Yale Collection of Western Americana, Beinecke Rare Book and Manuscript Library, Yale University, New Haven, Connecticut

On Mountains of the Green River, Smiths Buttes, 1868
Published in *The Great West Illustrated*
Albumen print, 13 x 16 (33 x 40.6)
Union Pacific Museum, Omaha

The Windmill at Laramie, 1868
Published in *The Great West Illustrated*
Albumen print, 9 x 11½ (23 x 29.2)
Union Pacific Museum, Omaha

FRANK M. SHERMAN
BORN: 1875, BIRTHPLACE UNKNOWN
DIED: 1921, LEBANON, OREGON

In 1903, Frank Sherman was running a photography studio in Colorado Springs while his brothers worked as cowboys in Hugo, Colorado. Frank went to Hugo that year to photograph the cowboys' spring roundup as a source of pictures for his postcard business. President Roosevelt's train passed through Hugo at the same time, and the cowboys delayed their roundup to prepare a chuckwagon breakfast for the president. Sherman captured the scene and produced a booklet called *President Roosevelt and the Hugo Cowboys* (1903). When he sold his business and moved to Oregon in 1906, his photographs were forgotten. It wasn't until 1966 that a group of glass plate negatives were discovered and Sherman's work was seen once again.

BOOKS:

President Roosevelt and the Hugo Cowboys: Photographs by a Cowboy Artist
By F.M. Sherman, half-tone plates by Frank Reistle
Colorado City, Colorado: F.M. Sherman, 1903
26 leaves; 8½ x 11 (21.6 x 28)
25 black-and-white reproductions of photographs by Sherman
State Historical Society of Colorado, Denver

LESLIE MARMON SILKO
BORN: 1948, ALBUQUERQUE, NEW MEXICO

Raised on the Laguna Pueblo, Leslie Marmon Silko received a BA (1969) in English from the University of New Mexico. She began to study law but instead chose a career as a writer and teacher. A book of her poems, *Laguna Woman* (1974), was a critical success and led to her first novel, *Ceremony* (1977), written in Alaska. She moved to Tucson in 1978, where she continues to live, write, and photograph.

BOOKS:

Rain
By Leslie Marmon Silko and Lee Marmon
New York: Library Fellows of the Whitney Museum of American Art, 1996
20 pp.; 12 x 9½ (30.5 x 24.1)
1 black-and-white reproduction of a photograph and one original photograph by Marmon, 16 laser prints of photographs by Silko
Copies 1 and 2: Library Collection, Whitney Museum of American Art, New York

FREDERICK SOMMER
BORN: 1905, ANGRI, ITALY

Raised in Rio de Janeiro, Frederick Sommer earned an MA (1927) in landscape architecture from Cornell University. He moved to Arizona in 1931 to recover from tuberculosis and became a US citizen in 1939. Sommer credits a meeting with Alfred Stieglitz for his decision to pursue a career in photography. He has received both NEA and Guggenheim Fellowships (1973 and 1974, respectively) and completed his PhD (1979) at the University of Arizona. He lives and works in Tempe, Arizona.

PHOTOGRAPHS:

Broken Glass, 1943
Gelatin silver print, 7½ x 9½ (19.1 x 24.1)
The Museum of Modern Art, New York
Nelson Rockefeller Fund

Rocks and Cactus, 1943
Gelatin silver print, 7⅝ x 9½ (19.4 x 24.1)
The Museum of Modern Art, New York
Purchase

Taylor, Arizona, 1945
Gelatin silver print, 7⅝ x 9½ (19.4 x 24.1)
Collection of Marc Harrison

Arizona Landscape, c. 1943
Gelatin silver print, 7⁹⁄₁₆ x 9⁷⁄₁₆ (19.2 x 24)
Collection of Marc Harrison

JOHN C. (CHARLES) VAN DYKE
BORN: 1856, NEW BRUNSWICK, NEW JERSEY
DIED: 1932, NEW YORK

John Van Dyke was admitted to the New York Bar in 1877, but instead of practicing law he became a librarian for the New Brunswick Theological Seminary, where he remained until his death. In his free time, Van Dyke pursued the study of art history and criticism, lecturing and publishing extensively. A favorite subject was the contemplation of natural beauty, which led to the publication of a series of popular books, *Nature for Its Own Sake* (1898), *The Desert* (1901), *The Mountain* (1916), *The Grand Canyon* (1920), and *The Meadows* (1926).

BOOKS:
see Chase, *The Desert*

ROBERT VENTURI
BORN: 1925, PHILADELPHIA

Robert Venturi received an MFA (1950) in architecture from Princeton University and soon afterwards won the Rome Prize Fellowship to study at the American Academy in Rome. Venturi returned to Philadelphia in 1956 to work at the firm of Louis I. Kahn and organized his own firm in 1964. Denise Scott Brown joined the firm in 1969, forming Venturi, Rauch, and Brown. An article by Venturi and Brown, entitled "A Significance for A&P Parking Lots, or Learning from Las Vegas," (1968) led to a collaborative research project with a group of students at Yale University. The resulting book, *Learning from Las Vegas* (1972), written with Steven Izenour, became a classic in architectural theory and contemporary urban design.

BOOKS:

Learning from Las Vegas
By Robert Venturi, Denise Scott Brown, and Steven Izenour
Cambridge, Massachusetts: The MIT Press, 1972
xvi, 189 pp.; 14¼ x 11 (36.2 x 28)
Color and black-and-white reproductions of maps, drawings, plans, advertisements, historic and contemporary photographs
Library Collection, Whitney Museum of American Art, New York

JoANN VERBURG
BORN: 1950, SUMMIT, NEW JERSEY

JoAnn Verburg received her MFA (1976) in photography from the Rochester Institute of Technology and has been the recipient of numerous awards, including a Guggenheim Fellowship (1986). She has often collaborated on projects with theater or dance companies, and developed a visiting artist program for the Polaroid Corporation. She served as project coordinator and photographer on the Rephotographic Survey Project, working with Mark Klett, Ellen Manchester, Gordon Bushaw, and Rick Dingus to produce the book *Second View* (1984). Verburg lives and works in Minneapolis.

BOOKS:
see Klett, *Second View*

PHOTOGRAPHS:

Eroded Sandstones, Woodman Road, Colorado Springs, Colorado, 1977
Diptych with William Henry Jackson's *Eroded Sandstones, Monument Park*, 1873
Published in *Second View*
Gelatin silver prints, 10 x 16 (25.4 x 40.6)
Rephotographic Survey Project, Tempe, Arizona

A.C. Vroman
Self-Portrait, 1899
Pasadena Public Library, California

A.C. (ADAM CLARK) VROMAN
BORN: 1856, LASALLE, ILLINOIS
DIED: 1916, ALTADENA, CALIFORNIA

Adam Clark Vroman was a Midwest railroad man who moved West and opened a book, stationery, and photo supply store in Pasadena that continues to operate today. An amateur photographer, Vroman made his first trip to Arizona in 1895 to photograph the Hopi Snake Dance. Over the next nine years, he made numerous trips around the Southwest to photograph its landscape, its missions and the daily life of Native Americans, often traveling in the company of photographer Frederick Monsen. Vroman worked on two expeditions of the Bureau of American Ethnology but primarily photographed for his own enjoyment and satisfaction, making his final trip in 1904 to Canyon de Chelly. His work was published in several books, including *Mission Memories* (1898), *The Genesis of the Story of Ramona* (1899), with T.F. Barnes, and *Ramona* (1913). Vroman also compiled albums of his work as gifts; shortly before his death, he donated sixteen of these volumes to the Pasadena Public Library.

BOOKS:

Arizona and New Mexico Pueblos
By A.C. Vroman
N.p., 1902
57 pp.; 10¼ x 9 (26 x 23)
55 bromide photographs by Vroman, prepared for H.E. Hoopes to commemorate a trip they took to the Southwest
The Denver Art Museum

see also Lummis, *Mesa, Cañon, Pueblo*

PHOTOGRAPHS:

Mesa Encantada (9), On the Way Up, 2nd, 3rd, and 4th Landings, 1897
Gelatin silver print, 6 x 8 (15.2 x 20.3)
Private collection

Mesa Encantada (7), South End of Mesa, 1897
Gelatin silver print, 6 x 8 (15.2 x 20.3)
Private collection

Mesa Encantada (1), the Mesa, from Acoma, 1897
Gelatin silver print, 6 x 8 (15.2 x 20.3)
Private collection

CARLETON (EUGENE) WATKINS
BORN: 1829, ONEONTA, NEW YORK
DIED: 1916, IMOLA, CALIFORNIA

Carleton Watkins moved to California in 1851 and apprenticed in the studio of daguerreotypist Robert Vance before opening his own studio in 1856. Watkins made the first of many trips to Yosemite Valley in 1861, and the photographs he took influenced President Lincoln's 1864 declaration to preserve Yosemite, a decision that led to the US National Parks system. He photographed Yosemite again for Josiah Whitney's California State Geological Survey, which published *The Yosemite Book* (1868). Clarence King, another member of Whitney's survey, later hired Watkins as photographer for King's own US Geological Exploration of the 40th Parallel, during Timothy O'Sullivan's absence in 1870.

The financial panic of 1874 led to bankruptcy for Watkins' Yosemite Art Gallery. He spent the next ten years attempting to re-photograph and copyright his lost work. In 1880, Watkins crossed Southern California and Arizona, photographing the Southern Pacific Railroad's new route. In 1906, his eyesight almost gone, Watkins lost his second gallery and negatives, this time to the San Francisco earthquake and fire. Soon after this, he was declared mentally incompetent and spent the last years of his life in the Napa State Hospital for the Insane.

PHOTOGRAPHS:

Cereus Gigantius, Arizona, 1880
Albumen print on board, 21¼ x 16½ (54 x 42)
The Bancroft Library, University of California, Berkeley

Tombstone Companies' 10-Stamp Water Mill and Tailings Dam, Town of Charleston, with Huachuca Mountains in the Distance, Arizona, 1880
Albumen print on board, 15⅜ x 21⅛ (39.1 x 53.7)
The Bancroft Library, University of California, Berkeley

Yucca Draconis, Mojave Desert, 1880
Albumen print on board, 16 x 21⅜ (40.6 x 54.3)
The Bancroft Library, University of California, Berkeley

EDWARD WESTON
BORN: 1886, HIGHLAND PARK, ILLINOIS
DIED: 1958, CARMEL, CALIFORNIA

Edward Weston, a founding member of the California Pictorialists, opened his first studio in Tropico (now Glendale) in 1911. Following a successful exhibition of his work in Mexico, Weston moved there (1923–26), associating with artists of the Mexican Renaissance such as Diego Rivera and José Clemente Orozco. Returning to California, Weston opened a studio with his son Brett, and began experimenting with detailed studies of shells and vegetables. These images were exhibited in his first one-artist show in New York (1930), which was organized by Orozco; they were published in his first book, *The Art of Edward Weston* (1932), designed by Merle Armitage. Together with Ansel Adams, he helped found the Group f/64 (1932), which denounced the Pictorialism he had once espoused.

Weston was the first photographer to be awarded a Guggenheim Fellowship (1937–39) and used the award to travel, with Charis Wilson, through California, Arizona, and New Mexico photographing the landscape. *Westways Magazine* supplemented Weston's Guggenheim grant in exchange for publishing options. During the next two years, twenty-one articles were published with Weston's photographs and Wilson's captions. The books *Seeing California with Edward Weston* (1939) and *California and the West* (1940) are compilations of these photographs, together with Wilson's text.

In 1941, Weston and Wilson traveled to Maine to collaborate on an edition of Walt Whitman's *Leaves of Grass*, but were forced to return home when Pearl Harbor was attacked. Weston was stricken with Parkinson's disease in 1948 and spent the final years of his life supervising the printing of his negatives by his sons, Brett and Cole Weston.

BOOKS:

Seeing California with Edward Weston
By Edward Weston
Los Angeles: Westways, Automobile Club of
Southern California, 1939
49 pp.; 13 x 10 (33 x 25.4)
Black-and-white reproductions of photographs
by Weston
Library Collection, Whitney Museum of
American Art, New York

California and the West
By Charis Wilson Weston and Edward Weston
A U.S. Camera Book
New York: Duell, Sloan and Pearce, 1940
127 pp.; 11½ x 10½ (29.2 x 26.7)
Map, 96 black-and-white reproductions of pho-
tographs by Weston. The original price was
$3.75
Copy 1: Library Collection, Whitney Museum of
American Art, New York
Copy 2: Private collection

PHOTOGRAPHS:

Dead Man, Colorado Desert, 1937
Published in *California and the West*
Gelatin silver print, 7½ x 9½ (19.1 x 24.1)
Center for Creative Photography,
The University of Arizona, Tucson

*Yucca, Mojave Desert (Joshua Tree, Mohave
Desert),* 1937
Published in *California and the West*
Gelatin silver print, 9½ x 7½ (24.1 x 19.1)
Center for Creative Photography,
The University of Arizona, Tucson

Yucca, Wonderland of Rocks, 1937
Published in *California and the West*
Gelatin silver print, 9½ x 7½ (24.1 x 19.1)
Center for Creative Photography,
The University of Arizona, Tucson

Badwater, Death Valley, 1938
Published in *California and the West*
Gelatin silver print, 7½ x 9½ (19.1 x 24.1)
Center for Creative Photography,
The University of Arizona, Tucson

Concretions, Salton Sea, 1938
Published in *California and the West*
Gelatin silver print, 7½ x 9½ (19.1 x 24.1)
Center for Creative Photography,
The University of Arizona, Tucson

Horse, KB Dude Ranch, 1938
Published in *California and the West*
Gelatin silver print, 7½ x 9½ (19.1 x 24.1)
Center for Creative Photography,
The University of Arizona, Tucson

*Old Bunk House, Twenty Mule Team Canyon,
Death Valley,* 1938
Published in *California and the West*
Gelatin silver print, 7½ x 9½ (19.1 x 24.1)
Center for Creative Photography,
The University of Arizona, Tucson

Zabriskie Point, Death Valley, 1938
Published in *California and the West*
Gelatin silver print, 7½ x 9½ (19.1 x 24.1)
Center for Creative Photography,
The University of Arizona, Tucson

Leadfield Club, Death Valley, 1939
Published in *California and the West*
Gelatin silver print, 7½ x 9½ (19.1 x 24.1)
Center for Creative Photography,
The University of Arizona, Tucson

Henry W. Bradley and William Herman Rulofson
George M. Wheeler, c. 1872
The National Portrait Gallery, Smithsonian Institution,
Washington, D.C.

GEORGE M. (MONTAGUE) WHEELER

BORN: 1842, HOPKINTON, MASSACHUSETTS
DIED: 1905, NEW YORK

West Point graduate George Wheeler planned
and led the United States Geographical Surveys
West of the 100th Meridian for the Corps of
Engineers, beginning in 1872; their purpose was
to create a ninety-five-sheet topographical and
geological atlas of the West. The Surveys developed from Wheeler's explorations of the Southwest in 1869 and 1871. Wheeler received $75,000
for operations during fiscal year 1873. Timothy
O'Sullivan, who accompanied Wheeler in 1871,
also documented the field seasons of 1873 and
1874.
    Wheeler made fourteen trips to the West
over the next eight years. The largest Wheeler
survey, in 1873, included field and office parties of

178 men, but competition with other surveys
brought an end to Wheeler's expeditions in 1879,
when his organization was discontinued by the
same law that established the US Geological
Survey. Wheeler supervised the completion of
his surveys' final reports and retired in 1888 with
the rank and pay of major.

BOOKS:
see O'Sullivan, *Photographs*

CHARIS WILSON

BORN: 1914, SAN FRANCISCO

Charis Wilson began posing for Edward
Weston soon after they met in 1934. She
became his collaborator and wife, traveling
across the Southwest with Weston for two
years on a Guggenheim Fellowship (1937–39)
and chronicling their trip in her daily journal.
Wilson collaborated with Weston on twenty-
one articles for *Westways Magazine*; these were
later published as *Seeing California with Edward
Weston* (1939) and *California and the West* (1940).
After her marriage to Weston ended, she went
on to write numerous articles as well as accompanying texts for *The Cats of Wildcat Hill* (1947)
and *Edward Weston Nudes* (1977). Wilson currently lives in Santa Cruz, and is working on
her memoirs.

BOOKS:
see Weston

PRECURSORS TO THE PHOTOGRAPHIC BOOK IN THE WEST

*Notes of a Military Reconnoissance [sic], from
Fort Leavenworth, in Missouri, to San Diego,
in California, Including Parts of the Arkansas,
Del Norte, and Gila Rivers*
By W.H. Emory, made in 1846–47, with the
advanced guard of the "Army of the West"
Washington, D.C.: Wendell and Van
Benthuysen, 1848
614 pp.; 9 x 5¾ (23 x 14.6)
Maps, 54 illustrations from drawings by John
Mix Stanley
Also published as *House Executive Document no.
41, 30th Congress, 1st Session*
DeGolyer Library, Southern Methodist
University, Dallas

Journal of a Military Reconnaissance, from Santa Fé, New Mexico, to the Navajo Country, Made with the Troops Under the Command of Brevet Lieut. Col. John M. Washington, Chief of Ninth Military Department, and Governor of New Mexico, in 1849
By James H. Simpson
Philadelphia: Lippincott, Grambo, and Company, 1852
140 pp., 74 leaves of plates; 9 x 5¾ (23 x 14.6)
Map, 74 black-and-white and color illustrations from drawings by Richard H. Kern and others
Also published as *Senate Document no. 64, 31st Congress, 1st Session*
Copy 1: Amon Carter Museum Library, Fort Worth, Texas
Copy 2: Collection of William S. Reese

Reports of Explorations and Surveys, to Ascertain the Most Practicable and Economical Route for a Railroad from the Mississippi River to the Pacific Ocean. Made Under the Direction of the Secretary of War in 1853–5, According to Acts of Congress of March 3, 1853, May 31, 1854, and August 5, 1854 (Pacific Railroad Surveys)
Washington, D.C.: A.O.P. Nicholson, 1855
Vol. 5; 11¾ x 9 (29.8 x 23)
The twelve volumes comprising the Pacific Railroad Surveys, published 1855–60, contain the reports of the four official surveys that sought the best route West. A dozen artists contributed more than seven hundred paintings and drawings, which were etched and lithographed for inclusion in the official reports, one of the most lavish government-sponsored publications of the nineteenth century.
Also published as *33rd Congress, 2nd Session, Senate Executive Document. no. 78*
Amon Carter Museum Library,
Fort Worth, Texas

Report on the United States and Mexican Boundary Survey, Made Under the Directory of the Secretary of the Interior
By William H. Emory
Also published as *34th Congress, 1st Session, Senate Executive Document no. 135*
Washington, D.C.: Cornelius Wendell, printer, 1857–59
3 parts in 2 vols.; 11¾ x 9¼ (29.8 x 23.5)
Maps, tables
Lieutenant Emory's Topographic Engineers were accompanied by artists Arthur Schott, John Weyss, and A. DeVaudricourt on their survey of the entire US-Mexico border.
DeGolyer Library, Southern Methodist University, Dallas

Report Upon the Colorado River of the West, Explored in 1857 and 1858
By Joseph C. Ives
Washington, D.C.: Government Printing Office, 1861
Published in 5 parts bound in one, each with separate pagination; 11¾ x 9¼ (30 x 23.5)
Maps, black-and-white and color illustrations, some drawn from photographs by Ives and sketches by Möllhausen and Egloffstein
Also published as *House Executive Document no. 90, 36th Congress, 1st Session*
DeGolyer Library, Southern Methodist University, Dallas

New Tracks in North America. A Journey of Travel and Adventure Whilst Engaged in the Survey for a Southern Railroad to the Pacific Ocean During 1867–8
By William A. Bell
London: Chapman and Hall, 1869
2 vol. (xiv, 236 pp., vii, 322 pp.); 8¾ x 5 (22.2 x 12.7)
Vol. 1: 23 black-and-white illustrations, drawn from photographs by Gardner
Yale Collection of Western Americana, Beinecke Rare Book and Manuscript Library, Yale University, New Haven, Connecticut

ILLUSTRATIONS:

Cañon of Chelly Eight Miles Above the Mouth. Sept. 8, 1849
By Richard H. Kern
Published in *Journal of a Military Reconnaissance*, no. 55
Wash on paper, 9¼ x 5⅝ (23.5 x 14.3)
Ewell Sale Stewart Library, Academy of Natural Sciences of Philadelphia

North West View of the Ruins of the Pueblo Pintado in the Valley of the Rio Chaco. Aug. 26, 1849
By Richard H. Kern
Published in *Journal of a Military Reconnaissance*, no. 20
Wash on paper, 6 x 9½ (15.2 x 24.1)
Ewell Sale Stewart Library, Academy of Natural Sciences of Philadelphia

Pueblo of Zuñi. Sept. 15th, 1849
By Richard H. Kern
Published in *Journal of a Military Reconnaissance*, no. 59
Wash on paper, 5⅝ x 9⅜ (14.3 x 23.8)
Ewell Sale Stewart Library, Academy of Natural Sciences of Philadelphia

Ruins of an Old Pueblo in the Cañon of Chelly. Sept. 8, 1849
By Richard H. Kern
Published in *Journal of a Military Reconnaissance*, no. 53
Wash on paper, 9¼ x 5 (23.5 x 12.7)
Ewell Sale Stewart Library, Academy of Natural Sciences of Philadelphia

As of April 22, 1996

BIBLIOGRAPHY

The following titles are recommended as introductions to American photographic books and the landscape of the arid West. Additional titles of books *by* (rather than *about*) the photographers featured in the exhibition may be found in the individual biographies, which are included in the catalogue of works beginning on p. 199.

GENERAL WORKS:

Anaya, Rudolfo A. *Heart of Aztlán*. Berkeley, California: Justa Publications, 1976.

Ansel Adams, New Light: Essays on His Legacy and Legend. San Francisco: Friends of Photography, 1993.

Ballinger, James K., and Andrea D. Rubinstein. *Visitors to Arizona, 1846 to 1980*. Phoenix: Phoenix Art Museum, 1980.

Bender, Gordon L., ed. *Reference Handbook on the Deserts of North America*. Westport, Connecticut: Greenwood Press, 1982.

Bush, Alfred L., and Lee Clark Mitchell. *The Photograph and the American Indian*. Princeton, New Jersey: Princeton University Press, 1994.

ew

n Muir

he

Coke, Van Deren. *Photographs, Photographically Illustrated Books and Albums in the UNM Libraries, 1843–1933*. Albuquerque: Art Museum, University of New Mexico, 1977.

——. *Photography in New Mexico: From the Daguerreotype to the Present*. Albuquerque: University of New Mexico Press, 1979.

Corle, Edwin. *Desert Country*. New York: Duell, Sloan & Pearce, 1941.

itlin,

's

Current, Karen. *Photography and the Old West*. Fort Worth, Texas: Amon Carter Museum of Western Art, 1978.

Davis, Keith F. *An American Century of Photography: From Dry-Plate to Digital. The Hallmark Photographic Collection*. Kansas City, Missouri: Hallmark Cards in association with Harry N. Abrams, 1995.

DeBuys, William Eno. *Enchantment and Exploitation: The Life and Hard Times of a New Mexico Mountain Range*. Albuquerque: University of New Mexico Press, 1985.

Dobie, J. Frank. *Guide to Life and Literature of the Southwest: Revised and Enlarged in Both Knowledge and Wisdom*. Dallas: Southern Methodist University Press, 1952.

Edwards, Gary. *International Guide to Nineteenth-Century Photographers and Their Works*. Boston: G.K. Hall & Co., 1988.

Fleming, Paula Richardson, and Judith Lynn Luskey. *Grand Endeavors of American Indian Photography*. Washington, D.C.: Smithsonian Institution Press, 1993.

Goldschmidt, Lucien, and Weston J. Naef. *The Truthful Lens: A Survey of the Photographically Illustrated Book, 1844–1914* (exhibition catalogue). New York: The Grolier Club, 1980.

Greenough, Sarah, et al. *On the Art of Fixing a Shadow: One Hundred and Fifty Years of Photography* (exhibition catalogue). Washington, D.C.: National Gallery of Art, 1989.

Hambourg, Maria Morris, et al. *The Waking Dream: Photography's First Century. Selections from the Gilman Paper Company Collection* (exhibition catalogue). New York: The Metropolitan Museum of Art, 1993.

Hollon, W. Eugene. *The Great American Desert: Then and Now*. New York: Oxford University Press, 1966.

Horgan, Paul. *Great River: The Rio Grande in North American History*. New York: Rinehart & Company, 1954.

Huth, Hans. *Nature and the American: Three Centuries of Changing Attitudes*. Berkeley and Los Angeles: University of California Press, 1957.

Hyde, Anne Farrar. *An American Vision: Far Western Landscape and National Culture, 1820–1920*. New York: New York University Press, 1990.

Ise, John. *Our National Park Policy: A Critical History*. Baltimore: The Johns Hopkins Press, for Resources for the Future, 1961.

Jackson, John Brinckerhoff. *American Space: The Centennial Years, 1865–1876*. New York: W.W. Norton & Company, 1972.

——. *Discovering the Vernacular Landscape*. New Haven, Connecticut: Yale University Press, 1984.

——. *The Necessity for Ruins and Other Topics*. Amherst: The University of Massachusetts Press, 1980.

——. *A Sense of Place, a Sense of Time*. New Haven, Connecticut: Yale University Press, 1994.

Jakle, John A. *The Tourist: Travel in Twentieth-Century North America*. Lincoln: University of Nebraska Press, 1985.

Jussim, Estelle, and Elizabeth Lindquist-Cock. *Landscape as Photograph*. New Haven, Connecticut: Yale University Press, 1985.

Krauss, Rosalind E. "Photography's Discursive Spaces: Landscape/View." *Art Journal*, 42 (Winter 1982), pp. 311–19.

Lamar, Howard R., ed. *The Reader's Encyclopedia of the American West*. New York: Thomas Y. Crowell Company, 1977.

Limerick, Patricia Nelson. *Desert Passages: Encounters with the American Deserts.* Albuquerque: University of New Mexico Press, 1985.

——. *The Legacy of Conquest: The Unbroken Past of the American West.* New York: W.W. Norton & Company, 1987.

——, Clyde A. Milner II, and Charles E. Rankin. *Trails: Toward a New Western History.* Lawrence: University Press of Kansas, 1991.

Lippard, Lucy R., ed. *Partial Recall: With Essays on Photographs of Native North Americans.* New York: The New Press, 1992.

Lyons, Joan, ed. *Artists' Books: A Critical Anthology and Sourcebook.* Rochester, New York: Visual Studies Workshop Press, 1985.

McPhee, John. *Basin and Range.* New York: Farrar, Straus and Giroux, 1980.

Malone, Michael P., and Richard W. Etulain. *The American West: A Twentieth-Century History.* Lincoln: University of Nebraska Press, 1989.

Margolis, David. *To Delight the Eye: Original Photographic Book Illustrations of the American West* (exhibition catalogue). Dallas: DeGolyer Library, Southern Methodist University, 1994.

Meinig, D.W. *Southwest: Three Peoples in Geographical Change, 1600–1970.* New York: Oxford University Press, 1971.

Meinig, D.W., ed. *The Interpretation of Ordinary Landscapes: Geographical Essays.* New York: Oxford University Press, 1979.

Milner, Clyde A. II, Carol A. O'Connor, and Martha A. Sandweiss, eds. *The Oxford History of the American West.* New York: Oxford University Press, 1994.

Nabhan, Gary Paul. *The Desert Smells Like Rain: A Naturalist in Papago Indian Country.* San Francisco: North Point Press, 1982.

Nadeau, Luis. *Encyclopedia of Printing, Photographic, and Photomechanical Processes.* New Brunswick, Canada: Atelier, 1994.

Nash, Roderick. *The American Environment: Readings in the History of Conservation.* Reading, Massachusetts: Addison-Wesley Publishing Company, 1968.

——. *Wilderness and the American Mind.* New Haven, Connecticut: Yale University Press, 1967.

Norwood, Vera, and Janice Monk, eds. *The Desert Is No Lady: Southwestern Landscapes in Women's Writing and Art.* New Haven, Connecticut: Yale University Press, 1987.

Novak, Barbara. *Nature and Culture: American Landscape and Painting, 1825–1875.* New York: Oxford University Press, 1980.

Ortiz, Alfonso, ed. *Handbook of North American Indians: Volume 9, Southwest.* Washington, D.C.: Smithsonian Institution, 1979.

Pomeroy, Earl. *In Search of the Golden West: The Tourist in Western America.* Lincoln: University of Nebraska Press, 1957.

Reisner, Marc. *Cadillac Desert: The American West and Its Disappearing Water.* Rev. ed. New York: Penguin Books, 1993.

Retratos Nuevomexicanos: A Collection of Hispanic New Mexican Photography (exhibition catalogue). Taos, New Mexico: Millicent Rogers Museum, 1987.

Roark, Carol E., Paula Ann Stewart, and Mary Kennedy McCabe. *Catalogue of the Amon Carter Museum Photography Collection.* Fort Worth, Texas: Amon Carter Museum, 1993.

Runte, Alfred. *National Parks: The American Experience.* 2nd ed., rev. Lincoln: University of Nebraska Press, 1987.

Sandweiss, Martha A. "Undecisive Moments: The Narrative Tradition in Western Photography." In Martha A. Sandweiss, ed., *Photography in Nineteenth-Century America* (exhibition catalogue). Fort Worth, Texas: Amon Carter Museum, 1991, pp. 98–129.

Scully, Vincent. *Pueblo: Mountain, Village, Dance.* New York: The Viking Press, 1975.

Sheridan, David. *Desertification of the United States.* Washington, D.C.: Council on Environmental Quality, 1981.

Smith, Henry Nash. *Virgin Land: The American West as Symbol and Myth.* Cambridge, Massachusetts: Harvard University Press, 1970.

Stegner, Wallace. *The American West as Living Space.* Ann Arbor: The University of Michigan Press, 1987.

Szarkowski, John. *Photography Until Now* (exhibition catalogue). New York: The Museum of Modern Art, 1989.

Trachtenberg, Alan. *Reading American Photographs: Images as History, Mathew Brady to Walker Evans.* New York: Hill and Wang, 1989.

Truettner, William H., ed. *The West as America: Reinterpreting Images of the Frontier, 1820–1920* (exhibition catalogue). Washington, D.C.: National Museum of American Art, Smithsonian Institution, 1991.

Tuan, Yi-Fu. *Topophilia: A Study of Environmental Perception, Attitudes, and Values.* Englewood Cliffs, New Jersey: Prentice-Hall, 1974.

Turner, Frederick Jackson. *The Frontier in American History.* New York: Henry Holt and Company, 1920.

Turner, Tom. *Sierra Club: 100 Years of Protecting Nature.* New York: Harry N. Abrams, in association with the Sierra Club, 1991.

Van Haaften, Julia. *From Talbot to Stieglitz: Masterpieces of Early Photography from the New York Public Library.* New York: Thames and Hudson, 1982.

Webb, Walter Prescott. "The American West, Perpetual Mirage." *Harper's Magazine,* 214 (May 1957), pp. 25–31.

——. *The Great Frontier.* Boston: Houghton Mifflin Company, 1952.

——. *The Great Plains.* Boston: Ginn and Company, 1931.

Weber, David J. *The Spanish Frontier in North America.* New Haven, Connecticut: Yale University Press, 1992.

White, Richard. *"It's Your Misfortune and None of My Own": A History of the American West.* Norman: University of Oklahoma Press, 1991.

PART 1:
SURVEYING AN UNFAMILIAR LAND

Bartlett, Richard A. *Great Surveys of the American West*. Norman: University of Oklahoma Press, 1962.

——. *The New Country: A Social History of the American Frontier, 1776–1890*. New York: Oxford University Press, 1974.

Billington, Ray Allen, and Martin Ridge. *Westward Expansion: A History of the American Frontier*. 5th ed. New York: Macmillan Publishing Co., 1982.

Danly, Susan, and Leo Marx, eds. *The Railroad in American Art: Representations of Technological Change*. Cambridge, Massachusetts: The MIT Press, 1988.

DeVoto, Bernard. *The Course of Empire*. Lincoln: University of Nebraska Press, 1952.

Dingus, Rick. *The Photographic Artifacts of Timothy O'Sullivan*. Albuquerque: The University of New Mexico Press, 1982.

Dippie, Brian W. *Catlin and His Contemporaries: The Politics of Patronage*. Lincoln: University of Nebraska Press, 1990.

Emory, William H. *Report on the United States and Mexican Boundary Survey Made Under the Direction of the Secretary of the Interior*. Volume I. Introduction by William H. Goetzmann. Austin, Texas: Texas State Historical Association, 1987.

Engstrand, Iris H.W. *Spanish Scientists in the New World: The Eighteenth-Century Expeditions*. Seattle: University of Washington Press, 1981.

Eskind, Andrew H., and Greg Drake, eds. *Index to American Photographic Collections*. 3rd ed. Boston: G.K. Hall & Co., 1995.

Galassi, Peter. *Before Photography: Painting and the Invention of Photography* (exhibition catalogue). New York: The Museum of Modern Art, 1981.

Goetzmann, William H. *Army Exploration in the American West, 1803–1863*. New Haven, Connecticut: Yale University Press, 1959.

——. *Exploration and Empire: The Explorer and the Scientist in the Winning of the American West*. New York: Alfred A. Knopf, 1966.

——. *New Lands, New Men: America and the Second Great Age of Discovery*. New York: Viking, 1986.

——., and William N. Goetzmann. *The West of the Imagination*. New York: W.W. Norton & Company, 1986.

——., Joseph C. Porter, and David C. Hunt. *The West as Romantic Horizon* (exhibition catalogue). Omaha, Nebraska: Center for Western Studies, Joslyn Art Museum, 1981.

Hales, Peter B. *William Henry Jackson and the Transformation of the American Landscape*. Philadelphia: Temple University Press, 1988.

Jackson, William H. *Time Exposure: The Autobiography of William Henry Jackson*. New York: G.P. Putnam's Sons, 1940.

Johnson, Brooks. *An Enduring Interest: The Photographs of Alexander Gardner* (exhibition catalogue). Norfolk, Virginia: The Chrysler Museum, 1991.

Manly, William L. *Death Valley in '49*. San Jose: Pacific Tree & Vine Co., 1894.

Naef, Weston J., and James N. Wood. *Era of Exploration: The Rise of Landscape Photography in the American West, 1860–1885* (exhibition catalogue). Buffalo, New York: Albright-Knox Art Gallery; New York: The Metropolitan Museum of Art, 1975.

Newhall, Beaumont, and Nancy Newhall. *T.H. O'Sullivan: Photographer*. Rochester, New York: International Museum of Photography at George Eastman House; Fort Worth, Texas: Amon Carter Museum of Western Art, 1966.

Palmquist, Peter E. *Carleton E. Watkins: Photographer of the American West* (exhibition catalogue). Fort Worth, Texas: Amon Carter Museum, 1983.

Powell, John Wesley. *Report on the Lands of the Arid Region of the United States, with a More Detailed Account of the Lands of Utah* (1879). Facsimile ed., with an introduction by T.H. Watkins. Cambridge, Massachusetts: Harvard Common Press, 1983.

Prown, Jules David, et al. *Discovered Lands, Invented Pasts: Transforming Visions of the American West* (exhibition catalogue). New Haven, Connecticut: Yale University Press, 1992.

Rabbitt, Mary C. *Minerals, Lands, and Geology for the Common Defence and General Welfare, Volume 1, Before 1879: A History of Public Lands, Federal Science and Mapping Policy, and Development of Mineral Resources in the United States*. Washington, D.C.: United States Government Printing Office, 1979.

Rudisill, Richard. *Mirror Image: The Influence of the Daguerreotype on American Society*. Albuquerque: University of New Mexico Press, 1971.

——., et al. *Photographers: A Sourcebook for Historical Research*. Brownsville, California: Carl Mautz Publishing, 1991.

——. *Photographers of the New Mexico Territory, 1854–1912*. Santa Fe: Museum of New Mexico, 1973.

Sandweiss, Martha A., ed. *Photography in Nineteenth-Century America*. Fort Worth, Texas: Amon Carter Museum, 1991.

Schmeckebier, Laurence Frederick. *Catalogue and Index of the Publications of the Hayden, King, Powell, and Wheeler Surveys*. Washington, D.C.: Government Printing Office, 1904.

Sichel, Kim. *Mapping the West: Nineteenth-Century American Landscape Photographs from the Boston Public Library* (exhibition catalogue). Boston: Boston University Art Gallery, 1992.

Snyder, Joel. *American Frontiers: The Photographs of Timothy H. O'Sullivan, 1867–1874* (exhibition catalogue). Philadelphia: Philadelphia Museum of Art, 1981.

Sobieszek, Robert. "Alexander Gardner's Photographs Along the 35th Parallel." *Image*, 14 (June 1971): pp. 6–13.

——. "Conquest by Camera: Alexander Gardner's 'Across the Continent on the Kansas Pacific Railroad'." *Art in America*, 60 (March-April 1972), pp. 80–85.

Stafford, Barbara Maria. *Voyage into Substance: Art, Science, Nature, and the Illustrated Travel Account, 1760–1840*. Cambridge, Massachusetts: The MIT Press, 1984.

Stegner, Wallace. *Beyond the Hundredth Meridian: John Wesley Powell and the Second Opening of the West*. Boston: Houghton Mifflin Company, 1954.

Stilgoe, John R. *Metropolitan Corridor: Railroads and the American Scene*. New Haven, Connecticut: Yale University Press, 1983.

Taft, Robert. *Artists and Illustrators of the Old West, 1850–1900*. New York: Charles Scribner's Sons, 1953.

———. *Photography and the American Scene: A Social History, 1839–1889*. New York: Macmillan Company, 1938.

Twain, Mark. *Roughing It*. Hartford, Connecticut: American Publishing Company, 1872.

Tyler, Ron. *Prints of the West*. Golden, Colorado: Fulcrum Publishing, 1994.

Unruh, John D., Jr. *The Plains Across: The Overland Emigrants and the Trans-Mississippi West, 1840–60*. Urbana: University of Illinois Press, 1979.

Van Haaften, Julia. *Tracking the West: A.J. Russell Photographs of the Union Pacific Railroad* (exhibition catalogue). New York: The New York Public Library, 1994.

Walther, Susan Danly. "The Landscape Photographs of Alexander Gardner and Andrew Joseph Russell." Ph.D. dissertation. Providence, Rhode Island: Brown University, 1984.

Weber, David J. *Richard H. Kern: Expeditionary Artist in the Far Southwest, 1848–1853* (exhibition catalogue). Fort Worth, Texas: Amon Carter Museum, 1985.

Welling, William. *Photography in America: The Formative Years: 1839–1900*. New York: Thomas Y. Crowell Company, 1978.

Wilkins, Thurman. *Clarence King: A Biography*. Rev. ed. Albuquerque: University of New Mexico Press, 1988.

PART 2: DISCOVERING A HUMAN PAST/INVENTING A SCENIC WEST

Apostol, Jane. *Vroman's of Pasadena: A Century of Books, 1894–1994*. Pasadena, California: A.C. Vroman, Inc., 1994.

Arrhenius, Olof W. *Stones Speak and Waters Sing: The Life and Works of Gustaf Nordenskiöld*. Mesa Verde National Park, Colorado: Mesa Verde Museum Association, Inc., [1984–86].

Athearn, Robert G. *The Mythic West in Twentieth-Century America*. Lawrence: University Press of Kansas, 1986.

Austin, Mary, with photographs by Ansel Adams. *The Land of Little Rain*. Boston: Houghton Mifflin Company, 1903.

Baur, John E. *The Health Seekers of Southern California, 1870–1900*. San Marino, California: The Huntington Library, 1959.

Belasco, Warren James. *Americans on the Road: From Autocamp to Motel, 1910–1945*. Cambridge, Massachusetts: The MIT Press, 1979.

Bunnell, Peter C., ed. "The Art of Pictorial Photography, 1890–1925." *Record* [of The Art Museum, Princeton University], 51 (1992), pp. 1–115.

Burdick, Arthur J. *The Mystic Mid-Region: The Deserts of the Southwest*. New York: G.P. Putnam's Sons, 1904.

Clark, Ira G. *Then Came the Railroads: The Century from Steam to Diesel in the Southwest*. Norman: University of Oklahoma Press, 1958.

Davis, Barbara A. *Edward S. Curtis: The Life and Times of a Shadow Catcher*. San Francisco: Chronicle Books, 1985.

Deutsch, Sarah. *No Separate Refuge: Culture, Class, and Gender on an Anglo-Hispanic Frontier in the American Southwest, 1880–1940*. New York: Oxford University Press, 1987.

Eldredge, Charles C., Julie Schimmel, and William H. Truettner. *Art in New Mexico, 1900–1945: Paths to Taos and Santa Fe* (exhibition catalogue). Washington, D.C.: National Museum of American Art, Smithsonian Institution, 1986.

Fiske, Turbesé Lummis, and Keith Lummis. *Charles F. Lummis: The Man and His West*. Norman: University of Oklahoma Press, 1975.

Fowler, Don D. *The Western Photographs of John K. Hillers: Myself in the Water*. Washington, D.C.: Smithsonian Institution Press, 1989.

Fox, Stephen. *The American Conservation Movement: John Muir and His Legacy*. Madison: The University of Wisconsin Press, 1981.

Goetzmann, William H. *The First Americans: Photographs from the Library of Congress*. Washington, D.C.: Starwood Publishing, 1991.

Henderson, James David. *"Meals by Fred Harvey": A Phenomenon of the American West*. Fort Worth: Texas Christian University Press, 1969.

James, George Wharton. *Reclaiming the Arid West*. New York: Dodd, Mead & Co., 1917.

———. *The Wonders of the Colorado Desert (Southern California)*. 2 volumes. Boston: Little, Brown, and Co., 1904.

Lyman, Christopher M. *The Vanishing Race and Other Illusions: Photographs of Indians by Edward S. Curtis* (exhibition catalogue). Washington, D.C.: Smithsonian Institution, 1982.

McCarthy, G. Michael. *Hour of Trial: The Conservation Conflict in Colorado and the West, 1891–1907*. Norman: University of Oklahoma Press, 1977.

McLuhan, T.C. *Dream Tracks: The Railroad and the American Indian, 1890–1930*. New York: Harry N. Abrams, 1985.

Mahood, Ruth I., ed. *Photographer of the Southwest: Adam Clark Vroman, 1856–1916*. Los Angeles: The Ward Ritchie Press, 1961.

Mitchell, Lee Clark. *Witnesses to a Vanishing America: The Nineteenth-Century Response*. Princeton, New Jersey: Princeton University Press, 1981.

Rae, John B. *The Road and the Car in American Life*. Cambridge, Massachusetts: The MIT Press, 1971.

Roosevelt, Theodore. *A Book-Lover's Holidays in the Open*. New York: Charles Scribner's Sons, 1916.

Smythe, William E. *The Conquest of Arid America*. New York: Harper & Brothers Publishers, 1900.

Spears, John R. *Illustrated Sketches of Death Valley and Other Borax Deserts of the Pacific Coast*. Chicago: Rand, McNally & Co., 1892.

Starr, Kevin. *Americans and the California Dream, 1850–1915*. New York: Oxford University Press, 1973.

———. *Inventing the Dream: California Through the Progressive Era*. New York: Oxford University Press, 1985.

Stineman, Esther Lanigan. *Mary Austin: Song of a Maverick*. New Haven, Connecticut: Yale University Press, 1989.

Stover, John F. *The Life and Decline of the American Railroad*. New York: Oxford University Press, 1970.

Strobridge, Idah M. *The Land of Purple Shadows*. Los Angeles: The Artemisia Bindery, c. 1909.

Van Dyke, John C. *The Desert: Further Studies in Natural Appearances*. New York: Charles Scribner's Sons, 1917.

———. *The Grand Canyon of the Colorado: Recurrent Studies in Impressions and Appearances*. Salt Lake City: University of Utah Press, 1992.

Webb, William, and Robert A. Weinstein. *Dwellers at the Source: Southwestern Indian Photographs of A.C. Vroman, 1895–1904*. Albuquerque: University of New Mexico Press, 1973.

White, G. Edward. *The Eastern Establishment and the Western Experience: The West of Frederic Remington, Theodore Roosevelt, and Owen Wister*. Austin: The University of Texas Press, 1989.

PART 3: MODERNIST VISIONS, TRADITIONAL VOICES

Adams, Ansel, with Mary Street Alinder. *Ansel Adams: An Autobiography*. Boston: Little, Brown and Company, 1985.

Broder, Patricia Janis. *The American West: The Modern Vision*. Boston: Little, Brown and Company, 1984.

Cohen, Michael P. *The History of the Sierra Club, 1892–1970*. San Francisco: Sierra Club Books, 1988.

Coles, Robert. *Dorothea Lange: Photographs of a Lifetime*. Millerton, New York: Aperture, 1982.

Green, Jonathan. *American Photography: A Critical History, 1945 to the Present*. New York: Harry N. Abrams, 1984.

Harvey, Mark W.T. *A Symbol of Wilderness: Echo Park and the American Conservation Movement*. Albuquerque: University of New Mexico Press, 1994.

Henderson, Randall. *On Desert Trails: Today and Yesterday*. Los Angeles: Westernlore Press, 1961.

Heyman, Therese Thau, Sandra S. Phillips, and John Szarkowski. *Dorothea Lange: American Photographs* (exhibition catalogue). San Francisco: San Francisco Museum of Modern Art, 1994.

———. ed. *Seeing Straight: The f.64 Revolution in Photography* (exhibition catalogue). Oakland, California: The Oakland Museum, 1992.

Krutch, Joseph Wood. *The Desert Year*. Tucson: The University of Arizona Press, 1951.

Lowitt, Richard. *The New Deal and the West*. Bloomington: Indiana University Press, 1984.

Luhan, Mabel Dodge. *Edge of Taos Desert: An Escape to Reality*. New York: Harcourt, Brace and Company, 1937.

McPhee, John. *Encounters with the Archdruid*. New York: Farrar, Straus and Giroux, 1971.

Meltzer, Milton. *Dorothea Lange: A Photographer's Life*. New York: Farrar, Straus and Giroux, 1978.

Newhall, Beaumont. *Supreme Instants: The Photography of Edward Weston* (exhibition catalogue). Tucson: Center for Creative Photography, University of Arizona, 1986.

Newhall, Nancy. *Ansel Adams: Volume I, The Eloquent Light*. San Francisco: Sierra Club, 1963.

Porter, Eliot. *Eliot Porter* (exhibition catalogue). Fort Worth, Texas: Amon Carter Museum, 1987.

Powell, Lawrence Clark. "An Essay on the Land." In Ansel Adams, *Photographs of the Southwest*. Boston: Little, Brown and Company, 1976, pp. xi-xxv.

Priestley, J.B. *Midnight on the Desert, Being an Excursion into Autobiography During a Winter in America, 1935–36*. New York: Harper & Brothers Publishers, 1937.

Quinn, Karen E., and Theodore E. Stebbins, Jr. *Weston's Westons: California and the West* (exhibition catalogue). Boston: Museum of Fine Arts, 1987.

Sandweiss, Martha A. *Laura Gilpin: An Enduring Grace* (exhibition catalogue). Fort Worth, Texas: Amon Carter Museum, 1986.

Sears, Paul B. *Deserts on the March*. Norman: University of Oklahoma Press, 1935.

Stewart, George R. *U.S. 40: Cross Section of the United States of America*. Boston: Houghton Mifflin Company, 1953.

Suran, William C. *The Kolb Brothers of Grand Canyon*. Grand Canyon, Arizona: Grand Canyon Natural History Association, c. 1991.

Worster, Donald. *Rivers of Empire: Water, Aridity, and the Growth of the American West*. New York: Oxford University Press, 1985.

———. *An Unsettled Country: Changing Landscapes of the American West*. Albuquerque: University of New Mexico Press, 1994.

PART 4: TRANSFORMED WEST

Abbey, Edward. *Desert Solitaire: A Season in the Wilderness*. New York: McGraw-Hill Book Company, 1971.

Adams, Robert. *Why People Photograph: Selected Essays and Reviews*. New York: Aperture, 1994.

Baltz, Lewis. *Rule Without Exception* (exhibition catalogue). Des Moines, Iowa: Des Moines Art Center, 1990.

Banham, Peter Reyner. *Scenes in America Deserta*. Cambridge, Massachusetts: The MIT Press, 1989.

Brower, David. *For Earth's Sake: The Life and Times of David Brower*. Salt Lake City, Utah: Peregrine Smith Books, Gibbs-Smith Publisher, 1990.

Coles, Robert. *The Old Ones of New Mexico: Photographs by Alex Harris*. Albuquerque: University of New Mexico Press, 1973.

Conniff, Gregory. *An American Field Guide: Volume 1, Common Ground*. New Haven, Connecticut: Yale University Press, c. 1985.

Engel, Leonard, ed. *The Big Empty: Essays on Western Landscapes as Narrative*. Albuquerque: University of New Mexico Press, 1994.

Evans, Terry. *Prairie: Images of Ground and Sky*. Lawrence: University Press of Kansas, 1986.

Foresta, Merry A., Stephen Jay Gould, and Karal Ann Marling. *Between Home and Heaven: Contemporary American Landscape Photography* (exhibition catalogue). Washington, D.C.: National Museum of American Art, Smithsonian Institution, 1992.

Frazier, Ian. *Great Plains*. New York: Farrar, Straus and Giroux, 1989.

Goldberg, Vicki. "A Terrible Beauty." *Art News*, 90 (Summer 1991), pp. 106–13.

Hagen, Charles, ed. *Aperture*, 120 (Summer 1990), issue entitled "Beyond Wilderness."

Hales, Peter B. "Landscape and Documentary." *Afterimage*, 15 (Summer 1987), pp. 10–14.

Hundley, Norris, Jr. *Water and the West: The Colorado River Compact and the Politics of Water in the American West*. Berkeley and Los Angeles: University of California Press, 1975.

Jenkins, William, ed. *New Topographics: Photographs of a Man-Altered Landscape* (exhibition catalogue). Rochester, New York: International Museum of Photography at George Eastman House, 1975.

Limerick, Patricia Nelson, and Thomas W. Southall. *Revealing Territory: Photographs of the Southwest by Mark Klett*. Albuquerque: University of New Mexico Press, 1992.

Nash, Gerald D. *The American West in the Twentieth Century: A Short History of an Urban Oasis*. Albuquerque: University of New Mexico Press, 1977.

Noriega, Chon A. *From the West: Chicano Narrative Photography*. San Francisco: The Mexican Museum, 1995.

Ratcliff, Carter. "Route 66 Revisited: The New Landscape Photography." *Art in America*, 64 (January-February 1976), pp. 86–91.

Reisner, Marc, and Sarah Bates. *Overtapped Oasis: Reform or Revolution for Western Water*. Washington, D.C.: Island Press, 1990.

Solnit, Rebecca. *Savage Dreams*. San Francisco: Sierra Club Books, 1994.

Szarkowski, John. *Mirrors and Windows: American Photography Since 1960* (exhibition catalogue). New York: The Museum of Modern Art, 1978.

Temple, Judy Nolte, ed. *Open Spaces, City Places: Contemporary Writers on the Changing Southwest*. Tucson: The University of Arizona Press, 1994.

Wallis, Michael. *Route 66: The Mother Road*. New York: St. Martin's Press, 1990.

Weisman, Alan, with photographs by Jay Dusard. *La Frontera: The United States Border with Mexico*. Tucson: University of Arizona Press, 1986.

Wolf, Daniel, ed. *The American Space: Meaning in Nineteenth-Century Landscape Photography*. Middletown, Connecticut: Wesleyan University Press, 1983.

MAY CASTLEBERRY is librarian and associate curator for Special Collections at the Whitney Museum of American Art. She has organized several exhibitions of books for the Museum, including "Fables, Fantasies, and Everyday Things." As editor of the Artists and Writers Series, she has produced fifteen fine press publications, including *The Magic Magic Book, Mesa Verde*, and *The First Picture Book*.

JOHN R. CHÁVEZ is associate professor of history at Southern Methodist University, Dallas. A specialist in Mexican-American history, he authored *The Lost Land: The Chicano Image of the Southwest*, and the forthcoming *Eastside Landmark: A History of the East Los Angeles Community Union*.

ROBERT COLES is professor of psychiatry and medical humanities at the Harvard Medical School and James Agee Professor of Social Ethics at Harvard University. He co-founded the Center for Documentary Studies at Duke University and is a member of its board of directors. Author of many articles and books, his most recent is *The Call of Service: A Witness to Idealism*.

EVAN S. CONNELL, the recipient of numerous honors, including the American Academy of Arts and Letters Award, is the author of many novels, short stories, and nonfiction works, among them *Mr. Bridge, Mrs. Bridge, Son of the Morning Star: Custer and the Little Bighorn, The Connoisseur*, and *The Alchymist's Journal*.

SUSAN DANLY is curator of American art at the Mead Art Museum, Amherst College. She co-edited *The Railroad in American Art: Representations of Technological Change*, and her most recent book is *Eakins and the Photograph: Works by Thomas Eakins and His Circle in the Pennsylvania Academy of the Fine Arts*.

WILLIAM H. GOETZMANN is Jack S. Blanton Senior Professor of History and American Studies at the University of Texas at Austin. He won a 1967 Pulitzer Prize for his book *Exploration and Empire: The Explorer and the Scientist in the Winning of the American West*; his other works include *Army Exploration in the American West, 1803–63* and *Sam Chamberlain's Mexican War*. He created the documentary series *The West of the Imagination* for PBS and co-wrote the accompanying book with his son, William N. Goetzmann.

WILLIAM N. GOETZMANN is associate professor of finance at the Yale School of Organization and Management and an expert on the economics of the art market. A former director of the Museum of Western Art in Denver, he co-authored *The West of the Imagination* with his father, William H. Goetzmann.

ANNE HAMMOND is the editor of *Frederick H. Evans: Selected Texts and Bibliography*. Co-editor of *History of Photography*, an International quarterly, and of the World Photographers Reference Series, she is currently completing a doctorate at Oxford University.

WILLIAM KITTREDGE turned to writing after spending years as a rancher in eastern Oregon; he now lives in Missoula, Montana. *Who Owns the West?* is his most recent book.

PATRICIA NELSON LIMERICK is professor of history at the University of Colorado, Boulder. She is the author of *Desert Passages: Encounters with the American Deserts, The Legacy of Conquest: The Unbroken Past of the American West*, and a co-editor of *Trails: Toward a New Western History*.

JULIE MELLBY is assistant curator of the Department of Printing and Graphic Arts at the Houghton Library, Harvard University. Formerly associate librarian of the Whitney Museum of American Art, she is the author of the exhibition catalogue *The Daniel Gallery* for the Zabriskie Gallery in New York City.

PETER E. PALMQUIST is an independent historian of photography. He was co-curator of and authored the catalogue for "Carleton E. Watkins: Photographer of the American West," which originated at the Amon Carter Museum. He is curator of the Women in Photography International Archive in Arcata, California.

LISA PHILLIPS, curator at the Whitney Museum of American Art, has organized more than thirty exhibitions and their accompanying catalogues, including "Richard Prince," "Image World: Art and Media Culture," and most recently "Beat Culture and the New America: 1950–1965."

MARC REISNER writes frequently about the environment. He is the author of *Cadillac Desert: The American West and Its Disappearing Water, Game Wars: The Undercover Pursuit of Wildlife Poachers* and co-author of *Overtapped Oasis: Reform or Revolution for Western Water*.

MARTHA A. SANDWEISS is director of the Mead Art Museum at Amherst College, where she serves as associate professor of American studies.

She edited and contributed to *Photography in Nineteenth-Century America*, and co-edited *The Oxford History of the American West*.

ROBERT A. SOBIESZEK is curator of photography at the Los Angeles County Museum of Art, where he organized "Robert Smithson: Photo Works" and "The Camera I: Photographic Self-Portraits from the Audrey and Sydney Irmas Collection." His most recent exhibition is "Ports of Entry: William S. Burroughs and the Arts."

THOMAS W. SOUTHALL, research fellow at the National Museum of American Art, has written many books, including *Revealing Territory: Photographs of the Southwest by Mark Klett*. He currently is working on an exhibition and publication on photographs of Native Americans by John K. Hillers.

KEVIN STARR is state librarian of California and professor at the School of Urban and Regional Planning at the University of Southern California. He has written several books, including *Americans and the California Dream, 1850–1915, Inventing the Dream: California Through the Progressive Era, Material Dreams: Southern California Through the 1920s, Endangered Dreams: The Great Depression in California*, and the forthcoming *The Dream Endures: California Enters the 1940s*.

RINA SWENTZELL writes and lectures on the philosophy and culture of the Pueblo world and its education, art, and architecture. She has written the book *Children of Clay*.

RON TYLER is director of The Texas State Historical Association and professor of history at the University of Texas at Austin. His most recent book is *Prints of the West*.

ADAM D. WEINBERG is curator of the Permanent Collection at the Whitney Museum of American Art. He has also curated "Vanishing Presence" at the Walker Art Center, and more recently he co-curated "Landscape as Metaphor: Visions of America in the Late Twentieth Century" at the Denver Art Museum.

TERRY TEMPEST WILLIAMS is a naturalist at the Utah Museum of Natural History in Salt Lake City. Her many books include *Refuge: An Unnatural History of Family and Place, An Unspoken Hunger: Stories from the Field*, and most recently, *Desert Quartet*.

SHARYN WILEY YEOMAN is a scholar of the American West who is currently completing a doctorate at the University of Colorado, Boulder.

ACKNOWLEDGMENTS

MAY CASTLEBERRY

Before acknowledging the many individuals and institutions who so generously participated in this exhibition and catalogue, I would first like to express my appreciation for the crucial, early support that launched this project. In 1991, David A. Ross, director of the Whitney Museum of American Art, encouraged my somewhat unlikely proposal concerning photographic books and changing ideas of the American desert. The future of the project was secured by grants from Joanne Leonhardt Cassullo and The Dorothea Leonhardt Foundation, Inc., The Nathan Cummings Foundation, and the National Endowment for the Humanities, which funded the extensive research necessary to realize the exhibition and catalogue. Without the support and challenging standards of these individuals and organizations, we could never have assembled so many fine works and contributions to the catalogue.

I warmly acknowledge the tireless efforts and lively participation of several staff members, who each worked consistently on this project for the better part of a year: Beth Handler, whose organization and diplomacy guided the exhibition to completion; Julie Mellby, whose research informed most aspects of the project and who compiled the artists' biographies; and Stacy Hoshino, who kept all of us and the exhibition installation on track. We owe a great deal to Tracy Edling, exhibits associate for The Newberry Library, Chicago, whose imaginative designs for this exhibition have been a constant inspiration.

All the essayists who contributed to this catalogue acted as advisers to the exhibition, and I hope this volume will stand as the best testament to their involvement and wise counsel. I am most indebted to Martha A. Sandweiss. Her scholarship on photography and narrative traditions in the American West laid the groundwork for many contributions to the catalogue, and her knowledge of Western photographic books greatly enriched the exhibition. Two Western correspondents were important to this project: Milan Hughston, director of the Amon Carter Museum Library, Fort Worth, and Amy Rule, archivist at the Center for Creative Photography, Tucson. Both wrote many of the entries in the catalogue of works and suggested some of the most interesting works and authors included in this catalogue.

It has been my privilege to work with many fine booksellers, whose learning and enthusiasm shaped this project, particularly Victoria Dailey, Los Angeles; Michael Dawson of Dawson's Book Shop, Los Angeles; David Margolis of Margolis & Moss, Santa Fe; Glenn Horowitz and Andrew Roth of Glenn Horowitz Booksellers, New York and Easthampton; and William Reese and the staff of the William Reese Company, New Haven.

I thank several friends and bookish professionals who read or revised proposals that helped me define the exhibition: Nan Richardson, photographic book editor; Michael Weintraub, bookseller; and Michael FitzGerald, my husband, an art historian who was a sounding board for many of my ideas. I am especially grateful to Susan Green, editor of the Huntington Library Press, San Marino, for her suggestions, which helped me organize the introductory essay in this catalogue.

Archivists, curators, historians, librarians, photography dealers, and many others offered advice for the overall project or helped us locate works of art. Special thanks are due Janet Borden, Terry Etherton, David Farmer, Ian Frazier, Maria Morris Hambourg, David Harris, Barry Lopez, Barbara McCandless, George Miles, Nicholas Olsberg, Eric Paddock, Peter E. Palmquist, Richard Pare, Sandra S. Phillips, John Rohrbach, Richard Rudisill, Andrew Smith, Thomas W. Southall, Constance Sullivan, and D.W. Wright. The staff of the United States Geological Survey in Reston, Virginia, generously checked many of our facts, and I cannot adequately thank them except to say that, despite limited resources, they uphold a proud tradition.

In addition, we would like to thank those who ensured the loan of a particular book or photograph, arranged for reproduction photography, or facilitated our research: Pierre Apraxine; Eleanor Barefoot; Frish Brandt; Ben Brantley; Richard Buchen; Christine Burgin; Bridget Burke; Alfred L. Bush; Eleanor Caponigro; Catherine Chermayeff; Kathy Clewell; Malcolm Daniel; Keith Davis; Virginia Dodier; H. George Fletcher; Jeffrey Fraenkel; Sharon Frost; Jane Fudge; Katherine B. Gully; Bonnie Hardwick; Therese Thau Heyman; Sinclair Hitchings; Elisabeth Hodermarsky; Kathleen Stewart Howe; Ben Huseman; Charles Isaacs; Claes H. Jacobson; Drew Johnson; Alan Jutzi; Amy Kelly; Austin Lamont; Leonard Lauder; Peter MacGill; Dan McLaughlin; David Martz; Laura Muir; Dianne Nilson; Thomas Phelps; Glenys Quick; Edward Ranney; William M. Roberts;

Jeff Rosenheim; Theresa Salazar; Merriam Saunders; David Scheinbaum; Aaron Schmidt; Keith Schreiber; Duane Sneddeker; Donald Snoddy; David T. Steere, Jr.; Errol Stevens; Joseph Struble; Rachel Stuhlman; Marcia Tiede; Joseph Traugott; Julia Van Haaften; Robert Vaughan; Kim Walters; Jennifer A. Watts; Mus and Stephen White; Matthew Whitworth; Mark Williams; Daniel Wolf; and Linda Kay Zoeckler. I also thank Malcolm Swanston, who designed and executed the maps that appear in each section of this catalogue and the exhibition.

The preparation of this volume was a substantial undertaking. Its realization depended on the guidance of Mary E. DelMonico, head, publications, at the Whitney Museum, and her excellent staff, including the ever impressive Sheila Schwartz, who edited all the essays with intelligence; Heidi Jacobs, whose patience and precision were essential to the completion of this publication; Nerissa Dominguez, who kept the production on schedule and managed, with Beth Handler, a massive rights and reproductions list; and José Fernandez, Denise M. Rompilla and Melinda Barlow, whose keen eyes for detail were invaluable. In addition, Corey Keller and Minou Roufail skillfully performed the tasks of typing, proofing, and correcting the texts according to editorial guidelines. This catalogue could never have come together without so many able hands.

Credit for the visual production of this catalogue is due two consummate professionals with whom it was an honor and a pleasure to work — Katy Homans, who designed the catalogue with sensitivity and imagination, and Robert Hennessey, who created the duotone and tritone film and oversaw the printing of the catalogue with a discriminating eye. To help us make the best possible reproductions, some of the lenders exceeded their obligations by providing original photographs for special halftone photography: The Ansel Adams Publishing Rights Trust, Mill Valley; Robert Adams; the Yale Collection of Western Americana, The Beinecke Rare Book and Manuscript Library, New Haven; Janet Borden, Inc., New York; the Boston Public Library's Print Department; Centre Canadien d'Architecture/Canadian Centre for Architecture, Montreal; Center for Creative Photography, The University of Arizona, Tucson; Linda Connor; Fraenkel Gallery, San Francisco; Lee Friedlander; Sondra Gilman and Celso M. Gonzalez-Falla; Hans P. Kraus, Jr.; and The Metropolitan Museum of Art, New York.

On a more personal level, I wish to thank several Western hosts and fellow travelers whose ideas or bookshelves helped immeasurably: Flora Miller Biddle, Sydney Biddle, Vija Celmins, Sue McBride, Jean Nathan, Nicholas Olsberg and, most important, Elizabeth and Frank Castleberry.

For their long-term support of the Library program — which is the foundation of this exhibition — I am indebted to Joan Hardy Clark and Brendan Gill, co-chairmen of the Library Fellows of the Whitney Museum of American Art, Joanne Leonhardt Cassullo, and the H.W. Wilson Foundation.

We are appreciative of the interns who volunteered their time for this project: Emily Finkelstein, Noga La'or, Alexandra Rowley, and Elizabeth Wolff.

Though I cannot name them all, thanks are owed to staff members in a number of departments at the Whitney Museum. I benefited greatly from the good will and collegial advice of Lisa Phillips, curator, and Adam Weinberg, curator, Permanent Collection. For their exceptional dedication and professionalism, I thank Steve Dennin, director of development, and Betsy Brady, associate director of development, grants. To Nancy Harm, assistant registrar, we owe an enjoyable, safe installation of all the works in the exhibition. I acknowledge the kind services of the exhibition staff, particularly Rich Gagliano, Lana Hum, Jack Martin, Christy Putnam, and Joshua Rosenblatt. I thank Mary Haus, director of communications, and Cecilia Bonn, associate director of communications, for their hard work and infectious enthusiasm, and Constance Wolf, associate director for public programs, for the creative educational programs she conceived for this exhibition. I acknowledge Loraine Baratti, Shirley Lyons, and Bernice Spandorf, who never let us down or neglected the care of the Library Collection. I warmly thank Willard Holmes, deputy director of the Whitney Museum, for his understanding, skillful management, and not the least, good humor.

And, finally, we thank the lenders to this exhibition: Robert Adams; Amon Carter Museum Library, Fort Worth; The Bancroft Library, University of California, Berkeley; the Yale Collection of Western Americana, The Beinecke Rare Book and Manuscript Library, New Haven; Bonni Benrubi Gallery, New York; Janet Borden, Inc., New York; Boston Public Library, Print Department; Christopher Cardozo Inc., Minneapolis; Christopher G. Cardozo; Center for Creative Photography, The University of Arizona, Tucson; Centre Canadien d'Architecture /Canadian Centre for Architecture, Montreal; Linda Connor; Victoria Dailey; Robert Dawson; Joe Deal; DeGolyer Library, Southern Methodist University, Dallas; The Denver Art Museum; Library, Denver Museum of Natural History; The Ewell Sale Stewart Library, The Academy of Natural Sciences, Philadelphia; Steve Fitch; Fraenkel Gallery, San Francisco; Lee Friedlander; George Eastman House, Rochester; Gilman Paper Company Collection, New York; Sondra Gilman and Celso M. Gonzalez-Falla; Howard Greenberg Gallery, New York; Hallmark Photographic

Collection, Hallmark Cards, Inc., Kansas City, Missouri; Karen Halverson; Alex Harris; Marc Harrison, I.D.S.A.; Philip Hyde; Len Jenshel; Mark Klett; Hans P. Kraus, Jr.; Jungjin Lee; Robert Mann Gallery, New York; The Metropolitan Museum of Art, New York; Robert Miller Gallery, New York; Richard Misrach; Missouri Historical Society, St. Louis; Museum of Fine Arts, Museum of New Mexico, Santa Fe; The Museum of Modern Art, New York; Joan Myers; Dorothea Lange Collection, The Oakland Museum, California; Barbara Norfleet; PaceWildensteinMacGill Gallery, New York; Peter E. Palmquist; Palm Springs Desert Museum, California; Mary Peck; The Pierpont Morgan Library, New York; Edward Ranney; William Reese Company, New Haven; William S. Reese; Rephotographic Survey Project, Tempe; Charles Schwartz; State Historical Society of Colorado, Denver; Special Collections, The University of Arizona, Tucson; Union Pacific Museum, Omaha; Anthropology Library, Yale University Library, New Haven; Geology Library, Yale University Library, New Haven; Yancey Richardson Gallery, New York; and several private collectors.

This publication was organized at the Whitney Museum by
Mary E. DelMonico, Head, Publications;
Sheila Schwartz, Editor; Heidi Jacobs, Copy Editor;
Nerissa Dominguez, Production Coordinator;
José Fernandez, Assistant/Design; and Melinda Barlow, Assistant.

Design: Katy Homans
Halftone photography: Robert Hennessey
Cartography: Malcolm Swanston
Printing: Litho Inc.
Binding: Acme Bookbinding
Printed in the USA